Designing for magazines

Common problems, realistic solutions

for: front covers,
contents pages,
flash forms (late-closing news),
departments, front and back,
editorial pages,
feature section openers,
new product and
new literature reports

Jan V. White

Second edition

R. R. Bowker Company

New York and London, 1982

Published by R. R. Bowker Company
1180 Avenue of the Americas, New York, N.Y. 10036
Copyright © 1982 by Jan V. White
Printed and bound in the United States of America

Library of Congress Cataloging in Publication Data
White, Jan V., 1928-
    Designing for magazines.

    Rev. ed. of: Designing covers, contents,
flash forms, departments, editorials, openers,
products for magazines. 1976.
    Sequel to: Editing by design.
    Includes index.
    1. Magazine design. I. Title.
Z253.5.W46 1982   741.65′2   82-4226
ISBN 0-8352-1507-5   AACR2

For Karla Weiss and *Chris*

CONTENTS

The hidden meaning of this frontispiece will become clear if you read page XII.

VIII

PREFACE

This is a companion volume to *Editing by Design*. It was assembled in answer to my students' request for examples of specific applications of the philosophy of *Editing by Design*. That philosophy (if one can honor plain old common sense with such a bombastic title) is simple:

As writers and editors we are always talking about "saying" things to our audience. That's a dangerous misnomer lying at the root of many of our problems. We — in publishing — never actually SAY anything. We SHOW. *Saying* is an aural means of communication whose essence is the direct relationship between speaker and hearer. It may be artificially multiplied by broadcasting technology, but that only mechanizes the one-to-one relationship. In publishing, when we speak of "saying" things, we actually mean printing our words on paper and then persuading the audience to read and absorb our thoughts through their eyes. That is a very different process from that of speaking since it requires the services of an interpreter: the designer. Being human, few writers trust that visual specialist to do right by their words; by the same token, few designers ever get as involved in the content of the material as they should. Instead, designers tend to concentrate on the superficial gloss of making it all look appealing.

If we are to communicate quickly and clearly (as we must, if we are to retain our audience), then we must accept the fact that WHAT we say is integral with HOW we say it. Visual form and verbal content are inseparable. That is why it is essential that verbal people become more sympathetic toward the visual aspect of their work (even if they don't all choose to become art directors) and why visual people must become more interested in the editorial purpose of the stories so they can express them cunningly and dramatically. They should, with justice, learn to consider themselves editors-who-use-design-as-a-tool, rather than pure designers grafting attractiveness onto strange materials. Graphic design is not something added to make pages look lively. It is not an end in itself. It is the means to an end — that of clear, vivid, stirring communication of editorial content.

This is so obvious that it hurts. What hurts more, though, is the sad fact that two separate editorial specialties have developed in our profession that create artificial barriers, and serve no useful purpose other than that rather shameful one of people needing someone to look down on and complain about. Sadly, few are the cases where respect and regard for each others' skills has melded a group of writers, editors, and designers into a team. Clearly, varying talents and different technical skills are needed for the common product. But those specializations must be overcome by the one overriding need: that of communicating effectively.

That implies, first and foremost, that the originators of the ideas (the writers) make up their minds about what it is they are trying to say, and what its significance to the reader is likely to be (i.e., the reason for publishing in the first place). Having articulated this to the designers, they can then rely on them to express those ideas in the most arresting manner, in order to hurtle them off the pages into the reader's mind.

Editing by Design is all about how the techniques of graphic design can be used to do just that.

Designing for Magazines is a compendium of case histories showing the ideas of editing by design in practice. Many are shown in before-and-after format. All of them describe the specific problems and reasons why the solutions took the form they did — THAT is the purpose of this book. The graphic appearance of the examples is a secondary result; very few have been picked for their flamboyant graphics. That is deliberately done — to show such flamboyance in this analytical context might be misleading, for it might be promising something that can only be accomplished under very special circumstances. There are annual collections of prize-winning graphics available showing such marvelous pages; they are celebrated, envied, and possibly even emulated. But one ought to learn to walk before attempting to run.

This, the second edition of *Designing for Magazines*, retains the original organization by page type found in most publications. No matter what publication you may be working on, be it consumer or business, in-house or national, small or large, rich or tightly budgeted, your Contents page, for instance, has problems that are common to all Contents pages and grow out of the material and purpose of the page. Those problems are analyzed in depth and then each chapter shows a series of annotated examples of various solutions. Many fresh examples have been added, and many outdated ones replaced. To broaden the utility of this book as a reference volume, I have inserted 116 examples culled from 103 publications of all kinds by 94 designers. Here you can, indeed, find the flamboyant, exciting design.

These are then followed by sketches of additional patterns or solutions. The only chapter that has not been given this broadened treatment is the first, on covers. Here the variety is so vast and the special format problems so specific to any one issue, that I found myself totally at a loss as to how to make sense of this vast array. So I took the coward's way out and did nothing. Instead, I suggest you visit your local newsstand or supermarket magazine rack; you will see how daunting such a choice process might be!

As an example of the realistic, down-to-earth approach followed here, let me explain the use of the many ruled lines shown in the analyzed example pages (as well as in the many other examples for whose design I was not responsible). I happen to *like* rules — but such a subjective reason ought to have the very lowest priority. I also believe rules to be useful:

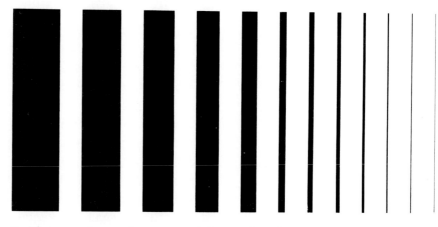

1. They are decorative — or can be made to be so.

2. They are cheap and always available from any printer on any typesetting machinery.

3. They are marvelously useful for organizing space by defining units within that overall space: they articulate the edges of things, they enclose elements, they contain.

4. They can be used as fences to separate neighbors .

5. They can be used as glue to attach elements to each other when space is tightened.

6. They can add "color" to the page by creating contrast between themselves and the type or between light, thin hairlines, and bold, heavy black bars.

7. They can be attached to type as underscores or overscores and help important words gain the desired emphasis.

8. They can become a subliminal patterning for a series of pages.

It is possible to see them utilized in all these ways in the examples shown. Seen cumulatively in this book, they are a bit overwhelming, I admit. But in the pages of a magazine there are fewer of them, more regularly used. And if they are used wisely and well, they can be made to belong to the editorial matter so logically that the reader does not even notice them — yet the product would be the poorer for the lack of them.

Now as to the frontispiece on page VIII: in my 31 years in publishing, I have worked with literally hundreds of editors and designers. Many of them were good to work with, others awful; some were fun, others dreadful. Some happened to be men, others women — and they fell into the good or bad categories regardless of gender: what matters is character and capacity and insight and responsibility and confidence and maturity and good judgment and seriousness of purpose and all the other attributes that good editors and designers must have. Gender (in this context) is totally immaterial.

As far as the other frontispieces in the book are concerned: let's face it, unless you are fascinated by contents pages or new products pages, this could be a very *dull* book! Something had to be done to spark it up with a bit of whimsy. So I went digging in the public domain and unearthed some old engravings that might yield that touch, given some judicious doctoring and inappropriate captions. All but three are from Gustave Doré's illustrations to the Bible dating back to 1869 (the illustrations, that is; the text goes back a bit farther).

It only remains to acknowledge with gratitude the help and cooperation of my many friends in publishing. It is obviously impossible to list them individually. It must suffice to list the publications kind enough to permit me to use their pages for the examples. They all have Publishers, Editors, and Art Directors — all clients and friends. To them all I am deeply grateful.

Westport, Connecticut, April 1982

ACKNOWLEDGMENTS

Architectural Record, McGraw-Hill, New York
Chemical Engineering, McGraw-Hill, New York
Construction Methods & Equipment, McGraw-Hill, New York
Data Communications, McGraw-Hill, New York
Dental Economics, PennWell, Tulsa, Oklahoma
Electrical Construction & Maintenance, McGraw-Hill, New York
Engenheiro Moderno, Serpel, Sao Paulo, Brazil
Engineering News-Record, McGraw-Hill, New York
Expansao, Editora Abril, Sao Paulo, Brazil
Golf Digest, New York Times Magazine, Norwalk, Connecticut
HoofBeats, U.S. Trotting Association, Columbus, Ohio
House & Home, McGraw-Hill, New York
Housing, McGraw-Hill, New York
Industrial Engineering, American Institute of Industrial Engineers,
    Atlanta, Georgia
Industrial Equipment News, Thomas Publishing, New York
Industrial Literature Review, Thomas Publishing, New York
Industrial Marketing, Crain Publications, Chicago
Industrial World, Johnston International Publications, New York
Kansas Farmer, Harvest Publications, Cleveland, Ohio
Library Journal, R. R. Bowker Company, New York
Medico Moderno, Edicom, Mexico City
Michigan Farmer, Harvest Publications, Cleveland, Ohio
Midwest Purchasing, Purchasing Management Association,
    Cleveland, Ohio
Modern Plastics, McGraw-Hill, New York
Nation's Schools, McGraw-Hill, New York
O Medico Moderno, Serpel, Sao Paulo, Brazil
Oil & Gas Journal, PennWell, Tulsa, Oklahoma
Scientific Research, McGraw-Hill, New York
Spotlight, Abraham & Straus, New York

The cover ought to attract attention...

COVERS

Everyone on a publication cares about — and worries about — the cover. That's because it is so many things to so many people: an attention-grabber on the newsstand; an attention-seeker on a desk or on the coffee table; a curiosity-arouser tempting one to look inside; in short, a showcase for the product. The editors are keenly concerned with the cover's drawing power since they want their product to be read and appreciated; the publishers are concerned, because they want their product to be successful — to be popular, useful, sell well, and thus be an increasingly valuable vehicle for advertising; the advertising sales people are concerned, because they need not just a good product, but a product with identity, a noticeable identity on which they can base their sales strategy; and circulation people are concerned, because they want to maintain the current circulation as well as increase it in quantity and improve it in "quality," through the perceivable excellence of their product. Excellence breeds confidence and a desire to invest in a subscription or a single issue at a newsstand. Equally, excellence breeds confidence in the advertiser, who wants his announcements within the magazine's pages to share in its aura.

The cover is what the public sees first: it is what registers uppermost in the viewer's mind. Obviously the inside contents are equally important, but they take time to examine, require intellectual effort to remember, visualize, and judge. The cover is much more accessible. It is undeniably there, staring up at you and you cannot help reacting to it in some way. No wonder so much attention is paid to it. It is the public package of the contents. It has to be manipulated in such a way that the reader, the buyer, the advertiser can all judge the book by its cover. It must express character as well as content; it must be believable, individual, have its own identity and its own image. The cover image becomes a major element in the overall image of the publication. It must impress a sense of urgency and importance; it must communicate a sense of worth, not just of the material packaged within, but also of *itself* as a product. As such, it is a symbol of the relationship between the

editors and the readers, so that the readers actually look forward
to receiving the next issue as a welcome, familiar, respected friend.

This sounds like a pretty tall order for a single page, and so it is.
Furthermore, there are not many covers that succeed in this complex
mission. They may succeed in most of their tasks most of the time,
but seldom in all jobs simultaneously. Which doesn't mean one
ought to give up and stop trying!

Fortunately there are guidelines based on experience, proven
market-effectiveness, successful experimentation and just plain
editorial instinct. Some of them are described below. But there is
one generally accepted dictum that unlerlies them all: *appeal to
the reader's self-interest.*

If the cover is "dull" — if it fails to sell the fascination of the
subject and, more importantly, the significance of that fascination to
the reader — if it doesn't persuade him of his need to have the
knowledge for fun and profit, then the chances are the cover has
failed: the prospective buyer won't buy, the prospective reader
won't open the magazine. The magnet will not have been strong
enough to win him over.

But don't think that the fault neccessarily lies in the cover
picture. The cover illustration, both in its subject and its graphic
treatment, isn't nearly as important as the editorial battle over its
choice would seem to indicate. *Of course* the pictorial image has an
effect: it can be attractive or repellent; felicitous or unbecoming;
to the point or irrelevant. But whatever it may be, it only acts as a
fleeting eye-catcher. It is the first step in rousing the potential
buyer/reader's attention. What ultimately hooks him and persuades
him to part with money and/or time are the words.

With the exception of the highly specialized publications that
deal with purely visual subject matter (such as photography,
architecture — or women) it is safe to say that the cover lines (the
billings) are far more important than the illustration. It is the words
that flash that signal of significance to the reader's self-interest.
They interpret the intended meaning of the picture (for a picture

without words is open to grave misinterpretation). They announce
the content, but, through the choice of words, they also imply the
slant of that content, so that the reader will understand the story's
probable importance *to him.*

Often several stories in the issue are signaled that way. If the
stories are chosen with care and described in intriguing language
where he cannot miss the descriptions, how can the reader fail
to respond?*

Covers are made up of four elements:

1. The basic format (the normal arrangement of the page, issue
   to issue)
2. The logo and ancillary information such as date, etc. (usually
   varying in color only)
3. The illustration (varying in subject and graphic treatment, issue
   to issue)
4. The cover lines (varying in words, of course, but also in
   position, if the format allows)

These four elements make a mix of potentially tremendous variety.
The precise mix for any one publication depends on the goals and
character of that publication. However, there are some basic
criteria involved in deciding the proportions of the particular mix.
And here are some of the most often asked questions and answers
about these criteria.

Should the format be standardized?

Yes. A standardized format has a definite recognition value and
gives the publication familiarity from issue to issue. Besides, the
production process is simplified (no small advantage). Also, paradoxically, the more the format is standardized, the greater the
freedom of graphic treatment of variables within that framework.

---

*Well, let's face it: it is amazingly depressing how often he can . . . but why
worry, there's always the next issue!

But such a sweeping generalization immediately needs qualifying by another which is equally sweeping: no matter how good a format may be, it is also essential that it be flexible enough to allow the form of expression required by any exigency that might come up. In short, systems are great, as long as they do not become straitjackets. Common sense and individual judgment, *plus departure from the system,* must be allowed in the equation as well. Reducing creativity to a series of computerized formats may, indeed, be cheaper, but the resultant printout cannot be anything but rigidly restricted to the formulas fed into the computer. The trouble with a good system is precisely its own excellence: it can become a substitute for thinking. When that happens in publishing, we might as well be dead.

Should the picture be big or small?

This depends on the availability of good pictorial images (photographs, illustrations, portraits, graphs — whatever the visual image may be). If they are available in a dependable quantity and quality (especially quality), then it is a reasonably good bet that a cover format can *and should* be built around a large image — perhaps full bleed — which can be relied upon to have the requisite poster impact. However, to have that impact, the picture should be unusual in either subject, treatment, coloration, handling — or a combination of them all — since full-bleed pictures are so commonplace that just plain size carries no weight.

Symbolic treatment of the subject is often preferable because of its surprise value, unless a truly realistic situation can be shown in a dramatic way. But the symbolism must be simple to be effective, or the startling effect is lost. Still-life photographs of unexpected combinations of items are highly effective, since they are surprising as combinations, and they are often quite simple to have made. Ingenuity and creativity of thinking are more important than money available for unusual or expensive reproduction technology.

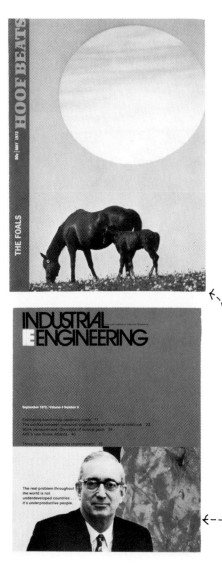

But — again — the ingenuity must be channeled to get the reader interested; thus, whatever brilliantly surrealistic imagery or flamboyantly artistic fireworks may appear on that front cover, if it doesn't achieve this one prime purpose it is no good (however many medals it might collect in design competitions).

One sure bet is people pictures. Everyone is curious about people: who the successful ones are (and what made them that way); what the leaders are thinking; what can be learned about them or from them that might come in handy.

What if the very subject of the publication does not lend itself to visual interpretation, or there is a dearth of illustrative material, no matter how clever the editors, designers, and cartoonists hired? Then, obviously, the format cannot be built around graphic images. Instead, it must be accepted that the pictorial element (if any) will be subdued in size and importance and the poster value of the cover obtained by other means. Large logo, perhaps? Large color area (with color changing from issue to issue)? Large type for the cover lines? In sum, it has to be a large something-else-other-than-picture, anyway. And it has to have a variation capability of color change or arrangement change so that variety between issues is assured, visibility secured, and recognition quality retained. Besides, it makes life so much easier not to have to strain to produce silk purses out of thin air (let alone sows' ears) issue after issue after issue after issue.

Starting on pages 28 and 18 are examples of the two extremes. The cover format of *HoofBeats* is predicated upon first-rate photography which speaks for itself. The strategic purpose of the cover is simply to present the glamour of the sport of harness racing. Full bleed is obviously useful, except where it is thought that variation therefrom might be more effective; absolute freedom of format is needed — and given. Contrast this to the cover of *Industrial Engineering,* for which illustrative material is scarce; the impact of the cover is based upon the overall impression of the design, rather than the picture, which is put in a position of less importance on the

page. The logo is large, the color area in which it floats is ample, and the cover lines glinting on this color announce the contents of the major stories clearly.

How should the logo be designed?

The logotype is the trademark of the publication. It is the symbol that ought to come to mind immediately when the magazine is mentioned. It is used not only on the front cover, but in all written materials for the publication: stationery, promotional material, circulation promotion letters. Wherever the publication's name is *seen* it ought to be *perceived* in terms of its logo. The name of the publication ought to be a personalized visual image — like a monogram; it ought, also, to be of the same family of type as the department headings inside the magazine, and ought to bear, if possible, a resemblance to the headline typeface used. This unity of visual character is a major link that ties the editorial matter together as a unified product.

Where should the logo go?

Newsstands dictate placing the logo at the top, of course. If copies are to be sold on newsstands, then the choice has been made for you. But, if the publication goes out by mail, the logo can fall wherever the designer may desire.

If the picture on the front cover is mediocre and the design depends heavily on the logo for graphic interest, then the logo ought to be the first element to be seen — and thus ought to go at the top of the page. (See *Industrial Engineering* examples, page 18.) For variety within this standard placement of the logo it is useful to have a design that will accommodate several treatments. Thus, *Chemical Engineering,* for instance, can be handled with light or dark "shadows," in color or black-and-white, or black-and-color, or

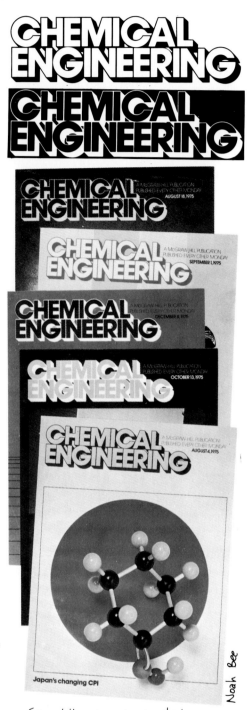

Japan's changing CPI

Noah Bee

Some of the many ways in which
a logo using "shadowed" lettering
can be manipulated to make the
most of color possibilities — yet
retain its original recognition
quality (AND simplicity in
production!)

white-and-color — depending on the best relationship of the logo to the picture.

If the picture quality is somewhat better and good illustrative matter may sometimes be available (and ought to be trumpeted on those occasions), then the format should be flexible enough to allow variation in placement. *Library Journal* allows such variations in placement, gaining diversity and flexibility therefrom (page 26).

If the picture is of poster quality, then the logo can be degraded to a minor element, used only as recognition label, and can (should) be placed wherever the picture dictates. (See the *HoofBeats* examples, on page 28.)

Should the cover have a frame?

It is safer not to use delicate frames around the edges of the cover since the trimming of the publication is often inaccurate; there are few things shoddier than poorly trimmed, crooked front covers. A design based on handsomely squared-off geometrical precision makes the crookedness more noticeable.

A full bleed makes the picture appear bigger because the bleeding implies that the image continues beyond the confines of the page and that what you see is just the central nucleus of a larger scene. This visual trick may well perform a useful service, depending on the subject matter: an oil well derrick in the Sahara needs to be seen against the enormity of a background extending to limitless horizons — and a bleed suggests this limitlessness; on the other hand, a jewel lying on a velvet cushion needs to be concentrated on — the expanse of surrounding velvet is immaterial, so a framed view is more appropriate. If a frame is used, however, it must be graphically strong in size and color to overcome whatever bad trimming might lie in store for it.

mēdico
moderno

mēdicomoderno mexico

<-- Version of logo rejected for
reasons of practicableness in
application : it would be fine for
a white background, but less so
for use over color illustration.

<---- Accepted version is much
simpler in concept and graphics

Should there be more than one cover line?

Yes, if there is more than one major story in the issue. If there is only
one cover line, then the illustration must have a direct relationship
to the story being announced. If there is more than one cover line,
then the cover picture can relate to any one of these lines (which
should then be handled by position and size to act as both cover
line and caption to the picture). The picture, however, does not
need to refer to the major story. Obviously this gives greater
freedom to those publications whose dearth of visual material often
dictates using illustrations of minor stories on the cover simply
because those illustrations are inherently interesting (or merely just
the best available).

The degree of graphic attention or stress the cover lines receive
varies with each publication. Some magazines which rely heavily on
newsstand sales superimpose cover lines in gaudy colors over the
background picture, some professional magazines run them in
demure black, neatly stacked at the foot of the page, other publications vary placement and handling of cover blurbs for each issue
according to the exigencies of the illustration and editorial judgment.
No single technique is better than another; any is good as long
as it intrigues and encourages the potential reader to open the copy.

Do white covers get dirty?

No. Well — maybe.

Anything will get dirty if the reader's thumb is covered with
axle grease. But if pristine whiteness is used as background color,
chances are that the reader will treat the issue with respect and
wipe the grease off on his pants first. It is folly to give up the useful
background color of white, which can make the cover so clean and
pure and charming, for the potential philistine spoiler. But, white is
not the only marvelous background color — so is good old,
solid black.

9

Magazine

Are black covers funereal?

No. Not if the black is used as a background, simply and forthrightly.

Black is, indeed, the color of mourning in some cultures (in others it happens to be white). However, to renounce the use of black for that reason is nonsense. Obviously, if other death symbols, like Old English typefaces, the word "alas," wreaths, or weeping willows are combined with the black, then the mourning sickness is reinforced! But if the black is treated as a raw material — as a pure color — then the artificially imposed funereal cliche is avoided, and a strong impression is created which is, perhaps, even more useful than that effected by white (see pages 22 and 23).

What do you do with a gatefold cover?

Assuming that the inside of the cover has been sold to an advertiser who will foot the bill for such an unusual event, then the gatefold front cover becomes an enormously stimulating problem. How do you make the most of it?

You do NOT make the most of a gatefold by treating it as two separate, individual pages, with one sort of material on one page and another sort of material on the other. That is a wasted opportunity if ever there was one. Instead you use the extra wide space to expand the image over the entire area at your disposal — making it larger in scale and double in impact value.

Naturally, the first image that is perceived is that part of the cover that is always seen (since the gatefold must be packaged folded under). However, the gatefold's inherent possibility of delivering a one-two punch when it is opened is where its potential greatness lies. The first intriguing glimmer of the idea appears on the front, always visible half of the cover; then it is expanded by the unfolded second half, so that the editorial meaning of the complete image communicates itself to the viewer with inescapable, unforgettable impact.

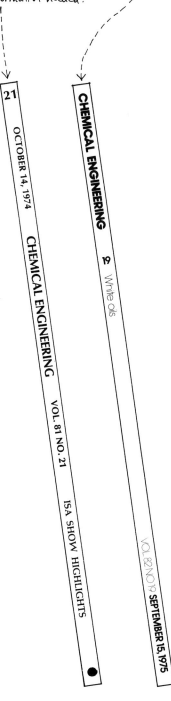

Before: all the information is equally black — there appears to be so MUCH of it and what a job it is to find the specific piece of information needed!

After: the name and date of the issue pop out because they are blackest — so are visible from afar. All the ancillary information is in very light type (though of the same size as the bold) and discernible only close up (where you need it).

What do you do with the spine?

This is the forgotten area of the cover, yet it has great sales value since it is seen even more often than the front cover; the spine is what is visible in a stack of publications on the shelf (standing or lying down).

It is, of course, necessary for reference purposes and filing ease to run the name, date, and volume and issue numbers on the spine, but they do not have to be enormous. It is much wiser to have other elements on the spine that do a little screaming for attention with materials that are more significant.

If possible, it is useful to have a standard spine treatment, preferably in color and on the entire spine: *Oil and Gas Journal's* yellow-striped spine is immediately recognizable; so is *National Geographic's.* Some magazines run a color over their logo, which becomes their symbol. Others run the logo itself in color. *Architectural Record* runs the issue number in red in the same position for each issue, which makes it easy to spot, easy to file, and easy to separate from the competition. If space allows (as it certainly does on the 9" x 12" format publications and some smaller ones whose logo is not too long) then the subject of the main story can be run on the spine, which is useful for future retrieval and recognition.

It is vital, however, to separate what is important from what is not, then express it as such in type size, color, and intensity. *Chemical Engineering's* spines were a dark, illegible, confusing mass; after analysis, they were changed and are more legible, more attractive, and — yes — more useful. The reader need not read everything to find what he is looking for, but can, by instinct, go directly to what he needs: he can identify the publication at a distance since the logo and date pop out at him; to find the specific material, he will be closer to the stack and can focus on the lightface story title and ignore the dark smudge of logo and date. It really works.

Development of format: change, growth, decisions

The examples here trace the changes in format of a local Portuguese-language medical magazine as it evolved into a leading multi-edition Latin American monthly.

The first format, at left, was innovative in its time, devoting as it did a large, formalized, framed area to a startling picture.. The thin, white frame set off the picture but suffered from poor trimming. The cover lines were restricted to the small box in the upper right.

The first change was a change in the wrong direction, at least as far as graphics is concerned. (Evidently the success of the publication was not hindered by the cover handling!). The cover lines were enlarged at the expense of the illustration which was reduced to the vertical sliver at left. The purpose was to focus attention on the contents by means of stressing the cover lines, yet retain the familiar square shape. The only good outcome of this move was to allow the logo a much larger space in which to be seen. But even that was dwarfed by the heavy cover lines which swamped all else. The result, a cover that was too busy, lacked poster quality, was ill-proportioned in its elements (so much so that the cover lines had to be set in an illegible condensed face to fit into their narrow space) and, worst of all, communicated an image which lacked the sophistication the publication demanded.

The latest development was a total redesign, based on the decision to make the most effective possible use of the graphic image inherent in the fascinating subject matter. Great attention is paid to the illustrations and their attention-getting capacity — not necessarily as startling but rather as communicative vehicles suited to their specific audience. All covers are full color, full bleed and the various national editions may use their own subjects. The highly individual logo is the element that holds them all together since it appears in prescribed position and size on the page.

médicomoderno
DEZEMBRO 1974

ARGENTINA / OCTUBRE 1973

médicomoderno

¿Qué
haremos con los
hospitales?

A Classe
julga a
vulgarização
do atestado

médicomoderno
VOL. XI / No. 11 / JULIO 1973

¿Será su
paciente
un "dios
con
prótesis"?

Arturo Alvarez Acevedo

The logo is the same in all
editions (three are shown:
Brazilian, Argentine, Mexican)
Its color varies according to the
requirements of the picture.
Its style is repeated in all
the department headings

Standard format with a square picture area allows variations that have a strong

Since this is a non-newsstand publication, the logo can be placed at the foot of the page with impunity; and, since this is a publication dealing with highly photogenic material, the graphic image on the cover can be relied upon to create the requisite poster impact. The square is used for two reasons: first, it is a satisfying geometric shape which works well in proportion to the white area left over at the foot of the page; and, second, it is the ideal compromise shape for accommodating photographs since about half the candidates for the cover are vertical and half are horizontal.

The top line, slightly separated from the others for emphasis, does double duty as caption as well as cover line. The large numeral is always run in bright red — as is its duplicate on the spine.

Red numeral, all other type in plain black

SAN ANTONIO MUSEUM OF ART, BY CAMBRIDGE SEVEN ASSOCIATES, INC.

KOHN PEDERSON FOX FIND VARIED FORM IN A NEW FUNCTIONALISM
PHOENIX' LATH HOUSE: CENTERPIECE FOR URBAN REVITALIZATION
ROUND TABLE: STEEL STRUCTURES IN ARCHITECTURE
BUILDING TYPES STUDY: FIVE NEW ENGLAND SCHOOL BUILDINGS
FULL CONTENTS ON PAGES 10 AND 11   SEMI-ANNUAL INDEX ON PAGES 198-201

ARCHITECTURAL RECORD

JUNE 1981 **6** A McGRAW-HILL PUBLICATION   SIX DOLLARS PER COPY

Alex Stillano

A year's-worth of covers

family resemblance

← Typical format
and two variations →
↓

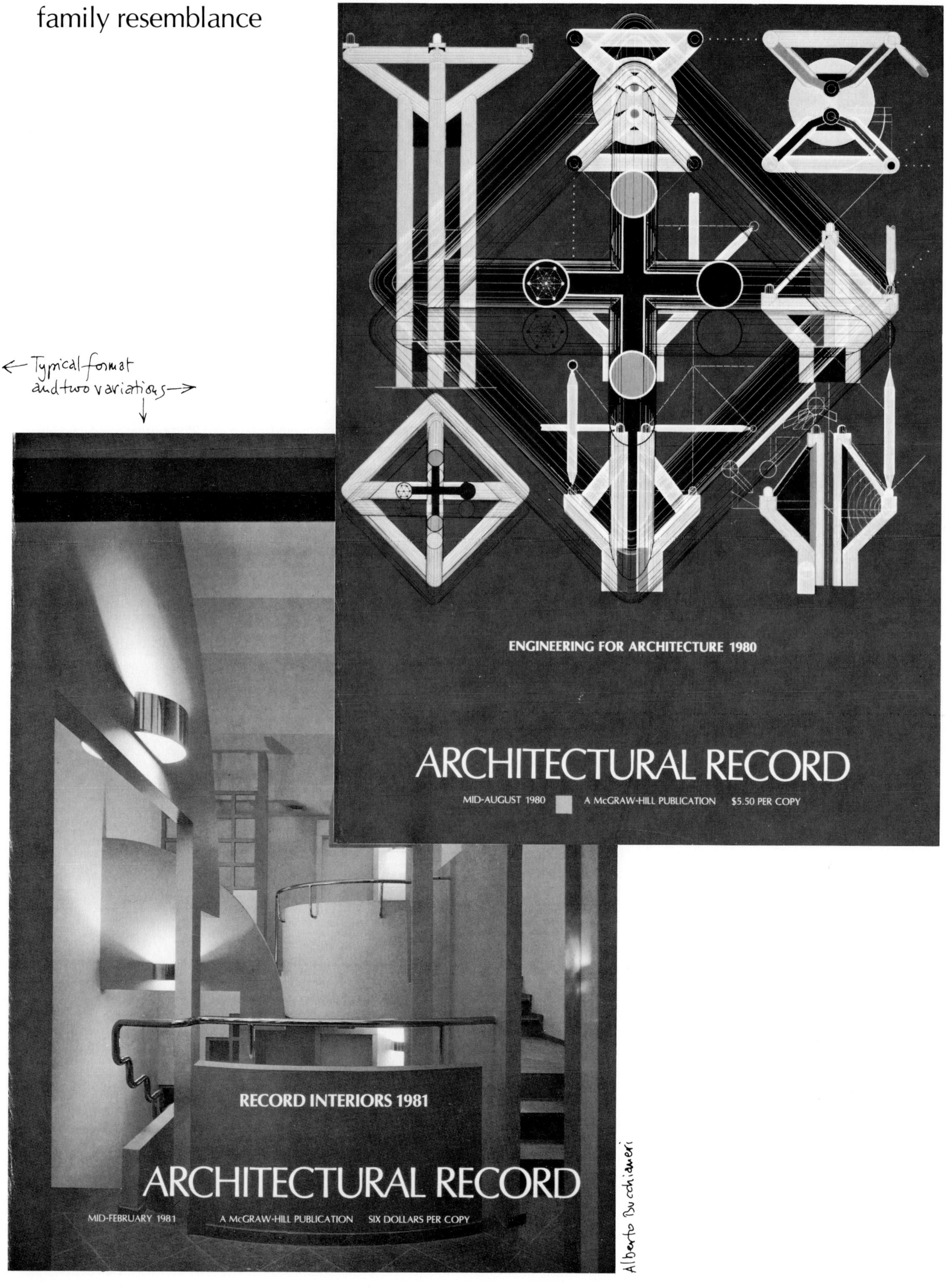

ENGINEERING FOR ARCHITECTURE 1980

ARCHITECTURAL RECORD

MID-AUGUST 1980 ◼ A McGRAW-HILL PUBLICATION $5.50 PER COPY

Anna - Maria Egger

RECORD INTERIORS 1981

ARCHITECTURAL RECORD

MID-FEBRUARY 1981 A McGRAW-HILL PUBLICATION SIX DOLLARS PER COPY

Alberto Bucchianeri

Easy-to-produce illustration clusters and color schemes

This tabloid size publication of new product reports had two problems: how to give the front cover a more vivid recognition quality, and how to make its production process less cumbersome. The solution served both purposes simultaneously: the pictures were clustered and their descriptions placed in the surrounding space (which also made the background color field appear larger); the logo area was simplified; the desired effect of colorfulness was enriched by the addition of the "shadows" cast by the logo words as well as the pictures, for the insides of the letters can be in one color, the shadows in a second, and the background in a third. A number of cluster panel mechanicals was made up with various proportions to fit likely photo sizes (six are shown opposite) and a chart showing two years' worth of color schemes was also prepared. The chart (opposite) shows both swatches of the color and process color tint percentages. Assembly became child's play: picking a cluster appropriate for the chosen photos and a color scheme that would work with them — and the rest is up to the printer.

Industrial Equipment News

A THOMAS PUBLICATION / FOUNDED 1933 / **JUNE 1980**

Industrial packaging, page 53

Valve operator

Epi-Torc actuator for 90 deg ¼ turn valves has self-locking epicyclic gearing, SPDT torque limiting and DPST travel limiting switches, and motor for intermittent or modulating service. Hand wheel provides for manual override. Housing is NEMA 4 and 7. **Keystone Valve Div,** Box 40010, Houston, TX 77040.   **IEN 2**

Strapping tool

Combination tension-sealer, a pneumatic magazine-equipped tool, secures non-metallic strapping to cartons, boxes, and crates. Once threaded, push of a button on new Model T-805 will automatically tension strap to preset level, then crimp seal and cut strapping. Scotch-Band polyester strapping comes in three thicknesses — 0.020, 0.025, and 0.030 in — and in three widths — ⅜, ½, and ⅝ in. Thickest size (No. 3630) has 1,150 lb breaking strength. **3M Company,** Dept PS80-14, Box 33600, St Paul, MN 55133.   **IEN 3**

Thermal glove

Non-asbestos three-piece glove gives the wearer complete over-the-wrist protection while providing an effective heat barrier. Inner leather glove (Tempo WAL) lined with wool and aluminized rayon protects to 500°F. Outer glove (Tempo Therm Shield) of woven fiberglass and Kevlar protects to 1,000°F. Economically replaceable slip-over covers offer additional heat protection and extend wear life. **Apex Glove, Inc,** 3820 W Wisconsin Ave, Milwaukee, WI 53208.   **IEN 1**

Scissors lift

Self-propelled Condor scissors lift comes in models with weight capacities from 750 to 1,250 lb and platform heights from 15 to 25 ft. With removable control box it can be operated from platform or ground. Features include 250 A.hr batteries, hydraulic brakes, solid or pneumatic tires, and two-speed drive with up to 3 mph travel speed. **Calavar Corp,** 9200 S Sorensen Ave, Santa Fe Springs, CA 90670.   **IEN 4**

⌐The unavoidable address sticker

Helen Hud

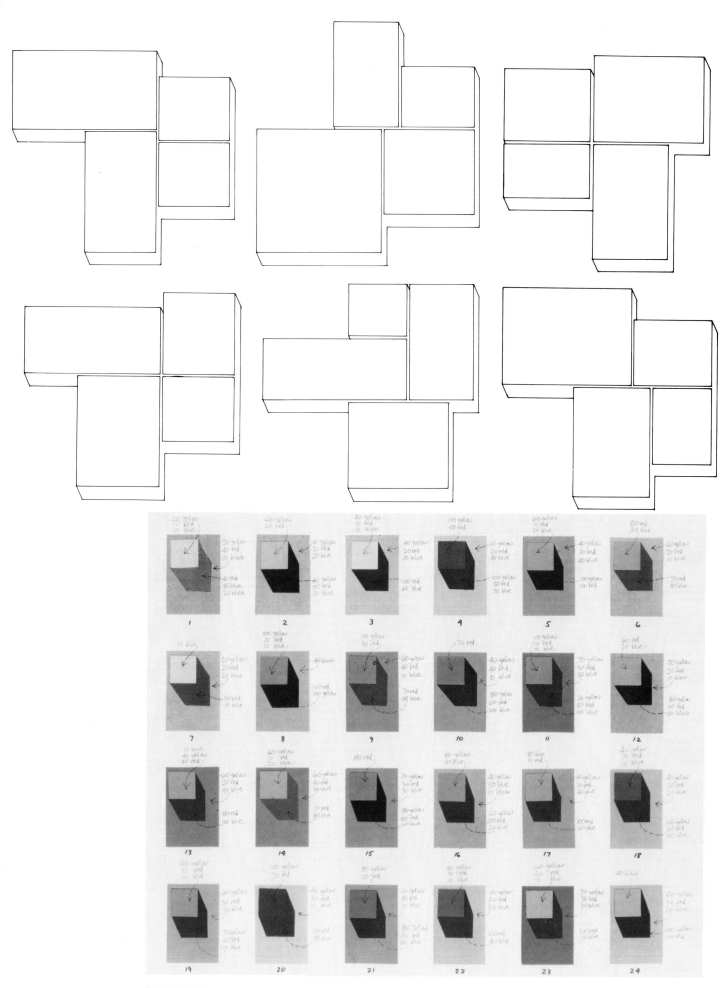

Cover design based mainly on graphics which include a picture

Here is a perfect example of the many publications whose subject matter is only tangentially photogenic and whose dearth of pictorial material results in constant struggles to conceive covers with impact. The examples at left show the results of such misdirected "freedom to create." Replacing this nebulousness with controllable techniques is one major way to improve the image of the magazine while allowing its editors to sleep better at night.

In this case, the picture area was reduced to a shallow strip across the foot of the page, thus automatically diminishing its evident importance. The rest of the cover is devoted to a strong color, different for each issue, of course, which can also be used to dress up the picture below as a duotone or as a tintblock with artwork. The logo is very large and obviously the major element of the design, which makes sense since the readers identify with it. The cover lines are large enough to be clearly legible; the bottom one is also the caption to the illustration. The date is dropped out in white from the color area and contrasts with the cover lines which are always in black.

Another example of this technique is shown on page 26.

September 1971 / Volume 3 Number 9

Principles of industrial systems engineering   20
IE salaries: past, present, and future   26
Better scheduling helps cut labor expense   34
Fisheries: newest frontier for IE's   40

Simulation model of an overhead crane system   13

as one element *

INDUSTRIAL
IE ENGINEERING
American Institute of Industrial Engineers

Use effective strategies and procedures
for applying techniques.

INDUSTRIAL
IE ENGINEER
American

* but not the <u>major</u> one

Using large size, medium size, and small size type in cover lines

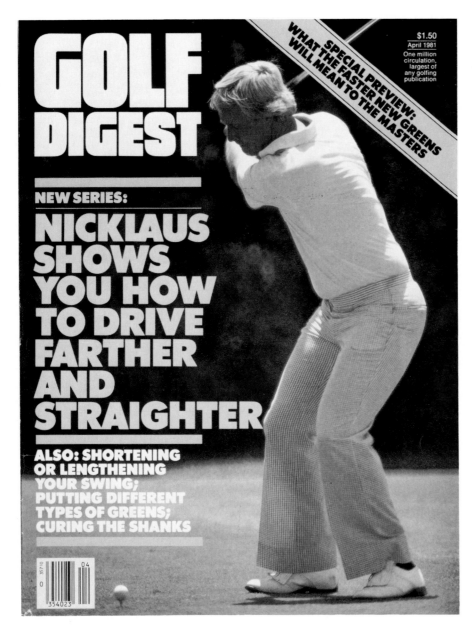

GOLF DIGEST

NEW SERIES:

NICKLAUS SHOWS YOU HOW TO DRIVE FARTHER AND STRAIGHTER

ALSO: SHORTENING OR LENGTHENING YOUR SWING; PUTTING DIFFERENT TYPES OF GREENS; CURING THE SHANKS

SPECIAL PREVIEW: WHAT THE FASTER NEW GREENS WILL MEAN TO THE MASTERS

$1.50
April 1981
One million circulation, largest of any golfing publication

How we see and handle the physical product affects the design of cover lines. For newsstand display, the logo obviously needs to be the largest element, in order to give immediate identification to the product. Next size down, yet still legible from several paces away, should be the type touting the major story. The largest type having done its work of attracting our attention, and perhaps beguiled us into picking up the magazine in our hands, the balance of the type can then be smaller, for it is to be read merely at arm's length. (When we start reading inside, we hold it 12 inches from our eyes, so the type can be smaller still.) This cover of *Golf Digest* designed by John Newcomb shows the triple typographic scale very clearly and elegantly.

Michigan Farmer, by contrast has a different need: it has no need to attract newsstand buyers, for it is delivered to subscribers. Nor does it have to attract attention to itself by screaming headlines: its attention-getting ploy is fulfilled by the illustration, which is always of some familiar evocative image to which the reader is likely to respond in a positive way. So much, then, for the long-distance appeal. The pick-me-up-and-read-me appeal is concentrated in the window, where four stories are signaled in topic terms as well as in straight headlines. True, the logo and headline windows are indeed intrusions into the background photograph — but the color of the picture helps to overcome them — a factor not discernible here in black-and-white.

MICHIGAN FARMER

AUGUST 2, 1980   70c
A HARVEST PUBLICATION

Looking toward harvest: **How crops and livestock will fare here**
Ron Ferrell: **Farmers must conserve more than soil**
Cricket business: **Just keeps chirping along**
Century-old seed: **Those weed seeds can outlive you**

To replace the problem of creating, week in and week out, homemade covers with poster value, the fundamental editing/ publishing decision was made to standardize the format. The picture area was designated for four-color photography; the cover lines, which, on a newsweekly, demand the latest possible closing time, were deliberately split away from the illustration. That allows the color separations for the illustration to have longer lead time, as they require, while permitting the cover lines literally last-minute revisions. The area in which the cover lines appear is reversed (i.e., white type on black) and the band containing the logo and dateline is also in black, with the logo in yellow. A sliver of space separates the bands from the color picture, both lightening the impression and making assembly much easier. The yellow spine, a well-known characteristic of the publication, was, of course, retained. The new design was introduced in 1970. An updated, fine-tuned amendment to the format done in 1981 is shown opposite.

August 3, 1970

OIL & GAS JOURNAL

PUBLISHED WEEKLY

Exclusive 13th annual report on pipeline installation and equipment costs 99

FPC switching from cost to market regulation of gas prices 37
Alaska unwraps data on North Slope's Prudhoe Bay discovery . . . 44
Water-quality problems and the solutions in waterflooding 92

the OIL AND GAS
JOURNAL
PUBLISHED WEEKLY   JANUARY 1, 1968

NEWS
Offshore rig building to hold high, thanks to hectic action abroad, U.S. lease sales   p. 29

Bulging Japanese refining capacity to jump a possible record volume this year   p. 48

TECHNOLOGY
Improve equipment, higher standards mean getting the most from pipeline radiography   p. 74

TRANSPORTING
LNG
Here are details on two systems — one a transoceanic project of high capacity, and the other a low-capacity domestic project.
p. 55

with black background

WEEK OF NOVEMBER 23, 1981
A PennWell Publication

OIL&GAS JOURNAL

PIPELINE ECONOMICS REPORT—Building cost inflation eases, p. 79

Offshore construction industry pulling out of doldrums, p. 45
NPC study sees big petroleum resource target in U.S. Arctic, p. 68
The modern shale shaker, key to improved drilling, p. 107
Nevada gets its fourth oil field at Bacon Flat, Nye County, p. 159

Nov.23,1981 Vol.79No.47

How gas processors can hold down dehydration costs, p.121

Surplus capacity, sagging demand pinch small U.S. refiners, p.71
Defense intelligence report: Soviets will meet energy targets, p.94
Pipelining natural gas from the Canadian High Arctic, p.145
A close look at the Atlantic's only oil giant: Hibernia, p.240

Sept.21,1981 Vol.79No.38
Oct5,1981 Vol.79No.40
August31,1981 Vol.79No.35
Dec.21,1981 Vol.79No.51
Jan.11,1982 Vol.80No.2

CUTTING DEHYDRATION COSTS
ANNUAL GEOPHYSICAL REPORT
New cleaning techniques, BEAUFORT SEA SEARCH
OGJ world sulfur survey
DEEPWATER DEVELOPMENT

Max Batchelder

23

To help the logo stand out, clean up its surroundings

There are notes of six different sizes of type around the "before" of *Engineering News-Record*. In the first "after," the housekeeping facts are pulled together into a relationship with the logo in small italic capitals; the cover line is the only element that appears in different type, as seems appropriate for creating the desired emphasis. The second "after" (by John de Cesare) simplifies the image further by reducing the logo to the acronym by which the publication is known by its readership, and concentrating everything in the single small-type line above. Cover lines are handled as each cover subject demands.

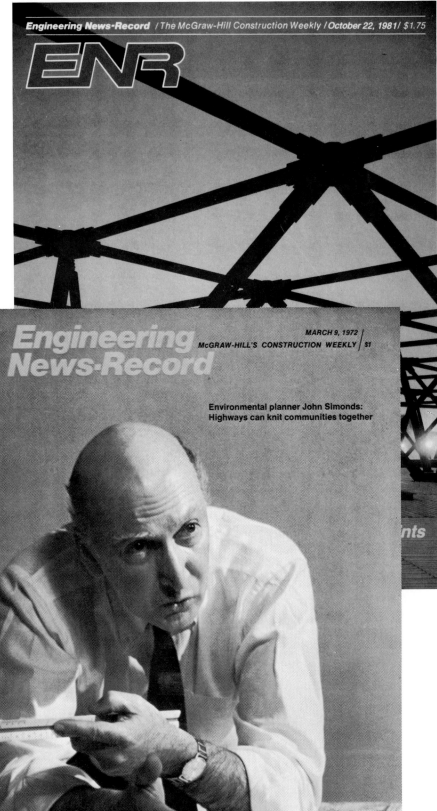

To make the product look bigger, silhouette the picture

Two fundamental departures from the original were made: strengthening the logo, and taking the photo out of full bleed.

The logo, set in a typeface of greater hard-edged strength, was amended to fit the two words into a single visual unit. Notice the overlap of the D and C, the double m, the ns ligature; there are many other detailed refinements of spacing and shaping to personalize the plain type into a monogram logo. All the tightening allowed it to be run much larger than before.

The photo is silhouetted for several reasons: (1) it focuses the reader's attention onto the subject, (2) it encourages unexpected enlargement and courageous cropping — yielding startling poster value, (3) it utilizes the white space as an expansive, bright contrast to the black logo, (4) it allows several cover lines to be placed on the page (here neatly aligned on the D in the logo).

Placement of decorative logo at head or foot of page to add variety

The three examples shown here illustrate the possibilities in logo and cover-line placement that have proved helpful in the design of the covers issue to issue. The logo and monogram as well as the color block in which they appear are deliberately large, for the poster quality of the cover may possibly depend upon them.

The outlined lettering (of the same family as the department headings and similar to the head-line typography inside) allows color manipulation that can be quite decorative. The outline itself can be in white, black, or color; the "inside" of the letters can be run in white, black, or color — as solid, tint, or mixed with a tint of black, or "transparent," as in the example opposite; the panel can be colorful, or grayish, or, as the last example shows, preempted by a full-bleed picture with no dire consequences to the visibility of the logo. The variety of effects thus achievable makes the problem of illustration choice far less crucial than it had been in the past when the cover stood or fell on the success of the visual image alone.

ALA CONFERENCE: NEW YORK
Scars and Gripes Forever: ALA gathers for its 93rd
New York, New York: a highly selective LJ restaurant guide
Places and Pastimes: a few New Yorkers share the city

JULY 1974 / ISSN 0000-0027

LJ LIBRARY JOURNAL

Top Priorities for LC: a Mini-Symposium
Placements and Salaries 1973
Price Indexes for 1974
Scientific, Technical, Medical, and Business Books To Come

Update on the Environment

Participatory Something or Other Through Bargaining
In the News: Top personnel of R.I. agency quit,
Boston's adult learning program, Canada cracks down
on U.S. publishers, textbook fights, federal $$ outlook

LJ LIBRARY JOURNAL

Complete freedom in logo placement is a luxury allowed only where the picture

The editorial purpose of the cover on *HoofBeats* is simply to show the glamour of the sport of harness racing. It is assumed that the reader will react with delight and recognition and will be unable to resist opening the issue. Obviously an ample supply of splendid pictures is essential for this ploy.

is the message

Two pictures are more likely to strike a responsive chord than just one

One of the major purposes of the front cover is to get the reader inside: to fascinate him enough so he turns from a mildly interested observer into an enthusiastic reader. Many newsstand magazines have enriched their appeal by adding a tiny picture or two to the large image already there (*Time, People,* etc.). The danger, of course, is that by dividing attention, it can cause dilution of impact and some confusion. However, if the trick is done for good reasons, it can serve publishing tactics well.

Housing's special issue covers two subjects of vital importance to its readership. It would be folly to show just one. By inserting the secondary image (coupled with the wording) into a relatively unimportant area of a very strong picture, the poster quality of the large photo is retained, yet the sales message is enhanced. Note, also, the unusual handling of the logo: it is an integral part of the picture.

To ensure legibility, it has, indeed, caused some problems in picture choice, since the top of all pictures must be dark enough and not mottled; however, it has given the product a distinct identity.

Kansas Farmer (just like *Michigan Farmer,* page 21) relies on photographs of familiar scenes to put the reader in an accepting mood. Yet it also needs to signal the fact that it is not an armchair travel book, but, rather, a hard-hitting, tabloid-size, biweekly newsmagazine. Since news photos are seldom of good enough quality to warrant full-bleed size, a format was devised that would allow an important news picture to be inserted into the enticing background in a box together with the accompanying headline. The news value of the photo is thus retained, yet the cover can hold on to its tempting mood. The graphics here are reminiscent of the *Industrial Equipment News* cover (see page 16); however, graphics are just the means to an end and the ends are very different.

Serving Kansas farmers and ranchers since 1863   A Harvest publication | 40¢ | January 6, 1979

Kansas Farmer

You may have a new school sooner than you think

The editors' chance to show off their wares

CONTENTS

Once the reader has opened the magazine (because the cover has done its work) chances are that he'll do one of three things:

1. He'll skim through the issue, riffle the pages, stop where fancy strikes him. There is little we can do to influence this kind of reader other than to give him an interesting product we hope will intrigue him.
2. He'll go straight to the cover story (or another story whose title he saw on the cover). Let us hope his interest will be sustained by our efforts and that he'll stay with the magazine for a while.
3. He'll check the contents page to see what else might be worth spending time on. So the contents page should be the instrument by which the editors lead the reader deeper into the issue. It is the editors' second chance to show off their wares.

To succeed, the contents page must be lucid, easy to absorb and simple enough to require no effort on anyone's part to figure it out.

Also, the contents page must appear important, underlining the inherent importance of the material covered by the publication.

Furthermore, the contents page must be easy to find; it must be noticeable as a page, as well as be in a strategic position where the reader cannot miss it. Normally page 3 or page 5 is where someone unfamiliar with the magazine might look for the contents page since they are the most common positions for it. But there are other positions (such as the inside front cover or the first page of the feature section) that can be used. The exact page used matters less than the regularity of its use, since regularity creates habit patterns and reader response. Forcing the reader to hunt for his guide-page is not the best way to win friends and influence people.

There are three kinds of readers who use the contents page:

1. Those who already know what they are looking for in the issue and are merely using the contents page as an index to find the page reference. For them, the editorial matter should be clearly organized and smoothly arranged so that they can skim the page efficiently.

2. Those who need to be sold on what the issue contains. For them, the big ideas (i.e., the headlines) should pop off the page quickly and clearly, and those headlines should be followed by a secondary supportive line that explains the significance of the story from the what's-in-it-for-you angle.

3. Those who would like to know the gist of the major articles without having to plow through them. This pertains less to the "vertical books" that specialize in a narrow segment of an industry or profession and whose readers are probably interested in or affected by everything the magazine has to report, than it pertains to the "horizontal books" which cater to a broad spectrum of readers who may be only peripherally interested in an in-depth study of a specialty not their own but who would like to know about its existence. For them, the contents page should provide a capsule summary of each article.

And then there is another class of contents page users: the many information hunters, such as librarians, or a reader who remembers seeing a story way back in 1967, or even an editor who might need to look up an old issue but is stymied by the index which doesn't have the proper cross-reference. These people need the contents page as a fast index. For them, the material should be efficiently organized, too, according to a system that is logical for the particular publication — either by interest area, by author, by subject, by date of development, by personality being written about, or other suitable organizing principle.

Quite obviously no one page arrangement can possibly succeed in pleasing all these groups. Nor should it try. As in all matters of design in publications, the editors must first make up their minds about what they want the page to accomplish. The publisher may be allowed some input here, too! Once the direction is set, a page makeup can be devised to fit the particular mix deemed appropriate and desirable.

But before we get into that, it is necessary to list all the many elements that need to be shoehorned into this page. Not all publications necessarily require every single one of them — yet it is amazing how much can be packaged into a little 8⅛" x 10⅞" rectangle. There are many publications that, mercifully, allow the various elements of front matter to be split among several spaces. But that is part of the *solution*. First, here's the problem:

* The table of contents itself, showing departments, headlines of the major stories (with, possibly, a secondary line for each), bylines, photographers' credits, interest-area labels, and, of course, page references.

* A label such as "contents". I have always waged war against this tautological requirement; after all, what else can this page be, IF it looks what it is?

* The logo for identification.

* The slogan of the publication, often helpful in defining the readership served.

* An historical reference to the longevity of the publication ("Founded in 1863") or the absorption of snob value antecedents ("Incorporating the *Cement Pourer*").

* The date of publication and volume and number information as required by law and librarians.

* Listing of the editorial staff shown in descending order of rank from the Editor down, giving name and function (some even with telephone numbers for quick access by the readership). To editors, their name and relative position in the hierarchy are of great concern. Changing the typographic makeup of these listings is perhaps the most dangerous of all ventures in magazine design and should never be attempted without protective armor.

  The business staff is also often listed below the editors, but the advertising sales staff is normally listed on the advertising index page and the advertising sales director usually appears on both.

  Some publications also require listing of professional advisors, publication committee members, association directors, and so forth.

* Association affiliations, usually in the form of heraldic emblems of questionable aesthetic value.

* The masthead: all the essential publishing information including the parent company, officers, address, etc.; also information about the frequency of publication, addresses of publication offices, where to submit manuscripts, where to complain about subscription problems or note change of address, and so on and so forth. The United States Post Office requires some of this material to appear within the first five pages of the periodical for it to qualify for second-class postage privileges. Hence — and to simplify makeup — much of the rest of the related material is run with it.

  This masthead information could go on a vertical one-third, combined with the list of editors; or it could be combined with a "Letter from the Publisher" and go on a vertical two-thirds; or it could become the gutter element in a full page, combined with the table of contents itself. Or it can become one element in a multipage sequence.

The word "masthead," strictly speaking, describes just the business information about the publication. It has, however, been broadened to cover the list of editors, and, by implication, the entire *space* in which it is run. So, sometimes, even the logo is misnomered the "masthead" (when it isn't being called the "flag").

✳ A miniature of the front cover, with its caption and credits.

✳ A paragraph or two announcing Coming Attractions.

✳ Miniatures of pictures to dress up the page (as editors say) or to act as signals for features inside.

✳ Trumpeting a special article by abnormal treatment in bold type, color, boxing, or even actual separation from the mainstream of the contents.

Obviously there is enough material. What happens when this plethora of raw information gets assembled without benefit of editing-by-design? Here are a few of the most typical errors.

⊘ Too much material for the space allotted — so much so that the reader turns away in terror, refusing to plow through all *that*, preferring to take his chances at finding something of interest by simply flipping through the pages. This is called the Blivet School of Contents Page Makeup (two kilograms of offal in a one-kilogram bag). It tends to be counterproductive.

⊘ Insufficient grouping; the page is gray all over. Size is a sign of importance; the editors must make sure that the hierarchy of type size corresponds to the editorial value each item has (though there must not be too many sizes). Also, the space between elements must be manipulated to group related subjects into visually logically organized arrangements — by tightening up within a group and enlarging the moats of space that separate one group from another.

⊘ Staff names too large (yes, that *is* possible) or, more likely, the job title overwhelms the name in the staff listings.

⊘ Masthead material set in a face so small and dark that it looks like a smudge.

⊘ The "Bugs" (the armorial bearings of the associations) too large by contrast to the surrounding typography, so that the eye cannot help but alight on them.

⊘ Slogan too overbearing.

⊘ Date and volume information too large.

⊘ The "coming next month" and "cover" information floats, fighting the table of contents. This happens because these two items are normally written as running copy, whereas the table of contents is written tersely in tabular fashion. The two kinds of writing (and its typographic visible form) do not work well together unless the nontabular matter is graphically treated as subservient to the tabular.

The way in which the material is organized on the page varies with the goals the editors have set. It also depends on the kind of publication being designed, the number of pages available, the number and kind of pictures to be accommodated, the nature of the readership, and the same considerations which affected the design of the cover also have a bearing here.

For instance, a publication whose pride lies in the distinguished roster of its authors must have a page arrangement that displays their names prominently; on the other hand, one whose source of pride lies in its breadth of coverage of an entire industry requires an arrangement that gives prominence to the interest-area labels which indicate that breadth.

Another example: A general interest newsmagazine requires a minimal listing of departments for quick reference to page numbers; on the other hand, a "slower," more specialized periodical is justified in devoting several pages to the contents using ample space to run short summaries of the authoritative articles.

Evidently, designing a page that *works* is a tricky business, requiring much finesse both in journalistic understanding (to express what the editors require) and in design capacity (to make that mass of unrelated bits and pieces sit on the page quietly, neatly, as if they belong, yet give the page an overall graphic quality that will make the reader stop and look).

Tricky though it be, there are some basic patterns that most contents pages follow, in spite of the fact that there are probably as many contents page designs as there are contents page designers. A number of these designs are shown in the examples that follow, some of them as "before-and-after" examples to make the style points clear. Following the example pages is a catalog of ideas in sketch form.

A sequential presentation of the entire issue with emphasis on the headlines

The material contained in the "before" as well as the "after" is identical: important headlines of each article; short descriptions of each article; bylines; department names; page numbers; and the ancillary logo, dateline etc.

By reorganizing the available space and articulating each story by means of horizontal rules that separate one from the next, a clear overview of the entire issue is achieved. The page numbers are in a row at the far right edge. The departments, which, as relatively minor elements on the contents page, merely require a page reference for ease of finding, are run ahead of and following the feature section in the sequence in which they appear in the issue. The feature section is emphasized by using the full page width, and by allowing the first several words of the headlines to be seen against clear white space. Note that the typeface of the headlines is no blacker or larger than that used in the "before" version. The white space at the top of the page allows space for expansion when more items are included in abnormally fat issues.

CONTENTS

VOLUME 3 NO. 7

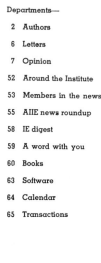

Cover: "The Thinker,"
Auguste Rodin, 1878-89.

Most magazine pages are designed to fit specifically on a left-hand page (or a right-hand page). To put them in a space for which they were not suited would spoil the scheme. To make it quite clear whether a page is a LEFT or a RIGHT, these curved lines indicating the page opposite are shown in all the examples in this book, where such understanding is essential.

IE INDUSTRIAL ENGINEERING CONTENTS

Two contents pages whose design is based on the importance of the headlines

This page from *Engenheiro Moderno,* the Brazilian publication, is designed to demonstrate the wealth of material in the issue: it is the "muchness" that matters primarily, and secondarily, the intrinsic interest of the articles themselves. The "April" logo (the month name is used in lieu of the word "contents") and the 1,2,3,4,5 emphasize this muchness. The numerals are also used at the head of each story inside the issue. The headlines and the story summaries are strong and highly visible, because they are staggered in the space, each element visible against the white, rather than mixed up together (as the heads and summaries are in the "before" example on page 38). The angular and somewhat heavy character of the typography and design is appropriate to the subject and professional readership of the publication. Departments are referred to at the foot of the page, and the cover is in the left-hand margin.

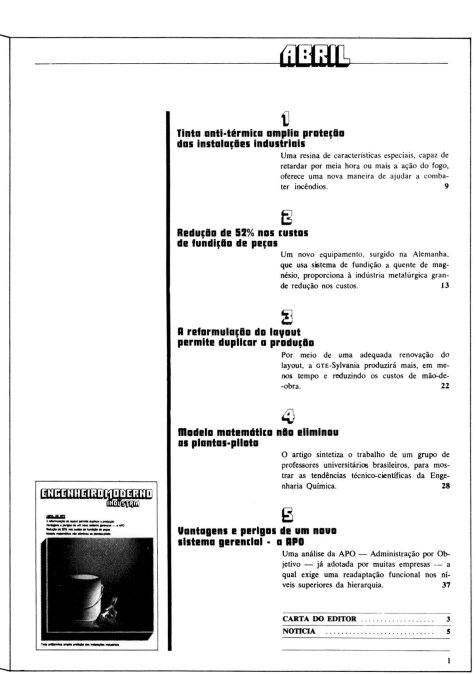

ABRIL

1
Tinta anti-térmica amplia proteção das instalações industriais

Uma resina de características especiais, capaz de retardar por meia hora ou mais a ação do fogo, oferece uma nova maneira de ajudar a combater incêndios.　　9

2
Redução de 52% nos custos de fundição de peças

Um novo equipamento, surgido na Alemanha, que usa sistema de fundição a quente de magnésio, proporciona à indústria metalúrgica grande redução nos custos.　　13

3
A reformulação do layout permite duplicar a produção

Por meio de uma adequada renovação do layout, a GTE-Sylvania produzirá mais, em menos tempo e reduzindo os custos de mão-de-obra.　　22

4
Modelo matemático não eliminou as plantas-piloto

O artigo sintetiza o trabalho de um grupo de professores universitários brasileiros, para mostrar as tendências técnico-científicas da Engenharia Química.　　28

5
Vantagens e perigos de um novo sistema gerencial - a APO

Uma análise da APO — Administração por Objetivo — já adotada por muitas empresas -— a qual exige uma readaptação funcional nos níveis superiores da hierarquia.　　37

1

Beneath the attention-getting frieze of random-size pictures that refer to their stories by page number, the entire contents are organized about the vertical column of page numbers. These run sequentially as in the issue, from top to bottom, down the middle of the page. The department headings and story summaries are placed to the right of this column spine, and the page could exist as it is and make sense.

But weaving across this vertical presentation, are horizontal modules defined by hairline rules, a single module per feature story. Story headlines extend to the farthest left edge of the page. They could be (and are) discerned by themselves: they are a simple list of titles, extremely easy to read, one after the other. Thus the page has a one/two punch: first the titles can be skimmed, then the summaries that might be of interest, and later the position of the items in the issue can be looked up. On the surface it looks like a complex system; but it is easy to figure out, especially since the heads are nice and black and pop out from the page. It also helps to read Spanish.

Both schemes make use of the two-level readership principle ("skim-reading"): primary information is shown large and bold, so it can be read easily and first. Secondary information, useful as supporting the primary, is run smaller and lighter. The reader can thus save time & effort by skipping what is uninteresting.

índice

This contents page has to include the staff list as well as the masthead, forcing the actual contents information into a vertical shape. To clarify the structure at first glance, the heavy vertical rule was inserted as a separator between masthead and contents, but the two elements are tied together by the logo that spans the entire page and acts as a headline for both.

In the masthead area, the staff names and functions were reset one to a line since there is ample room available; the logo of the parent company was pushed into the logical position next to the business information about the publication (the masthead, which was kept unchanged).

The illogical placement of the miniature reproduction of the front cover picture was changed: it had no relationship whatever to the masthead material (though the *width* of the column, as a shape, was appropriate — but that is a very wrong reason for putting an item in a space!). Instead, the picture was shifted into direct relation with the cover story headline where it makes complete editorial sense. Not only does this

LIBRARY JOURNAL

XEROX

Editor-in-Chief: John N. Berry III; *Associate Editors:* Shirley Havens, Karl Nyren; *Production Editor:* Norman Parrish; *Assistant Editors:* Ellen Mangin, Noël Savage, Nancy Brown; *Editorial Assistants:* Maureen Crowley, Albert Miller; THE BOOK REVIEW: *Editor:* Janet Fletcher; *Associate Editors:* Irene Stokvis Land, Anneliese Schwarzer; *Senior Review Editor:* Robert R. Harris; *Production Editor:* Marlene Charnizon; *Assistant Editors:* Carey A. Horwitz, Linda Feirstein, Katharine Scott, Kyle Ahrold, Janet Milstone, Deborah Pritchett; *Editorial Assistants:* Bette-Lee Fox, Ann Sankar; *Media Editor:* Phyllis Levy; ADVERTISING: *Director:* Erwin Baker; *Production:* Maureen J. Rose; *Publisher:* Paul J. Carnese.

LIBRARY JOURNAL is published by R. R. Bowker Co., a Xerox company. Direct editorial and advertising correspondence to 1180 Avenue of the Americas, New York 10036. Telephone: (212) 581-8800. All other correspondence to R. R. Bowker Company, Dept. C, Box 1807, Ann Arbor, Michigan 48106. Publications Offices at 300 North Zeeb Road, Ann Arbor, Michigan 48106. Issued twice a month, September through June, monthly in July and August. Second class postage paid at Ann Arbor, Michigan and additional mailing offices. Copyright © 1973 Xerox Corporation. LIBRARY JOURNAL is indexed in *Library Literature, Library & Information Science Abstracts,* and *Reader's Guide to Periodical Literature.* SUBSCRIPTIONS: USA: 1 year $16.20; 2 years $29.15; 3 years $42.10. Canada and Postal Union of the Americas and Spain, add $2 per year; elsewhere, add $3 per year. Single copy $1.35. Spring, summer, and fall announcement numbers and children's book issues, $3.25 each. POSTMASTER: Please send Form 3579 to R. R. Bowker Company, Dept. C, P.O. Box 1807, Ann Arbor, Michigan 48106. LIBRARY JOURNAL reserves the right to make its own independent judgment as to the acceptability of advertising copy and illustrations in advertisements. Advertiser and advertising agency assume liability for all content (including text, representation and illustrations) of advertisements printed, and also assume responsibility for any claims arising therefrom against the publisher. Offers to sell products, which appear in LIBRARY JOURNAL, are subject to all laws and regulations and are void where so prohibited.

FEATURES

DEPARTMENTS

THE BOOK REVIEW

Cover: Clockwise, starting from the bottom, these new libraries are: the Skokie Public, Illinois; the James Michener Branch,* Bucks County, Pennsylvania; Lyndon State College, Vermont; Loyola-Notre Dame, Baltimore; and the Cherokee County Public, South Carolina (*Lawrence S. Williams, Inc. photo)

3483

remove the necessity of running a separate descriptive caption for the picture, but it also dresses up the contents column, and it allows the headline to act as caption, too. The cover story gains importance just by this simple change.

The contents themselves are displayed in the sequence in which they occur in the issue, item by item. However, the clarity of presentation is muddied by the necessity of expressing three levels of importance for these elements. On the first level of importance are the *Features* and the *Book Review*. (Hence the bold rules and the all-cap logos.) The second level is the *News* — not deserving of bold rules, but requiring long listing of item heads and a boldface logo. On the lowest level of importance are the individual departments which are designated simply by name and page reference and a separating hairline rule. Whether this ranking is effective is debatable; whether it is even necessary is also questionable. In a page as complex as the contents, the simpler and more logical it can be, the better.

EDITOR-IN-CHIEF: John N. Berry III
ASSOCIATE EDITORS: Shirley Havens
Karl Nyren
PRODUCTION EDITOR: Ellen Mangin
PRODUCTION: Nancy Brown
ASSISTANT EDITORS: Noel Savage
Albert Miller
EDITORIAL ASSISTANT: Maureen Crowley

BOOK REVIEW/EDITOR: Janet Fletcher
ASSOCIATE EDITORS: Irene Stokvis Land
Anneliese Schwarzer
SENIOR REVIEW EDITOR: Robert R. Harris
PRODUCTION: Marlene Charnizon
ASSISTANT EDITORS: Carey A. Horwitz
Linda Feirstein
Katherine Scott
Kyle Ahrold
Janet Milstone
Deborah Pritchett
EDITORIAL ASSISTANTS: Betty-Lee Fox
Ann Sankar

ADV. SALES MANAGER: Richard H. Brown
ADVERTISING PRODUCTION: Maureen J. Rose
PUBLISHER: Paul J. Carnese

XEROX

LIBRARY JOURNAL is published by R. R. Bowker Co., a Xerox company. Direct editorial and advertising correspondence to 1180 Avenue of the Americas, New York 10036. Telephone: (212) 764-5100. Subscription inquiries and changes of address should be directed to R. R. Bowker Company, 300 North Zeeb Road, Ann Arbor, Michigan 48106. Publications Offices at 300 North Zeeb Road, Ann Arbor, Michigan 48106. Issued twice a month, September through June, monthly in July and August. Second class postage paid at Ann Arbor, Michigan and additional mailing offices. Copyright © 1974 Xerox Corporation. LIBRARY JOURNAL is indexed in *Library Literature, Library & Information Science Abstracts,* and *Reader's Guide to Periodical Literature.* SUBSCRIPTIONS. USA: 1 year $16.20; 2 years $29.15; 3 years $42.10. Canada and Postal Union of the Americas and Spain, add $2 per year; elsewhere, add $3 per year. Single copy $1.35. Spring, summer, and fall announcement numbers and children's book issues, $3.25 each. POSTMASTER: Please send Form 3579 to R. R. Bowker Company, Dept. C, P.O. Box 1807, Ann Arbor, Michigan 48106. LIBRARY JOURNAL reserves the right to make its own independent judgment as to the acceptability of advertising copy and illustrations in advertisements. Advertiser and advertising agency assume liability for all content (including text, representation and illustrations) of advertisements printed, and also assume responsibility for any claims arising therefrom against the publisher. Offers to sell products, which appear in LIBRARY JOURNAL, are subject to all laws and regulations and are void where so prohibited.

New York Public Library Photo by Jerry Cooke

Full spread devoted to contents separates the "road map" from the summaries

The "before" and "after" examples from *Chemical Engineering* contain the same material, but the "after" has been rearranged to emphasize what is editorially important: service to the reader. And it attempts to do it as clearly and flexibly as possible within a tight framework. This is a typical case of *editing*, using that term in an organizational, visual, graphic, and placement sense. It is also a case of quite simple rearrangement of space and emphasis through typographic sizing and "color."

The "before" left-hand page appears spotty (though each individual element on it is certainly nicely visible.) It is not sequentially organized, however, because it pulls the feature report out of its proper turn and separates the regular features from the other stories. This organization reflects the editors' judgment of the relative importance of the various elements, but it does so at the cost of muddling the reader who finds it hard to know where to look or how to use the page as a reference guide.

The right-hand page also leaves much to be desired in its basic arrangement: much valuable white space is wasted at the top (if the logo weren't so large, then the white space might possibly have been useful in attracting attention to the spread; but the large logo PLUS all this space is overkill). The summaries themselves — which are the main point

---

Chemical Engineering
CHEMICAL TECHNOLOGY FOR PROFIT-MINDED ENGINEERS

Contents

THE COVER

Symbolized are two potential danger areas that are receiving new and effective emphasis: hazardous spills and pipelines. For details, see articles starting on pp. 56 and 94.

IN THE NEXT ISSUE

Installed cost of corrosion-resistant piping, changes in the engineering construction business, properties of chemicals (Part 5), homogenized fuels. Part 20 of the engineering economics refresher series, preparing for painting, Polish natural gas, management by objectives.

Print order this issue 72,393

Highlights Of This Issue

A LID ON HAZARDOUS CHEMICALS—56
This week, a tough law governing the handling and transport of hazardous substances, particularly chemicals, is scheduled to go into effect. Though enforcement will be delayed while the regulatory parameters are better defined, the new law ups penalties to $5 million and hits hard at barge transport.

INFLATION HITS MAINTENANCE, TOO—60
A recent survey of petroleum refiners identifies where the major rises in maintenance costs are coming. As might be expected, the chief culprits are the higher costs of labor and materials.

GOOD TOPICS CROWD AIChE AGENDA—64
The program for the Salt Lake City meeting of AIChE was better than usual and both attendance and interest were high. Discussed here are coal processing, ammonia production, and electroorganic syntheses.

METHANATION COMES OF AGE—68
Substitute natural gas based on coal or heavy oil is too low in heating value for general fuel uses, because of its high hydrogen/carbon monoxide makeup. Several nickel-catalyst schemes are now able to methanate the raw SNG to a high-Btu fuel of pipeline quality.

LOGIC DIAGRAMS FOR BATCH PROCESSES—101
This last article of a series on Boolean algebra and logic diagrams shows how "flipflops" can be used in logic diagrams. It also shows how rather-complicated batch processes can be represented.

SPECIFYING CONTROL VALVES—105
Sizing and selecting control valves requires an extensive knowledge of process plant design and valve manufacturers' practices—a knowledge that is further extended by recent innovations in valve design. This article brings into one description the scattered information required to handle the problem.

YOUR MONEY'S WORTH FROM MEETINGS—116
Was the last meeting you attended a disaster? Did you return with a single idea worth the time and money you spent attending it? Meetings are too frequently disappointing. You can make even a poor meeting worthwhile—pick up useful information and make valuable contacts—if you prepare properly.

SELECTING DUST-CONTROL SYSTEMS—120
In designing a dust-control system, it is important that the correct design be selected from the very beginning to provide room for expansion, to minimize costs, and comply with OSHA and EPA regulations.

September 2, 1974; VOL. 81, NO. 18—Chemical Engineering (with Chemical & Metallurgical Engineering) is published biweekly with an additional issue in October by McGraw-Hill, Inc. James H. McGraw (1860-1948), Founder.

Executive, Editorial, Circulation and Advertising Offices: McGraw-Hill Building, 1221 Avenue of the Americas, New York, NY 10020. Telephone (212) 997-1221.

Subscriptions: Available only by paid subscription. Chemical Engineering solicits subscriptions only from engineers and other technical personnel in the Chemical Process Industries. Position, company connection, nature of company's business, products and approximate number of employees must be indicated on subscription applications forwarded to address below. Publisher reserves the right to refuse nonqualified subscriptions. Subscription rates per year for individuals within field of the publication, U.S. & U.S. Possessions $9.00, Canada $10.00 (single copies $1.50, except Desk-book Issues $2.50); elsewhere, upon request. Unconditional guarantee: The Publisher upon written request from any subscriber, agrees to refund the part of the subscription price for copies not yet mailed.

Publication Office: 99 N. Broadway, Albany, NY 12204. Second Class postage paid at Albany, New York and at additional mailing offices and postage paid in Montreal, Quebec. Title reg (R) in U.S. Patent Office. Copyright (C) 1974 by McGraw-Hill Inc.

All rights reserved. The contents of this publication may not be reproduced either in whole or in part without consent of the copyright owner.
Officers of McGraw-Hill Publications Company: John R. Emery, President; J. Elton Tuohig, Executive Vice-President-Administration. Paul F. McPherson, Group Publisher-Vice-President; Senior Vice-Presidents: Ralph Blackburn, Circulation; John B. Hoglund, Controller; David G. Jensen, Manufacturing; Gordon L. Jones, Marketing; Jerome D. Luntz, Planning & Development; Walter A. Stanbury, Editorial.
Officers of the Corporation: Shelton Fisher, Chairman of the Board and Chief Executive Officer; Harold W. McGraw, Jr., President and Chief Operating Officer; Wallace F. Traendly, Group President-McGraw-Hill Publications Company and McGraw-Hill Information Systems Company; Robert N. Landes, Senior Vice-President and Secretary; and Ralph J. Webb, Treasurer.

Subscribers—Send change of address notice correspondence regarding subscription service or subscription orders to Fulfillment Manager, Chemical Engineering, P.O. Box 430, Hightstown, NJ 08520 (Send all other correspondence to appropriate department at 1221 Ave. of the Americas, New York, NY 10020.) Change of address notices should be sent promptly; provide old as well as new address; include zip code or postal zone number if any. If possible, attach address label from recent issue. Please allow one month for change of address to become effective.

of the whole page — are squeezed between an unnecessary headline and the masthead at the foot of the page. The summaries certainly read as a *listing,* but there is a slowness, a lack of urgency, an ordinariness about them, which detracts from their purpose of exciting the reader and encouraging him sufficiently to open the issue and find out more about the fascinating material outlined here.

The "after" shows the ruthless reorganization of the same material deemed necessary to make the most of the hidden opportunities. First of all, the available space was reorganized: the masthead was pulled off the right-hand page and set in a narrow vertical column hidden in the gutter of the left-hand page. That way the right-hand page was freed of encumbrances and could be developed as a full page of important-looking summaries. The space remaining on the left side of the left-hand page could be used for placing a simplified sequential listing of the entire issue in a single, wide column. This page pretends to be nothing more than a listing — and, as such, is excellent for reference. It sells nothing, summarizes nothing, dresses up nothing. All it does is *inform.* The selling job is left to the summaries on the opposite page. The cover blurb and next-issue blurb are run at the foot of this listing to separate them from the summaries.

The result of the reorganization is that instead of four intertwined columns of material crossing the spread, there are now just three; but each of these three is clearly self-contained, naturally expressive of its own material. The shapes and the contents fit each other — that's what makes the spread easy to understand.

Two details should be noted: the features listed on the left-hand page are set bold and run in color to give them extra visibility; and the various articles emphasized on the right-hand page are classified by their departments by means of the free-standing headings, so that initial reference as well as cross-reference to the listing opposite can be made easily.

Annotations: Run in color · Sequential listing · Masthead · Department · Folio · Summary

CHEMICAL ENGINEERING
Chemical technology for profit-minded engineers

THE COVER
Choosing the correct piping for a given job can influence the economics of an entire process operation. For details on how to make the best selection for corrosive service, see report starting on p. 94.

IN THE NEXT ISSUE
Featured: Special report on materials of construction for handling acids. Also, heat from nuclear power, primer on partial molar properties, homogenized fuels, engineering and unionism, world energy conference, panel-type heat exchangers, substitute tobacco, how to prepare a resume.

Chemical Engineering with Chem-Metallurgical Engineering is published biweekly with an additional issue in October by McGraw-Hill, Inc., James H. McGraw (1860-1948) Founder.

Executive, Editorial, Circulation and Advertising Offices: McGraw-Hill Building, 1221 Avenue of the Americas, New York, NY 10020. Telephone (212) 997-1221.

Subscriptions: Available only by paid subscription. Chemical Engineering solicits subscriptions only from engineers and other technical personnel in the Chemical Process Industries. Position, company connection, nature of company's business, products and approximate number of employees must be indicated on subscription applications forwarded to address below. Publisher reserves the right to refuse nonqualified subscriptions. Subscription rates per year for individuals in the field of the publication: U.S. & U.S. Possessions $9.00. Canada $10.00 (single copies $1.00, except Deskbook Issues $2.50); elsewhere, upon request. Unconditional guarantee: The Publisher, upon written request from any subscriber, agrees to refund the part of the subscription price for copies not yet mailed.

Publication Office: 99 N. Broadway, Albany, NY 12204. Second Class postage paid at Albany, New York and at additional mailing offices, and postage paid at Montreal, Quebec. Title reg. (R) in U.S. Patent Office. Copyright (C) 1974 by McGraw-Hill, Inc. All rights reserved. The contents of this publication may not be reproduced either in whole or in part without consent of the copyright owner.

Officers of McGraw-Hill Publications Company: John R. Emery, President; J. Elton Tuohig, Executive Vice-President-Administration; Paul F. McPherson, Group Publisher-Vice-President; Senior Vice-Presidents Ralph Blackburn, Circulation; John B. Hoglund, Controller; David G. Jensen, Manufacturing; Gordon L. Jones, Marketing; Jerome D. Luntz, Planning & Development; Walter A. Stanbury, Editorial.

Officers of the Corporation: Shelton Fisher, Chairman of the Board and Chief Executive Officer; Harold W. McGraw, Jr., President and Chief Operating Officer; Wallace F. Traendly, Group President-McGraw-Hill Publications Company and McGraw-Hill Information Systems Company; Robert N. Landes, Senior Vice-President and Secretary; and Ralph J. Webb, Treasurer.

Subscribers—Send change of address notice, correspondence regarding subscription service or subscription orders to Fulfillment Manager, Chemical Engineering, P.O. Box 430, Hightstown, NJ 08520. (Send all other correspondence to appropriate department at 1221 Ave. of Americas, New York, NY 10020.) On change of address notices should be sent promptly, provide old as well as new address; include zip code or postal zone number if any. If possible, attach address label from recent issue. Please allow one month for change of address to become effective.

Dec. 31, 1975
Volume 4, No. 8
Number of copies: 16,095

NEWS 40 **Contractors have a full house**
Despite shortages of manpower and materials, most engineering and construction companies serving the chemical process industries will admit that they have seldom had it so good. As a result, contracts today are nearly all on the cost-plus basis.

NEWS 44 **A solar/hydrogen economy?**
Teamed up or individually, solar energy and hydrogen are expected to play important roles as the U.S. moves away from a fossil-fuel economy. The prospects of these energy sources was debated at the 9th Intersociety Energy Conversion Engineering Conference.

NEWS 48 **Synthetic lubricants seek niche**
Though cost-prohibitive for most uses, silicones, polyalkylene glycols and phosphate esters have been taking away some markets from petroleum-based lubricants, particularly high-temperature applications.

PROCESS TECHNOLOGY 52 **Ammonia feedstocks are changing**
Natural gas has long been the number-one starting material for ammonia because of its wide availability and low cost. In various parts of the world, changes for the worse in both factors now augur a shift to heavy oil and coal precursors. Here's a rundown on technology and economics of each.

FEATURE REPORT 99 **Cost of corrosion-resistant piping**
Corrosion-resistant piping possibilities are narrowed down by cost comparisons of complex and straight-run piping systems. Materials of construction for piping and fittings are considered, as well as labor costs for various fabrication techniques.

ENGINEERING 107 **Inflation: impact on costs**
This concluding article of the series explores the limitations and scope of discounted-cash-flow methods, reviews the categories of company finance and the associated cost of capital, and takes a close look at inflation. It also shows how to calculate the effects of rising costs on the sales price of a product.

ENGINEERING 113 **Hydrogen halides: HF, HC1, HBr, HI**
These anhydrous hydrogen halides are industrially important in the production of many organic, inorganic and specialty chemicals. Their physical and thermodynamic properties are presented in graphs for the easy availability of data.

YOU & YOUR JOB 124 **Management-by-objectives**
Management-by-objectives is more than a principle of management. It is a comprehensive system that affects the basic nature of the relationship between supervisor and subordinate. Its ramifications bear upon almost all aspects of a manager's job.

OPERATION & MAINTENANCE 130 **Preparing for painting**
Before a structure is painted, it should be properly designed so as to minimize painting problems. If the structure already exists, it must be inspected and undergo proper surface preparation, such as cleaning by sandblasting or shotblasting.

MEDICO MODERNO / VOL. X / N.º 7   INDICE

1

This is a variation of the spread shown in the preceding example; the two pages are used similarly. Page 1, here, has a clearly placed sequential listing of the contents of the whole issue. The page numbers form the demarcation line between features and departments. The departments branch off to the right (and are styled to look like miniatures of the logo). The feature titles lead into the numbers from the left.

Page 2 repeats the feature titles and the pattern of the page numbers but fleshes out each title with a summary of the article. The outside space, used for department headings on page 1, is utilized here for the attention-getting pictures.

As a point of interest: these two pages were redesigned, combined into one, when space in the publication became scarce. The page shown here, therefore, is the ''before''; the ''after'' is on page 41.

INSTANTANEA DE MM

VACACIONES EN EL CARIBE MAS BARATAS QUE EN EUROPA 38

Durante sus próximas vacaciones usted puede salir de lo común, viajando al Caribe: Jamaica, Cayman Islands, Haití, Bahamas. Más cerca y más barato que Europa, encontrará lugares maravillosos para el descanso en medio del singular ambiente afroantillano. Planee su viaje preferido y tenga en cuenta las siguientes indicaciones.

10 COCTELES PARA DAR VIDA A SUS REUNIONES SOCIALES 52

Sus convites pueden ganar incomparablemente en éxito y cordialidad con estas bebidas sabrosas, originales y bien presentadas, que dejarán un recuerdo duradero en el paladar y la memoria de sus agasajados.

GUIA PARA PERFECCIONAR SUS FOTOGRAFIAS EN COLOR 72

Ud. puede iniciarse en los secretos de las técnicas para perfeccionar sus fotos en color, aprovechando estas indicaciones producto de la experiencia de peritos en este arte.

ESQUEMA PARA INSTALAR EL SONIDO EN SU CONSULTORIO 80

Tener un buen sistema de sonido en su consultorio depende menos del precio que del equilibrio entre sus elementos y la adecuada disposición de las cajas acústicas, según le demuestran aquí algunos peritos y varios colegas suyos.

COMO PUEDE UD. IMPORTAR INSTRUMENTAL SIN PROBLEMAS 86

Traer al país instrumental científico es menos complicado y oneroso de lo que generalmente se cree. Esta sencilla guía lo orientará acerca de los trámites previos que usted deberá realizar para importar el equipo que ambiciona.

3

Contents on a page and a spread

The "before" and "after" shown in this example illustrate a comparatively superficial redesign. The spaces were already well defined: the first page is a "road map" of the issue as a whole, the succeeding spread contains the summaries of the articles in this Brazilian business magazine. The redesign merely clarifies the elements, improves their legibility, and adds a little decorative color.

On page 1, the page numbers become the organizing spine for the page; the interest-area designations read in from the left, the headlines read out at the right. This format is much more legible than the "before" handling which just overlaps the same material, and uses the available space to its full potential. The masthead lines are widened, becoming a base for the whole page, and the logo is placed higher. The date becomes the focal point for the page.

In the succeeding spread, the logo is dropped altogether since the miniature of the front cover, suffices to identify the page. Removing this element allows smooth alignment of the tops of the four text columns, which is emphasized by the double rule that runs across both pages. This smoothness becomes a good contrast to the pictures, which are taken out of alignment and are toyed with in random, overlapping fashion. In the presentation of the summaries, the page numbers are, again, emphasized by a variety of techniques, including underscoring. Beneath the underscore are the headlines. Bunching of the type on the left-hand edge of each headline leaves clean, white gaps at the right-hand edges which act as foils to the type, making it appear darker than it in fact is. The pattern of typography within each column is strong enough to allow random column lengths at the foot of the page (the columns "hang" down from the horizontal rule). This makes makeup somewhat easier. The vertical rules between columns help to "clean up" each column.

before →

after →

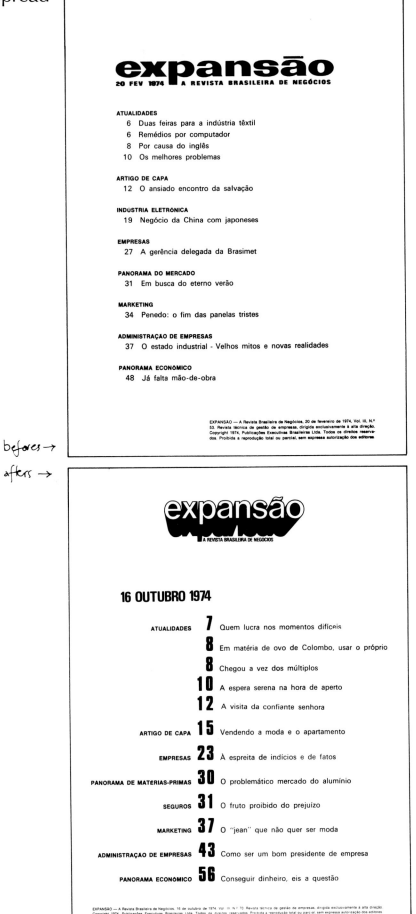

EXPANSÃO — A Revista Brasileira de Negócios, 20 de fevereiro de 1974, Vol. III, N.º 53. Revista técnica de gestão de empresas, dirigida exclusivamente à alta direção. Copyright 1974, Publicações Executivas Brasileiras Ltda. Todos os direitos reservados. Proibida a reprodução total ou parcial, sem expressa autorização dos editores.

EXPANSÃO — A Revista Brasileira de Negócios, 16 de outubro de 1974 Vol. III N.º 70 Revista técnica de gestão de empresas, dirigida exclusivamente à alta direção. Copyright 1974, Publicações Executivas Brasileiras Ltda. Todos os direitos reservados. Proibida a reprodução total ou parcial, sem expressa autorização dos editores.

Stephen Bogyo, diretor-superintendente geral da Fábricas Peixe, conta como conseguiu, com uma equipe de executivos profissionais, recuperar a empresa que há vários anos vinha perdendo dinheiro.

(Foto de Ulrich Svitek)

pág. 6

pág. 6 pág 19 pág. 27 pág. 34

expansão *O conteúdo resumido deste número*

Duas feiras para a indústria têxtil 6
Os negócios fechados na XVII Fenit chegaram a 200 milhões de dólares, segundo o diretor da Feira, Pedro Paulo Lamboglia. Uma quantia superior em cerca de 60% à da feira do ano passado. Em 1974, como a procura de produtos têxteis e de equipamentos para fabricá-los cresceu muito, haverá duas Fenits. Na de junho (de 8 a 16), não entrarão as máquinas e as vendas serão de artigos para o próximo verão.

Remédios por computador 6
Em São Paulo, uma farmácia incomum está demonstrando até que ponto a máquina pode competir com ou substituir o homem. Implantada há três meses, depois de uma experiência coroada de êxito na cidade de Rio Claro, interior de São Paulo, a Droga Mec já realiza cerca de duzentas vendas diárias. E pretende duplicar essa marca em pouco tempo.

Por causa do inglês 8
O problema de Hamilton Borges de Queirós era aparentemente simples: como milhares de pessoas, ele precisava falar inglês. Porém, esbarrava sempre em dificuldades de tempo, dinheiro, inibição ou motivação. Até que resolveu acabar com elas e criou o Sistema Integrado do Dynamic English Course (Sidec). O êxito foi tão grande que ele agora prepara a incursão de sua empresa por outras áreas educacionais.

Os melhores problemas 10
Para os empresários do auto-serviço, o ano de 1973, marcado pela escassez de produtos como carne, leite em pó e outros, mostrou que é preferível enfrentar a falta de produtos do que a de compradores. Os problemas causados pela escassez não foram suficientes para impedir um crescimento das vendas da ordem de 50% nem para arrefecer esperanças para 1974, ano em que se prevê crescimento ainda maior.

O ansiado encontro da salvação 12
Em janeiro de 1972, quase três anos depois de o grupo Brascan assumir o seu controle, a Peixe (Indústrias Alimentícias Carlos de Britto S. A.) não só ainda não tinha recuperado nem um pouco do mercado perdido para a concorrência, desde meados da década de 60, como a sua situação se deteriorara mais, com os prejuízos crescendo sem parar. Foi aí que um novo grupo de administradores, o quarto desde 1969, decidiu aplicar a "teoria do efeito do guarda-chuva", e acabou encontrando nela o ansiado caminho da salvação da empresa.

Negócio da China com japoneses 19
A Sharp S. A. Equipamentos Eletrônicos é uma empresa que procura intensamente aproveitar, de forma racional, as oportunidades criadas pelo *boom* desenvolvimentista. Se em Manaus fica mais barato instalar uma fábrica, por que não ir para lá? Em menos de quatro anos, conseguiu ocupar 60% do mercado de calculadoras eletrônicas (segundo seus diretores) e está lançando seu televisor através do sistema de venda direta ao consumidor.

A gerência delegada da Brasimet 27
As múltiplas atividades da Brasimet Comércio e Indústria S. A. asseguram sua rentabilidade. E, por estranho que pareça, é justamente a autonomia delegada às gerências de departamentos que garante os bons índices de rentabilidade em todos os setores. A partir de 1971, a empresa abriu seu capital e, em pouco tempo, saldava compromissos de longo prazo, diminuía custos financeiros e amealhava um capital de giro capaz de dar aos seus executivos a tranqüilidade suficiente para continuarem traçando ambiciosos planos de desenvolvimento do setor industrial.

Em busca do eterno verão 31
O mercado de bronzeadores apresenta um crescimento considerável e constante de 15% ao ano, mas está apenas começando no Brasil. Para os fabricantes, o deslanche depende apenas da educação dos consumidores, que, por enquanto, mal se iniciam nesse indelével culto à cor da pele.

Penedo: o fim das panelas tristes 34
A Penedo tinha a imagem de uma indústria acanhada. E só conseguiu mudá-la no dia em que decretou o fim das panelas tristes, lançando uma moderna e colorida linha de utensílios de cozinha. Tanto bastou para se lhe abrirem as portas antes inacessíveis dos grandes supermercados e magazines do país. Depois disso, as vendas não pararam mais de crescer, quase que duplicando em apenas um ano.

O estado industrial — Velhos mitos e novas realidades 37
Em *The New Industrial State*, J. K. Galbraith descreveu a indústria moderna como um conjunto de colossos inflexíveis e que satisfazem a si próprios. Indícios recentes, apresentados pela primeira vez neste artigo, originalmente publicado na *Harvard Business School*, mostram que Galbraith descreve o "velho" estado industrial, não o novo. Da mesma forma, o autor sustenta que os remédios drásticos que ele e seus seguidores receitaram para colocar de novo as grandes companhias "sob controle" — nacionalização, controle de preços e medidas semelhantes — são irrelevantes no caso.

Já falta mão-de-obra 48
A economia paulista cresceu menos que a brasileira no ano passado, 11 contra 11,4%. Mas, na verdade, a economia de São Paulo continua saudável como nunca. O percalço paulista se explica pelo fato de o cálculo do PIB só levar em consideração os acréscimos na produção, justo onde a agricultura do Estado, cujos rendimentos crescem cada vez mais, mostrou resultados menos notáveis no ano passado. O problema número um do Estado é a escassez de mão-de-obra, que já atinge alguns segmentos do setor de serviços, elevando os salários e reduzindo as rendas das empresas.

2 EXPANSÃO 20 FEV 1974 — EXPANSÃO 20 FEV 1974 3

Adolpho Lindenberg, da construtora que leva seu nome, conta, no *Artigo de Capa* desta edição, sua estratégia para construir e vender imóveis de alto padrão. (Foto de Michel Zabé)

12

8

23

31

37

7
Quem lucra nos momentos difíceis
Com a escassez de papel, muitas fábricas de formulários para computadores instaladas no país ficaram em situação difícil. Uma delas, contudo, a Moore Formulários Ltda., não só previu esta crise como conseguiu ampliar razoavelmente sua participação no crescente mercado brasileiro.

8
Em matéria de ovo de Colombo, usar o próprio
Como símbolo para seus produtos, a Basf Brasileira descobriu um "ovo de Colombo" — o próprio, devidamente encaixado, de pé, entre as letras S e M da palavra *Som*. Enquanto procura fixar sua imagem com aperfeiçoamentos nas fitas de gravação e com lançamentos de discos, a empresa prepara-se para aumentar sua penetração nos mercados interno e externo.

8
Chegou a vez dos múltiplos
Com a falta de crédito e os efeitos da inflação sobre o poder aquisitivo do consumidor, o mercado de arte brasileiro vai perdendo a euforia que caracterizou os últimos meses de 1973. Contudo, este problema parece não preocupar a Jabik Centro de Arte Multiplicada, instalada há quatro meses em São Paulo: seguindo uma tendência já estratificada na Europa e Estados Unidos, vai comercializar trabalhos em série a preços acessíveis.

10
A espera serena na hora de aperto
Motoo Adachi, presidente da representação da Japan Trade Center em São Paulo, não parece assustado com os prováveis reflexos das crises que afligem o comércio mundial. Pelo menos a decisão brasileira de limitar a importação de bens supérfluos deverá afetar as vendas de equipamentos de som no mercado brasileiro. Mas nem isso convenceu Adachi e sua equipe a romper uma certa passividade oriental.

12
A visita da confiante senhora
No Brasil para o lançamento da Skin Life, uma nova linha de produtos de beleza, *miss* Mala Rubinstein, sobrinha e herdeira de Helena Rubinstein, passeou o seu ar satisfeito, devido à aceitação da marca em todas as faixas de consumo, e sua confiança no desenvolvimento desse setor do mercado.

15
Vendendo a moda e o apartamento
A Construtora Adolpho Lindenberg percebeu que, para se diferenciar da concorrência, precisaria não apenas se preocupar em vender apartamentos e escritórios de luxo para os estratos de melhor poder aquisitivo da população. Era preciso vender uma certa moda em construção, para dar aos negócios a rotatividade de que precisava.

23
À espreita de indícios e de fatos
A Siemens S. A., braço brasileiro de uma avantajada corporação multinacional, não acredita que a atual desordem econômica mundial represente ameaça imediata para uma indústria que, como ela, não produz para o mercado consumidor final. Mas, cautelosamente, ela se aproxima dos clientes para acompanhar de perto os seus negócios, e reflete sobre alguns indícios de problemas futuros, entre eles a queda de 5% nas vendas para a indústria de eletrodomésticos.

30
O problemático mercado do alumínio
A produção brasileira de alumínio só dá para atender à metade da demanda interna e, por isso mesmo, a indústria que usa o metal como matéria-prima é escrava dos desígnios do mercado mundial, onde não há CIP que dê jeito nas livres inclinações altistas.

31
O fruto proibido do prejuízo
À primeira vista, a Companhia de Seguros do Estado de São Paulo (Cosesp) pode parecer mais uma empresa pública sem chance de ganhar dinheiro. Operando numa ampla faixa do mercado, entretanto, a empresa atingiu um lucro líquido no ano passado correspondente a mais da metade do seu capital social de 29,7 milhões de cruzeiros. Em áreas de nítido interesse social, onde seria sua obrigação perder dinheiro — é o caso do seguro rural —, a Cosesp sai lucrando.

37
O "jean" que não quer ser moda
A Levi Strauss do Brasil, subsidiária de uma empresa que vende semanalmente 3,5 milhões de *jeans* no mundo, está vendendo aproximadamente 50% do que pretendia em suas previsões iniciais. O que fazer? A Levi's está-se reorganizando para superar esta fase de recessão do consumo.

43
Como ser um bom presidente de empresa
Os problemas mais sérios de uma organização comercial exigem e devem merecer a atenção exclusiva do principal homem da empresa. E mais: parece que há razões inequívocas para que estes problemas sejam cercados invariavelmente de silêncio e sigilo. No artigo transcrito da Harvard Business Review, o professor Joseph C. Bailey mostra que há um denominador comum para aqueles que sabem enfrentar os problemas mais sérios em suas empresas.

56
Conseguir dinheiro, eis a questão
Com a redução do prazo de permanência dos recursos externos no país de dez para cinco anos, o governo espera obter um fluxo de 6 bilhões de dólares, até o final do ano. As dificuldades no mercado mundial porém persistem e não dão mostras de um afrouxamento pelo menos por enquanto. As taxas de juros sobre os empréstimos variam, ainda, entre 42 e 46% ao ano — perspectiva pouco animadora para quem necessita de cobrir um acentuado déficit em sua balança comercial.

2 EXPANSÃO 16 X 1974 — 3 EXPANSÃO 16 X 1974

A spread, whose arrangement identifies the five sectors of the publication

Quite a different approach to spatial organization is shown in this contents page solution. The sequential flow of the material is there, the various headlines are there, but the organization is based on yet another criterion: reflecting the book's division into five sectors. But two important elements must be disposed of first: the logo and dateline and the staff listing. The former are in the best, most visible reference position on the spread — the top right-hand corner. And the staff listing, in its light and restrained type dress, is positioned at the far left. This, too, is an important position on the spread (but, then, the staff listing is also important). The use of pale type helps to separate the listing visually from the contents and its many boldface elements.

The space left over after the logo and staff listing are positioned, is then defined by the very strong horizontal rule, which becomes the major graphic organizing element of the spread.

Suspended from the rule are five separate columns, each dealing with one sector of the issue — all familiar to the readership. The strength of the horizontal element is such that it allows the columns to be of random length, as the material requires.

The sequence of placement of the elements within the columns follows the sequence in which they appear in the issue (with a few minor exceptions). The reference to next month's issue is an element that does not quite fit the pattern, and, as such, is somewhat jarring. However, placing it at the very end of the flow minimizes the problem; it seems impossible to invent a system that will fit all exigencies.

The miniature reproduction of the front cover illustration appears, with its credits and description, perched atop the horizontal rule and, therefore, is clearly the starting point of the entire sequence, in much the same way that a large upstanding initial draws the eye to the start of a column of text.

Cover: House in Massachusetts
Architects: Peter Forbes & Associates
Photographer: Paul Ferrino

EDITOR
WALTER F. WAGNER, JR., AIA

EXECUTIVE EDITOR
MILDRED F. SCHMERTZ, FAIA

SENIOR EDITORS
HERBERT L. SMITH, JR., AIA, Administration
ROBERT E. FISCHER

ASSOCIATE EDITORS
GRACE M. ANDERSON
DOUGLAS BRENNER
CHARLES K. GANDEE
MARGARET F. GASKIE
BARCLAY F. GORDON
CHARLES K. HOYT, AIA
JANET NAIRN

ASSISTANT EDITOR
ANDREA GABOR

PRODUCTION EDITOR
ANNETTE K. NETBURN

DESIGN
ALEX H. STILLANO, Director
ALBERTO BUCCHIANERI, Senior associate
ANNA-MARIA EGGER, Associate
MURIEL CUTTRELL, Illustration
J. DYCK FLEDDERUS, Illustration
JAN WHITE, Consultant

EDITORIAL CONSULTANTS
EDWARD LARRABEE BARNES, FAIA
JONATHAN BARNETT, AIA, Urban design
GEORGE A. CHRISTIE, JR., Economics
ERNEST MICKEL, Hon. AIA, Washington
PAUL RUDOLPH, FAIA
Foreign architecture
L'Architecture d'Aujourd'hui, Paris

McGRAW-HILL WORLD NEWS
MICHAEL J. JOHNSON, Director
9 domestic and 10
international news bureaus:
Bonn, Brussels, Buenos Aires,
London, Milan, Moscow, Paris,
Singapore, Tokyo, Toronto.

CIRCULATION DIRECTOR
RICHARD H. DI VECCHIO

BUSINESS MANAGER
JOSEPH R. WUNK

REPRINT MANAGER
PATRICIA MARKERT

MARKETING SERVICES MANAGER
CAMILLE H. PADULA

DIRECTOR-NATIONAL ACCOUNTS
HARRINGTON A. ROSE

ASSISTANT TO PUBLISHER
ELIZABETH HAYMAN

PUBLISHER
PAUL B. BEATTY

THE RECORD REPORTS

13 **Editorial**
Housing in the 1980s
Can't we do more than just *stand* here?

4 **Letters/calendar**

33 **News in brief**

35 **News report**
Annual Building Products Executive
Conference is held in Washington.
Central Park is being renovated.
Architects and engineers support bill for
supplement to liability insurance.
Whitney Museum opens out-of-state
branch. CCAIA holds its annual
convention.

40 **Buildings in the news**
White River Park, in Indianapolis, is
planned by team of architects. Venturi,
Rauch and Scott Brown design new zoo
in Philadelphia.

46 **Design awards/competitions**
Eleven projects receive awards for
excellence from the North Carolina
Chapter of the AIA. The Prestressed
Concrete Institute cites nine buildings in
the United States and Canada in its 1981
awards program.

51 **Books received**

150 **Office notes**

ARCHITECTURAL BUSINESS

53 **Image-building for architects:
a guide to public relations**
Public relations expert James P.
Gallagher offers practical counsel on
winning the goodwill of fellow
architects, community leaders, and
potential clients.

57 **Causes and effects of 1981's
office building boom**
In sharp contrast to most segments of
the construction industry, office building
contracting reached record totals this
year. Economist Robert A. Murray
analyzes the factors that contributed to
this extraordinary activity, and assesses
the likelihood of continued vigor.

50

51

Contents page designs based on flexible picture-and-caption units

In *Construction Methods & Equipment* magazine, the feature stories are deliberately played up on the contents page, and the departments merely listed alongside. Each story must be shown not only with a headline, but with a summary and a picture as well. Naturally, the headlines have to be long, the summaries flexible in length, and the pictures of any shape necessary . . .

To make the assembly of such hopelessly complex pages possible without each one turning into a major design problem, a series of predesigned grids was worked out, such as the ones shown here. The principle behind this technique, of course, is the one of camouflage, or misdirection of the reader's consciousness from the comparative messiness of the items themselves, to the smooth neatness of the containers in which they are encased. It is packaging, pure and simple — but it works, especially when the grid is run in color. The examples shown here are typical of the single-page and spread versions of the system.

Single-page version. The "net" of rules is run in color

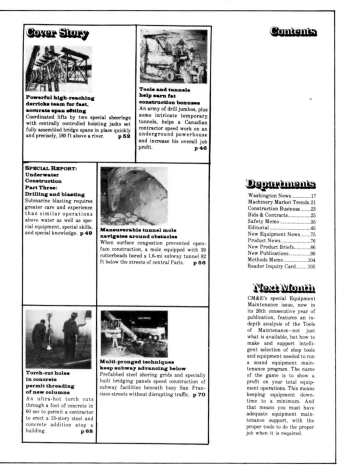

Cover Story

Powerful high-reaching derricks team for fast, accurate span setting
Coordinated lifts by two special sheerlegs with centrally controlled hoisting jacks set fully assembled bridge spans in place quickly and precisely, 180 ft above a river. **p 52**

Tools and tunnels help earn fat construction bonuses
An army of drill jumbos, plus some intricate temporary tunnels, helps a Canadian contractor speed work on an underground powerhouse and increase his overall job profit. **p 46**

SPECIAL REPORT: Underwater Construction Part Three: Drilling and blasting
Submarine blasting requires greater care and experience than similar operations above water as well as special equipment, special skills, and special knowledge. **p 49**

Maneuverable tunnel mole navigates around obstacles
When surface congestion prevented open-face construction, a mole equipped with 39 cutterheads bored a 1.6-mi subway tunnel 82 ft below the streets of central Paris. **p 56**

Torch-cut holes in concrete permit threading of new columns
An ultra-hot torch cuts through a foot of concrete in 60 sec to permit a contractor to erect a 13-story steel and concrete addition atop a building. **p 68**

Multi-pronged techniques keep subway advancing below
Prefabbed steel shoring grids and specially built bridging panels speed construction of subway facilities beneath busy San Francisco streets without disrupting traffic. **p 70**

Contents

Departments

Next Month

CM&E's special Equipment Maintenance issue, now in its 26th consecutive year of publication, features an in-depth analysis of the Tools of Maintenance—not just what is available, but how to make and support intelligent selection of shop tools and equipment needed to run a sound equipment maintenance program. The name of the game is to show a profit on your total equipment operations. This means keeping equipment downtime to a minimum. And that means you must have adequate equipment maintenance support, with the proper tools to do the proper job when it is required.

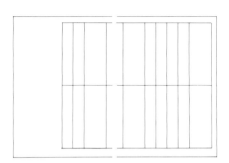

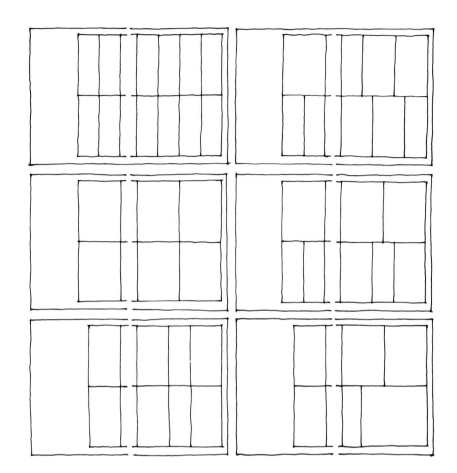

This simple column grid is the basis for the six arrangements at right. → Many more are possible - as required to accommodate the requisite number of stories in the issue (or their relative importance shown by size).

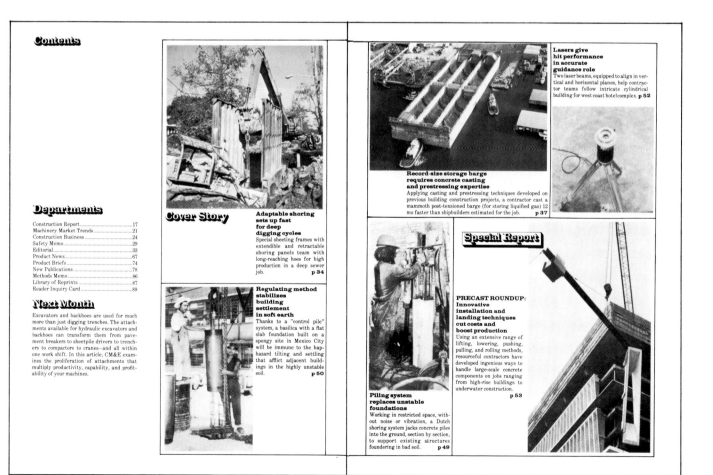

Contents

Departments

Next Month

Excavators and backhoes are used for much more than just digging trenches. The attachments available for hydraulic excavators and backhoes can transform them from pavement breakers to sheetpile drivers to trenchers to compactors to cranes–and all within one work shift. In this article, CM&E examines the proliferation of attachments that multiply productivity, capability, and profitability of your machines.

Cover Story

Adaptable shoring sets up fast for deep digging cycles
Special sheeting frames with extendible and retractable shoring panels team with long-reaching hoes for high production in a deep sewer job. **p 34**

Regulating method stabilizes building settlement in soft earth
Thanks to a "control pile" system, a basilica with a flat slab foundation built on a spongy site in Mexico City will be immune to the haphazard tilting and settling that afflict adjacent buildings in the highly unstable soil. **p 50**

Lasers give hit performance in accurate guidance role
Two laser beams, equipped to align in vertical and horizontal planes, help contractor teams follow intricate cylindrical building for west coast hotel complex. **p 52**

Record-size storage barge requires concrete casting and prestressing expertise
Applying casting and prestressing techniques developed on previous building construction projects, a contractor cast a mammoth post-tensioned barge (for storing liquified gas) 12 mo faster than shipbuilders estimated for the job. **p 37**

Special Report

PRECAST ROUNDUP: Innovative installation and landing techniques cut costs and boost production
Using an extensive range of lifting, lowering, pushing, pulling, and rolling methods, resourceful contractors have developed ingenious ways to handle large-scale concrete components on jobs ranging from high-rise buildings to underwater construction. **p 53**

Piling system replaces unstable foundations
Working in restricted space, without noise or vibration, a Dutch shoring system jacks concrete piles into the ground, section by section, to support existing structures foundering in bad soil. **p 49**

Four-column makeup

Esquire, April Silver

Working Woman, Tony Iannotta Petrella

Simple sequence with pictures placed in relation to story headlines. Page/Topic/Title/Byline/Description clearly shown.

Sequential listing emphasizes story topics. Deep indenting allows folios to stand out (even in very light type). Picture frieze decorates top of page.

Geo, Susanne Walsh

Next, Lester Goodman

Sequential story listing placed on page surrounding one large photo. Unusually generous margins help communicate the expensive touch.

Grouping of cover stories, features, departments, and columns. Strong contrast of color in the typography has hard-hitting character.

Mechanix Illustrated, Andrew Steigmeier

Four areas of interest defined clearly, each in its own column. Ancillary material scattered on rest of page in unrelated patterning.

Cincinnati

Two degrees of importance implied: features in the upper box, everything else in the lower box. Pictures overlap from column to column in unexpected ways.

Le Nouveau Photocinéma, Henry Chaucheprat

Arbitrary, geometrical breakup of space into 12 square modules allows organization of subjects by categories (more or less) with pictorial infill.

Los Angeles, William Delorme

20% screen of black over whole page except central panel emphasizes features. Department list conveniently balanced between front and back.

Three-column makeup

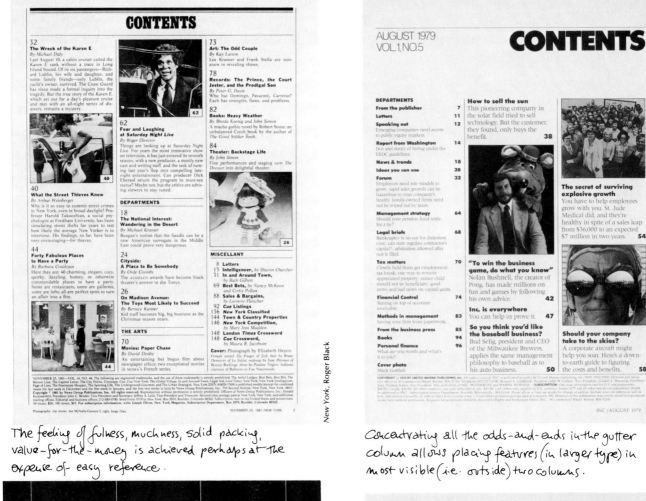

New York, Roger Black

Inc, Paul Schaffrath

The feeling of fullness, muchness, solid packing, value-for-the-money is achieved perhaps at the expense of easy reference.

Concentrating all the odds-and-ends in the gutter column allows placing features (in larger type) in most visible (i.e. outside) two columns.

Look, Regis Pagniez

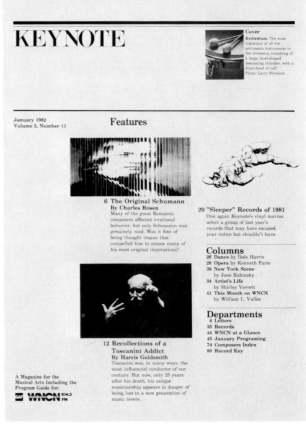

Keynote, Edward Spong

Sequential flow emphasized by rules bleeding top and bottom. Running page in white on black sacrifices legibility for visibility.

The luxury of enough space: a relaxed arrangement whose structure shows through the surface irregularity.

Folio:
THE MAGAZINE FOR MAGAZINE MANAGEMENT

NOVEMBER 1981 VOL. 10 NO. 11

Cover design: Steve Phillips

NOVEMBER 1981 3

Folio, Steve Phillips

Pictures placed in central column, cross-referenced by page number to articles listed in flanking columns.

Adventure Travel
VOLUME 2/NUMBER 11 APRIL 1980

USPS 430-910

Adventure Travel, Gail Segerstrom, Dugald Stermer

The picture column dominates the page because of its extra-wide proportion — emphasizing the importance of graphics in this publication.

NORTH SHORE
The magazine of Chicago's northern suburbs   Vol. 4, No. 9 September, 1981

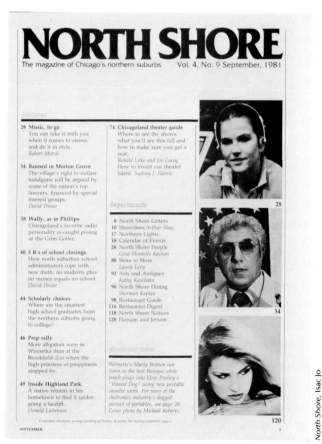

Wilmette's Marty Britton can listen to the best Baroque while pooch plugs into Elvis Presley's "Hound Dog" using new portable cassette units. For more of the electronics industry's dogged pursuit of portables, see page 28. Cover photo by Michael Roberts.

Controlled circulation postage pending at Skokie, IL 60206. See mailing statement, page 6.

SEPTEMBER   5

North Shore, Isac Jo

Placing people-pictures in the outside, far-right column enlivens the image of the page at first glance.

DISCOVER
THE NEWSMAGAZINE OF SCIENCE

NOVEMBER/1980   VOLUME 1, NUMBER 2

Page 34   Page 46   Page 66

THE COVER:
Computer-drawn map of the sun's corona by the High Altitude Observatory and the Solar Maximum Mission

Discover, Leonard Wolfe

The arbitrary placement of story titles in three columns of irregular length is anchored by the strong frieze of pictures across the top.

One-column makeup

AVENUE.
FEBRUARY 1979/VOL. 2 NO. 5

COVER PHOTOGRAPH BY ERNST HAAS, DRAWING BY JOY BILLOUT. PHOTOGRAPHS BY DAVID COX, MICHAEL EVANS, HENRY GROSKINSKY, ALEN MACWEENEY, ARNOLD NEWMAN, NIG BELARIA, JOHN STEWART, DAN WYNN, ILLUSTRATIONS BY STEVEN GUARNACCIA AND PAT WARNER.

Avenue Magazine, Inc. 75 East Fifty-fifth Street, New York, N.Y. 10022. Telephone: (212) 758-9517. Judith Price / President and Publisher. David Breul / Editor. Bob Ciano / Design Director. Lou Rena Hammond / Calendar Editor. Matthew Carrara/ Art Associate. Mary Dunphy / Production Manager. Copyright © 1979 by Avenue Magazine, Inc. All rights reserved. No part of this periodical may be reproduced without the permission of the publisher. Subscription price: $20. Avenue is published exclusively for residents of selected neighborhoods in New York City and is not for sale on newsstands. Printed by Colorcraft Offset, N.Y.C.

FEBRUARY, 1979/AVENUE 5

Avenue, Bob Ciano

Another example of the luxury of ample space: formal, clean, uncluttered, easily scanned listing, with a minimum of verbiage. Lines defined with rules.

CONTENTS

Cover photography: Michael Sullivan

Technology Illustrated, Peter Hudson

Folio/topic/description/byline — the pattern in each feature listing creates informal tabulation. Rules define full page width, overlap picture.

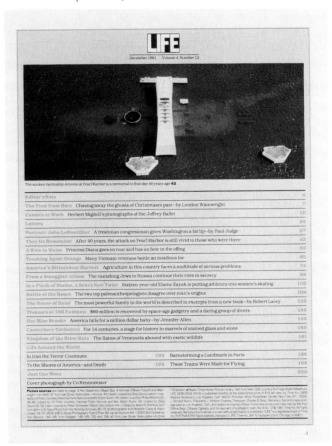

LIFE
December 1981   Volume 4, Number 12

The sunken battleship Arizona at Pearl Harbor is a memorial to that day 40 years ago! **42**

Life, Bob Ciano

Topic/description/byline/folio flush right; all in color on colored background. Space above type devoted to ingenious handling of pictures.   **58**

Like a detour around a landslide that blocks a road, coronary bypass surgery routes the heart's blood supply around obstructions in the coronary arteries. Perhaps no surgical treatment for disease has been as instantly accepted and provoked such intense debate over its usefulness. Painting by Lou Barlow.

contents
SEPTEMBER 1978
VOLUME 1, NUMBER 9

Human Nature, Ira Silberlicht

Apparently a 1/3, 2/3 page breakup, this qualifies for a 1-column place because of its handling of first lines: byline/title/description start/folio.

CameraArts
JANUARY/FEBRUARY 1982 VOLUME 2, NUMBER 1

Turn to page 53 for the first 13-page magazine gatefold, including a 6-page reproduction of Kenneth Snelson's Times Square.

Camera Arts, published by Ziff-Davis Publishing Company, One Park Avenue, New York, New York 10016. Richard P. Friese, President; Selwyn Taubman, Treasurer; Bertram A. Abrams, Secretary. COPYRIGHT © 1981 BY ZIFF-DAVIS PUBLISHING COMPANY. ALL RIGHTS RESERVED.

2

Camera Arts, Thomas Ridinger

Defining the width of the two columns by means of the horizontal rules allows the type to be set ragged right, and even accepts the amusing interruption in the center.

SOMMAIRE L'EXPRESS

N° 1594 du 29 janvier 1982
Ce numéro a été tiré à 600 000 exemplaires

61, avenue Hoche 75380 PARIS Cedex 08
Tél. : 755.97.98. Abonnements : 375.67.00

Printed in France. Second class postage paid a New York N.Y. 10022 US mailing agent: expeditions of the printed word Ltd. Annual subscription price 94 $ US. Commission Paritaire 2° classe // permis à 982. Port payé à Montréal.

L'EXPRESS - 29 JANVIER 1982

MAUROY
Nationalisations retardées, opposition requinquée : de gros soucis pour le Pouvoir (p. 36).

TURQUIE
La junte du général Evren mise au banc des accusés par le Conseil de l'Europe (p. 29).

DOCUMENT
Premier retour à Oran, dix-sept ans après (p. 68).

3

L'Express, Pascale Lentillon

Left-hand half contains full listing, right-hand half picks out three stories for emphasis. Departments are bunched up under "ET AUSSI" — and also.

AUDUBON
The magazine of the National Audubon Society

March 1981 / Volume 83, Number 2

Russell W. Peterson / Publisher
Les Line / Editor
Daniel J. McClain / Design Director
Gary Soucie / Executive Editor
Roxanna Sayre / Managing Editor
Kathleen Fitzpatrick / Senior Editor
Martha Hill / Picture Editor
Ruth Norris / Associate Editor
Leslie Ware / Associate Editor
Linda Morrissey / Picture Associate
Schellie Hagan / Researcher
Robert Cahn / Washington Editor
Frank Graham Jr. / Field Editor
George Laycock / Field Editor
John G. Mitchell / Field Editor
Ellen Rundo / Assistant to the Editor
Robbin Gourley / Design Associate
Carmine Branagan / Advertising Director
Robert A. Bridges / Circulation Manager

THE COVER: Wave-polished stones on a beach at St. Mary's Lake, Glacier National Park, in a photograph by Glenn Van Nimwegen.

Audubon, Daniel J. McClain

Right-hand half is devoted to listing of contents, the left to miniature cover picture, masthead, indicia etc. Whole page is boxed.

contents
prime time
Volume I, Number 11   November 1980

27
42
100

Cover: Photographs, clockwise from upper left: Marilyn Silverstone/Magnum, Gregory Edwards, Antoine Pradock, Francesco Scavullo.

PRIME TIME 3

Prime Time, Judy Fendelman

Stretching definition of 2-column makeup a bit: 1/3 pictures, 2/3 listing set wide. Features at top, departments below.

Channels, Dean Morris

Time, Rudolph Hoglund

Two rows of five stories across in an appropriate storyboard pattern: picture/folio/title/byline/description all rag right, vertical rule at left.

Six columns across. Three stories picked out for emphasis with pictures. Tiny type, yet eminently legible — and worth reading.

Exxon Marine, William Snyder

L'Expansion, Jean Pierre Montagne

With only a few items to list, elegantly restrained typography contrasts with empty area to yield drama. Background in pale ocean-hue.

Upper box, divided into columns of varying widths, contains descriptions of five stories. Titles repeated in full listing below.

Publisher and Editor-in-Chief
LEDA GIOVANNETTI SANFORD
Editor
JOAN SCHLESINGER
Design Director
PAUL HARDY
Articles Editor
DONALD DEWEY
Associate Editor
GWENDA BLAIR
Contributing Editors
NICHOLAS ACOCELLA
JOANNE BARKAN
EVELYN DELLA CORTE
PAOLO FORMANI
RICHARD GAMBINO
NIKA HAZELTON
CHARLES MANN
JOHN MARIANI
WILLIAM WEAVER
Assistant to the Editor
WENDY FISHER
Assistant Copy Editor
JEAN GRASSO FITZPATRICK
Editorial Assistant
BETTYANN LOPATE
Design Assistant
MILES ABERNETHY
Production Coordinator
ROBERT SANFORD
Advertising Sales Director
JOHN LOGSDON
Advertising Coordinator
JUNE GRECO
Circulation Director
HARVEY SWAINE
Circulation Assistant
BARBARA ROSENFELD
Assistant to the Publisher
LOIS TUREL
Business Manager
ALDO IAVARONE
Business Coordinator
RHODA LEVENBERG

Cover Photograph by Pete Turner

Attenzione
SEPTEMBER 1979 VOL. 1, NO. 3

Attenzione, Paul Hardy

At first glance flamboyant, this is a conservative, functionally organized scheme: masthead at far left and contents at right are as simple as can be. Picture areas (and huge folios) are handled courageously indeed!

Welcome to the third issue of *Crops Quarterly.*

We know that getting ready for a new growing season makes the first few months of the year a busy time for you. We want you to know that PAG Seeds and your local PAG dealer sincerely want to help in any way possible.

That's why we call this important period PAG Prime Time. It's a time especially set aside by your dealer when he will give you hybrid performance information, help with hybrid selection, and provide information on seed storage, pickup and delivery.

We know that useful information is important to you. And Prime Time is our way of getting "localized" informa-tion to you in time to help you this planting season. Your PAG dealer will have up-to-the-minute hybrid performance reports on the PAG hybrids that are standouts in your area.

Many PAG dealers will be sponsoring special prime time events or making special Prime Time promotional offers. Take advantage of these. You'll find they'll be a good way to get your 1980 planting season off to a good start!

Dick Endres
Dick Endres
General Manager
PAG Seeds

SPRING, 1980 VOLUME 2, NUMBER 1

CROPS QUARTERLY CONTENTS

Editor
Gary Ashbacher
Art Director
Gordy Wilkinson

CROPS QUARTERLY is an agricultural publication emphasizing ideas and crop management practices that enable farmers to get top yields. PAG Seeds, a Division of Cargill Inc., P. O. Box 9480, Minneapolis, Minnesota 55440 publishes this magazine four times a year. It is distributed by PAG Seeds dealers throughout the United States. While the information contained herein is believed to be reliable, PAG makes no representation as to accuracy or completeness. Any statement non-factual in nature constitutes current opinions, which are subject to change.

Editorial, design and printing by The Webb Company. Correspondence should be directed to Editor, Crops Quarterly, 1999 Shepard Road, St. Paul, MN 55116. ©1980 PAG Seeds. Printed in the U.S.A.

Crops Quarterly, Gordy Wilkinson

This scheme, too, plays off simple text against imaginatively handled graphics: vast space separates editorial message from the four columns of listings and picture area. Note the liveliness that partial silhouetting can impart.

ACKNOWLEDGMENTS

Cover—Construction by Nicholas Fasciano, photographed by
Dan Kozan, background by Sarah Oliphant, products courtesy
of Georgia-Pacific, American Can, Black & Decker, Emtark, International Business Machines, Kraft, AMF, Emhart, Aluminum
Co. of America, General Electric, Burlington Industries, Polar-
oid, International Paper, Outboard Marine, Du Pont, Borden,
Beech & Lomb. 6—Dan Kozan. 41,44—Chartmakers Inc. 47—
Hugh P. Brown. 8. Burch. 59—Ellsworth Davis—Washington Post.
105,108,112—Michael McGinn. 116,117—William Rivelli. 121,
122—Courtesy General Electric Co. 127—William Rivelli. 133,
134—Kilbourn courtesy Continental Awards, photographed by
Al Pretti, courtesy General Electric, Henry Grossman, Tom
Ebenhoh, Julian Wasser. 140—William Redszus, courtesy NBC,
Richard Howard—Black Star. 156,157—Ricardo Watson, Michael
Evans, Roddey S. Mims, Diana H. Walker, Richard Frank, Rod-
dey S. Mims. 171—Courtesy Cadillac Motor Car Division. 198—
Courtesy Sotheby Parke Bernet. 192—Courtesy Preview Inc.
245—Courtesy George Elkins Co. 211—Bernard Diederich for
Time. 252—The New Studio. 226—George Phillippe. 236—Steve
Delaney, Susan T. McElhinney. 225. Greenaddys Stewart. 225
258—AP photograph, Patrick Studio. 262—Patrick Studio. 290—
William Redszus. 308,310,314,319—TV screens by Peter Vandore
and Eric, chart by Louis Dan Johnson. 322—Patricia Byrne. 357—
Lora Jones, Alan Reingold.

FORTUNE (ISSN 0015-8259) May 4, 1981, Vol. 103, No. 9
Issued biweekly by Time Inc., 3435 Wilshire Blvd., Los Angeles, CA
90010. Second-class postage paid at Los Angeles, CA and at
additional mailing offices. Subscriptions U.S. U.S possessions, one year
$30. Canada, one year $32, elsewhere one year $36 to $57. Single
copy $2.50. Address all subscriptions and correspondence concerning
them to FORTUNE, 541 North Fairbanks Court, Chicago, Illinois 60611.
Principal offices: Time & Life Building, Rockefeller Center, New York,
N.Y. 10020. Address correspondence concerning editorial matters to
FORTUNE, Time & Life Building, Rockefeller Center, New York, N.Y.

For the cover, Nicholas Fasciano built a shelf
system in the shape of a 500 and filled it with
products made by companies representing the
ten top industrial classifications in the FORTUNE
500. It was photographed by Dan Kozan.
Articles about this year's list begin on page 114,
and the directory itself begins on page 322.

Fortune, Ronald N. Campbell

Clear, sequential presentation with departments at left, narrow, and features at right, wider. Special items picked out in red ink. The pictures placed straddling the gutter, where they are visible when the book is fully opened — their function is more decorative than essential.

In diesem Heft

Capital, Jürgen Kryszons

Complex contents presented tabulated by topics in two central columns (Special Advice, Money, Careers, Economy etc). Outer halves of pages devoted to informal stories about stories, some with pictures and even captions. Tan background with red display helps hold it all together.

Eastern Review, John Van Hammersveld

Cheerful, colorful atmosphere to divert in-flight passengers. Effect of delightful, miscellaneous bits and pieces is created by the narrow-column makeup, strong color contrast in type, apparently random insertion of pictures. "Preview, Review, Overview" headings are hardly visible — but that doesn't detract from success of presentation.

OGJ — Jan.12,1981 Vol.79No2

OGJ Report: West Africa

Oil production from this region looms ever more vital in view of the continuing shutdown of flow from Iran and Iraq and the trend toward imposition of production ceilings by other major oil exporting countries. Conditions are difficult—both politically and from an operations standpoint. But potential is high, activity is brisk, and new countries are joining the list of West African oil producers. OGJ's International Editor covers it all in this on-site report.

(Continued)

Technology

Drilling/production

Alaskan study—1:
New study analyzes Alaska OCS areas 73
Peter T. Hanley and William W. Wade. Of 10 upcoming OCS lease sales in Alaska, six have been evaluated. Part one of this two-part article sets out the important technical parameters for each of the six areas.

Drilling and development costs studied for offshore gas fields 95
Konthi Kulachol and S.S. Marsden. A study of the development of offshore gas fields has resulted in relationships for determining the costs of drilling, subsea equipment and completions, manifolds, flowlines, platform, floor gas processing equipment, and transportation.

Refining/processing

Stretford plants proving reliable 80
Thomas J. Kresse, Ernest T. Lindsey, and Ted Wadleigh. Stretford tail gas cleanup plants have proved reliable handling an acid-gas stream containing up to 12% H_2S from a Sulfinol plant and natural gas containing 30 grams H_2S/100 scf for Natural Gas Pipeline Co. of America.

Refinery catalytically cuts NO_x emissions 99
Joe B. Blair, Gene Maxey, and Herbert Hill. A California refinery reduced its NO_x emissions while increasing its heater efficiency with a project prompted by an expansion.

Transportation

Guidelines can aid in chartering LNG vessels 88
Alex Vedeler. Shipping is a highly specialized element in an LNG project. It is important that key parts of the shipping agreement be considered fully by all parties early in project planning.

This week's cover

Sundown over the Malongo fields off Cabinda, West Africa. Special OGJ report on critically important West African producing region in today's tight worldwide crude-supply situation begins on page 47. Photo courtesy Gulf Oil Corp.

The Oil and Gas Journal (ISSN 0030-1388) is published weekly by Petroleum Publishing Co., 1421 S. Sheridan Rd., Tulsa, Okla. Box 1260, 74101. Second-class postage paid at Tulsa, Okla. Copyright 1981 by Petroleum Publishing Co. All rights reserved.

Oil & Gas Journal, Max Batchelder

Both sides of heavy stock card tipped in following inside front cover. Extremely complicated publication requires detailed grouping of full spectrum of contents for specialized readership.

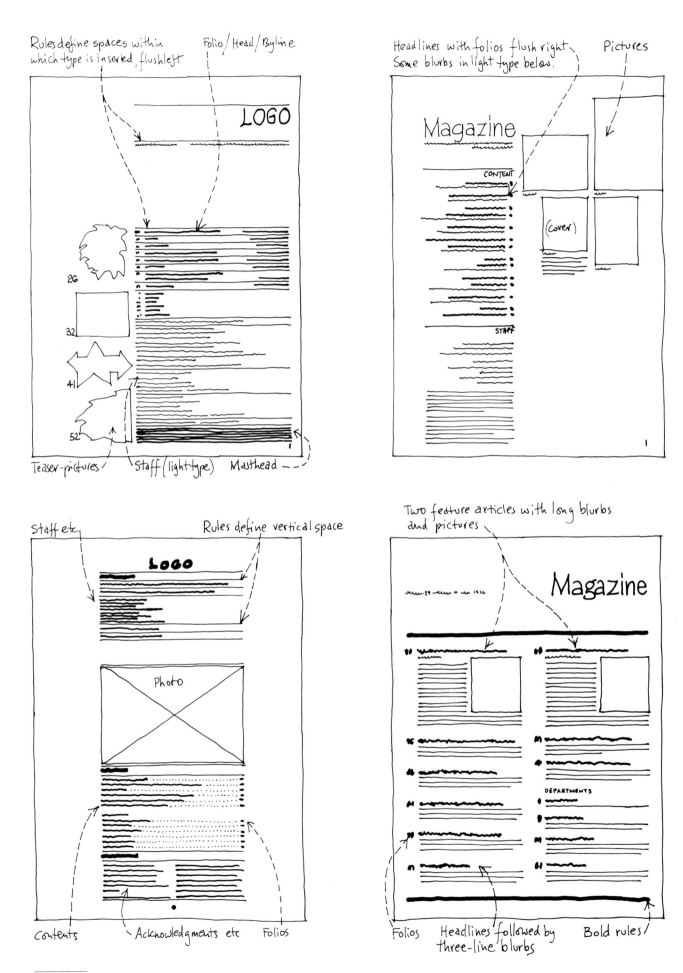

Rules define spaces within which type is inserted, flushleft

Folio / Head / Byline

LOGO

26

32

41

52

Teaser-pictures

Staff (light type)

Masthead

Headlines with folios flush right. Some blurbs in light type below.

Pictures

Magazine

CONTENT

(cover)

STAFF

1

Staff etc

Rules define vertical space

LOGO

Photo

Contents

Acknowledgments etc

Folios

Two feature articles with long blurbs and pictures

Magazine

1976

DEPARTMENTS

Folios

Headlines followed by three-line blurbs

Bold rules

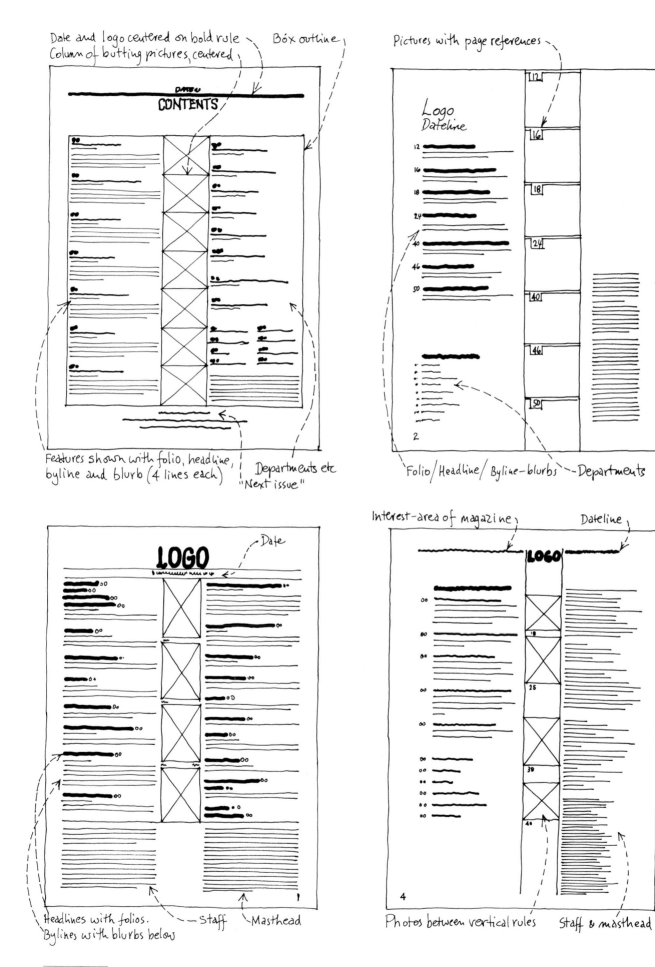

Date and logo centered on bold rule
Column of butting pictures, centered

Box outline

DATE

CONTENTS

Pictures with page references

Logo
Dateline

12
16
18
24
40
46
50

2

Features shown with folio, headline,
byline and blurb (4 lines each)

Departments etc
"Next issue"

Folio/Headline/Byline-blurbs

Departments

Date

LOGO

Interest-area of magazine

Dateline

LOGO

Headlines with folios.
Bylines with blurbs below

Staff

Masthead

4

Photos between vertical rules

Staff & masthead

Rules define each story presentation
Pictures arranged axially

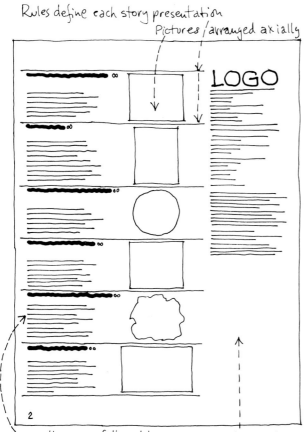

LOGO

Headlines are followed by
the folio. Blurbs set ragged right.

Staff & masthead

Sequential listing: Folio / Headline / Blurbs
Dateline acts as "headline"

LOGO

Attractive photo frieze separates contents above
from staff lists etc. below

Date

LOGO

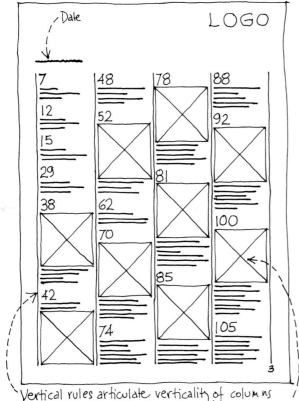

Vertical rules articulate verticality of columns
into which items fit (in sequence) with pictures

Staff listings

Magazine

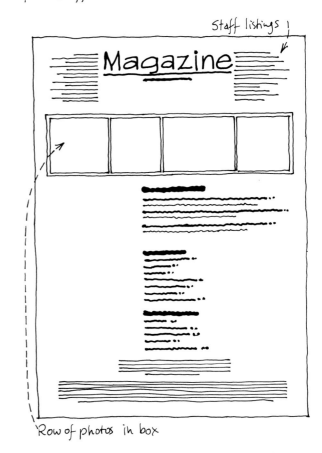

Row of photos in box

Bold and light rules organize space. Bold and light type indicates importance

Byline/Folio/Headline pattern followed throughout

Grid of horizontal rules equally spaced,

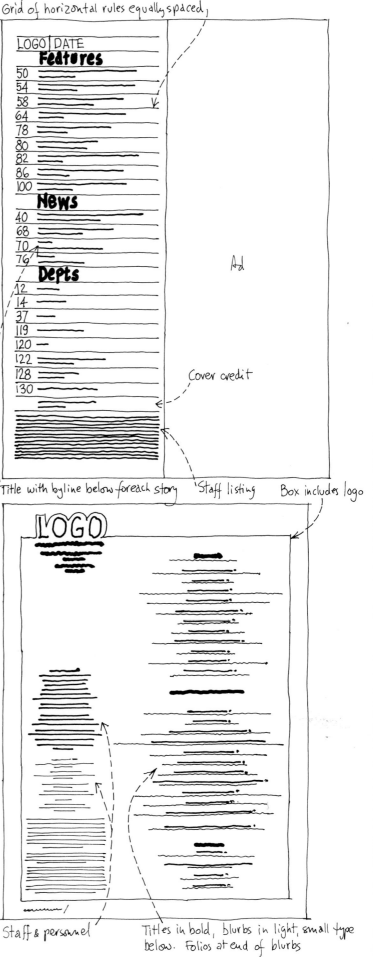

Features
50
54
58
64
78
80
82
86
100

News
40
68
70
76

Depts
12
14
37
119
120
122
128
130

Ad

Cover credit

Title with byline below for each story   Staff listing   Box includes logo

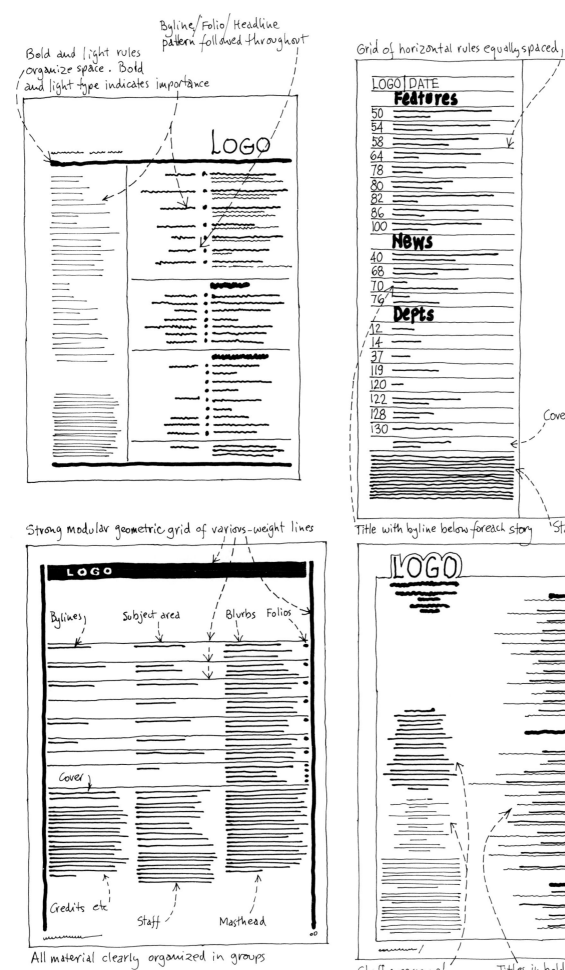

Strong modular geometric grid of various-weight lines

Bylines   Subject area   Blurbs   Folios

Cover

Credits etc   Staff   Masthead

All material clearly organized in groups

Staff & personnel

Titles in bold, blurbs in light, small type below. Folios at end of blurbs

FLASH! STOP PRESS! URGENT!

FLASH FORMS

Many publications have a "flash form" — a four- or eight-page sheet that goes to press at the very last moment (i.e., it "closes late" — that's why it is called the "late-closing" form). It is bound into the magazine as the last step in production; it can therefore carry the latest stop-press news. Of course such news can't possibly be as up-to-the-minute as that in today's newspaper, since production and distribution of the periodical takes time. However, it is generally accepted that such a group of late-closing pages is a positive attribute of specialized publications and, as such, deserves to be handled wisely and subtly, in order to bring out its maximum potential.

(!!)

Many publications do not have a true late-closing form, but nevertheless, recognizing its sales and public relations value, they ape the real thing by plagiarizing the design techniques that the honest ones use. The sham becomes transparent once the page is read, but the fact that pages which have the look of flash forms are there seems to add extra value to the publication.

Whether the flash form pages are honest or sham is, alas, immaterial as far as page design goes. The effectiveness of graphic image is not affected by the freshness or the staleness of the content — so here are some of the elements often used, which combine to give the required look. How they are combined, how the subtlety of proportion and spacing and typographic "color" are handled can make all the difference between a page that looks fresh and interesting and a page that is obviously a rip-off, a cliché, a pastiche of all the other "News from Washington" pages the editors have seen over the past years.

What are the basic elements?

1. Color of stock. If the late-closing form is, indeed, a true late-closer, it is often economically possible to print on a paper of different color and texture from the rest of the publication. Here is the prime method of calling attention to this section of the magazine, since it looks different (it can even be seen at the edge of the closed issue) and feels different (rougher, softer) than the surrounding stock. Usually it is a yellow or buff-colored paper since this seems to be visible yet restrained enough to appear obviously "editorial" (with the commensurate dignity required) and thus cannot be mistaken for an advertising insert which is likely to be colored more flamboyantly. Other commonly used colors are pale blue, pale orange, pale green, and sometimes, though not too often, thank goodness, pale pink. In any case the color is likely to be pale, because the paleness ensures that the black type printed on it will be easily legible; the contrast between the ink and the paper color are crucial.

What do the quasi-late-closers do? To help their pretense of having a make-believe insert, they use cans and cans of ink to print a second color full-bleed over the page. (The hue is normally brighter, more unsubtle, cruder than actual colored paper.) This coating of colored ink may actually create the illusion of a second stock — assuming that both sides of the page get the full treatment. But this seldom happens because the way the pages are laid out for printing prior to folding and trimming makes coloring both sides of a page impractical. The advertisers get preference, obviously, which is only right, since they are footing the bills. So you often find an "insert" that *appears* to be an insert all right, until you turn the page and discover that the emperor has no clothes: one side of the paper is colored, but the other side is not, and so the illusion is shattered. Nevertheless, whether the ink is printed on one side or both, the tactile and textural difference between the two paper stocks is nonexistent — although the color-inked side probably will be somewhat more slimy and shiny than the neighboring pages, because of all that glossy ink. So the trick seldom, if ever, works the way the editors hope it will.

2. *The logo.* There must be some sort of department heading that links the flash form to the other departments clearly, making it into an element in a chain of elements, albeit a most important one. Usually the slug reads "Washington," since most industry and professional news of political consequence or indicating future trends emanates from there. However, there are publications which merely call this page "Late News" and yet others who invent their

own label usually based on a pun or inside joke of some sort, such as *Chemical Engineering*'s "Chementator" or *Modern Plastics'* "Plastiscope." Whatever the wording, the typography must be of-a-piece with the rest of the department headings.

3. The date. This information is often run in conjunction with the logo, to reinforce further the impression that this page is a newsletter being sent to the recipient as a sort of bonus bound into the magazine.

4. The writer's name and/or picture. If the report is written by a special writer retained by the publication to inform the readers of the inside scoops, then his name rightfully belongs on the page, not merely because he probably deserves the byline, but because his very presence brings credit to the publication. Sometimes, the name of the editor is used if he is known and respected by the readership and can thus add a degree of lustre (or credibility) to the information.

5. The typography. There are three schools of thought here — each has its adherents, each its detractors and drawbacks. Examples of each can be found on the pages that follow.

(a) Large-type, wide-measure, heavy-handed school, that trumpets its items few to the page, possibly using some boldface lead-ins for emphasis
(b) Normal-type, normal-measure school, which relies on headlines to do its trumpeting (and there are lots of headlines per page)
(c) Typewriter-type school, that carries the newsletter-bound-into-the-issue illusion to its ultimate graphic conclusion

The choice of type is further complicated by the problem of headlines. This is, obviously, not just a design consideration, but must be integral with the thinking of the editors and the way the items are written.

Thus school (a) can eschew the use of boldface lead-ins and substitute headlines in some way: either stacked in the left-hand margin, or run as single-liners, poking out into the left-hand margin. Or it can compromise and run boldface lead-ins as outriggers in the left-hand margin.

School (b) can stack headlines, run them as outriggers, span two columns, three columns, or whatever; the danger here is that the more "normal" the page arrangement, the less "special" it is, losing some of its importance in the process.

School (c) has a problem with headlines since typewriter type comes in one size only. As soon as different sizes are combined, the illusion of that typewritten letter is weakened (even though people are becoming accustomed to copy from typewriters with interchangeable typefaces). The entire illusion, however, goes out the window when real boldface typset type is thrown in to make the headlines bolder. If typewriter type must be used, then its limitations must be accepted and a design format devised that will overcome them (see page 83).

6. *Decorative elements* (such as rules and borders, etc.). The same principles apply here as in other situations where extraneous graphic material is brought into play: there is no reason why decorative elements should not be used, as long as they are used with a specific purpose in mind. Decoration, in itself, is a perfectly acceptable purpose, but when coupled with another good reason, the likelihood is that the solution will make good sense and create graphic character with impact and serious value.

What are such good reasons? Creation of "color," for instance, by making contrast between very thin elements and very black elements, such "color" adds a liveliness to the page that it would lack if it were in plain type. Or creating a "box" that individualizes this page from all the others, thereby giving it its aura of extra importance. Or running two hairline rules up the page, bleeding top and bottom, creating a tall, thin channel, within which the material is placed — not terribly useful on a single page, but extremely useful on a multipage insert where the vertical rules act as railroad tracks from page to page, linking the pages together with minimal bumps. Or placing "masts" up the center of the page from which to suspend the items on either side. Or running color rules between items, both to split them up, as well as to create a "net" within which the items are disposed. Or for one of the purposes suggested by the examples on the next few pages.

PERSPECTIVAS: PRODUCCION

Helio polaco con tecnología inglesa
Una instalación de avanzada para elaborar gas natural permitirá a Polonia obtener gas rico en metano, y al mismo tiempo convertirá a ese país en importante proveedor mundial de helio. La nueva tecnología a utilizarse en la planta se basa en un proceso originado por la Petrocarbon Developments Ltd., de Manchester, Inglaterra. El gas natural del sudeste de Polonia posee gran proporción de nitrógeno y un contenido de helio relativamente elevado. Con el empleo de dos tubos verticales destiladores y temperatura relativamente baja, conforme a una organización análoga a la de una planta de oxígeno, el nuevo proceso reducirá la proporción de nitrógeno, proveyendo productos de metano para zonas industriales situadas a distancias de 120 y 150 millas. También se recupera y se licua aproximadamente el 88% del helio del gas de carga.

Envases de metal más delgado
Los fabricantes de envases metálicos cilíndricos (vulgarmente "latas") continúan su pugna con los productores de frascos y botellas en el mercado de los envases. Los fabricantes de latas han venido esforzándose por reducir el espesor de las paredes de los envases a fin de abaratar los costos. Recientemente la American Can Co. ha producido un diseño de dos piezas, llamado MiraForm II, que reduce la cuantía del metal necesario más o menos en un 15%. El espesor del tipo con paredes aceradas es de sólo 0.004 de pulgada, y de 0.005 de pulgada el aluminico. En el fondo de la lata hay un rebajo grande. Al desplazarse dicho fondo bajo la presión de empacado, el rebajo forma una nueva y estable superficie de asiento.

Los fabricantes de aluminio reducen la energía
El alza en el costo de la energía ha obligado a los fabricantes de aluminio a buscar una nueva tecnología para disminuir el consumo de las caídas de reducción. Utilizando revestimiento de grafito alrededor de los ánodos para que éstos se coloquen con menos facilidad. Sumitomo Chemical ha reducido el consumo eléctrico. En la planta de la ciudad de Tokio el nuevo sistema resulta en una demanda de 13.5 MWh por tonelada, mientras que los fabricantes de aluminio norteamericanos necesitan alrededor de 16 MWh por tonelada. Sin embargo, Alcoa está construyendo una planta en Palestina, Texas, donde se espera que el consumo baje a 9 MWh por tonelada cuando se ponga en funcionamiento a principios del año próximo.

Nuevo plástico estructural con fibras desplazables
Un nuevo tipo de plástico estructural moldeado debe gran parte de sus características ventajosas a un método de fabricación de propiedad exclusiva que dirige las fibras de vidrio de refuerzo a los lugares del molde donde

son necesarias para aumentar la resistencia. El resultado es un material estructural que es igual o superior, pero más barato, que los otros plásticos reforzados con fibras de vidrio, la madera contrachapada o los paneles "sandwich" de chapas metálicas y material alveolar. Soporta bien la humedad, los golpes y las trepidaciones (cuando se lo utiliza como recubrimiento de camionetas de remolque). Una máquina de moldeado por inyección reactiva produce paneles de plástico blanco brillante de 8 pies por 40 pies, que se pueden clavar, remachar y cortar fácilmente. Escribir a Contact Xentex Co., 23 Industrial Rd., Londonderry, N.H., USA 03053.

Colada automática de metal para fundiciones
Roto-Pour es un nuevo sistema para transferir y colar metales fundidos, desarrollado por General Motors Corp. Mejora el rendimiento al eliminar el exceso de las coladas y reducir las pérdidas por desechos. El metal caliente fluye en cantidades controladas desde un horno de conservación hasta una de las cucharas que están distribuidas alrededor de la máquina giratoria. La cuchara llena se traslada a la sección de moldes y se alinea con el molde correspondiente. El régimen de la colada se controla por la inclinación de la cuchara. El sistema utiliza elementos de lógica neumática y motores neumáticos para controlar todos los componentes. General Motors ha otorgado la licencia a Roberts Corp. (P.O.Box 239, Lansing, Mich., USA 48902) para construir y vender el sistema Roto-Pour.

Telar sin lanzadera
Los productores de telas en los EE.UU. están luchando contra la competencia que las presentan los fabricantes de tejidos de punto, tanto nacionales como extranjeros, incrementando el número de telares sin lanzaderas, que son hasta cinco veces más rápidos que los telares comunes. En este nuevo tipo de máquina, un proyectil (1) toma el hilo de grandes conos (2) y lo dispara mediante una cámara de aire a presión a través de la urdimbre (4), luego retorna al lado opuesto por otro disparo. Este sistema fue primeramente desarrollado por Sulzer, de Suiza, pero existen otros modelos fabricados por firmas de Francia, Alemania Occidental y España. Una versión japonesa utiliza una corriente de agua bajo alta presión para transportar el hilo de la trama a través del telar. Una firma norteamericana, Crompton & Knowles (345 Park Ave. New York, N.Y., USA 10022), tiene un modelo para telas multicolores con una capacidad de producción de siete a ocho yardas lineales por hora.

INDUSTRIAL WORLD EN ESPAÑOL, NOVIEMBRE DE 1975

Short items: the essence of the material

It doesn't matter how the items are arranged on the page, as long as this one crucial feature comes across immediately: each item is short. This is not merely a characteristic of the material to be played up in order to make the most of it visually, but is also a useful reader-attractor since short items always receive the most attention. (It looks as though it is no work to go through a group of little snippets, whereas a page of solid gray type would seem much more threatening drudgery.)

This example from *Electrical Construction and Maintenance* is about as simple a presentation as can be devised: separation is achieved by means of rules between the items; boldface lead-ins are used in lieu of headlines; there is lots of white space to make the page stand out — yet it remains part of a continuum by virtue of the logo which is reminiscent in design of all other department headings.

WASHINGTON REPORT

Signs that inflation is in fact here and increasing are beginning to multiply, and pressure for stronger economic measures to combat it is building up, both within government and out. Business economists and financial experts, and some government economists, agree that the time is already past when the Administration should take decisive action to curb this inflation before it gets out of hand. The big question is what action to take to provide the needed restraint to the economy, and relieve some of the pressures which are contributing to inflation.

Late last month, President Johnson reaffirmed that he did not want to push for an anti-inflationary tax increase prematurely, and cited a number of economic trends that are having some dampening effect on the economy. These included tax actions already adopted, a slowdown of the money supply and growth of business loans, and a 17% drop in housing starts in February.

Spending for new plant and equipment will rise $8 billion to $60 billion this year, according to the latest quarterly survey conducted by Dept. of Commerce—Securities & Exchange Commission. This forecast is generally causing concern among officials, who fear it could overextend the construction and equipment industries, adding to inflationary pressures. In 1965's final quarter, capital-investment spending was at a $55,350 million annual rate, and 1966's first quarter was expected to total $57,200 million. The average annual rate predicted for the second half of this year is $62,200 million.

An additional 200,000 tons of copper was released from the Federal stockpile late last month by President Johnson, chiefly to meet mounting need for the metal in the Vietnam war. This action was also expected to dampen pressure for a copper price increase.

A pay raise for Federal employees of exactly 3.2% was proposed by President Johnson early in March. This conforms to the Administration's wage guideline for labor and industry. Federal employee's pay has increased by more than 16% since 1961.

Estimates for 1966 gross national product (GNP) keep climbing as business activity keeps accelerating and defense spending, with its multiplier effect on the rest of the economy, keeps going up. Forecasts now range from $724 billion to $735 billion, versus earlier forecasts of $720 to $725 billion.

Unemployment in February dropped to 3.7% of the total labor force, the lowest rate since 1953. The rate was down to 2.6% during the Korean War.

Industrial output rose to a record during February, when it was 151.3% of the 1957-59 average. A year earlier it was 139.2%. During the same month personal income jumped $4 billion, at a seasonally adjusted annual rate, to a record $556.3 billion.

9

Two-columns-per-page organization

In this page from *Dental Economics* the individual items are kept within a maximum of five and minimum of three lines apiece; with this basic visual definition of the raw material, it is possible to devise a page arrangement that will make the staccato rhythm come across unequivocally, giving the page its individuality. Here the heavy, horizontal rules are run in color, helping dress up the page even further. (See page 182 for another example of a department from this publication and compare the differences and similarities of graphic treatment of the two sets of materials.)

rules
in color

Newsclips

The 8 per cent increase in appropriations for capital spending by the Nation's business firms improves the year-long business outlook.

The sales picture for Japanese television manufacturers was less than rosy last year. Now Japanese-made sets are being "dumped" in this country at less than prices charged in Japan.

The chances of being punished for a serious crime in the U S today are 3 in 100. Only 12 per cent of all reported major offenses lead to arrests, only 6 per cent to convictions, and only 1 per cent to prison.

The FDA will require child-proof packaging for all liquid household drain cleaners containing more than 10 per cent sodium hydroxide or potassium hydroxide, should a proposed regulation be adopted.

Auto prices continue to rise. Ford increased prices three times last year, to $187 per car; $232 for General Motors, and $119 for Chrysler.

George Wallace, Alabama's new governor, has his eye on the 1972 national scene, according to political observers.

A plastic house has come off the drawing boards at Du Pont as an outgrowth of research in polymers. Except for the structural framework, the showcase home is made entirely of plastics.

American Express, Diners Club, and Carte Blanche all report a significant increase in the number of establishments abroad accepting credit cards and in the number of customers using them overseas.

A serious threat to the economy is posed by the possibility of a strike in the steel industry, following next summer's wage negotiations.

Recovering remarkably from a last-summer slump, the Italian lira is expected to be safe from devaluation in the near future, according to Swiss bankers.

Cargo shipping is expected to surpass passenger revenue for the Nation's airlines.

The gift industry anticipates big sales in silver anniversary presents this year for the over 2 million U S couples who married in 1946, the year following the end of World War II. This was the largest number of weddings recorded in one year before or since.

Those bomber-size aircraft flying into Cuba from Russia are equipped with advanced gear for submarine detection, seriously concerning Uncle Sam.

The average European absorbs approximately $22 a year for government-sponsored research and development costs. The cost to a U S citizen averages $34.

A change in political direction in the Democratic party is anticipated in the near future. The realists are said to be taking over—the extremists will have "less to say," and the influence of the moderates of the center, and just left of center, will be felt more.

Western Union's flat-rate Public Opinion Message permits John Q. Public to express himself on a current issue to the President or to his congressman for only $1.

The problem of oil spills could soon be eliminated by the inoculation of the spill area with microbes which would eat the oil.

There are 4.5 million Americans who suffer from partial blindness; that is, 1 million who are unable to read newsprint and 3.5 million with some permanent, noncorrectable eye defect.

By 1975, it is predicted that 30 million women will be employed outside the home. This rise in the number of working women will increase the demand for appliances and convenience foods.

There is so much interest in do-it-yourself activities that Harvard's Doctor R. D. Buzzell recommends that more retailers turn to repair businesses and home maintenance.

The number of people moving into Southern states in the past ten years exceeds those leaving. Nearly one-third of the U S population lives in the South.

...or a single, extra-wide column organization

This is the important first page of a multipage news section. As such it must carry the major news stories as well as act as "opener." The extra wide setting (highly uncharacteristic of the magazine as a whole) and the geometrically simple page arrangement (which is, indeed, quite characteristic of it) meet both these requirements. The boldface lead-ins to the items ought to be restricted to one line only, and, to help legibility as well as continue the shortness-of-items principle, the items ought not to exceed five lines apiece. The variety produced on the page by the different item lengths is a positive factor — as variety — but one wonders whether a couple more short items culled from the long ones, might not make the page even more successful.

NEWS IN BRIEF

THE RECORD REPORTS

NEWS REPORTS
BUILDINGS IN THE NEWS
HUMAN SETTLEMENTS
REQUIRED READING

A bill now in Congress would allow a construction union to shut down an entire construction site. If passed, HR 5900 will permit a union to force a general contractor off the project by picketing everyone on the site, even if he is not involved in the disagreement. The bill, known as the Common Situs, would abolish the existing rule that allows a construction union to strike and picket a firm in dispute, but not to willfully picket or to pressure any firm on the site that is neutral in the dispute. The change would enable any of the building trade unions having a dispute with one of several firms on the site to picket indiscriminately and to shut down the entire project. Details on page 34.

The U.S. Supreme Court has agreed to review Federal court authority to countermand state licensing rules for design professionals. The case in point involves a three-judge constitutional court in Puerto Rico which struck down a provision that only citizens can get full licenses from examining boards of architects, engineers and surveyors. The high court, will look at the legality of banning alien architects. The lower court order to the board to license Mexican and Spanish applicants is stayed until the Justices rule in the term beginning October 6.

Candidates are now being considered for the AIA/NBS Architect in Residence Program sponsored by the American Institute of Architects and the U.S. Department of Commerce, National Bureau of Standards. Among the goals of the program is maintaining linkages between the architectural profession and research and development in planning and construction technology. The appointment offers a stipend of $15,000 and runs from September 1, 1975 to June 30, 1976. For further information, contact: John P. Eberhard, AIA Research Corporation, 1735 New York Avenue, N.W., Washington, D.C. 20006.

Wage settlements in the construction industry are averaging 10.1 per cent so far this year, up from 9.6 as reported in April. These figures are compiled by the Associated General Contractors of America and reflect 153 settlements reported to its national office. Approximately 3,500 contracts expire this year.

Bankers are now wary of PUD costs, according to a *Business Week* interview with mortgager Robert L. Cashion, board chairman of North Carolina National Bank. He states: "The amount of development capital required, the amount of risk exposure generated, is just oo much for any one leader or consortium of lenders to accept."

Owens-Corning Fiberglas Corporation announces its Fourth Annual Energy Conservation Awards Program. The program recognizes architects, engineers and building owners who have made significant contributions to energy management in the design and construction of commercial, industrial and institutional buildings. Deadline for submitting entries is August 31. For further information, write Owens-Corning Fiberglas Corporation, Fiberglas Tower, Toledo, Ohio 43659.

Joseph A. D'Amelio of Sweet's, and Saul Horowitz Jr. of HRH Construction Company died on June 24 in the crash of an Eastern Airlines jet landing at New York's John F. Kennedy International Airport. Both men were returning from the annual convention of the Construction Specifications Institute in New Orleans. Mr. D'Amelio, a registered architect was vice president of development for the Sweet's Division of McGraw-Hill Information Systems Company, and had previously been an assistant professor of architecture at Cooper Union in New York. Before joining McGraw-Hill, he was also a designer in the New York offices of Skidmore, Owings and Merrill; Gruzen and Associates; and Edward Durell Stone. Saul Horowitz Jr., chairman of the HRH Construction Company, one of the largest privately owned building concerns in New York, was also the current president of The Associated General Contractors of America. Last year, he was named "Construction's Man of the Year" by *Engineering News-Record* and among the buildings constructed by his firm are the Whitney Museum of American Art and the Waterside housing development in New York City.

Columbia University is seeking films and video-tapes dealing with built environments for a film festival to be held in November. This year's festival focuses on the urban reality and on process of urbanization. A jury of prominent urban specialists will award money prizes to those works selected and all entries must be received between September 15 and October 1st. Deadline for indicating interest is July 31st. For more information, contact Francois Contino, 410 H Avery Hall, Columbia University, New York, New York 10027.

John Merrill Sr., retired partner in Skidmore, Owings & Merrill died June 10 at the age of 78. He lived in Colorado Springs. Mr. Merrill, who retired in 1958, was a Fellow of the American Institute of Architects and past president of the Chicago Chapter. Among his most notable achievements was the design and construction of Oak Ridge, Tenn., the nuclear-research installation where the atomic bomb was developed.

Peter Blake has been appointed chairman of the Boston Architectural Center's School of Architecture. Mr. Blake architect and editor of *Architecture Plus*, will move to Boston from New York and assume his duties at the BAC later this year. The BAC is one of the oldest and largest architectural schools in the U.S., with more than 550 students admitted under an open-door policy, with a volunteer faculty of more than 200 professionals.

Longer items require strong headlines to entice the reader's scrutiny

The two examples shown here are similar solutions to the problem of getting the reader interested in slightly longer items. In fact, the texts are not all that long, though the large (twelve point) type makes it appear as though they were. The contents, however, are of great importance to the readership and thus warrant a stentorian tone of voice, one with obvious authority. Big type, set widely, is the most forthright visual signal of such tone, assuming that the typeface itself has the right character. Baskerville (*Engineering News-Record's* body copy face) and Century Expanded (*Construction Methods and Equipment's* face) both are dignified and strong enough to do the job.

The headlines that jut out like outriggers into the white space of the left-hand margin are highly visible and help lead the eye right into the text. They are visible because of their blackness (in spite of the fact that the type size is only twelve point) and because of the white space against which they contrast.

The outrigger boldface lead-ins in the example on the next page are better at pulling the eye into the text, since they lead directly into it; however, technical typesetting requirements dictate that the boldface headlines in both the examples here be set on separate lines.

ENR WASHINGTON OBSERVER

Transportation measures clear Congress in waning hours

Major legislation affecting highways, airport development and railroad construction moved through final congressional steps in the closing days of the congressional session. In a last-minute move, the House approved by a vote of 410 to 7 the federal highway aid bill (H.R. 8235), which extends the Highway Trust Fund for two years and provides an unspecified amount for the Interstate program. The measure also includes $800 million for the primary road system, $400 million for the secondary system, $800 million for the urban system and $400 million for the urban extension system. Senate-House conferees must now meet to resolve differences with the Senate's S. 2711, which has lower funding levels.

In a separate action, the House approved its aid to airport development bill (H.R. 9771) after restoring a provision for terminal improvements. Funding was set at $2.3 billion over three years. Both houses of Congress passed a $6.5-billion railroad aid bill (S.2718) that includes $2.4 billion for construction improvements in the Northeast corridor. The fate of the measure is in doubt. Transportation Secretary William T. Coleman recommends a veto, prompting congressional leaders to withhold the bill until Congress returns, to block a potential pocket veto by the President.

AGC fights expansion of small contractor surety bond program

The Small Business Administration (SBA) surety bond guarantee program for small construction contractors is coming under fire from the Associated General Contractors (AGC). The contractors' association claims that marginal firms, lacking the stability to secure bonding on the open market, are unfairly propped up by a plan under which SBA provides guarantee assistance for companies with an annual volume up to $2 million. The program encourages companies to take "unnecessary risks on jobs for which they do not have the qualifications or experience to obtain commercial bonding," AGC officials are telling congressional committees.

AGC wants Congress to make it clear to SBA that it should not have raised the volume ceiling of $750,000, which was in effect until two years ago. The agency adjusted the amount upward after determining that many general contractors with higher gross receipts were unable to obtain bonds.

Trade commission joins battle for professional advertising

The Federal Trade Commission (FTC) in separate challenges involving physicians and optometrists has joined the Justice Department in its battle against advertising bans on professional services. Commission spokesmen will not say whether similar action against construction design organizations is to be expected, but clearly all restrictions on professional advertising will be challenged by one or the other of the federal agencies.

The FTC filed complaints against the American Medical Association, charging that its policies prevent physicians from advertising and against ophthalmologists and optometrists over eyeglasses advertising. In both cases, the commission is demanding that the groups "cease taking any action which interferes with a . . . (professional's) right to advertise his services or to otherwise engage in open and free competition" with other professionals.

Export Expansion Act still alive

Don't give up hope for the Export Expansion Act. It may still become law, but probably not before next year.

The construction industry has a large stake in the bill. John E. Quinn, executive secretary of the National Constructors Assn., has said approval would mean an increase of $2 billion to $3 billion annually for the 35 companies in NCA.

The bill is complex, but two provisions are particularly important to the construction industry. One would authorize several U.S. firms to enter into cost sharing contracts with the Commerce Dept. to develop export programs in various ways, including the preparation bids on foreign projects.

Another provision would establish a Commission on Foreign Procurement Practices which would recommend federal government action to assure that bids by firms in individual foreign countries receive no more favorable treatment in the U.S. than that accorded to bids by U.S. firms in that country.

Among these provisions is one offering an antitrust exemption to U.S. firms forming a combine for bidding on foreign work. U.S. international contractors have long argued that the antitrust laws have worked at a disadvantage to them in attempting to win foreign work.

The bill (S.2754), sponsored by Sen. Warren Magnuson (D-Wash.), has now been divided into six separate pieces of legislation to get around problems of congressional jurisdiction.

In Congress' rush to get away for the summer political conventions, the measures are unlikely to move very far. Magnuson, however, is among the most powerful of Senators and as chairman of the Commerce Committee he is in a position to see to it that the issue is kept alive.

International banks may be cut

The Administration's proposal for appropriations for international banking authorities may be cut by Congress again this year.

These requests are stalled at the subcommittee level pending Congressional action on the authorization legislation for security assistance. Action on the appropriations is not likely before fall and all face substantial cuts in the House where Rep. Otto Passman (D-La.) has great influence as chairman of the Foreign Operations Subcommittee of the House Appropriations Committee. Passman is highly critical of Nixon's policy of putting more foreign aid through multilateral institutions which Passman believes dilutes the control of Congress and loses export business for U.S. companies.

Although the U.S. construction industry has complained in the past that the procurement practices of the international financial institutions are weighted against American firms, U.S. contractors still stand to get some business from the multilateral agencies. U.S. contractors and engineering firms in recent years have done quite well in bidding on projects financed by international development institutions, winning a share of the business roughly comparable to the U.S. contributions to those institutions.

Two-columns-out-of-three used as basis for design variations

The two versions of *Modern Plastics'* "Plastiscope" section show the two degrees of importance assigned to the material on the pages: the more important, stop-press material, right, is set in larger scale, using double-column width with long outrigger-type boldface lead-ins to carry the eye into the text. The department's second division, opposite, (which starts on a new page in the back of the book) carries the more mundane, less important stories; the normal column width is used, with free-standing headlines that are positioned similarly to the outriggers, but here span the full page, also covering the illustrations which are placed in the far left column.

The tone intended by the editors becomes quite evident when the two pages are compared — yet makeup is absolutely standard and simple.

NEWS AND
INTERPRETATION

THE PLASTISCOPE

Plastics respond to the general business level   A study of the past three 6-month periods for plastics indicates that the industry's sales pattern follows that of general industry with little modification. The once fashionable idea that because of its new markets and its successful invasion of old markets, plastics could increase while general business declined, probably can now be abandoned.

Plastics sales in the first six months of 1966 continued the upward climb that had been going on for several years in nearly all business, and contributed to the record sales set in 1966 (see table, below). But the figures show that most sales began to level off in mid-1966. They were still high compared to other years, but the rate of growth had slowed, as it had in most other industries.

The first-half sales of 1967 remained at about the same level as the second half of 1966 with a slight over-all decline, except in three or four instances to be discussed later. If this first-half figure is doubled, it may give an indication of what the total for 1967 is going to be, but most sales managers feel that the second half will exceed the first half by a small percentage.

How the major plastics stacked up at mid-year   The following table contains U.S. Tariff Commission consumption figures for the first and second halves of 1966 and the first half of 1967, covering the large-volume resins. Statistics for such materials as nylon, acetal, polycarbonate, etc., are not reported by the Commission in its monthly publication. (Figures below are in thousands of pounds).

Material	First 6 months of 1966	Last 6 months of 1966	First 6 months of 1967
Polyethylene, low density	1,261,254	1,264,718	1,248,410
Polyethylene, high density	437,833	451,397	476,386
Polypropylene	250,628	293,639	299,686
PVC and copolymers	1,071,304	1,080,809	1,032,343
Styrenics, total	1,182,543	1,243,932	1,143,963
Molding	629,306	621,263	563,797
Extrusion	174,903	164,310	174,186
Epoxy, unmodified	71,621	66,831	64,985
Polyester	202,890	194,753	212,703
Phenolic types, total	406,690	392,441	389,196
Molding	138,040	133,354	123,497
Laminating	41,829	36,075	33,069
Urea and melamine	276,484	267,179	271,793
Laminating	16,928	15,351	16,081
Cellulosics	90,276	92,659	86,291

For the polyolefins, it's a case of "high hopes"   Low density PE consumption is expected to be about the same in 1967 as in 1966, namely, 2.5 billion pounds. It could even go to 2.6 billion, but through September there was as yet no indication of the kind of big raise that would have to come to produce that volume. Film-grade resin sales, which account for almost 50% of domestic sales, were 506.3 million lb. in the first half of 1967 versus 543 million lb. in the same period of 1966. The 1967 film figure could have been influenced by a large inventory buildup in the last few months of 1966 by extruders. In 1967, the industry expects a sale of at least 2.25 billion lb., a little over 1966. The low density PE export market is not yet clear—it varies considerably from month to month, but at last count was slightly under 1966.

Of even more importance to the industry than sales volume was the price

43

THE PLASTISCOPE

German breweries introduce test beer bottles — blow molded from PVC

The long-awaited entry of polyvinyl chloride bottles into volume food markets may be beginning in Germany, with the introduction of test bottles for beer—first shown at the International Exhibition of Fine Foods, Cologne, in early October. (They were also shown at the Kunststoffe show in Dusseldorf.)

The fillled bottles were distributed (free) at the Exhibition by Paderborner Brauerei GmbH,. Paderborn, and Stern-Brauerei Carl Funke AG, Essen, both of West Germany. Spokesmen for Chemische Werke Huels, of Marl, which developed the bottles with the two breweries, says there are no chemical reaction problems in storing the beer in PVC bottles. Data on formulation of the PVC compound, including use of heat stabilizers, was not available at the time the bottles were introduced.

Another problem, that of containing a liquid that can build up gas pressure, and of maintaining flavor, is solved in the use of PVC, the chemical company says. While the Paderborner bottle is conventional in shape (see photo), the brewer reportedly has no qualms about its ability to contain the liquid. Stern-Brauerei, on the other hand, has deliberately chosen a shape that resembles two connected globes, with the cap resting on the top globe. The globe design is believed more capable of resisting the build-up of gases within the container. Another spherical beer bottle, recently patented in Germany by Helmut Lower, of Dransfeld, is said to provide four to six times the pressure resistance of cylindrical constructions, plus giving uniform wall thickness.

Horst Launer, president of Paderborner, claims that the economics of the PVC bottle favor it over glass when the brewer maintains a blow molding machine on the premises, even exclusive of gains in handling and shipping. The PVC bottles are one-third the weight of throw-away glass containers.

Resin combinations in fluidized bed coatings are tailored to the job

A wider market for fluidized bed and electrostatic coatings is foreseen with the introduction of blends of plastics and resin powders that combine the advantages of two polymers with gains in economy and performance. So far, the system has been used to successfully blend vinyl with polyethylene, epoxy, butyrate, and polyester; to blend nylon with epoxy and PE; and to combine epoxy with PE and polyester.

The blending technique was developed by B. L. Downey Co. Inc., of Vernon, Calif., and is currently being used to coat a line of silverware display racks. The system can also be adapted to lay down laminates of two or more resins; one such use is in a vinyl/polyester laminate for aluminum chairs, to be used in an outdoor cafe (see photo).

Reductions in costs are claimed for the blending system, since more expensive resins may be combined with such commodity types as PVC and PE. For instance, the silverware display racks combine epoxy and PVC in a 75:25 ratio. Epoxy sells for about three times the price of PVC.

But there are processing and performance advantages from the blending system as well. For instance, in the epoxy/PVC mix, the epoxy provides good adhesion to the metal frame; vinyl alone would require a separate priming step. Also, epoxy alone would be brittle, and probably could not survive flexing of the metal rack; the vinyl adds flexibility to the coating. A third benefit comes with blending special colors into a coating that might be difficult to obtain with one resin.

The company reports that there are special techniques involved, which include the blending of compatible powders in the right proportions, and using particles of similar size. There is reportedly no problem in curing dissimilar materials, even when different melt temperatures are involved. Nylon (450° F. melt index) and PE (300° F.) have been blended and cured successfully. Experiments are under way with nylon and chlorinated polyether, and other exotic combinations.

In the process, mixed powders are suspended in a tank by about 1 lb. air pressure. At the same time, the tank is vibrated to move the particles horizontally and maintain a controlled turbulence. Metal parts to be treated are first preheated in an oven at about 600° F., and then dipped into the tank for coating. After dipping, excess particles are vibrated off the part, and it travels to the curing oven.

The largest market for standard pow-

Tan-colored stock insert is the major recognition factor of four-page section

Chementator

The tough new 1-ppm. ceiling for worker exposure to vinyl chloride in ambient air was upheld Jan. 31 by a three-judge panel of the U.S. Court of Appeals for the Second Circuit, in New York.

The Soc. of the Plastics Industry (SPI) and some 20 chemical and plastics firms challenged the standard after OSHA announced it last fall (*Chementator*, Oct. 14, 1974, p. 52), mainly on the grounds that it is unnecessarily harsh and technologically infeasible. But the court disagrees, saying in part that the companies "simply need more faith in their own technological potentialities."

The ruling opens a possibility of easement for PVC fabricators. OSHA's new regulation covers them at present, as well as companies that make or polymerize vinyl chloride; but the court says that if vinyl chloride levels prove to be sporadic and low at PVC fabricating plants, the fabricators might be exempted (or subjected to a less rigorous standard).

The 1-ppm. ceiling was originally to go into effect Jan. 1, but in December SPI won a stay pending the (Jan. 31) decision. As of now, the effective date is April 1. At presstime, SPI has not decided whether to appeal the new ruling.

China might become a major natural-gas supplier to Japan. A Japanese trade mission now in Peking discussing gas projects says the Chinese are strongly interested in getting Japanese technical help for building natural-gas-liquefaction plants "several tens of times" bigger then the 150,000-ton/yr figure initially mentioned by the Japanese group itself during the discussions. A substantial part of the output, derived from the offshore Taiko oil-and-gas field situated in the Gulf of Pohai, would be shipped to Japan.

Today, Japan's gas imports consist of 1 million tons/yr from Alaska and 2.4 million from Malaysia. This total is nearly twice what Japan produces from its domestic wells.

And Japan is looking closer to home for oil, too, via an agreement with the U.S.S.R. over exploration and development of petroleum (and gas) resources off Sakhalin Island, just north of Japan and east of Siberia. The Japanese are talking with Gulf Oil about possible participation, as a supplier of capital and knowhow.

Under the agreement, Japan's Sakhalin Oil Development Cooperation Co. will extend to the Soviets a $100-million credit repayable only if oil and gas are found, plus a $52.5-million regular credit. Once oil production starts, the U.S.S.R. will supply Japan with 50% of it over a 28-yr period—at a price 8.4% below the prevailing international level, for the first ten years.

Two other Japanese-Soviet agreements for Soviet oil or gas development, in the Tyumen and Yakutsk regions, are currently stalled because of staggering capital requirements. Japanese observers give the Sakhalin venture a better chance of success, because its closeness to Japan will keep transportation investments down. If the project materializes, it should considerably ease Japan's heavy dependence on Middle East oil.

Westinghouse still expects to make a go of its offshore-nuclear-plants venture at Jacksonville, Fla., even though Tenneco Inc. has bailed out by selling Westinghouse its 50% interest.

The joint operation, Offshore Power Systems (OPS), was founded in 1972 after feasibility studies by the two companies for an assembly facility to make floating

---

Chemical Engineering's biweekly flash form is the best read and most informative collection of essential news available to its readership. It is one of the most important elements in the publication and must, therefore, be instantly accessible. The familiar, colored stock can be discerned just by looking at the edge of the closed issue, and when the pages are flipped, the section is impossible to miss. The colored stock is the department's prime recognition symbol.

The "before," left, shows the typographic arrangement as it was imposed on the stock: the legibility and arrangement were perfectly satisfactory, merely lacking sparkle. This was, perhaps due to the choice of rather tired typefaces; and the logo was much too large (why gild the lily when the stock itself does the attention alerting?).

The "after," opposite, retains the wide-column setting, actually somewhat wider to accommodate the same number of characters per line as before but allow for the wider Baskerville type that replaced the narrow Times Roman. The two vertical rules alongside the column were introduced not just to make the page look "different" or to give it some vague image of "printout" or "galley"; they were brought in because, in some mysterious way, they manage to tie the four pages together into a smoothly flowing unit, a single strand instead of four individual page-long segments.

The outrigger lead-ins were therefore sacrificed and brought flush with the left edge of the type column. To signal the start of each item and to reinforce the blackness of each headline, a six-pica-long stub overscore was placed above each lead-in.

The logo is handled the same way as all other department headings; the dateline is smaller but still very much in evidence; folio and footline are centered.

New catalysts for automobile catalytic converters withstand leaded gasoline combustion products. Developed by Du Pont, and now undergoing tests, the catalysts are billed as a "major breakthrough" by company scientists.

The basic ingredient is a synthetic crystal, resembling perovskite in structure, that is built up from lanthanum, strontium and cobalt oxides. The crystal incorporates active catalytic components such as platinum, ruthenium and palladium, while screening these materials from lead and other poisons. U.S. Patent No. 3,897,367 was issued for the invention in late July.

Besides resistance to lead, Du Pont claims the formulation has many other advantages over conventional catalysts, including durability, thermal stability, and resistance to phosphorus, sulfur and, under most conditions, halogens. To back up these claims, the company is conducting automotive tests, and so far has chalked up over 20,000 miles on 1975 vehicles.

Perchloroethylene and 1,1,1-trichloroethane do not cause cancer, according to Dow Chemical Co., which has reported preliminary results of more than two years of inhalation experiments on rats. This conclusion, if it holds up to critical review, would clear the way for substitution of the two solvents for trichloroethylene, which the National Cancer Institute singled out in a March "memorandum of alert" as a possible carcinogen.

Of all the 192 animals exposed to 1,1,1-trichloroethane, and an equal number exposed to perchloroethylene, only one suspicious liver tumor was found (several others were of a type common to rats). The liver tumor occurred in a female that had been inhaling 1,750 ppm of 1,1,1-trichloroethane—or about four times the peak vapor-exposure-limit recommended by the American Conference of Governmental Industrial Hygienists. But Dow scientists concluded that the statistical incidence of this type of tumor was the same in control and exposed rats; hence, 1,1,1-trichloroethane is not indicated as a cancer-producing agent.

Studies on other chlorinated solvents produced by Dow are in various stages at the company's Midland, Mich. laboratories. Perchloroethylene and 1,1,1-trichloroethane were given top priority.

Polyimide resins capable of withstanding temperatures of 700°F are being groomed by Gulf Oil Chemicals Co., as the company nears completion of the first commercial plant to make a major component for the resins, BTDA (benzophenone-tetracarboxylic dianhydride).

While getting ready to produce BTDA, Gulf purchased technology from Hughes Aircraft Co. for the resins. Described as a new class of addition-curable thermosetting polyimides, these resins are claimed to exhibit exceptional thermal stability and ease of processing. Conventional polyimides withstand temperatures of no more than 550°F. The resins can be used as adhesives, or to bind molybdenum disulfide (at ratios of about 70:30 resin-to-moly), and then be compressed under heat to yield not an adhesive but a solid lubricant.

The multimillion-dollar BTDA facility at Gulf's Jayhawk Works in southeastern Kansas, near Pittsburg, should begin operation at the end of this month. No production unit exists yet for the polyimide resins, except for bench-scale facilities that provide the U.S. Air Force with small quantities. On a commercial basis,

Last minute news, hot off the typewriter

These two examples are both from *Industrial Marketing*. The "before," right, uses both typewriter type and blue ink tinting over the whole page in an attempt to create the impression of a super-rush late-closing. One assumes that the reader will accept the implication that the logo and the typeset heading were preprinted and that the typewritten matter is imposed thereon as on a letterhead.

The "after" version, opposite, eschews the use of colored ink altogether, preferring to give the illusion of a "letter" by means of the ruled box which seems to define the edge of a piece of paper placed on the page. Neither version can be as realistic or successful as if the "letter" had actually been typed and then a photograph of it reproduced as a halftone, with a "shadow" cast by the letter completing the illusion.

Fortunately neither version uses regular typeset type for headlines as is too often done: obviously the introduction of material that cannot possibly have been set on a typewriter must immediately destroy the hot-off-the-typewriter illusion that the editors are trying to create.

The "before" illustrates a very normal typewritten page makeup, with the indentions, underscorings, capitalizations, and spacings that come naturally to the medium. The "after" adds a degree of graphic play to this *natural* use of the medium: by manipulating the space, it allows more imaginative use of the lead-ins, tucking the headline sentences into the white space that "belongs" to the preceding story. Thus much greater attention-grabbing capacity is built into the format. Yes, the page is gray all over, but that is a deliberate ruse and a positive attribute IF the typewriter illusion is deemed desirable.

Blue tint
↓

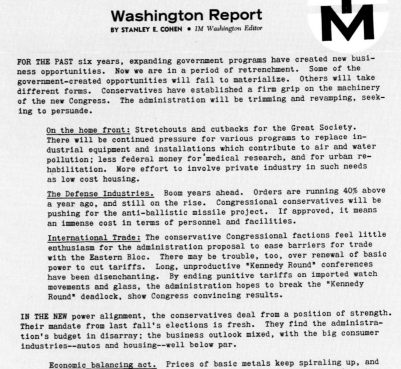

Washington Report
BY STANLEY E. COHEN • *IM Washington Editor*

FOR THE PAST six years, expanding government programs have created new business opportunities. Now we are in a period of retrenchment. Some of the government-created opportunities will fail to materialize. Others will take different forms. Conservatives have established a firm grip on the machinery of the new Congress. The administration will be trimming and revamping, seeking to persuade.

<u>On the home front</u>: Stretchouts and cutbacks for the Great Society. There will be continued pressure for various programs to replace industrial equipment and installations which contribute to air and water pollution; less federal money for medical research, and for urban rehabilitation. More effort to involve private industry in such needs as low cost housing.

<u>The Defense Industries.</u> Boom years ahead. Orders are running 40% above a year ago, and still on the rise. Congressional conservatives will be pushing for the anti-ballistic missile project. If approved, it means an immense cost in terms of personnel and facilities.

<u>International Trade:</u> The conservative Congressional factions feel little enthusiasm for the administration proposal to ease barriers for trade with the Eastern Bloc. There may be trouble, too, over renewal of basic power to cut tariffs. Long, unproductive "Kennedy Round" conferences have been disenchanting. By ending punitive tariffs on imported watch movements and glass, the administration hopes to break the "Kennedy Round" deadlock, show Congress convincing results.

IN THE NEW power alignment, the conservatives deal from a position of strength. Their mandate from last fall's elections is fresh. They find the administration's budget in disarray; the business outlook mixed, with the big consumer industries--autos and housing--well below par.

<u>Economic balancing act.</u> Prices of basic metals keep spiraling up, and the amber light still flashes for investments in plant and equipment. Meanwhile, the government pumps money into the mortgage market, in an effort to bring down interest rates and stir up more home building.

<u>The six percent surtax:</u> Will continue to hang as a threat over the economy. Congress hopes to avoid it. But if it is going to push for projects like the anti-ballistic missile, it will fall far short of bringing budget deficits down to manageable levels.

<u>Postage rates:</u> The pressure is on to help pay for postal mechanization to move rising mail volumes and to ease the $1.2 billion post office drain on the Treasury. Real goal probably is a settlement along these lines: 6¢ letter; three annual 10% increases for magazines and newspapers; a 4¢ bulk third class rate.

<u>Government statistics:</u> White House will fight to save its Census of Business and Manufactures from the economy ax. Due to be taken in early 1968, it provides fresh benchmarks for marketers as well as economic analysts. Major new ingredients: Breakdowns showing channels of distribution for industrial products, the first since 1958. A census of construction industries, the first since 1939.

IM

By STANLEY E. COHEN, IM Washington Editor

Our increasingly
interdependent
society is accustomed to rising government influence over the kinds of products that are made and how they are sold. Probably that's why there is so little dismay, despite the rapid strides in these directions in recent months. Health and safety have become major justifications for federal action. Federally enforced safety standards for gas pipelines and electric utilities are high on this year's legislative agenda. So are tougher flammability standards for fabrics. A law covering the design of color TV sets and other equipment that emits radiation is in the drafting stage. In the executive branch, air and water pollution standards will require changes in product design. Automobile makers are beginning to respond to the requirements of the automobile safety law. Tires are

Legal liability
is another
consideration
which opens
the way for expanded federal intervention. The new Commission on Product Safety, likely to be authorized this year, will become a repository for new ideas. It wants to find out who tests potentially dangerous products; who imposes safety regulations; how much liability the manufacturer has if the product fails. How to sell it: Anti-trust takes on more sophisticated concepts. In the ABC-ITT merger litigation, Justice Department stressed "reciprocity" as a questionable practice. Recent Supreme Court decisions, such as the Schwinn case, narrow the manufacturer's influence over dealers. Other government activity is keyed to demands for more "consumer information." "Truth-in-Packaging" and "Truth-in-Lending" try to define the kinds

Government sees
itself as a
helper as well as
a regulator. After numerous false starts, Commerce Department finally seems to be organizing itself to look out for the interests of marketers. Through its new distribution advisory committee, it'll be encouraging joint efforts to explore such problems as: how to improve the public image of business; how to recruit bright young people into marketing and advertising; how to examine the contribution of advertising to economic growth. Government plays other roles, too: Export stimulator--New Kennedy Round tariffs yield concessions in the 50% range for about a third of our exports. Commerce Secretary Alexander Trowbridge urges marketers to take a close look. Marketing statistics--Even agencies like IRS are trying to provide data that helps define markets. Post Office Department's ZIP has become a marketing tool, too. Self Regulation--New Commerce Department procedures will make it easier for industries to agree on "voluntary" standards. And anti-trust law no longer precludes self-regulation-with-teeth.

next. They will have to have a built-in "ply-gauge." And there will be new standards for tires by load capacity.

of information sellers must give to buyers.

HOUSING HOTLINE
LAST-MINUTE NEWS

Fannie Mae jumped into the mortgage pass-through arena last month with a $250 million offering backed by seasoned mortgages carrying rates of 9% to 11%. The mortgage pass-through certificates are available in $25,000 denominations. FNMA chairman David O. Maxwell said the program will be expanded to include new mortgages early this year. More developments: Fannie Mae will now purchase second mortgages made by lenders *and*, in some cases, by homesellers. In another vein, a tax bonanza is what Fannie Mae will get if it's successful in its bid to apply operating losses to income taxes paid during the past ten years. If the move comes off, Fannie Mae will get a $900 million tax refund instead of a paltry $450 million.

Rent control took a beating at the polls last year, claims the National Multi Housing Council. Pointing to overwhelming voter rejection of rent control initiatives in local elections in four communities, NMHC co-chairman Preston Butcher declared, "This public backlash against rent control is the most dramatic evidence to date that voters no longer view rent control as an answer to their housing problems." The four communities that torpedoed rent control recently are: Ventnor, N.J., San Bernadino and San Rafael, Calif. and Minneapolis, Minn. Rent control may be reeling, but it's hardly down for the count. Nearly 200 communities nationwide still impose varying forms of limitations on rents.

U.S. Home Corporation swapped $15.3 million of debt for 901,592 shares of stock—a move that increased stockholders' equity by $15.3 million and resulted in a $3.2 million tax-free gain. But other recent reports on the nation's largest homebuilder are very gloomy. The company announced a $2.4 million loss for October, and an analyst with investment firm Smith Barney, Harris Upham & Co. said U.S. Home could show a loss of $7.5 million or more for 1981's fourth quarter. Poor earnings could also trigger loan covenants that would prohibit U.S. Home from paying a February dividend.

BEPS was bleeped for yet another year, reports James C. Cashman, a member of the National Assn. of Home Builders' BEPS Task Force. And when the Building Energy Performance Standards finally do become effective in August, 1985, they'll be voluntary guidelines instead of mandatory standards. The DOE-sponsored BEPS sought to establish energy-design standards for virtually all newly constructed buildings. But under heat from builders, Congress delayed the effective date of the standards for two years and eight months. A recent amendment to an appropriations bill achieved the additional year's delay and the conversion to voluntary compliance.

Don't tamper with the home mortgage interest deduction! That was the message the Senate sent to the administration last month in an 83-to-0 vote on a resolution re-affirming the deductibility of interest expense on home mortgages. Senator Lloyd Bentsen (D-Tex) introduced the resolution to head off what he called "ominous rumblings" from the Treasury Department that an annual cap of $5,000 or $10,000 for such expense was being considered as a way of shrinking budget deficits. "Once they established such a cap," Bentsen said, "it would be relatively easy to continue to lower it in stages until it was finally eliminated." The government estimates interest deductions on home mortgages save taxpayers $25.3 billion a year.

Merrill Lynch plans to acquire Advance Mortgage Company in an estimated $42 million transaction. Roger E. Birk, chairman of Merrill Lynch, said an "agreement in principle" had been reached to acquire Advance through Merrill Lynch's real estate financing subsidiary, Merrill Lynch Hubbard, which already has a $2.7 billion first mortgage portfolio. Advance Mortgage, a subsidiary of Oppenheimer & Co. and one of the largest mortgage bankers in the country, now services over $4.8 billion in first mortgages. News of the planned acquisition touched a sore spot at Citicorp, the New York City-based bank holding company, which reluctantly divested itself of Advance Mortgage in September, 1979 under orders from the Federal Reserve.

HOUSING/JANUARY 1982   13

Housing, Joe Davis

Full, sense-making topic sentences in bold lead into rest of paragraph. Yellow tinted page, red logo.

Turner, CBS Hold Merger Talks, But Neither Displays Much Enthusiasm

ATLANTA—Ted Turner, founder of Cable News Network, met recently with top officials of CBS to discuss a possible merger. No agreement could be reached. That much is agreed upon by both sides. The rest of the tale depends on who is telling it.

Turner revealed in a gathering at the National Press Club in Washington, DC, that the meeting had occurred.

"CBS came down to Atlanta to try to acquire CNN" four or five weeks ago, Turner said. "I didn't let them make an offer. I was too busy telling them I was going to bust them."

CBS tells it differently. A network spokesman said, "Gene Jankowski [president, CBS Broadcasting group] and William Leonard [president, CBS News] flew to Atlanta at Ted Turner's invitation. As good business people, we look at and listen to opportunities presented to us. We'd be remiss if we didn't. At the Atlanta meeting Turner suggested that we meet again in

New York and, yes, at that time he and Mr. [Thomas] Wyman were introduced." Wyman is president of CBS Inc.

Despite Turner's quick rejection of the deal, he agreed to meet with CBS executives a second time about three weeks ago. When asked why, Turner replied, "I thought it would be interesting." When pressed, he said, "Why should I sell? I like what I do."

He said CBS initiated the discussions because CBS board chairman William Paley was "incensed" over the ABC-Westinghouse announcement of their joint cable venture.

According to Turner, the meeting took place at the Atlanta Airport Hilton because Jankowski and Leonard did not want to be seen in Turner's office. Turner termed both of them "lightweights" and set up a meeting in New York's two weeks later with Jankowski and Wyman.

Apparently, little came of the meeting, although Turner boasted he "could sell CNN for a tidy piece of change." He predicted that CNN would grow to such a size that in a few years he could merge with CBS and be boss. As a parting remark, he said he would like to acquire one of the major networks. "Don't laugh," he said. —*Susan Sewell*

'NY Post' Task Force To Study Putting Out Sunday Paper

NEW YORK—The *New York Post* has announced plans to set up an editorial task force that will look into publishing a Sunday edition, according to Roger Wood, the *Post's* executive editor.

"We're looking into developing the format—but we have no doubt that eventually we will put out a Sunday paper, but I can't say *when*," said Wood. "We hope to make the circulation no less than our daily is now [850,000], and we most likely will add to our editorial staff."

Wood said the growth the *Post* has shown over the last few months—an increase from a Sept. 30 ABC audited 760,000 circulation to a currently guaranteed 850,000—has enabled the paper to proceed with plans to publish seven days a week.

The *Post* launched a Sunday edition in the fall of 1979 when *The New York Times* and *Daily News* were shut down by strikes. Several weeks after those papers resumed publication, the *Post* folded the edition. □

Heublein Taps Conn. Shop

HARTFORD, CONN.—Heublein International, Farmington, Conn., recently named Maher, Pastor & Stevens, Hartford, to handle several creative assignments involving its Inglenook and Portuguese wines.

The agency will create International Wine Brand Portfolios for Inglenook, Beaulieu, Fonseca Vineyards and Lancers Wines.

The efforts will include point-of-purchase materials, graphics and print ads adapted for the various international wine markets.

Green Is New MPA Chief

George J. Green, president of the New Yorker Magazine Inc., is the new chairman of the Magazine Publishers Association. He has been a member of the MPA board since 1976 and has served as the organization's treasurer for the last two years. Other new officers include Jack D. Rehm, president of Meredith Corp.'s Publisher's Group (MPA vice-chairman); Raymond Eyes, president and publisher, The McCall Publishing Co. (MPA treasurer); and John J. Bené, president/chief executive officer, Parents Magazine Enterprises Inc. (MPA secretary) Joan S. Conners, president and publisher of American Express Publishing Corp., is a new member of the MPA board of directors. □

LATE NEWS

BROWN & WILLIAMSON TOBACCO CORP., Louisville, Ky., announced late Friday that it has moved its Viceroy cigarette account from McCann-Erickson, New York, to Grey Advertising, New York. McCann-Erickson retains B&W's Barclay cigarette accounts. Cunningham & Walsh, Chicago, continues as agency for planning and placement of media marketing for all brands, including Viceroy. Billings were not disclosed. In 1979, billings were $16.5 million. In 1980, billings were $13.8 million.

THE U.S. SUPREME COURT HEARD ORAL arguments last week in a two-year-old case involving the city of Boulder, Col., and Telecommunications Inc. that will determine whether cities can be sued by cable companies or other businesses on antitrust grounds. The landmark case involves a building moratorium that the city imposed on TCI, a multiple-system operator, halting the cable company's expansion in Boulder. TCI brought an antitrust suit against Boulder, claiming it was unfairly restraining trade. If TCI wins its case, some attorneys believe that cities will be open to a host of antitrust suits from cable companies. The court is expected to issue a decision before the end of the year.

READER'S DIGEST WILL PUBLISH a monthly Greek edition starting next February. A premiere issue will appear in November. The new edition brings to 17 the number of languages in which the Digest publishes, and, with an expected circulation of 50,000, it will be the 41st edition of the magazine. The Greek Digest will be called Epiloges apo to (Selections from). Headquarters will be in Athens.

USA NETWORK, GLEN ROCK, NJ, has opened a New York City office in the Simon & Schuster building at 1230 Ave. of the Americas. The office will house the advertising sales department, comprised of account executives and an advertising sales manager, to be named shortly. In a statement issued by the network, Jeffrey Lowenna, vice president, said, "We . . . believe that a New York presence for USA firmly establishes the network along 'Broadcast Row' as a leading cable television company."

THE LONDON OFFICE OF DANCER Fitzgerald Sample has continued its new-business spree by winning travel-operator Hoseason's $3 million advertising account from British agency Abbott, Mead, Vickers SMS. The office has added $7.5 million to billings in the last six weeks, including $2 million for rubber-glove brand Marigold, and $2.5 million for air-freshener brands Airbal and Tobacco Clear.

Adweek, Walter Bernard

Late news boxed column is set off from rest of publication by dark italics set ragged right. Yellow tint in box, red logo.

LOOK AHEAD

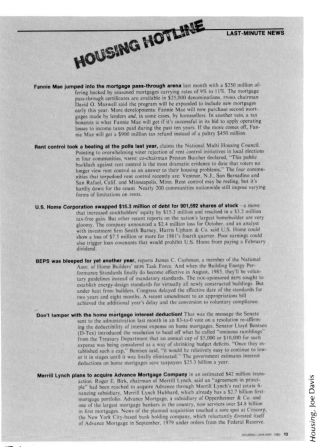

UNIVAC'S NEW GENERATION	Sperry Univac plans to unload a bombshell at the NCC, a spanking new architecture for its large scale processors. While other mainframers scrambled to respond to IBM's 4300 Series by slashing prices and changing model numbers, Sperry's computer arm will be unveiling a new generation of processors which have been secretly in the works for several years. The machines will be compatible with -- and still be numbered in -- the 1100 Series, but will use multiple microprocessors as their basic building blocks. (The chips are thought to come from Motorola.) First off the line will be a cpu of about the same power as Univac's 1100/40, which it will replace. The big surprise will be in the price -- about one-third that of the 40.
... AND A DISTRIBUTED PROCESSOR, TOO	After years of stalling, Univac finally has decided to take the wraps off its Distributed Communications Architecture (DCA), announced with some fanfare in November 1976. At the NCC, the Blue Bell, Pa., mainframer is expected to unveil its Distributed Communications Processor (DCP), the first substantive product release to come out of the company's DCA development drive. When it announced DCA two-and-a-half years ago, Univac touted a DCP which industry insiders claim was nothing more than the company's 3760 front-end processor with a new coat of paint. Also bundled into the offer was the Telcon software package. The born again DCP is the real thing this time. The system is designed to function as a front-end processor, nodal processor, or as a terminal concentrator. The company hopes to demonstrate the new setup at the show and expects initial deliveries of the system and software to begin in July.
AND AGAIN FROM HONEYWELL	It probably won't happen at the June NCC but Honeywell, too, has an upcoming announcement. It's readying a replacement for its 66/85, ballyhooed as its biggest machine ever back in late '77, then dropped in the spring of '78. It will be in the 66 family, will be the family's biggest, and will support Honeywell's Distributed Systems Environment (DSE) but it probably won't use common mode logic (CML) technology. Honeywell blamed the expense of CML when it decommitted the 66/85.
FIVE MORE FOR NATIONAL CSS	National CSS, the information services company which may be acquired by Dun & Bradstreet pending approval by the Securities & Exchange Commission, plans to announce five new computers to extend and add depth to its 3200 series. One of the products will be a faster 3200 cpu; two others will be special purpose versions, one for back-end applications work, the other for heavy front-end communications loads. Both will be available, according to the

MAY 1979   17

Datamation, Cleve Marie Bontell

Typewritten memo format with free-standing heads separated in left-hand rubric. Brown ink on brown tint.

UPDATE

MULTILAYER ICs	**Semiconductor topologies soon will resemble** multilayer printed-circuit boards, says Tom Longo, Fairchild Semiconductor's VP of R&D. Fairchild is already developing a CCD imaging device with three layers of polysilicon interconnect. Longo expects to see five interconnect layers — three polysilicon, two metal — when circuit densities reach 100,000 gates/chip.
SPEECH MODULE	**Texas Instruments has expanded** its TM990 microcomputer module family to include a speech module containing an industrial vocabulary of over 160 words. Designated the TM990/306, the module has an amplifier capable of driving an 8-ohm speaker at 2.5 watts. For more power, an external amplifier can be connected to the preamplifier output of the $1280 unit.
COMPUTER LINKS	**IBM researchers in Zurich** are investigating the use of infrared light communication between mainframes and terminals to overcome the immobility of cabled systems. The system controller is a satellite station wired to the host computer and mounted in the ceiling of a room containing computer work stations. An array of LED's on the satellite exchanges data with similar arrays on the terminals. Reflected infrared light floods the entire area, so line-of-sight transmission is not necessary.
LINEAR CHIPS	**Linear integrated circuits** with sensors for temperature, light or magnetic fields built onto the same chip offer a giant potential market, says Robert Dobkin, director of advanced linear circuit development at National Semiconductor. Integrated temperature sensors that can already handle up to 200°C should find wide use in industry, predicts Dobkin. All other temperature sensors (i.e.—Nichrome or platinum wires, thermocouples, thermistors, bi-metal strips) are non-linear, require lots of costly electronics, and need to be calibrated. Integrated temperature sensors can deliver linear outputs, and on-chip trimming can set voltage reference values to 0.01%, he says.
64-K RAM MARKET	**The market for 64-K dynamic RAM** (random-access memory) chips will be over $1 billion, and will be even larger than the TTL logic market, predicts Dr. Richard L. Petritz, president of INMOS. One reason for the big market for 64-K RAMs, added Petritz, is that the learning curve for these complex devices will make it difficult for systems companies to compete economically with in-house facilities. This will be one of the early products of the new firm he heads, funded by $100 million from the British government. Plants will be built in Colorado Springs and in England to manufacture VLSI products.
JAPAN PLANS R&D	**Innovative materials R&D projects** will begin this year in Japan once plans developed by the Science & Technology Agency are OKed. Four study themes recommended include research on amorphorous and superconducting materials, as well as on high-efficiency ceramics and ultra-high pressure materials. The projects would continue for 3 to 10 years with government funding of ¥1-4 billion (about $4.25-$17 million). Different laboratories under the Agency's jurisdiction (such as the Research Development Corp. of Japan), as well as university and industrial labs will be invited to join the programs. Each program will be

(2)

High Technology, Virginia Murphy-Hamill

Stylized typewriter format; topic heads in margin lead into boldface lead-ins then into text. Grey tint.

Business outlook

William B. Franklin, Chief Outlook Editor / December 28, 1981

A gradual consumer pullback as the slide steepens

Consumers are becoming more cautious in response to slowing economic activity. But the data do not yet show the abrupt retrenchment that usually accompanies recession.

After adjustment for inflation, the figures reveal that consumers have gradually been reducing their spending since early last spring. They are dragging their feet a bit more these days, but have not cut back to the extent that they did during the 1980 recession.

Business executives have recently slowed their pace of capital investment, but plans for early 1982 still call for some modest increase, even after adjustment for inflation.

While the initial reaction of both consumers and businessmen indicates that they were not spooked early in the recession, that is now changing. The downturn in business activity is picking up speed; it may turn out to be neither short nor mild.

It is not clear how far production will fall. What is clear is that it is still falling, and the decline is accelerating. Production is declining rapidly in response to rising inventories and falling sales. The BUSINESS WEEK index is in a steep decline (page 2).

Nor is it clear how quickly the unemployment rate will rise and how high it will go. New claims for unemployment compensation, seasonally adjusted, soared to almost 600,000 in the first week of December, for the largest number since the economic slide began.

A toboggan ride in factory output would quickly turn the modest plus in capital spending plans into a sizable minus. At the same time, a sharp increase in the unemployment rate would almost certainly pull the rug out from under retail trade.

Retail spending brings mostly bad news

The most recent consumer spending figures provide little Christmas cheer, despite a recent uptick. The good news is that spending in retail stores during November rose 0.8%. Since this includes part of the important holiday selling season, that seemed to offer some hope that maybe the yearend surge would not turn out too poorly, after all.

The bad news is that the October sales figures, which had earlier been estimated to have declined 1.5%, were revised downward to show a much larger decrease of 2.1%.

Sales for the two months averaged $87.1 billion, seasonally adjusted. If they held even in the year's final month—which may well be only a wistful hope—sales would be off 1.2% for the quarter, compared with the previous quarter. And this is in current dollars. After adjustment for inflation, the decline in real terms would be about 2%. This brings merchants' real volume some 3.5% below its peak, touched last March.

If unemployment is still on the upswing, as it appears to be, retailers can expect a poor post-holiday selling season, also.

Retail sales can hold up—and have—even during recession, as long as the

Business Week, John R. Vogler

Caption: Rough, tan-colored stock is characteristic of four such newsletter inserts in each issue.

BUSINESS THIS WEEK

Busting up

America's justice department dropped its antitrust suit against AT&T. The telephone company agreed to spin off its 22 operating companies in return for freedom to enter new fields of data processing and telecommunications.

The justice department also dropped its 13-year-old antitrust suit against IBM. Its case was too "flimsy", it said.

American unemployment reached 8.9% last month—a rise of two percentage points, or 2m ex-workers, since July, 1981.

European steelmakers prepared to counter the export-blocking effects of anti-dumping suits brought by American steel companies.

General Electric reckons Mr Reagan's sanctions against Russia will cost it $175m in lost orders for the Siberian gas pipeline.

De Beers diamond sales dropped by 46% to $1.47 billion last year.

General Motors agreed with union leaders to match wage cuts with lower car prices.

Chip-maker Intel reported profits of $27.4m for 1981—72% below 1980's results.

Unctad proposed a facility to give export credits at low interest rates to exporters from developing countries.

Stricken Belgian steelmaker Cockerill-Sambre negotiated a $720m debt rescheduling with its government.

Olivetti announced 1981 sales of $2.3 billion, 30% higher than 1980's.

Australia's Woodside Petroleum delayed plans for offshore gas developments, because of the oil glut and the reluctance of its Japanese backers.

Coalminers in New South Wales and Queensland struck for more pay.

Government investigators reckon that American oil companies have paid $650m less in production royalties than they should.

International Harvester plans to axe 6,700 jobs to win $200m in payroll savings this year.

Christina Onassis was elected to the board of the Union of Greek Shipowners.

Gold fell to $380 an ounce—its lowest price since October, 1979.

IN BRITAIN

Busting in

Australian Robert Holmes à Court made an offer for Lord Grade's Associated Communications Corporation.

Companies' pre-tax profits rose 11% in the third quarter of 1981—and not just thanks to North Sea gas. Profits outside the oil industry were up 13%.

Central government borrowing seems likely to be within its £11.5 billion target for 1981-82, despite the tax-gatherers' summer strike.

Manufacturers' wholesale prices rose ½% in December, the smallest rise for seven months. Raw material prices stayed flat.

Claims for flood and snow damage may cost frost-bitten insurance companies £100m.

British Rail threatened to suspend striking train drivers.

BL airlifted components to keep output up despite the big freeze.

The monopolies commission blackballed both bids for the Royal Bank of Scotland.

The government told leaders of 530,000 civil servants that their claim for a 13% pay rise was unrealistic.

Lloyds Bank signed an £80m leasing deal for a North Sea oil rig.

Northern Foods bid $69m for the American company Keystone Foods, supplier to McDonald's restaurants.

The CBI wants £1 billion more investment in nationalised industry.

Key indicators: **Major economies**

The Economist

Caption: News items reduced to telegraphic single-sentence reports run in narrow columns.

Radar

O Congresso não pode tocar nos atos

Na terça-feira pela manhã, a lei do Congresso que restabelecia a memória histórica do presidente Juscelino Kubitschek, anulando todas as punições que lhe foram impostas por leis de exceção, estava integralmente vetada pelo presidente João Figueiredo. Só à tarde é que surgiu no Planalto, depois da interferência do senador José Sarney, presidente do PDS, a fórmula conciliatória do veto parcial, que apenas mantém a devolução das condecorações cassadas ao presidente — devolução esta já feita há várias semanas pelo Executivo. A decisão do presidente Figueiredo de vetar a reabilitação de JK pelo Congresso transbordou o campo do simbolismo e tornou-se um exemplo de que as artérias da abertura começam a dar sinais de obstrução. O veto quer dizer simplesmente que o Executivo não dá ao Congresso o direito de comutar, sob pena de póstuma e simbolicamente, penas impostas pelos atos institucionais.

Petróleo novo alivia os russos

Os russos fizeram uma importante descoberta de petróleo no Casaquistão, uma província da Ásia central. Testes nas vizinhanças da cidade de Caraganda parecem revelar um campo bastante rico e nos últimos meses encomendaram 10 milhões de dólares em equipamento de perfuração a empresas ocidentais. Essa descoberta pode ser de importância vital para a URSS, pois é sabido na comunidade de informações internacional que a década de 80 começou com a ameaça de uma severa crise de petróleo sobre o Kremlin.

Ou o padre sai, ou é expulso

O padre italiano Vito Miracapillo, da prelazia de Ribeirão, a 80 quilômetros do Recife, que se recusou a celebrar missa comemorativa do aniversário da Independência, deixará sua paróquia e o Brasil. O governo federal não absolveu a atitude do religioso e, com base no novo Estatuto dos Estrangeiros, pode e quer expulsá-lo do país. Só não o fará se, burocraticamente, a própria hierarquia católica remover Miracapillo.

O senador é general aposentado

O senador Luís Cavalcanti (PDS-AL) criticou na semana passada o ex-presidente Ernesto Geisel por receber proventos como ministro aposentado do STM e uma pensão como ex-chefe do Executivo. Segundo o senador, o ex-presidente "acumula empregos e aposentadorias". Por certo o senador nada vê de ilegal nisso. Afinal, o general Luís Cavalcanti acumula a aposentadoria pelo tempo que serviu ao Exército com os vencimentos do senador Luís Cavalcanti. Faz isso porque é de seu legítimo direito. Afinal, trabalhou no Exército, contribuiu para o dia em que se aposentasse e hoje, com

VEJA, 24 DE SETEMBRO, 1980

Dívidas deixam estatais amarradas

O calote das empresas estatais fechou o mês de agosto em 70 bilhões de cruzeiros. Essa dívida vencida, somada à que vence a curto prazo, eleva o número para 100 bilhões. Com esses números na mão, a Secretaria de Planejamento acredita que dispõe de um sólido argumento para desestimular novos projetos e investimentos de empresas que não pagam sequer o que devem.

A CVM espera por Galvêas e Langoni

Será na segunda semana de outubro o julgamento, pela Comissão de Valores Mobiliários (CVM), do "caso Vale". Seu presidente, Jorge Hilário Gouveia Vieira, não quer anunciar a decisão da CVM sem que o ministro da Fazenda, Ernane Galvêas, e o presidente do Banco Central, Carlos Geraldo Langoni, estejam no país. Ambos terão suas próximas semanas ocupadas pela reunião do Fundo Monetário Internacional, em Washington, e ambos são personagens do imbroglio.

Dos 22 ministros, só três em Brasília

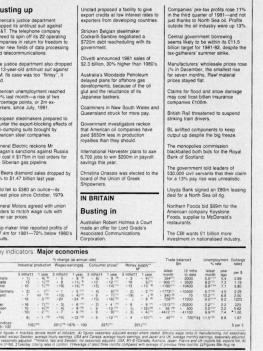

Juscelino: cassado

Na sexta-feira, o Brasil foi governado por um Ministério itinerante. No Planalto estavam o presidente João Figueiredo, os generais Golbery do Couto e Silva e Octávio Medeiros e o almirante Maximiano da Fonseca. O resto era a imensa solidão do cerrado: dos 22 ministros, dezenove estavam fora da capital. Os paulistas (Delfim Netto, Amaury Stabile e Murillo Macedo) estavam em São Paulo. Os mineiros (Abi-Ackel e Eliseu Rezende) em Belo Horizonte. O ministro (Jair Soares) embarcou de manhã para Porto Alegre. Enquanto cada um garantiu um fim de semana antecipado fora da capital, outra bateria estava no exterior. Waldyr Arcoverde, da Saúde, foi para os Estados Unidos. Eduardo Portella, da Educação, para a Iugoslávia. César Cals, das Minas e Energia, está na Checoslováquia. Walter Pires, do Exército, no Chile. Ramiro Guerreiro, das Relações Exteriores, na Bélgica.

Figueiredo não assiste à posse americana

Figueiredo: só

Está fora de cogitação a possibilidade de o presidente João Figueiredo ir aos Estados Unidos, em janeiro, para a posse de Jimmy Carter ou de Ronald Reagan. No receituário da Itamaraty prevê-se a possibilidade de Figueiredo ir até duas vezes à América do Norte no próximo ano, mas ambas no segundo semestre. Numa etapa, visitaria os Estados Unidos. Noutra, o Canadá.

Veja, Pedro De Oliveira

Caption: Blue-tinted stock; photos run in horizontal line screen ("radar"?); normal news format.

---

business newsletter

Carbide wraps up Phase 1 of an expansion . . .
Union Carbide put the finishing touches on the first phase of a 200-million-lb/year vinyl acetate monomer (VAM) expansion in its complex at Texas City, Tex. Capacity at the plant, which produces VAM from ethylene and acetic acid, has been boosted from 350 million to 450 million lb/year. The second phase, says Carbide, "will bring capacity up to 550 million lb in 1982." Just one year ago, Carbide disclosed plans to increase by 100 million lb/year the acetic acid capacity of its Coatings Materials Div. plant at Brownsville, Tex. Says Division President N.L. Zutty: "These expansions will enable Union Carbide to maintain its position as one of the nation's leading producers of acetic acid and vinyl acetate—demand for which is expected to increase at a rate of 4-5% per year through 1985."

. . . and increases its lines of credit
In an unrelated action, Carbide says it has lifted its lines of credit from $800 million to $1 billion. Chairman William S. Sneath notes that maintaining the present pace of the company's construction program at a cost of more than $1 billion/year will require additional long-term external financing. "The availability of the [new] credit arrangements," says Sneath, "gives Union Carbide considerable flexibility with regard to the timing of long-term financing." The last previous increase in the company's lines of credit, from $600 million to $800 million, was in 1976.

Socal ponders a new offer for Amax
Stiff resistance from Amax management was behind Standard Oil of California's withdrawal of its proposed $4-billion merger offer for Amax (CW, Mar. 25, p. 15). The acquisition would have been the largest ever if it had been approved. Industry observers, however, are guessing that Socal may return with an upgraded offer sometime in the near future, especially considering that it already owns 20% of Amax stock and had previously tried to purchase the diversified mining company in 1978. Moreover, Socal refuses to say whether it has nailed the lid shut on any further attempts to take over Amax. Says one company spokesman: "I don't think we really know ourselves at this point." The company, he says, "still believes that its offer was fair and that a merger of Amax would be to the advantage of the stockholders of both companies and in the national interest."

Du Pont gives up on an antiknock plant
Scratch one of the six plants that manufacture lead alkyls in the U.S. The unit to be shut down by Aug.

1—the only one west of the Rockies—is part of Du Pont's complex at Antioch, Calif.; other units at that seaport site will not be affected. Du Pont says the closure is necessitated by declining U.S. demand for gasoline antiknock additives based on tetraethyl lead and tetramethyl lead. The dwindling demand, of course, reflects the federal government's decision to phase out the use of those additives. Du Pont will continue to produce TEL and TML in its Chambers Works at Deepwater, N.J. Other producers are all on the Gulf Coast: Ethyl at Baton Rouge, La., and Pasadena, Tex.; PPG Industries at Beaumont, Tex., and Nalco Chemical at Freeport, Tex.

Du Pont's economist foresees an upturn
The economist in charge of forecasts for the nation's largest chemical company is looking ahead to a new boom period for chemicals and for the economy as a whole. Chemical production, says Du Pont's Charles B. Reeder, will grow at an annual rate of 6% this year—two percentage points faster than overall U.S. industrial production—and 6.3% in 1982. While his forecast plays 1981 as a transition year, Reeder told a chemical marketing group in New York last week that the business cycle has definitely hit its nadir and now is pointing back up again. His prediction for inflation-adjusted gross national product: Up 2.7% this year and a further 4.3% next. Reeder contends that inflation, which ran nearly 10% last year, will ease to 8.5% this year, and to, at most, 8% in 1982. "Frankly," he says, "it's hard for me not to be optimistic."

Cash-poor Kennecott will wed for wealth
Kennecott, the largest U.S. copper producer, is still a cash-poor company with 60,000 shareholders; but by the end of this month, with the grace of the Federal Trade Commission, it will have just one stockholder—and be cash-rich. That one stockholder: Standard Oil of Ohio, a big beneficiary of the Prudhoe Bay oil bonanza in Alaska. Last week, Kennecott's numerous present owners ratified the plan for Sohio to buy up all Kennecott stock for $1.77 billion, or $62/share. Kennecott Chairman Thomas D. Barrow was jubilant, pointing out that "Sohio is in a position to assure Kennecott the needed funds—$1.6 billion over the next five years—for modernization and expansion." Anaconda, the country's second-largest copper company, was acquired by Atlantic Richfield four years ago. There has been gossip about a possible attempt to take over Phelps Dodge, No. 3 in the copper industry, but during P-D's annual meeting last week, Chairman George B. Munroe scoffed at those rumors, asserting that "there's nothing to them."

Chemical Week, Robert T. Martinott

Caption: Trim, light-ruled box encloses page, typical of several similar ones. Crisp logo.

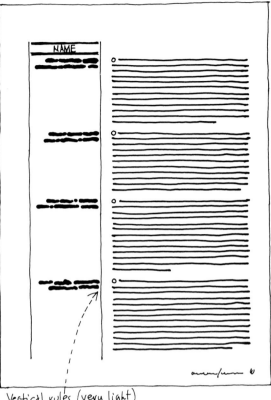

Vertical rules (very light)
contrast with bold heads

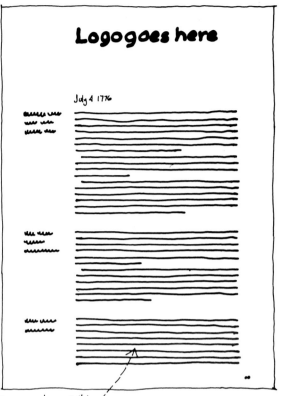

Key words within copy
emphasized in boldface

Some graphic symbol (e.g. a black square)
signalling the start of each new item

Maximum line length is standardized
but placement on page is staggered

Overall department slug.   sub-department (boxed)

DEPARTMENT

WASHINGTON

Regular column

Each news item starts
with boldface words   Charts with color

slug

NATIONAL

Headline goes here

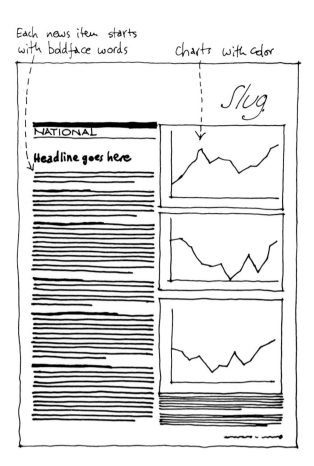

Bold rules

newsletter

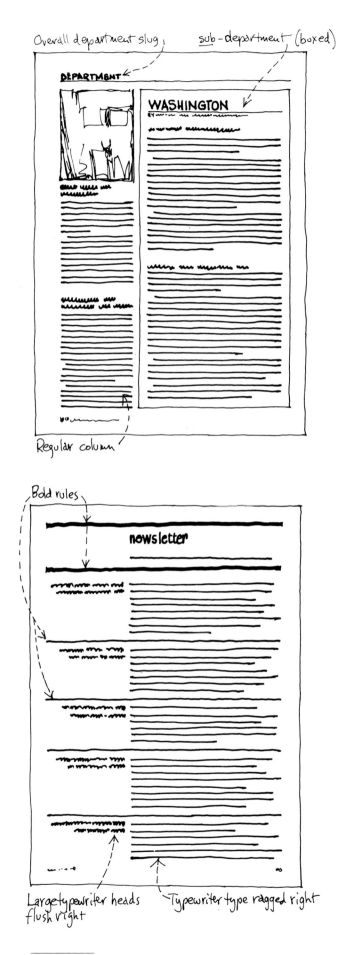

Large typewriter heads
flush right   Typewriter type ragged right

Color over whole page and letterhead-style
heading plus lots of white space

WASHINGTON NEWS

Underscoring of typewriter type
(instead of boldface headlines)

The battle for the readers attention between edit and ads

DEPARTMENTS

This is a generic term, referring to all the pages normally run in a publication that are not "feature stories," the cover, or advertising pages. Thus, strictly speaking, all the other chapters in this book discuss "departments." However, since it is logical to break various departments out of the total package for separate treatment, this chapter deals with general principles — whatever isn't covered elsewhere.

Department pages are, by definition, individual pages scattered throughout the publication, somewhere among the ads. There are, of course, many exceptions to this generalization: sometimes a department is so important and so large that it begins to be the tail wagging the dog, or sometimes, where it is a good tactical ruse, it is positioned within the "editorial well" (i.e., the feature section). But, for most publications, the scattered-throughout-the-magazine definition holds true. It holds true in enough cases to warrant thinking of the pages that way and to design them in such a way as to make the most of them.

Designing departments, surrounded as they are by flamboyant visual materials in the ads, is not easy. Certain basic principles must be accepted and followed. The most basic principle is to recognize the problem — and this, in itself, is none too easy. Editors are often too close to their work to allow them this perspective. They are given X number of page positions to fill and the advertising department fills the others. The printer is the first to see the two sets of pages together in one place, after him, the reader. When an editor "looks at" his publication, he "sees" only a part of it — perceiving the editorial pages and seldom noticing the ads, except where the ads impinge on his consciousness through some magic quality of their own, or when they clash with the editorial matter in some embarrassing way. From this perspective the editor sees each successive space as an entity, each one a separate problem with its own solution. The essential interrelationship between these entities is a factor editors tend to forget, simply because they automatically conceive of those spaces as being interrelated, after having worked hard on *all* of them. The trouble is, of course, that the reader does NOT think of them as separate entities for two reasons: first, he doesn't know how many there are, since they appear one by one and, second, he doesn't recognize them for what they are because they do not look related.

For the reader to notice the scattered pages and realize that they belong together, it is necessary for them to have a rigidly adhered-to format which will give them a family resemblance that is so undeniably strong it will come through even with the most casual fast-glance and in spite of the distracting will-o'-the-wisp images in the surrounding ads.

Unless the editors accept the necessity of this family resemblance, they will have difficulty living within whatever format restrictions may be the overall design policy of the publication. There is a problem here: editors are indoctrinated to make the most of everything and to make it look interesting. One of the ways to achieve that quality of "interestingness" is to make each bit of material look "different" from all the other material. Journalists tend to seek freedom of expression and here they are being asked to limit themselves voluntarily. To get their cooperation it is important that they understand the problem from the broad, publication-as-a-product point of view. Let us assume that such insight has been reached. Where do you go from here?

1. Underplay the presentation

To make the most of the material on the scattered editorial pages, it is necessary to make them as different from the ads as possible, while, at the same time, making them as similar to each other as practical. Since the ads are all very different from each other and vie for the reader's attention through unpredictable arrangement, color, black headlines, etc., perhaps it is wisest to go to the opposite extreme and make the editorial pages appear serene, quiet, and predictable. The ads will act then as foils to the edit pages, and edit pages will become noticeable by their very grayness.

2. Make up a colorful dullness

An outgrowth of the underplayed presentation principle mentioned above, this is a more *realistic* approach to the problem. Assuming that the publication has a lot of gray type that needs to be accom-modated (*eo ipso* "dull" in appearance), the only way to create the required liveliness that a page must have to make it memorable (while still retaining its disciplined serenity in contrast to the ads) is to give it a few spots of "color," and such color means simply "black ink." On pages 94 and 95 a "before" and "after" example of the opening page of a major section of *Library Journal* is shown. The purpose of the contrast is merely to illustrate the possibility of creating "color" through the judicious application of bold type contrasted with thin rules, light type, and some white space. There is, indeed, less copy on the "after" page than on the "before," but the sacrifice was deemed worth making for the sake of the attention-getting design qualities appropriate to the opening page of a major section.

On the next two pages are other examples from the same magazine, showing the way other departments are handled as part of an overall discipline, with the "color" designed in by different ways (though nowhere as strongly as on the news section and the book review section openers).

The way in which the department headings are used, the spaces retained, and vertical rules inserted all lead to the next principle. . . .

3. Repeat patterns rhythmically

It is not necessary to describe a specific pattern that is to be repeated. Whatever it may be, its value derives from the repetition itself — not just an echo, or a vague, slightly altered repetition, but an exact, absolutely precise repetition. This is the only kind of repetition, so precise that its simplicity cannot be missed, that works effectively.

If the repeated material consists of ruled lines, they must be of equal weight in all cases and begin and end in the same position to give the appearance of deliberate repetition.

If the repeated material consists of pictures, such pictures must be placed in the same position on each page, and their proportion must be precisely the same, or they won't look as though a deliberate interrelationship was intended. It is not good enough just to have a picture in the top right-hand corner, hoping that that will do the trick. Nor is mere similarity of shape adequate, though geometrical peculiarity is a great help (like making it unequivocally square, perhaps). But repetition of exact size is crucial.

If the repeated material consists of nothing but white space such as a deep margin at the head of the page, then that white space must be utterly clean and of clearly articulated depth (or it will look accidental, IF it is noticed at all!). To ensure such precision, perhaps it might be best to define the edges of the white space with a graphic element such as a box, two horizontal rules, a bullet in each corner, or whatever may "read".

If the repeated material consists of graphic signals of some sort, then those signals must be designed as a coordinated group, so that they have the quality of repetition even though each individual signal may need to show a different word or image. See the headings within the copy on pages 198 and 199.

4. Invent a peculiar format

If the material lends itself to such manipulation, it might well be useful to package it in a fresh way — anything other than the normal three-column format. Two illustrations of this alternative are shown on pages 98 and 100. Both are based on a centered-trunk principle, from which the heads branch out and beneath which go the stories; both depend on having short items so that enough headlines seem to "grow out" of that central trunk.

On pages 102 and 103 are two examples based on other gimmicks (let's call a spade a spade): the one on page 102 uses a standardized underscoring-cum-vertical-hairline attached to the flush-left edge of the column. The ragged-right setting of both the heads and the text make it appear as though the text was attached to the vertical rule, especially since the vertical rule is chopped off flush with the last line of the item. Thus we achieve a unitization of stories: making-little-things-within-a-big-context.

On page 103 is an example which attempts to do the same thing, i.e., unitize each story separately. However, in this case, pictures and long headlines are involved; a four-column format is used, which devotes the left-hand side to a subdepartment and the right-hand to normal stories.

5. Relate to the cover and the feature section

The editorial product is a totality. In conjunction with the ads, it is packaged as one three-dimensional article. This is how the reader receives it, and this is how he thinks of it: one object.

Although this chapter concentrates on departments, it is necessary to remember that the departments are merely a part of that object. It is important, therefore, to remember that the graphic image the departments transmit must be produced in the context of that unified product. Thus it is highly advisable that the typography be the same in the departments as in the features, certainly as far as text face is concerned. It is perhaps even more important, though, that the headline type be of the same family, since display typography is attention seeking, visible, and thus, very important. If the body copy has a consistent quality of texture and color, and the display type retains a family resemblance, then the publication is well on its way to unity. If, then, the department headings are visually related to the logo on the cover and both logo and department heads relate to the display typography, little else can be done to ensure that visual unity. *Industrial World*'s logo shows a three-dimensional version of Helvetica (custom-made); department headings are an outline version of Helvetica (custom-designed with the rule), and article headlines are machine set Helvetica of some sort. There is no question of their "belonging."

Pages 104 and 105 show an example from *Industrial Engineering* magazine which takes the process one step further: since each of the articles requires a short summary for information retrieval, the summaries are always placed in a four-line box at the top of the first page of the article, together with the writer's byline and affiliation. The one inch high unit thus becomes a readily recognized symbol of story starts. The same one inch high unit is used in the departments for housing the department heading (flush left or flush right, depending on page position). The two sets of signals work as a series of links in a chain throughout the publication.

Logo

Department headings

Headlines

A coordinated system of handling diverse pages based on graphic consistency

L *NEWS*

NIXON SIGNS $32.9 BILLION BILL; RELEASES IMPOUNDED $$

President Nixon has finally signed into law a bill appropriating $32.9 billion for fiscal 1974 programs under the Department of Health, Education, and Welfare and the Department of Labor. Other versions of the bill had been vetoed previously by the President, and Congress—unable to override the veto—had enacted continuing resolutions to fund library programs on a temporary basis. Congress did reduce its appropriations demands by about $1 billion in the current bill, which still exceeds Nixon's budget request by $900,000. In a related action, Nixon released $1.1 billion in education and health money that had been impounded—an action seen by critics as a strategem aimed at preventing the release of appropriations exceeding his budget targets. The impoundment policy has been assailed by a flood of lawsuits—30, at last count—charging the administration with illegally withholding funds. In most cases the White House has lost its argument in federal district courts, which have ordered the release of some $966 million, but the Administration is appealing many of these decisions. Before Nixon decided to release some of the impounded funds, Congress had already refused to accede to a proposal that would have, in effect, nullified the anti-impoundment lawsuits.

Sarah Case of ALA's Washington headquarters told *LJ* that some of the impounded funds soon to be released will support various library programs. She noted that the court suits that were won at the district court level were taken into consideration when the Administration decided which funds to release. Thus far, the HEW has announced that these funds are to be returned: $51,770,000 in impounded Library Service and Construction Act funding is to be returned to the states; $10 million in funds earmarked for books under Title II of the Elementary and Secondary Education Act; and $48 million for AV, equipment, and remodeling under Title III of the National Defense Education Act (NDEA). One source, she said, indicated that libraries will have two years to spend impounded funds, but she noted that the HEW has not yet come out with a firm policy on a deadline for the spending of impounded funds.

Paul H. O'Neill, associate director of the budget office, in charge of human resources and community affairs, told a *New York Times* reporter that about $600,000 of the released funds would be spent in the current fiscal year, which ends next July 1. The released funds, he said, cover the full range of education and health programs, and programs involved will receive increases varying from five percent to a doubling of their budget—depending on variations in the law. O'Neill predicted, "There will be a surge in programs in the pipeline." Some $13.5 billion in funds for other programs, including $6 billion for water treatment plants, have not yet been released by the Administration.

Released funds for library service, said Case of ALA-Washington, will be distributed in accordance with the formulas of the various grants. LSCA, for example, stipulates that block grants are to go to the state library agencies, which will subsequently decide exactly where the money is to be spent.

Commenting on the prospects for libraries under Revenue Sharing, Case said that libraries are in a much stronger position financially than they have been for quite some time. They will be receiving large blocks of impounded funds: the regular appropriations provided by Higher Education Act, LSCA, ESEA and related acts; plus Revenue Sharing funds allocated by both states and localities. Nixon, she said, used his RS plan "as an excuse to zero out money earmarked for libraries," but RS "theoretically" was not supposed to replace regular appropriations. She predicted that this new and separate funding will continue to support library services. As for the future of the categorical aid programs, Case noted that last year Congress amended the Higher Education Act, thus providing funding from that source for five years. LSCA was amended in 1970, and Congress will have to decide whether or not to extend it by June 30 of 1976.

She pointed out that the current appropriations bill does not provide money for library construction, but she noted that some $15 million in impounded funds covering library building is to be released to the states. Many states and localities, incidentally, have allocated large chunks of RS funding for one-shot improvements like library buildings.

The current appropriations bill contains a provision whereby Nixon can cut total appropriations by $400 million; but any single appropriation or program can get no more than a five percent cut, and those programs which do not exceed the President's budget cannot be axed at all. What follows is a rundown of funds appropriated for various library programs—appropriations which can be reduced by only five percent. Under the Elementary and Secondary Education Act, $1,810,000,000 has been allocated for educationally deprived children; $95,000,000 for school library resources and instructional materials; $146,393,000 for supplemental educational centers; $41,500,000 for state education departments; $50,000,000 for the education of handicapped children; and $53,000,000 for bilingual education programs.

Under LSCA, $46,479,000 is to go for library services and $2,730,000 for interlibrary cooperation. National Defense Education Act appropriations include $30,000,000 for equipment and minor remodeling and $13,360,000 for language development.

Under the Higher Education Act, $15,000,000 is to go for the community service program; $10,500,000 for college library resources; $3,000,000 for library training; and $1,500,000 for research. Also: $8,098,346 has been earmarked for the Library of Congress' Acquisition and Cataloging; $99,992,000 for developing institutions; $2,100,000 for fellowships; $12,500,000 for undergraduate equipment and materials. Subsidized loans for higher education facilities amount to $31,425,000.

Other appropriations include: the sum of $75,000,000 for the National Institute of Education; $10,000,000 for the Postsecondary Innovation Fund; $3,000,000 for State Postsecondary Commissions; and $12,000,000 for the Right to Read program. These amounts have been allocated for Older Americans Act programs: $68,000,000 for community programs and $10,000,000 for training. Money available in state grants under the Adult Education Act totals $56,300,000; $16,500,000 will go to ETV (educational television) facilities; $25,871,000 under the Medical Library Assistance Act, including an allocation for the National Library of Medicine; $4,226,750 for the National Agricultural Library; finally, $82,371,150 for the Library of Congress; $406,000 for the National Commission on Libraries and Information Science; and $36,471,000 for the Superintendent of Documents.

National Book Committee Moves: Director Jack Frantz reports the new address is 1564 Broadway, New York, N.Y. 10036 (at 47th St.). Phone: (212) 575-1070.

On this and the following pages are shown typical departments from *Library Journal*. They have been chosen to illustrate the consistency of the overall solution as well as the subtle differences between each department treatment, since each needs slightly different handling to express its particular content most effectively.

The differences are manifested in the headline treatment and the composition of the pages; the raw materials, however, remain the same: same typefaces, same strong contrasts between body and headline type, same hairline rules between columns adding texture and interest, same heavier rules above headlines, same department headings, same spacing between elements.

The two major department openers (the News page, opposite, and the Book Review opener on page 97) have more white space than the others. This serves two functions: it makes them stand out, and it is a necessary foil to the bold, heavy type of the department heading. Compare this solution to the "before" version at right, which uses the same body type-

of color, texture, scale

face. In its attempt at elegance and simplicity the "before" succeeds admirably; and, since most of the other pages are equally restrained in handling, they contrast with the ads admirably. Unfortunately their very paleness tends to make them a trifle dull; hence the introduction of the strong headline typography and the other color-creating rules, and the resultant compromise between the retained well-mannered paleness and the lively boldfaces.

The Checklist and People pages show how the pictures are pulled together and run as groups beneath the logos with the text run separately beneath. This makes the most of the available illustrations (grapes look like "more" in bunches than as individuals rolling around), and it makes page assembly much easier.

The Viewpoint page, a sort of outside editorial, uses the lower line of the logo as the top edge of its own box; the text is set in two-column measure to add that degree of importance that the pronouncement seems to deserve. See also the Editorial page on page 129.

LJ. NEWS

Publisher-library relations study planned by Indiana U.

The National Science Foundation has awarded a $117,000 grant to the Graduate Library School of Indiana University for a major study aimed at promoting publisher-library cooperation at the national level. The proposed study is one response to the widening rift between publishers and libraries now at odds over what rights and obligations are connected with copyright. Recent actions by publishers indicate a trend toward a stronger stand on the copyright question. Among them: the Williams and Wilkins suit against the National Library of Medicine, opposition by publishers to the cooperative acquisitions plans of the New York Public Library-Columbia-Yale-Harvard consortium, and the outspoken recommendations of the Authors League of America for a successor to L. Quincy Mumford as Librarian of Congress.

Dean Bernard Fry, who heads up the Indiana investigatory team, noted that unless a basis for cooperative action is worked out now, "libraries and publishers are likely to take unilateral actions that will commit them to adversary roles which can only harm the entire communications system." Publishers, he noted, are raising their subscription rates by 15 to 20 percent annually, and libraries, consequently, are cutting back on journal buying and relying increasingly on interlibrary shared resources.

Said Fry, cooperative library arrangements aimed at cutting acquisitions costs "could have quite serious side effects on the unstable economic mechanism which has allowed the publishers of...research journals to maintain a narrow margin of economic viability." These publishers are seeking alternatives to the print format, but "the traditional journal remains the most widely used tool offered by the present system for the storage and communication of scholarly and research information."

The Indiana study on the "Economics and Interaction of the Publisher-Library Relationship in the Production and Use of Scholarly Journals" will be undertaken by an advisory committee representing learned associations, university presses, professional society publishers, commercial publishers, libraries, the Center for Research Libraries, and the Federal Library Committee. Becker and Hayes, Inc. has subcontracted to assist the study team in gathering and analyzing data.

The researchers plan to propose within a year "joint actions aimed at achieving cooperative and reasonable results agreeable to all involved communities." In addition to identifying relevant practical and legal problems, the study team is to "recommend changes of an institutional, organizational, and philosophic nature that must be brought about in order to create the kind of environment necessary for a direct attack on the broad systems planning problems that lie at the heart of the matter."

Choices for new LC librarian named by ALA & Authors League

Looking to the retirement of L. Quincy Mumford as Librarian of Congress, the American Library Association has named its candidates for this post. They are: Page Ackerman, university librarian, University of California, Los Angeles; Lillian Bradshaw, director, Dallas Public Library; Charles Churchwell, associate provost, Miami University, Oxford, Ohio; Keith Doms, director, Free Li-

Streaking in Michigan: Flint Public Library staffer Patty Price streaked in a library PR stunt, but the local paper later decided not to print the above pic

LJ MAGAZINES

Bill Katz, PROFESSOR, SCHOOL OF LIBRARY SCIENCE, STATE UNIVERSITY OF NEW YORK, ALBANY

British History Illustrated

1974. Bimonthly. $9. Ed: Barrie Pitt. Historical Times Ltd., London. Subs to: 330 Walnut St., Boulder, Colo. 80302. Illus. adv. Aud: Ga, Ac, Hs. (Subject: History. Issues examined: Vol. 1, Nos. 1-3, 1974).

Here is a more modest version of the familiar *American Heritage* magazine with a concentration on British history. Within its 65 heavily illustrated pages (black and white, as well as sepia photographs and line drawings) are four to five articles by experienced writers and historians. There are no footnotes, and the magazine is purposefully written for the educated layman - not the expert. Still, as with its American counterpart, the writing is authoritative and appears to be accurate and objective while maintaining a fast "I was there" stylistic approach. The editor notes the magazine will cover the broad tapestry of British history, "from Roman Britain to Churchill, from the heartland of London and the Home Countries to the farthest colony over which the flag of Britain flew." Issues examined indicate the editor is quite correct. This does not replace the equally excellent British based *History Today*. The latter is directed to the same audience, but is considerably broader in its scope. In view of the writing style, the fine illustrations and the obvious qualifications of its contributors, *British History Illustrated* is highly recommended for all libraries. *BK*

Motive Power International

1973. Quarterly. $5. Ed: B. R. Garratt, Box 39, Poet Moody, British Columbia, Canada. Illus. Aud: Ga. (Subject: Hobbies-Models. Issue examined: No. 1, Fall 1973)

A specialized hobby magazine for the man or woman interested in locomotives of the world. (The 22 pages is in no way limited to Canada or North America features material on engines from England and abroad.) There are three to four articles and statistical information on various types of engines. A few black and white photographs. Somewhat similar in purpose and scope to *Trains* and *Railroad Magazine*, although most emphasis here is on the locomotive. At any rate, the railroad fan will want to rush a sub for this one, as will an involved librarian. - *BK*

Living Hand

1973. Semiannual. 4 issues, $8. Eds: Mitchell Sisskind & Paul Auster, 525 Hawthorne Ave., Chicago, Ill. 60657. Illus. Aud: Ac. (Subject: Little Magazines. Issue examined: Vol. 1, No. 1, Fall 1973)

A well printed and edited vehicle for new writing from both the United States and Europe. (One of the editors lives in Paris.) Probably of most interest for translations of heretofore little represented authors in the English language, e.g. Paul Celan and Georges Bataille in the first number. Bits of prose and prose poems, too. An impressive little with more than a touch of the traditional literary magazine. A good addition for larger academic collections, and a title to watch in the years ahead. *BK*

Small Press Book Club

1974. Bimonthly. Ed.: Robert R. Miles. Box 1906, San Pedro, Calif. 90733. Aud: Ac, Ga. (Subject: Little Magazines.)

This may be a long-needed breakthrough for both librarians and small magazine editors and publishers. It's a BMOC-type plan for the alternative press, made feasible by the support of such respected figures as Richard Kostelanetz and Tom Montag. Every other month you'll receive a listing of 8-12 books, each annotated and exerpted, and chosen to represent the best of the small press scene. And chosen by authorities. Every other mailing will include a "mag-bag," consisting of three to four little magazines, for roughly $3.95. Since every library should have some selections from the small press world, this is an ideal route. The stature of the advisors, and the commitment represented by advertising contracts already signed, assure that this will last. All libraries should get on the mailing list without delay. Just one "mag-bag" a year will give you a sampling, and once the water's tested you'll find it's not that bad: in fact, they should become a standing order. Not only recommended, but required. *Don Dorrance, South Milwaukee Public Library, Wisconsin*

Trellis

1973. Irreg. (Two issues plus two supplements). $5. Box 656, Morgantown, W.V. 26505. Aud: Ac, Ga. (Subject: Poetry. Issue examined: Vol. 1, No. 1, Spring 1973)

While this is a poetry magazine of over 100 well printed pages, a good deal of emphasis is on anthologizing, i.e. a number of the poems and short essays have appeared elsewhere (where previously printed is duly noted). The result is a much better than average poetry magazine with such entries as William Matthews, Gregory Orr, Richard Grossinger, Margaret Anderson, Ron Padgett, etc. About one-third of the entries are either prose poems or short essays dealing with poetry. And while out of West Virginia, the scope is international. The editors offer a nice way of giving the smaller library a good, solid cross section of modern poetry at a low price. (Although issued irregularly, at least one issue and a supplement will come out each year.) *BK*

Northern Journey

1973. Semiannual. $3.50. Northern Journey Press, P.O. Box 4073, Station E, Ottawa, Ontario. Illus. Aud: Ac. (Subject: Little Magazines. Issue examined: No. 3, 1973)

The Canadians seem to be enjoying a celebration of little magazines, most of which are surprisingly high in quality. This is no exception. In 100 well designed pages are included graphics, photographs, prose, poetry, and essays primarily by the younger creative writers. A fine autobiographical-critical piece is contributed by veteran George Woodcock, as

2458 LJ/OCTOBER 1, 1974

LJ CHECKLIST

Libraries & the disadvantaged

The Office for Library Service to the Disadvantaged of the American Library Association has recently released the following publications: *Reflections on Library Service to the Disadvantaged* by Clara S. Jones, director, Detroit Public Library (which covers a talk given by Ms. Jones at ALA's June 1973 conference, at the first sponsored meeting by the advisory committee for OLSD); *Chicago's Study Unlimited: College Courses in the Library* by Jane Reilly (a summary of a program jointly operated by the Chicago Public Library and the City Colleges of Chicago); and *Library Services to Farmworkers: the Need for a Survival Information Center 1974* by Martin J. Zonligt. Free copies of each publication may be obtained by sending 20c in stamps for each item, plus a self-addressed mailing label to Office for Library Service to the Disadvantaged, American Library Association, 50 East Huron St., Chicago, Ill. 60611.

Library service for the deaf

Library Services with Deaf People: a Guide to Concepts, Activities, Resources is a publication of the Virginia State Library. Based on a workshop held at Gallaudet College, Washington, D.C., in February and concepts taken from various other brochures, this pamphlet is intended for libraries in Virginia, but the services could be applicable to other areas. The information is arranged under such headings as: establish priorities, explore resources, plan and initiate programs and services, and evaluate programs. Copies are available free from Library Development Branch, Virginia State Library, Richmond, Va. 23219.

U.S.S.R. medical care

Medical Care in the U.S.S.R. reports on the study of medicine and public health in the Soviet Union. It contains selected documents covering all phases of Soviet medicine and health in an effort to improve cooperation between clinicians, health scientists, and health administrators in the U.S. and U.S.S.R. Copies of this report (HE 20.3702: Un 3/3 S/N 1753-00006) are available for 75¢ each from the Superintendent of Documents, U. S. Government Printing Office, Washington, D.C. 20402.

Soviet public health plan

The Soviet Five-Year Plan for Public Health, 1971-1975 was prepared under the auspices of the Soviet-Eastern European Studies Program of the Fogarty International Center. It tells how the Soviet Union has sharply reduced infectious diseases and has improved the overall health conditions of its citizens. Copies of this 30-page report (HE 20.3702: So 8 S/N 1753-00018) are available for 55c each from the Superintendent of Documents, U.S. Government Printing Office, Washington, D.C. 20402.

On detente

The Meaning of Detente is a new publication of the Department of State, and one of its General Foreign Policy Series. Based on a recent statement by Arthur A. Hartman, assistant secretary of state for European affairs, this booklet briefly explains detente (a relaxation of tensions) as it applies to the Soviet Union and the United States. It outlines its dimensions, the laying of its foundation, its accomplishments, and its impact on military strength and negotiations. The full text of the Subcommittee hearings, House of Representatives, on detente will be published early in 1975 and will be available from the U.S. Government Printing Office. Copies of this booklet may be obtained for 35c each from the Superintendent of Documents, U.S. Government Printing Office, Washington, D.C. 20402.

1974 standards catalog

The 1974 Catalog of the American National Standards Institute (ANSI) lists more than 5600 American national standards and more than 3000 international standards and recommendations. The American standards are those approved through October 31, 1973. The international standards are those received by ANSI from the International Organization for Standardization, from the International Electrotechnical Commission, and from the International Commission on Rules for the Approval of Electrical Equipment. The catalog also lists special publications dealing with various aspects of standardization such as metric conversion and occupational safety and health. Copies of this catalog are available free from American National Standards Institute, 1430 Broadway, New York, N.Y. 10018.

Consumer finance

Finance Facts Yearbook 1974 contains "the latest facts about consumer financial behavior and the consumer finance business." Written by Dr. S. Lees Booth, senior vice president and director of the National Consumer Finance Association, Washington, D.C., the book is designed as a convenient reference source for those who require accurate and current information about various aspects of the consumer sector. Information is provided on population, labor forces, education, consumer income, expenditures, savings, and the use of credit. In addition, it looks ahead at the U.S. economy for the balance of the year. Copies are available free from: Order Department, National Consumer Finance Association, 1000 Sixteenth St., N.W., Washington, D.C. 20036.

NYC transportation report

Transportation Policy and the New York Environment is a recent publication of the Council on Environment of New York City, and the third in the Council's series of reports entitled *Citizen's Policy Guide to Environmental Priorities for New York City, 1974-1984*. Michael Gerrard, policy analyst for the Council and author of the report, presents the majority opinion of 19 transportation experts for reducing the adverse environmental and energy effects of transportation in New York City during the coming decade. According to the Council, Mr. Gerrard includes data never before compiled in this comprehensive study of New York's transportation patterns and problems. Charts are included to clarify and substantiate the many proposals and facts. Copies are available for $1.50 each from Council on the Environment of New York City, 51 Chambers St., Room 228, New York, N.Y. 10007.

Alternatives' booklist

New York Book Fair Catalog lists the publications of over 230 small, independent publishers, along with graphics highlighting the feminist, third world, and avant garde literary coalition, who presented their wares in New York during the ALA annual conference. For free copies of this catalog, send a stamped (25¢), self-addressed, 6" x 9" envelope to: WARM NECK, 23 Bay St., Cambridge, Mass. 02139.

2136 LJ/SEPTEMBER 15, 1974

LJ PEOPLE

P. HOGAN

M. RIDGEWAY

C. SPALDING

T. SHAW

JEAN ANDERSON, formerly Library Manager, Cities Service Research and Development Company, Cranberry, N.J., has been appointed Associate Librarian, University of South Florida, Fort Myers Educational Center Library, Fort Myers.

ELIZABETH ANN BREEDLOVE, formerly on the staff of the University of Pennsylvania and Washington University Libraries, has been appointed Assistant in Academic and Research Libraries at the Bureau of Academic and Research Libraries, New York State Library, Albany.

VIVIAN Y. BROWN, formerly assistant to the Young Adult Coordinator, Nassau Library System, Garden City, N.Y., has been appointed Young Adult Consultant in the Programs and Services Department of the Queens Borough Public Library, Jamaica, N.Y.

SUSAN T. BURTON, formerly Bibliographic Searcher, Pacific Northwest Bibliographic Center, University of Washington, Seattle, has been appointed Reference Librarian, Undergraduate Library, University of Texas at Austin.

JOHN CALDWELL, formerly Head of Technical Services, California State College, Stanislaus, has been appointed Director, Denkmann Memorial Library, Augustana College, Rock Island, Ill.

VIRGINIA CLARK, formerly Editor of ALA's *Books for College Libraries*, has returned to *Choice* magazine. In her new post as Humanities Editor, she will be responsible for reference, religion, philosophy, and communications and performing arts reviews.

DAVID COHEN, formerly Librarian of the Plainview-Old Bethpage High School Library, New York, has been appointed Adjunct Associate Professor at the Queens College Library Science Department, Flushing, N.Y.

F. GILLIS DOUGHTIE, formerly Coordinator of Extension Services, Montgomery City-County Public Library, Alabama, has been appointed Director of MCCPL.

PAUL E. DUMONT, formerly Systems Librarian, San Antonio College, Texas, has been appointed Chief of Materials Processing, Dallas Public Library.

IVA W. FOSTER, Librarian of Bates College, Lewiston, Maine since 1957, has retired after 40 years of service at the college library.

GEORGE GARDNER, formerly manager of technical services at the Card Catalog Corporation, Minneapolis, Minnesota, has been appointed Assistant Library Division Manager for Technical Services at the Hennepin County Library, Edina, Minn.

ERNESTINE GILLILAND, formerly Associate Director of the North Central Kansas Library System, Manhattan, has been appointed Kansas State Librarian.

JOSEPH HELFER, formerly with the Connecticut Department of Environmental Protection, has been appointed Associate Editor for Science, *Choice* magazine, Middletown, Conn.

PATRICIA HOGAN, formerly Head of the Department of Public Services, Schaumburg Township Public Library, Ill., has been appointed Information Librarian, North Suburban Library System, Morton Grove, Ill.

THOMAS JAQUES, formerly Personnel Consultant, Mississippi Library Commission, Jackson, has been promoted to the post of Assistant Director of Library Development.

RICHARD KRUG, Director of the Milwaukee Public Library, Wisconsin, has retired.

GERALDINE LEMAY has retired from the post of Library Director, Savannah Public and Chatham Effingham-Liberty Regional Library, Savannah, Ga.

JAY K. LUCKER, formerly Associate University Librarian at Princeton University, New Jersey, has been appointed the Director of Libraries at the Massachusetts Institute of Technology, Cambridge.

DONALD W. LYONS, formerly Assistant Librarian, Kentucky State University, Frankfort, is now Associate Librarian.

JACK MULKEY, formerly Management and Administrative Consultant, Mississippi Library Commission, Jackson, has been promoted to the post of Assistant Director of Administrative Services.

BARBARA R. RAU, Director of the Bethlehem Public Library, Delmar, New York since 1955, has retired.

MICHEL H. RIDGEWAY, formerly Acquisitions Librarian, U.S. Military Academy, has been promoted to Assistant Librarian, Collection Development and Technical Services.

C. SUMNER SPALDING has retired as Assistant Director (Cataloging) of the Processing Department at the Library of Congress a post he has held since 1968. His career at LC started in 1940. Among the posts held: Chief of the Catalog Maintenance Division, Chief of the Serial Record Division, and Chief of the Descriptive Cataloging Division. Spaulding was the general editor of the *Anglo-American Cataloging Rules*.

DANIEL YANCHISIN, formerly Senior Reference Librarian, North Carolina State University, Raleigh, has been appointed Head, History and Travel Department, Memphis and Shelby County Public Library and Information Center, Memphis, Tenn.

DEATHS

LUCILLE GOTTRY, director of the Rochester Public Library, Rochester, Minn. from 1943 through 1968, died at the age of 71, on December 30, 1974. A charter member of the Minnesota State Commission for the Status of Women, Ms. Gottry was president of the Minnesota Library Association in 1947.

DOROTHY W. LYON, head of the Children's Room of the Salt Lake City Public Library, Utah, for 18 years, and a staff member for 31, died January 5.

THOMAS SHULER SHAW, nationally known expert on reference, bibliography, and government publications, died February 15 in Baton Rouge, La. Mr. Shaw served for 32 years on the staff of the Library of Congress, retiring in 1962 from his post as Head of the Public Reference Section. He was a member of the faculty of the Graduate School of Library Science at Louisiana State University from 1962 until 1972, when he retired. Mr. Shaw was winner of the 1968 Isadore Gilbert Mudge Award, the American Library Association's highest award in the field of reference work, for his work in the development of the reference collections and aids at the Library of Congress. He was a founding member of ALA's Reference Services Division and assisted in the passage of the Revised Depository Law of 1962. Very active in professional associations, Shaw served as an officer and committee chairman of ALA's Association of College and Research Libraries, and Reference Services Division. When he retired from his faculty position at Louisiana State University, Shaw was cited through a resolution for "his numerous contributions to the State, to the LSU Graduate School of Library Science, and to the profession."

LJ/APRIL 15, 1975 725

LJ LETTERS

Resurrection

Paul Bixler
Managing Editor, Antioch Review

The Antioch Review shall rise again. In fact, it is already rising. Contrary to a lugubrious letter to subscribers written by its former editor, the magazine is alive and well. Instrumental in our rehabilitation is a recent grant of $44,500 from the Ohio Board of Regents. The project is innovative, supporting cooperation in small magazine editing and education between privately financed Antioch College and two public institutions of higher learning, nearby Wright State University and Central State University.

We ask that libraries (they make up two-thirds of our established subscribers' list) please bear with us while we turn the confusion of transition into regular performance. Some librarians may remember that I edited this magazine once before.

Disgusted NOW

Carol Swaim
National Organization for Women, Chicago, Illinois

I am thoroughly disgusted with your cheap shot at NOW in the *LJ Hotline*, June 17, p. 2. You should get your facts straight before commenting on our policies.

The facts are these: NOW distinguishes between 1) voluntary activities which serve to maintain women's dependent and secondary status and 2) change-directed activities which lead to more active participation in the decision-making process.

Volunteer labor for social service is an extension of unpaid household work. Humanitarianism for some on the backs of others ends by being exploitation. The volunteer system reinforces economic dependence of a woman by preventing her from earning money of her own. Reference: *Volunteerism: What It's All About*, obtainable from NOW, 5 South Wabash, Chicago, Ill. 60603.

As a professional librarian I am appalled at the exploitation of women by libraries. In the Harrisburg District Libraries women volunteers (?) are paid (if paid at all!) as low as 50c a hour for 20 hours a week. This can come out of overdue money, and therefore no tax accounting is necessary. Some women volunteers have worked as long as ten years at this low wage. And, of course, there are no benefits such as Social Security credit, paid vacations, etc. Have you ever considered why most of the volunteers are women?

I could go on for pages, but I think you get the message. NOW recognizes the importance of pay for volunteers, but more important is the recognition that volunteers (especially in libraries) are used to pick up the slack in government negligence or in the organization's fund-raising. They are often exploited and ridiculed by professionals, rarely have decision rights, real responsibilities, or challenging tasks.

NOW and the dollar

Lillie Struble
Library Board, Annville Free Library, Pennsylvania

May I register a protest against the statement of the NOW organization as quoted in *LJ Hotline* that women should not engage in volunteer work because "If the work is worth doing, it is worth being paid for." It seems that the members of NOW have not thought out the results of such a position. They would have women motivated only by the almighty dollar with no regard for the welfare of others. We have always deplored the businessman whose only interest is in amassing a fortune and who shows no concern for service to society. Fortunately, many of our financial leaders do care and give much time, serving without pay on boards of schools, libraries, colleges, YMCA's, Boy Scouts, hospitals, Red Feather, and other agencies. And Jaycees all over this land have honored such service by choosing those broad-minded citizens for their community service awards.

Perhaps the officers of NOW have never experienced the satisfactions that come from volunteer work, from doing something over and beyond what is expected, and the reward that comes from doing something for others without any thought of recompense. Many libraries in this country were started and manned by volunteers until funds could be found to pay trained workers. Still, much of the work in libraries does not require any special training and volunteers can be very helpful. Hospitals use volunteers to great advantage, and I have heard doctors maintain that the volunteers are often better than the regular paid workers. Schools are now also asking for volunteers. Surely if women are to achieve equality with men, they should not be deprived of the rewards and satisfactions that come with volunteer work.

Boob tube set

Marvin H. Scilken
Publisher, *The U*N*A*B*A*S*H*E*D Librarian*, Orange, New Jersey

I'd like to protest the elitist attitude in Bill Katz's Review of the *National Star* (*LJ*, June 15, p. 1687): *The National Star* . . . is "no more necessary in a library than the *National Enquirer* or for that matter *The Readers Digest*, but the same people ["the boob tube set"] that made these . . . . a part of their reading may want to have a copy about. Otherwise the average librarian can pass this only at his or her supermarket checkout stand."

Apparently Bill feels that libraries should not have truck with anything popular with the "boob tube set" except, of course, if they happened to be minority boob tubers. The issues of the *National Star* I have read have had useful information presented in a popular manner. It belongs in any library that wants to be of service to this segment of its community.

I have felt that many *readers* don't use libraries because they detect or expect to detect the Katz attitude (even if we have it we really don't want it—and you either) in the library staff. It seems to me that libraries should first serve the masses before they go casting about for other groups to serve.

Freeze-dried books

Erwin C. Surrency
Professor of Law and Law Librarian, Temple University, School of Law, Philadelphia, Pa.

I have been amused by the letters (*LJ*, December 1, 1973, p. 3491; January 15, p. 82; July, p. 1741) from different librarians reporting on the success of the recovery process following the fire in the Temple University Law Library. The library profession has had the benefit of the opinions of these experts, none of whom have examined the materials which were salvaged. I understand that a conservation conference has been held using the results of the Temple University Law Library experience as a basis of discussion on how future libraries can be saved after a disaster. The librarian was not asked to attend or express his views.

2108 LJ/SEPTEMBER 15, 1974

96

LJ BOOK REVIEW

The Contemporary Scene

Bernard, Jessie. **The Future of Motherhood.**
Dial. Sept. 1974. 352p. LC 74-13391. $10. SOC SCI
Another fine contribution from this astute sociologist/social philosopher and futurist. As Bernard dissects the multitude of social trends affecting motherhood, she notes the coercive social forces which have pressured women to become mothers and challenges the myth of the "motherhood instinct." The survey doesn't report on any new sample or study; but current research and literature are creatively used and integrated, and such issues as the emergence of cohabitation, the role of the woman as worker, day care centers, etc. are clearly presented. This most authoritative survey should be read by those concerned with parenting and with the emergence of new role definitions.—*Roger W. Libby, Inst. for Family Research & Education, Syracuse Univ., N.Y.*

Gettleman, Susan & Janet Markowitz. **The Courage to Divorce.**
S. & S. 1974. 228p. bibliog. index. LC 74-945. $7.95. SOC SCI
Not a do-it-yourself guide nor a rule book for coping with divorce problems, but rather a philosophical survey of the obstacles to divorce (and of the need to eliminate these). The message is clear: a clean divorce is better than a bad marriage. The authors, both clinical social workers, question the longstanding belief that the nuclear family is sacrosanct; they also dispel such myths as the damage incurred by the child of divorce, asserting instead that the child may be liberated by exposure to an extended environment in the stepfamily. From experience, they caution against therapists who perpetuate the "save the marriage concept," imposing bias in the guise of treatment. A brief section is devoted to the history of divorce in the Hebrew and Roman cultures and in the Catholic and Protestant faiths. None of the sections on the cultural, historical, or legal development of divorce is definitive; therefore, for those contemplating divorce, this book will best serve as a counsel to alleviate society-implanted guilt feelings and to support the search for alternative life styles. *Ruth E. Almeida, North County Lib., Glen Burnie, Md.*

Kane, Paula & Christopher Chandler. **Sex Objects in the Sky.**
Follett. Sept. 1974. 160p. LC 74-80327. $5.95. TRAV/SOC SCI
A sobering antidote to the "Coffee, Tea, or Me" school of thought, this angry book examines the workaday realities behind the ultra-glossy image of the stewardess as swinging geisha of the Technological Age—the humiliation she endures at the hands of jet-lag jocks, as well as the very real dangers she faces from radioactive cargoes, from the industry's laxity (which leads to unnecessary casualties of both flight attendants and passengers), etc. The book's well backed with statistics and case histories, and achieves an added personal dimension in ex-stew Kane's description of her own metamorphosis from the airborne Barbie-doll image. Another well-deserved dart to industries that package and market women as commodities; general collections will want.—*Patricia Goodfellow, Leaside P.L., Toronto, Canada*

CONTENTS

Library Journal **reviews are indexed in** ***Book Review Index*** **and in** ***Book Review Digest.***

REFERENCE

African Encyclopedia.
Oxford Univ. Pr. 1974. 554p. ed. by W. Kajubi & others. illus. maps. index. $13. REF
Originally intended to serve as a general encyclopedia for African students, this volume will also be of great value to American students and to teachers of African studies. The articles cover a broad range of topics, both current and historical. These articles are informative and written in a style easily comprehensible to secondary school students. A good index, plus a subject guide; copiously illustrated with photos and maps. This most welcome addition to the growing list of reference books on Africa is recommended for both school and public libraries.—*Nancy R. Northrup, Dept. of History, UCLA*

Christopher, Joe. R. & Joan K. Ostling, comp. **C. S. Lewis: an annotated checklist of writings about him and his works.**
Kent State Univ. Pr. (Bibliographies & Checklists). 1974. 389p. LC 73-76556. $15. LIT/BIBLIOG
While disclaiming completeness, Christopher and Ostling have supplied an excellent bibliography of secondary source material, including the most important reviews of Lewis' publications. Their introduction, which proclaims a cut-off date of July 1972 indicates, as well, best bibliographies of primary sources and libraries with strong C. S. Lewis collections. The annotations are remarkably thorough and indicate a familiarity with each item surveyed. Material is arranged in groups according to subject content.

LJ BOOKS TO COME

383 Reprints To Be Published September 1, 1974—January 31, 1975

REFERENCE

Aldington, Richard. *A List of Complete D. H. Lawrence Works.* reprint. Bern Porter. Nov. $12.50.

Child, Hamilton. *Grafton County Gazetteer and Directory.* reprint, 1890. 1172p. photogs. New Hampshire Pub. Oct. $25.

Lossing, Benson J. *Harper's Encyclopaedia of United States History, from 458 A.D. to 1905: with special contributions covering every phase of American history and development by eminent authorities.* 10 vols. reprint of 1905 new ed. illus. maps. Gale. Sept. $185. LC 71-175736.

Moore, Francis & others. *Old Moore's Almanack.* reprint, 1701, 1801, 1901, 1930. 208p. British Bk. Centre. Oct. $12.

ART

Finden, William & Edward Finden. *Ports and Harbours of Great Britain.* reprint, 1836. 262p. illus. British Bk. Centre. Oct. $22.50.

Prior, Edward S. *A History of Gothic Art in England.* reprint, 1900. 480p. illus. British Bk. Centre. Oct. $25.
Survey of English churches & cathedrals.

Seymour, Charles, Jr. *Michelangelo's David: a search for identity.* reprint, 1967. 224p. illus. Norton. Sept. $2.95.
Reconstructs the state of mind of young Michelangelo & the cultural texture of Renaissance Italy.

Smith, H. Clifford. *Jewellery.* reprint, 1908. 457p. British Bk. Centre. Sept. $27.50.

BIOGRAPHY

Anderson, A. A. *25 Years in a Wagon.* reprint, 1888. (Africana collectanea, Vol. 48). 435p. maps. photogs. Verry. Nov. $22.50.

Ballou, Adin. *Autobiography of Adin Ballou, 1803-1890.* reprint, 1896. (American Utopian Adventure). ed. by William S. Heywood. 604p. illus. Porcupine Pr. Nov. $22.50.

Behan, Beatrice. *My Life with Brendan.* reprint. Nash, dist. by Dutton. Sept. $8.95.
Brendan Behan's wife tells of her life with this controversial literary figure.

Campbell, John. *Travels in South Africa.* reprint, 1815. (Africana collectanea, Vol. 47). 448p. maps. Verry. Sept. $25.

Hammond, John Hays. *The Autobiography of John Hays Hammond.* 2 vols. in 1. reprint, 1935. (Gold: Historical & Economic Aspects). 813p. illus. Arno. Sept. $44. LC 74-351.

Lawrence, Frieda. *"Not I, But the Wind . . . ."* reprint, 1934. 324p. illus. photogs. Southern Illinois Univ. Pr. Sept. $10.

Parton, James & others. *Eminent Women of the Age: being narratives of the lives and deeds of the most prominent women of the present generation.* reprint, 1869. (Women in America: from Colonial Times to the 20th Century). 656p. illus. Arno. Sept. $34. LC 74-3968.

Paton, Lucy Allen. *Elizabeth Cary Agassiz: a Biography.* reprint, 1919. (Women in America: from Colonial Times to the 20th Century). 454p. illus. Arno. Sept. $24. LC 74-3969.

Rodney, Thomas. *Diary of Captain Thomas Rodney, 1776-1777: papers of the historical society of Delaware VIII* reprint, 1840. (American Constitutional & Legal History). 53p. Da Capo. Sept. $9.50.

Thompson, Silvanus P. *Life of Lord Kelvin.* 2 vols. reprint, 1910. Chelsea Pub. Sept. $—.

Stein, Leon & Annette K. Baxter, eds. *Fragments of Autobiography.* reprint. (Women in America: from Colonial Times to the 20th Century). 366p. illus. Arno. Sept. $23. LC 74-3982.

———, eds. *Grace H. Dodge: her life and work.* reprint. (Women in America: from Colonial Times to the 20th Century). 302p. illus. Arno. Sept. $16. LC 74-3987.

Wilson, T. G. *Victorian Doctor: being the life of Sir William Wilde.* reprint, 1942. 350p. illus. British Bk. Centre. Oct. $19.50.

BUSINESS & ECONOMICS

Carpenter, Kenneth E., ed. *Gold and Silver in the Presidential Campaign of 1896.* reprint. (Gold: Historical & Economic Aspects). Arno. Sept. $17. LC 74-366.

———, ed. *Gold Mining Company Prospectuses. Pt. 1: California.* 8 articles. *Pt. 2: Alaska, Arizona, Colorado, Idaho, Utah.* 7 articles. reprint. (Gold: Historical & Economic Aspects). illus. maps. Arno. Sept. $26. LC 74-365.

———, ed. *Speculation in Gold and Silver Mining Stocks.* reprint. (Gold: Historical & Economic Aspects). Arno. Sept. $9. LC 74-367.

Committee on Banking and Currency. *Gold Panic Investigation: 41st Congress, 2d Session, House Report, No. 31, U.S. House of Representatives, Committee on Banking and Currency.* reprint, 1870. 483p. Arno. Sept. $25. LC 74-363.

Coughlin, Charles E. *Father Coughlin on Money and Gold.* reprint. (Gold: Historical & Economic Aspects). Arno. Sept. $18. LC 74-368.

Emmons, William Harvey. *Gold Deposits of the World: with a section on prospecting.* reprint, 1937. (Gold: Historical & Economic Aspects). 562p. illus. Arno. Sept. $30. LC 74-350.

Letcher, Owen. *The Gold Mines of Southern Africa: the history, technology, and statistics of the gold industry.* reprint. (Gold: Historical & Economic Aspects). 580p. illus. maps. Arno. Sept. $33. LC 74-353.

Preshaw, G. O. *Banking Under Difficulties, or, Life on the Goldfields of Victoria, New South Wales & New Zealand: by a bank official.* reprint, 1888. (Gold: Historical and Economic Aspects). 179p. Arno. Sept. $11. LC 74-357.

Ross, Ishbel. *Ladies of the Press: the story of women in journalism by an insider.* reprint, 1936. (Women in America: from Colonial Times to the 20th Century). 642p. illus. Arno. Sept. $33. LC 74-3972.

Russell, Henry B. *International Monetary Conferences: their purposes, character, and results with a study of the conditions of currency and finance in Europe and America during intervening periods, and in their relations to international action.* reprint, 1898. (Gold: Historical & Economic Aspects). 477p. Arno. Sept. $25. LC 74-359.

Seyd, Ernest. *Bullion and Foreign Exchanges Theoretically and Practically Considered: followed by a defence of the double valuation, with special reference to the proposed system of universal coinage.* reprint, 1868. (Gold: Historical & Economic Aspects). 716p. Arno. Sept. $37. LC 74-360.

fiction

Evans, Max. *One-Eyed Sky.* reprint. Nash. Sept. $5.95.

Gorki, Maxim. *Bystander.* reprint, 1930. tr. from Russian by Bernard Gilbert Gurney. 736p. Oriole. Nov. $14.50. LC 74-79547.
Tetralogy covering forty years in Russia, 1880 to 1917.

TABLE OF CONTENTS

Listings are based upon the fullest data available from publishers at press time. Dates and prices are subject to change.

For information, please write to Irene Stokvis Land, Editor, Books To Come.

LJ VIEWPOINT

Gerald R. Shields, SCHOOL OF INFORMATION & LIBRARY STUDIES, STATE UNIVERSITY OF NEW YORK, BUFFALO

A tail wagging the ALA puppy?

Robert Wedgeworth, executive director of the American Library Association, labeled as a "personnel matter" the recent resignation of the editor and two assistant editors of *American Libraries.* Yet in his subsequent remarks to the final session of Council in New York last July he revealed that it was more likely a *policy* matter. Wedgeworth read to the ALA Council a statement prepared and presented the previous day to a joint meeting of the Publishing Board and the Editorial Committee. He claimed that for two years he had been attempting to get the editor of *AL* to implement a policy which would allow the magazine to have a reporter cover the Washington D.C. scene. Wedgeworth stated that such a concept was "dependent upon the editors of *American Libraries* sitting down with the directors of the Washington Office, developing a workable plan for covering the Association's affairs so that we do not cross swords on the Washington scene, and respecting the right of *American Libraries* to cover the news and the Washington Office's responsibility to implement Association policy."

I had known that the Washington Office had on occasion been unhappy with some of the stories and letters printed in *AL* but I was unaware during my tenure as editor (1968-1973) that there was supposed to be some sort of agreement as to what news was "fit to print."

As I mulled over Mr. Wedgeworth's remark I became more concerned. If his remarks had been extempore, it would be easy to assume that it didn't mean what it said. But the remarks were prepared and consequently must be taken seriously. Those remarks revealed a policy. How deep and how long has it been a part of the Association?

Could that *unwritten* policy explain the cold shoulder given to Zoia Horn when she was involved in the trial of the Harrisburg *five*? Was accepting her challenge to librarianship considered too embarrassing to the Washington Office during a time when the federal government was attempting to squelch critics of the Vietnam War?

Is it possibly the explanation for the foot-dragging over Michael J. McConnell's demand that the Association back up its policy that an individual is appointed to a position of professional merit and does not lose it because of choice of object of affection? Does the Washington Office feel that to be associated in defense of a man who sought a marriage license with another man is damaging to its "responsibility to implement policy"?

Does this "policy" explain the convoluted goings-on over the investigation into the fair employment practices at the Library of Congress? Was it acceptable to the Washington Office to censure the Rodman Public Library in Ohio but not an agency of the U.S. Congress?

In reviewing the events arising out of actions of the ALA executive branch over the past few years there seems a possibility that the policy mentioned by Wedgeworth runs deeper than whether there is a reporter on the *AL* staff who meets the approval of the Washington Office. Certainly some of the positions taken by the Committee on Intellectual Freedom in the areas of oppression and censorship could be viewed with alarm by many politicians. Has the libertarian stance of ALA intellectual freedom activity been played down on the Washington scene?

Does this newly revealed policy have anything to do with some of the problems encountered by the formation of the Government Documents Round Table which is very visible in several Washington arenas? And it is certain that some of the activities of the Social Responsibilities Round Table have "crossed swords" with the Washington Office.

So, the act of resignation by J. Gordon Burke, Mary Lux, and Jill Reddig self-proclaimed as a matter of policy is supported obliquely by Wedgeworth, thus opening up a new vista for Council to contemplate. Is the purpose of ALA to be the operation of a legislative program tailored to be acceptable to a majority of federal funders and policy designers? If so, fine, if that is what the membership wants. All I would ask is that such a program be made a clear matter of policy.

It is clear that we can not have it both ways. Wedgeworth's seemingly contradictory statement made that Friday is understandable in light of his policy. He said he would continue to support *AL* as a most effective membership organ. "But, I must remind you," he cautioned, "that this is not an independent magazine."

It will help in reading that journal to know the basis upon which the news that appears has been selected. If the selection is based on Washington Office policy, so be it. Just say so on the masthead and in a formal policy statement passed by Council.

LJ FIRST NOVELISTS

Eleven new writers—fall 1975 discuss their first published novels

Harvey Aronson & Mike McGrady
Establishment of Innocence
(*Putnam—November*)
"Writing is what I do in this life. I've been a newspaper reporter and columnist, I write magazine pieces, and I've written two nonfiction books, *The Defense Never Rests* with F. Lee Bailey, and *The Killing of Joey Gallo.* I quit my job at *Newsday* five years ago to freelance, and they've been the best years of my life. I like what I do.

"Working on *Establishment of Innocence* was the most fun I've had as a writer. The reason why is that it's a novel, and it helped that the book was a cooperative venture with my longtime friend, Mike McGrady. Our system was for each of us to write a chapter and then give it to the other person to rewrite. Each of us had the option of changing the changes back to their original form, but that was an option neither of us ever exercised. And although we had a few discussions about the novel, we never had an argument.

"We tried to write a good book, an entertaining book and a book that would sell. The novel concerns the way things seem to be and the way they really are, and it touches on political corruption, investigative reporting and loneliness in suburbia. A murder is essential to the plot, and we hope this carries an element of suspense.

"As for the future, I'm currently working on a nonfiction novel—a real-life story about the compromises prosecutors have to make to achieve what passes for justice in our society. After that, I'd like to try fiction again."

Harvey Aronson

"Although I might cite many influences on my decision to become a novelist, I must say that nothing impressed me quite so much as a meeting I once had with Harold Robbins. The meeting took place at the Plaza Hotel and Mr. Robbins was ebullient—understandably so, since that very day he had received a $2 million advance on his next novel. The novel was not yet written or even outlined. In fact, he received that advance on the basis of nothing more than this title: *The Adventurers.* I have often been paid 'space rates' and the Harold Robbins pay scale—$1 million a word—struck me with enormous impact.

"Another influence was a subsequent meeting with J. P. Donleavy, the critically acclaimed author of *The Ginger Man* and other artistic successes. Mr. Donleavy was asked why he was a novelist and his answer remains with me to this day: 'One of the reasons for being a writer is money. The other reasons are money and fame and money and girls and sometimes just money all alone, by itself.'

"As a newspaperman, I interviewed many other prominent novelists, people such as the late Jacqueline Susann and Irving Wallace. As I read their books, and the other best-selling novels of our time, I realized it would be possible for anyone—*anyone*—to make a fortune in this racket.

"This past year has served only to reinforce this belief. I work an hour or two a day and the financial rewards have been enormous.

"The only thing that surprises me is that more people don't do it. It would seem to be a most lucrative hobby for housewives, for motel clerks, for—oh, anyone with spare time and difficulty making ends meet."

Mike McGrady

Judith Chernaik
Double Fault
(*Putnam—July*)
"In my first novel, *Double Fault,* I have tried to explore the crisis of a woman in her mid-30's who is forced suddenly to come to terms with failures in her marriage, her work, her conception of herself as a decent human being. I suppose I am a traditionalist in literary matters; I believe that fiction must be about real men and women, about their primary relationships. I believe that contemporary fiction, while it seeks to define a contemporary world, must still address itself to universal human concerns, the difficulty of loving, the barriers that isolate people from one another. Ultimately fiction is a form of self-discovery, its motive a profound discontent, a persistent dissatisfaction with one's life and character, and, of course, the vanity that pushes the writer to pass on his special vision of life to others.

"While my own early reading was dominated by the great sprawling 19th-Century English and European novels, I like economy in fiction, spare, taut writing that implies more than it states. I admire novelists who 'write to the moment,' the psychological realism of Richardson, Henry James, Nathalie Sarraute. This is the quality I would like to aim for in my own fiction, and I am convinced that it can only be achieved by struggling with the problems that matter most to one, and are least amenable to solution."

Rick DeMarinis
A Lovely Monster
(*S. & S.—January*)
"I wanted to write a Frankenstein novel from the point of view of the monster. It occurred to me that a creature made up of a variety of donor organs would first of all not be in robust health. In novels of this kind, the monster is usually endowed with terrifying physical strength right from the outset. That has never seemed plausible to me. Therefore, my monster, 'Claude,' begins life in a post-operative twilight: weak, dazed, frightened. He also starts out a terrible hypochondriac. That too seemed probable to me. After all, his survival depends on the successful interdependence of many organs, each alien to the other. The danger of massive rejection is ever-present. Claude does become powerful and a bit frightening, but only after he takes up a regimen of jogging and weightlifting. Thus, his strength is never super-human even though it is formidable. Other things occurred to me.

A page of short items organized about a central spine

This is a page typical of some half dozen such short-item report pages packaged under different headings. The "before" version, at right, shows the way in which the items used to be imposed on the page: somewhat lackluster fashion in spite of the second color headlines. It is a perfectly acceptable solution, workable, simple, easy to live with on an issue-to-issue basis, but it is a bit unimaginative.

The "after" calls for no substantive changes in the items or the way they are written, though widening the column width and allowing greater column height allows two or three extra items per page. The only difference: the makeup man shifts the headlines in the left-hand column to a flush-right position and rules above each headline that appear to grow out of the double-line vertical spine are inserted. The logo and the spine are standing artwork.

The folio and footline are centered and act as visual echoes of the centered logo at the head of the page.

At far right is a version of this page squeezed into a vertical two-thirds space.

OUTLOOK | WORLD BUSINESS

Forecasting world production and trade

An international team of economists is putting together a system or model to forecast trends in international trade. Called Explor Multitrade, it will consist of data—such as a forecast of production, consumption, government spending, prices, costs, profits, investments, labor, foreign trade—of 50 to 80 industries of 10 countries which, collectively account for two thirds of the world's trade. They include Belgium-Luxembourg, Canada, France, Germany, Italy, Japan, the Netherlands, Spain, the U.K. and the USA. The research program is being worked on by Batelle's Pacific Northwest Laboratories (Batelle Blvd., Richland, Washington, A 99352). Forecasts are now available for these countries for the years 1975, 1980 and 1985.

Data bank on new products and patents

Subscribers to Patindex, a new product information service, receive a computerized printout of what's new in about 250 major product categories covering 17 industries in 21 countries. The printout describes a product or process, its stage of development, patent status, countries available for licensing and whether a joint venture or knowhow agreement is required. Subscribers specify their area of interest. Cost is $500 a year. For details, write to Patents International Affiliates 540 Madison Ave., New York, N.Y., USA 10022.

High oil bills for this year

Major oil consuming countries will need considerable sums to pay for their imports of the fuel this year. For example, Japan's bill will come to $11,000 million, $33,000 million for Europe's Common Market countries, and $10,000 million for the U.S. Where will some of them get the money to pay? A high level delegation of Japanese industrialists and bankers who visited the U.S. this month said that Japan must intensify its export drive to pay for the oil. But it will not be as aggressive as in past years. The constraints they cite are: shortage of raw materials, rising concern over environmental pollution, and pressure from overseas countries for Japanese companies to manufacture right in consuming countries.

IRELAND: Big alumina plant at Shannon

Alcan Aluminum Ltd. of Canada will construct a $230 million, 800,000 metric tons a year capacity alumina plant on a thousand acre island in the estuary of the Shannon River, opposite Shannon airport. Construction begins this year and production is scheduled by 1978. Most of the bauxite will come from West Africa. The ingots will be exported to Britain and Europe. The plant will be operated by Alcan Ireland Ltd., a new subsidiary owned 70% by Alcan, 20% by A/S Ardal OG Sunndal Verk of Norway, and 10% by Granges Essem AB of Sweden, both Alcan affiliates.

BRAZIL: Growing use of powder metal

Markets are expanding at a fast rate for powder metal (PM) parts. The automobile makers, especially Volkswagen do Brasil, are the biggest users. So are the manufacturers of sewing machines, motorcycles, bicycles and appliances. The industry consumes 1,200 metric tons of iron powder a year and 300 metric tons of copper powders, mostly imported from the U.S. and Europe. There are four PM companies and two in-plant operations which make PM parts for shock absorbers and sewing machines.

SPAIN: Ford's Valencia plant begins work

Bulldozers have leveled 500 acres of the site for Ford Motor Co.'s main assembly plant, a $500 million investment that will be turning out 250,000 cars a year by late 1976. Almost half of the components of each car will be imported by Ford but two thirds of the plant's output will be exported. The facility is situated at Almusafes, some 12 miles from Valencia.

TAIWAN: Manufactured goods main exports

Unlike most Asian countries whose main exports are primary products or agricultural goods, Taiwan's total exports last year were 92.6% industrial, according to the Ministry of Economic Affairs. They totaled $4,140 million. Big export gains were in products such as bicycles, plastics, electric machinery and metal products.

WORLD BUSINESS TRENDS

Europe to use more minicomputers

Over the next ten years through 1984, the use of minicomputers in Europe will increase 60-fold, from a $10 million level last year to an estimated $600 million. The largest potential market will be in production control applications where the units will replace existing hard wired controllers, according to a market study by Frost & Sullivan, Inc. of New York. Process industries and utilities will also take up big shares of the industrial control market. The study finds that France, Germany and the U.K. will account for two thirds of European minicomputer usage. While U.S. products now dominate the market, European and Japanese minicomputers are now becoming available.

Saudi Arabia plans to industrialize

Buoyed by oil revenues estimated at more than $30,000 million a year, Saudi Arabia has allocated about $100,000 million for big industrial projects. Over the next five years, these projects will include petrochemical, steel, gas, fertilizer, methanol and aluminum plants, among others. Other countries will be providing additional funds for 50-50 joint ventures, thus boosting total spending for the five-year industrialization drive to $150,000 million.

Chile rehabilitates industries

As part of a program to stimulate industrial development, Chile's National Economic Development Agency (CORFO) is granting $13 million worth of credits to large and medium sized industrial firms suffering from low productivity and in need of funds to modernize or diversify. Credits will also be granted to the building of new plants. The Inter-American Development Bank has loaned $10 million of the total costs of the program.

Timken Co. modernizes worldwide

The Timken Co. of Canton, Ohio, a U.S. major manufacturer of bearings, will be spending $60 million over the next five years to boost capacity, modernize equipment and build new plants in six countries where it now operates. These are in Australia, Brazil, England, Canada, South Africa and France.

Mexico makes its own stainless steel

An integrated stainless steel project, costing $83.6 million, will ensure Mexico a domestic supply of the metal. At present, the country imports all of its stainless steel products. To be built in stages at San Luis Potasi, between Monterrey and Mexico City, the initial phase will be the construction of a 40,000 metric ton a year cold rolling mill, followed by facilities for hot rolling and metal production. The financiers of the project are the Fundidora Monterrey S.A. Group, Pechiney-Ugine-Kuhlmann of France, the International Finance Corp., three Mexican companies and other local investors.

High prices slowdown use of nitrogen fertilizer

Eastern Europe is and will be the largest producer and consumer of nitrogen products through 1985; North America will continue to be the second largest ammonia producer, but will be surpassed by Asia in nitrogen fertilizer consumption. These are among the forecasts in a 41-country study, *World Nitrogen Supply & Demand,* prepared by Predicasts, Inc., (11001 Cedar Ave., Cleveland, Ohio, USA 44106.) A copy of the study costs $375. It projects worldwide nitrogen fertilizer consumption to rise to 86 million tons by 1985, from 35 million tons in 1972. It notes, however, that in the past several years, fertilizer consumption has been slowed due to rising prices, capacity shortages, and lack of investment capital for expansion.

Oil pipeline along Panama Canal

A $100 million, one million barrel a day capacity pipeline running parallel to the Canal is being planned by the Panamanian government. It would carry oil from Ecuador, Peru and Bolivia for transport to U.S. and Caribbean ports. Terminals at both ends of the line will be able to handle 120,000 DWT tankers. Construction will take 18 to 24 months, and the pipeline could be opened by 1977, according to the government.

Romania wants MFN status from U.S.

Romanian-US trade could soar to $1,000 million by 1980 from the current $400 million a year level if the U.S. would accord most-favored-nation status to Romania, according to a joint-country trade study. Romania is ready to purchase $100 million worth of U.S. industrial goods as soon as this status is given. It is shopping around particularly for NC machine tools, foundry equipment, earthmoving machinery, cranes and shipyard equipment.

Jamaica readies new trans-shipment port

At a cost of $45 million, Jamaica hopes to transform Kingston into a major trade distribution center for the Caribbean on "the scale of a Hong Kong, Beirut or Halifax." Phase one of the project, now nearing completion, consists of a 40 ft deep channel, 2,400 ft of ship berths served by four gantry type container cranes, each rated at 40 tons (two cranes now operational). Phase two is a 100 acre free trade zone contiguous to the port where manufacturers may set up assembly and other export-oriented plants, with the benefit of a 10-year, 100% tax holiday on profits. The new free zone is being promoted as an ideal distribution site because it is the center of shipping routes in the area, equidistant between North and South America, and located on direct trade routes through Panama between the Far East and Europe.

INTERNATIONAL, LTD.
Department 8700
Wood-Ridge, New Jersey
07075 U.S.A.

Tel. 201-777-2900
Telex 133-350

UNITED STATES
San Diego, California
Chicago, Illinois
Houston, Texas

UNITED KINGDOM
Woking, Surrey, England

EUROPE
Brussels, Belgium
The Hague, Holland
Rome, Italy
Hamburg, West Germany

MID AND FAR EAST,
PACIFIC AREA
Kuwait
Singapore
New Delhi, India
Auckland, New Zealand

WORLD BUSINESS TRENDS

Japan's exports to Middle East are up sharply

"We are spending most of our reserves on buying Arab oil, and we must try to get some of it back," a Japanese businessman told Nadim Makdisi, editor of the Arabic magazine *Alam Attijarat* during a recent trip to Tokyo. Japan's steel exports to the Middle East in the first three quarters of 1974 were 2.6 times that of a year earlier, while chemical exports were up 2.5 times. The decline of traditional markets in southeast Asia, Europe and America, have focused Japanese attention on the oil-rich lands. Numerous contracts have been concluded or are under negotiation for large scale industrial orders. By October of last year, the Middle East took 8% of Japan's exports compared with 4.7% a year earlier.

West Germans invest more in the U.S.

According to official West German statistics, that country's direct investments in the U.S. were $205 million in the first half of 1974—a sizable increase over the $136 million invested in all of 1973. This brought total West Germany investment in the U.S. to about $1,000 million compared with $6,000 invested by U.S. firms in Germany.

Continued expansion seen for ammonia fertilizers

An enormous increase is underway in production of ammonia fertilizer. During the past 10 years, approximately 150 large scale fertilizer ammonia plants (600 tons a day or more) have been put into operation or are now being built, the M.W. Kellogg Co. estimates. Most new construction centers on plants of 1,000 to 1,500 short tons a day. While this capacity range will continue in the near future, Kellogg feels there will also be interest in giant plants of 2,000 short tons a day and greater, associated with cheap natural gas feed—such as in the Middle East and North Africa. Kellogg also says that "coal-based operations can be justified in locations where the unit cost of coal is low, where gas does not exist, and where the alternative is expensive imported oil, as in South Africa and India."

Taiwan Power Company to build third nuclear plant

Taiwan Power Company is planning to build its third nuclear power plant, which will have two generators with an installed capacity of 950,000 kW each. The generators are expected to be completed in March 1984 and April 1985. The company's two other nuclear power plants, both in northern Taiwan, are now under construction.

Brazil plans major expansion in steel capacity

Brazil's steel production capacity will grow from about eight million tons per year to over 22 million tons by 1979. Major expansion will be carried out by three government-owned mills—CSN, COSIPA and USIMINAS—as well as a number of smaller mills. The three major companies account for half of the steel produced in Brazil and for virtually all flat rolled steel. In December, the Inter-American Bank announced two loans totalling $103 million to CSN and COSIPA. The loan to CSN, for $63 million, will help it carry out a $1,600 million expansion program, which will increase capacity of its Volta Redonda plant from 2.3 million to 3.5 million tons per year by 1978.

Several pages suspended from central axis

Here the problem is to make the most of a typical house organ news section with its many short items, some copiously illustrated and others just text reports; simultaneously, the problem is to avoid the typical three-column strait-jacket that seems to be the only way to handle such material.

First decision: editorial judgment agrees that this section deserves good play, and that it therefore deserves enough space to do it justice.

Second decision: it is justified to "waste" one column out of the potential three-to-a-page, place the remaining two columns centered about a strong vertical rule, and encroach onto the extra-wide margins thus left over with long, outrigger headlines and with larger pictures.

The resultant freedom of makeup allows interesting-looking pages with ample variety that avoid appearing messy because of that strong structural central axis about which they spin.

NEWS & NOTES

A&S scholarship winners honored

A reception for the 1973 A&S Scholarship winners and their parents was given in the Executive Board Room in Brooklyn.

Shown here with President **Edward Goodman** are (left to right) Sheri Katzelnick, daughter of **Rhoda Katzelnick**, Budget Dresses, Manhasset; Janice Herbert, daughter of **Russell (Roger) Herbert**, Supervisor of Merchandise Handling, Brooklyn; James Sorace, son of **Alfred Sorace**, Ladies' Shoes, Garden City; Robert Tepper, son of **Roslyn Tepper**, Gift Shop, Manhasset; Eva Capobianco, daughter of **Evelyn Capobianco**, Junior Sportswear, Babylon; Mary Moran, daughter of **Hannah Moran**, Flying Squad, Huntington; and Rose Glassman, daughter of **Helene Glassman**, Staff Artist, Brooklyn. Invited but unable to attend was Robert Master, son of **Meyer Master**, Collection Manager, Brooklyn.

3

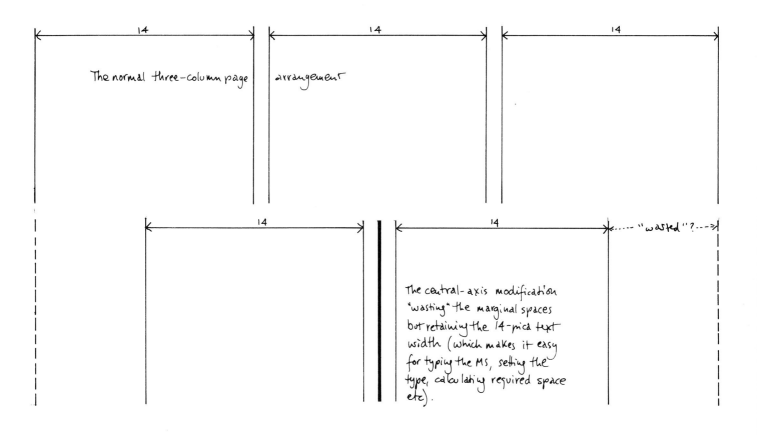

The normal three-column page arrangement

The central-axis modification "wasting" the marginal spaces but retaining the 14-pica text width (which makes it easy for typing the MS, setting the type, calculating required space etc).

"wasted"?

Artists and customers create contemporary crafts

WOODBRIDGE A back-to-school special event on August 23 was called "Make it a Day at A&S." Artists from the Museum of Contemporary Crafts on 53rd Street in New York City participated with customers in "Make It. Wear It. and Share It" events. Projects included body and clothing painting; jewelry from fresh flowers and garden goodies; hats and bags from just about everything; and "pop top treasures" from what else but pop tops.

More employees schooled in emergency first aid

HEMPSTEAD. Participants in the class are shown here. *Clockwise:* William Mangels, Camera Man; **Ronald Patell**, Security; Theresa Ennis, Nurse; **Sylvia Angielski**, Personnel, Garden City; **Harriet Demos**, and **Al Opperman**, Service Supervisors; **Gloria Williams**, Carle Place; **Dorothy Summa** and **Sarah Schor**, Service Supervisors.

Teen board cooks out with cerebral palsy center

WOODBRIDGE. A&S Teen Board members held a One-to-One Cookout with the Cerebral Palsy Treatment Center in Edison, N.J. on July 12 at Roosevelt Park. The store sponsored the entertainment and distributed raffles for the benefit of the Treatment Center to Teen Board members. The prize, a ten-speed bicycle, will be awarded at a free concert in Roosevelt Park on September 9.

Before the cookout, Teen Board members visited the Treatment Center to learn more about how it operates and what services are provided.

Super sleuths honored at special breakfast

SMITH HAVEN. The figures for the Smith Haven 1973 Shortage Contest added up to a first — a group of three-time winners. The June "Super Sleuths" were the Junior Dress Department and the Budget Sportswear Department. Shown here are **Marie Polizzi**, Sales and **Dolores Wallace**, Department

Manager, Junior Dresses; and **Eva Petillo**, **Jackie Pechner**, **Ronnie Crofton**, all of Sales, **Paula Berger**, Assistant Department Manager, **Alice Fraticelli**, and **Lilly Avramenko**, Sales Budget Sportswear. The Bridal Department was also a June winner for the second time.

At the July "Super Sleuth" breakfast, members of each winning department received a corsage and a weekly lottery ticket. And the special three-time winners were awarded "super" corsages of carnations and roses and a chance at $1,000,000 — a special lottery ticket. After the breakfast, Assistant Store Manager **John Lloyd** praised the winners for their efforts to prevent shortage and wished everyone luck in the September lottery.

4

Andy award captured by advertising department

A&S won out over all the big Madison Avenue advertising agencies when it received an Andy Award for the best newspaper campaign of 1972.

The Advertising Club of New York at its 10th Annual Andy Awards program awarded Abraham & Straus its coveted Andy for their 1972 Christmas newspaper campaign series. It was one entry in 3,753 and the store is showing off its trophy in the 9th floor Advertising Department where the campaign was created.

Each year the A&S Christmas series focuses on a theme that selects outstanding merchandise assortments based on customers' current life-styles. The entire staff participates in a brainstorming session; categories are selected, and merchandise presented in an amusing, provocative way. This is the second year in a row that A&S received a top award for its Christmas series. Last year it won the NRMA (National Retail Merchants Association) outstanding advertising award for its Lifestyle '71-'72 series.

This year's award went to four ads selected from a series of 12 with a common theme focused on current merchandise trends: cuffed junior pants (CUFF IT!), big tote carryalls (SCHLEP IT!), indoor planters (DIG IT!), and gourmet fish cooking utensils (POACH IT, fry it, bouillabaisse it, even gefilte it!).

5

Unitization of individual stories yields recognizable character

This example shows a perfectly simple three-column page — with a difference: each item is clearly defined in length, so each signals its start and its end quite clearly. (This is a useful attribute in increasing readership, for people like to read short pieces, especially when they see exactly how short they are.)

The headlines and text are actually set simply flush left and ragged right, with standardized spacing between the headlines and between the items. Superimposed over them are ruled grids, made from existing templates. The only variable: to make the vertical rule end flush with the last line of the item. The horizontal rules are, of course, calculated to coordinate with the line-by-line setting of the text, so that the complex-appearing makeup is, in fact, a perfectly simple laying-down of galley as it comes from the typesetting machine.

The grid (with variations for other situations in the magazine) becomes the recognition symbol of the departments, aided by the department headings, of course.

noticiario internacional

Los inmigrantes de las ciudades son más receptivos a la medicina

En los países en desarrollo, los recién llegados a las ciudades parecen ser más receptivos a la Medicina moderna que los antiguos residentes. El Dr. Robert W. Morgan de la University of Lagos College of Medicine, dice que esto sucede a pesar de que los inmigrantes son generalmente pobres, viven fuera del perímetro urbano y tienen menos acceso a las facilidades médicas. Sus conclusiones se basan en tres encuestas sociomédicas hechas en Lagos, capital de Nigeria. El investigador cree que hay una clase de "personalidad inmigrante" y sugiere como innovación que los programas médicos sean inicialmente destinados a los recién llegados a la ciudad.

Las mujeres italianas continúan amamantando a sus bebés

Un estudio demostró que las mujeres italianas continúan amamantando a sus bebés, prácticamente en la misma proporción que sus madres y abuelas.
De 70 a 80% de 3.746 bebés nacidos en la clínica pediátrica de la Universidad de Roma entre 1967 y 1969 mamaron por lo menos 30 días.
Igual estadística para el periodo de 1933 a 1937 en Messina demostró que 69% mamaron en el primer mes y 84% de 1938 a 1942.
El estudio realizado en Roma, sin embargo, reveló un declinio en este tipo de alimentación hasta los 4 meses de edad. Entre 1940 y 1950, cerca de 50% de los bebés eran amamantados por 4 meses. La cifra ahora disminuyó entre 22 y 28%.

Estudio sobre el suicidio

Una investigación del Cornell University Medical College, de tres años sobre intentos de suicidio, dirigida por el siquiatra Ari Kiev, establece, por ejemplo, que el medio social en el cual el intento se produjo es mejor indicio de las posibilidades de que se repita el atentado que la forma en que se produjo el primero. Y si el acto es debido a un esfuerzo para llamar la atención, es muy posible que se repita dentro de un año. "Contra lo que muchos podrían esperar, dice el Dr. Kiev, el tipo de desórdenes siquiátricos no influye en las probabilidades de un nuevo atentado contra la vida. La actitud de las otras personas y del paciente con relación a sí mismo son más importantes que la naturaleza de los síntomas como elemento de juicio para pronosticar el caso."

La incompatibilidad sanguínea ABO causa abortos espontáneos

La incompatibilidad sanguínea ABO entre la madre y el feto es una de las principales causas de aborto espontáneo, informan los investigadores de la University of British Columbia, Canadá. Según K. Takano y el Dr. J. R. Miller, estudios de 78 fetos abortados indicaron que 35 de ellos tenían grupo sanguíneo incompatible con sus madres, una proporción más alta que la que ellos esperaban. Sin embargo, no parece haber una interacción entre las incompatibilidades ABO y Rh.
De las 229 mujeres que tuvieron abortos espontáneos antes de las 20 semanas de gestación, el 52% tenía tipo sanguíneo O, un porcentaje más alto que en la población general; 37,1% tenía tipo A; 9,2% tipo B; y 1,7% tipo AB. Los investigadores canadienses están seguros de que obtendrán la relación exacta del grupo sanguíneo en cada aborto espontáneo, checando por la técnica de la aglutinación mixta los tipos ABO de los fetos abortados.

El nivel de la alfafetoproteína para calcular la edad gestacional

El nivel de la proteína del suero fetal puede ser mejor para medir la edad gestacional que el peso en el nacimiento, afirma un grupo de investigadores suecos. El Dr. C. G. Berstrand y sus colegas del Hospital General y de la Universidad de Lund encontraron que, entre 165 recién nacidos el nivel de la alfa fetoproteína fue esencialmente el mismo en niños de igual edad gestacional pero de peso diferente. Sin embargo, entre aquellos, con peso igual pero diferente edad gestacional, el nivel de la fetoproteína varió. Los investigadores todavía no pueden decir exactamente qué papel tiene la proteína del suero en el crecimiento del feto.

Breaking a standard-size page into a four-column format allows the small stories to be handled as self-contained squared-off units, separated from each other by means of rules. This kind of rigid precision is appropriate in the context of engineering which is the subject matter of this Brazilian magazine.

The left-hand half is actually a subdepartment. The heavy rules act as both separators of stories, as well as attention-adders to the headlines to which they are tied with rigidly prescribed spacing measurements. The resultant color and texture is what gives the pages their distinctive appearance. Incidentally, the fully packed and bold handling of headlines, in some measure reminiscent of newspaper brashness, adds to the "newsy" feeling of the page.

NOTÍCIA

Componentes brasileiros para mercado de reposição dos EUA

A Case do Brasil está exportando componentes de máquinas rodoviárias e agrícolas para os Estados Unidos, a fim de atender à demanda do mercado de reposição tanto no país importador como no Canadá. Em 1973, as exportações da Case deverão ultrapassar de 500 mil dólares, o que representa um bom volume de divisas para o Brasil.

Bombeiros conhecem na indústria equipamento especial antifogo

A Mercedes-Benz do Brasil-SP, possui em sua fábrica um dos mais eficientes e modernos sistemas de prevenção de incêndio. Graças a um treinamento intensivo dos próprios operários, tem-se conseguido debelar 80% dos inícios de incêndio, mesmo antes da chegada dos bombeiros ao local, utilizando extintores manuais e carretas com pó pressurizado, espuma ou CO_2.

Recentemente visitou a MB um grupo de oficiais do Corpo de Bombeiros de São Paulo, para conhecer melhor sobre os equipamentos especiais de combate a incêndio, montados em veículos Mercedes-Benz.

Durante a visita, os bombeiros puderam observar vários aspectos do sistema da Mercedes-Benz, que conta com 33 bombeiros próprios e 5 viaturas, caixas de aviso que dão o alarme diretamente no painel eletrônico na sala de plantão. Existem também, distribuídos do teto, dispositivos automáticos que, em caso de superaquecimento, dão sinal indicativo no painel eletrônico.

Fábrica baiana recebe equipamento elétrico

Continuando o fornecimento de todo o sistema elétrico contratado pelo Grupo J. Macedo, para sua fábrica de Feira de Sant'Ana, BA — Pneus Tropical S.A., a Siemens do Brasil enviou seis subestações abaixadoras com capacidade unitária de 1 000 kVA, que receberão energia de 4 150 V, para baixar para 440 V e distribuir para a alimentação dos motores das máquinas. Seguirão também mais quatro subestações com capacidade unitária de 150 kVA, para o sistema de distribuição de luz.

Segundo contrato, a Siemens terá o projeto e execução de todo o "engineering" da instalação elétrica, incluindo fornecimento, montagem e colocação em funcionamento dos equipamentos e a administração de materiais adquiridos de terceiros através de seu pessoal.

CAT recomeça exportações

Pelo navio "Delta Mexico", seguiram no dia 3 de fevereiro para o México, mais 33 motoniveladoras brasileiras fabricadas pela Caterpillar Brasil.

Esse país, gozando das regalias oferecidas pela ALALC, tem-se mostrado um excelente importador deste e outros produtos da indústria brasileira.

Trijato mais silencioso

A partir de 1974 os que moram perto de aeroportos verão um trijato que não fará aquele barulho ensurdecedor e não deixará no céu um rasto de fumaça. É que começarão a operar no Brasil os aviões DC-10.

Os novos aviões serão equipados com motores General Electric CF-6 e são, no mínimo, 10 decibéis mais silenciosos que os aviões intercontinentais do projeto anterior com quatro turbinas, e no entanto as novas turbinas possuem o dobro de empuxo das usadas anteriormente.

O primeiro motor General Electric CF-6 era de 40 mil libras de empuxo, utilizado nos trijatos DC-10. Posteriormente, a GE colocou em operação o motor CF6-50 com 50 mil libras de empuxo e que já está em serviço regular desde dezembro do ano passado.

Além dos DC-10 a GE está equipando o avião europeu "Airbus A 300-B", um bijato atualmente em testes de vôo na França, onde é conhecido como A 300-B. Este ano a Boeing começará a testar o seu 747-300, que terá motores General Electric CF6-50, com 51 mil libras de empuxo na decolagem, o único com empuxo acima de 50 000 1b.

Summaries in the feature stories set the graphic pattern for department headings

An abstract of each article is one of the requirements in this magazine, the official publication of the American Institute of Industrial Engineers. Run at the head of each opening page, the summary can also act as a curiosity-stimulator in conjunction with the headline. It also gives a standard out-of-the-way position for the byline and author's affiliation material.

The four-line abstract is placed within a one inch high space, defined by two rules. This same one inch high space is used for the department headings. As the magazine is examined page by page, the rhythm of that one inch space becomes a characteristic element of the product, tying all the pages together by virtue of that sameness despite the distinctive handling required by the various departments. The one inch headings are strong enough to overcome the discrepancies.

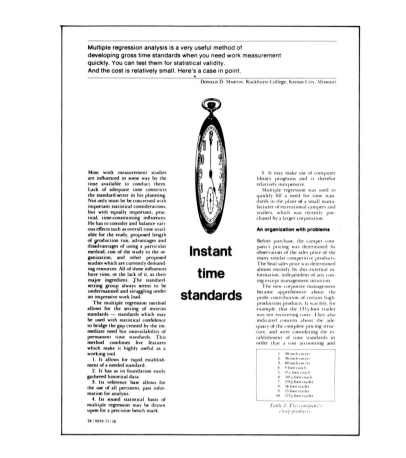

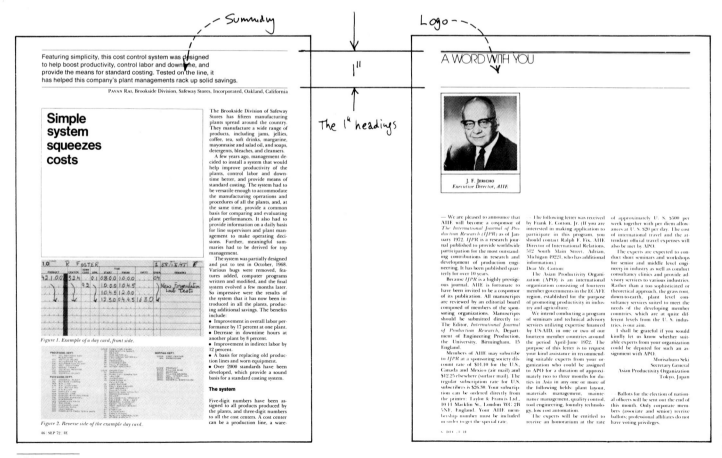

Industrial engineering in fisheries is still new. The IE needs much knowledge before he can communicate intelligently with fishery scientists. But it's a challenging and rewarding world that awaits him.

Michael S. Inoue, Oregon State University, Corvallis, Oregon
Walter T. Pereyra, National Marine Fisheries Service, Seattle, Washington

Fisheries : newest frontier for IE's

Today, industrial engineers are called on to solve problems of high complexity and of far-reaching significance to society. The objectives of studies must now include careful consideration of the preservation and propagation of resources as well as their utilization. This is especially significant when such resources form an integral part of a production system. Such is the case in fishery, forestry, dairy, and other agricultural activities.

Of the various natural resources, fisheries present the most challenging problems to industrial engineers because of the complex factors involving the resources and their environment. Fishery resources, for instance, are such that their population growth and decay must be studied as a dynamic system in time and space, taking into consideration modifying ecological and oceanographic parameters. From a simplistic viewpoint the population can be thought of as a dynamic pool in which recruitment and growth are increasing the population's total size, while mortality factors, both natural and man-caused, are operating to reduce its size. The picture becomes progressively more complicated when one takes into consideration the environment, other related species, and the fact that fishery populations are not homogeneous structures. The fishery population is best described as collections of subsystems which exhibit a varying degree of dependency. Many mathematical techniques used in "population dynamics" are similar to the correlation analysis techniques used by industrial engineers in demand forecasting and other applications, but are more involved because of the need to consider multidimensional aspects.

As part of resource assessment, the magnitude of the potential yield must be evaluated in order to permit optimum allocation of the resource over time. Determination of yield levels is not in itself a final solution as we still have the problem of detecting the exact location of the appropriate fishing grounds. This complication arises because the population is not static like a field of corn. Rather, it is undergoing continual changes in its time-space distribution and aggregation in response to changes in the environment (e.g., temperature, salinity, or oxygen levels), or the animal itself (e.g., spawning).

All of these factors must be taken into account, in addition to the usual consideration of costs and revenues in reaching the fishing grounds, harvesting the fish, and returning to the port where the catch will command the best market price. Also, a fishery system must consider harvesting, processing, and marketing problems. In this way, the total system can be optimized without the usual pitfalls of suboptimization.

Challenge of natural systems

The breakeven analysis of a fishing vessel operation is complicated by the inclusion of independent variables. For example, the simple two-dimensional situation shown in Figure 1-A becomes complicated with the inclusion of just one independent variable that is a function of nature, Figure 1-B.

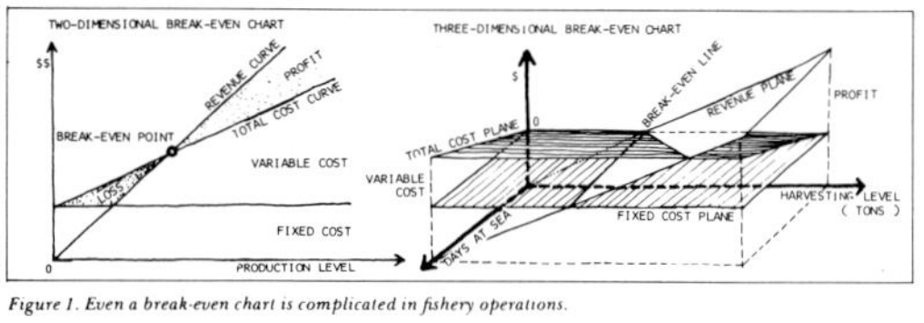

Figure 1. Even a break-even chart is complicated in fishery operations.

In an ordinary factory, the cost and revenue variables can be considered functions of the controllable variable of production level. But, when applied to a fishing vessel, the number of days at sea controls the major expense, while the amount of catch is the main factor that will determine the revenue. Since the two independent variables are only stochastically related, a breakeven line must be analyzed rather than a breakeven point, Figure 1. To optimize such a system, it becomes necessary to consider a dynamic, and preferably an adaptive, decision model.

Even under the simplest assumptions, the decision will involve the determination of days at sea that will maximize the profit.

$$\text{Expected Profit} = \int_o^t R(t',x)P(x|t')dt' - \int_o^{t+\tau} c(t')dt'$$

Where

$R(t',x)$ = the average revenue for X tons of catch on day t' assuming a fixed time (τ) requirement for return journey,

$P(x|t')$ = the probability function for harvesting X tons during t' days.

$c(t')$ = the operating cost of vessel for t' days.

The expression can quickly become overwhelmingly cumbersome if more realistic assumptions are made.

The function $P(x|t')$ will depend greatly on how the vessel schedules its itinerary. For instance, even if the vessel is fully informed of expected catch, variance at each location, and expected weather conditions on nearby fishing grounds, the routing algorithm will require more than a simple traveling-salesman solution by a branch-and-bound technique. Whereas, a traveling salesman terminates his journey upon completion of visits to a fixed number of states, a fishing vessel's return is dependent on the carrying capacity of the vessel, the abundance of fish at the destinations, maximum time that fish can be held, assuming they are not frozen, and landing timetables established by the buyer. The tagging value on the branch-and-bound decision tree, moreover, depends on the time and date of arrival, the port, and the quality, size, and type of fish caught. All these difficulties are minor, however, compared to the problem of obtaining reliable data to use with these models.

Role of industrial engineering

In spite of all these seemingly insurmountable difficulties, it would appear that an industrial engineer is one of the best equipped partners to work with the fisheries scientist. As an example of how an industrial engineer might become part of a fisheries research team, it is useful to look at our major federal fisheries agency, the National Marine Fisheries Service (NMFS), its functions, and how these relate to industrial engineering. NMFS has a responsibility to collect, process, and disseminate information on fishery resources. As part of its overall mission, it aids all marine fishery resource users, including those associated with commercial fishing, sports fishing, and the general public. This assistance is realized by carrying out research and providing services in such related areas as resource assessment (including exploratory fishing), resource allocation, fishing and sampling systems, materials handling, food processing, marketing, etc.

The close relationship between the activities of NMFS and the field and techniques of industrial engineering is illustrated in Table I. In general, an industrial engineer might participate in the following areas:

Systems analysis. The data collection and processing techniques of systems analysis are largely applicable even in natural system studies. These may involve experimental design, stopwatch timing, work sampling, audio-video recording, quality control techniques, etc. Testing of parameter estimation, regression and correlation analysis are widely utilized in fisheries research.

Model-building and simulation. Ecological problems involving the interaction of natural populations with the environment and man's activities lend themselves to simulation modeling. Models have been built and used to analyze such fishery problems as the value of Bristol Bay sockeye salmon forecast (Mathews, 1966); New Bedford industrial trawl fishery (Gardner, 1971); and the allocation of a salmon run (Rothchild and Balsiger, 1971). A population dynamics study, for instance, using a dynamic, first- or

AIIE NEWS ROUNDUP

Spokane gives support to student chapter

Russ Estes, Vice President of the **Spokane Chapter**, presented a $100 check to Jerry Glantz, a senior at Montana State University and President of the student chapter. The chapter is lending support in the hope of establishing closer ties with students. The money will be used for the publication of a newsletter, and for establishing an outstanding senior award at Montana State University in conjunction with the national contest.

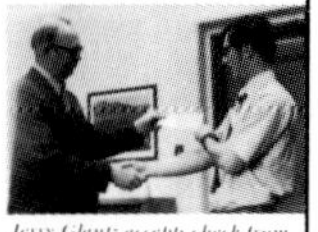

Jerry Glantz accepts check from Russ Estes.

Three members serve advisory board

Three members of the **Winston-Salem Chapter** volunteered to give professional advice by serving on the Forsyth Technical Institute Advisory Board. They are Harry Driscoll, Past President of the chapter and a Senior Engineer at Western Electric Company; Perry Taylor, Manager of Operations at Westinghouse Electric Company; and R. P. Kelley, Superintendent of Resources and Statistical Control at Piedmont Aviation.

The Advisory Board is composed of professional and technical people of the community considered well qualified in their fields. The Board, which is organized into committees, advises the school on curricula, equipment and student placement. The three chapter members are also serving on the Manufacturing Engineering Technology Committee.

The IE function at Armstrong Cork

Dan Power, Plant Industrial Engineer at Armstrong Cork Company in Macon, Georgia, explained the work IE's do at the plant and the dollar savings goals that are made each year. Speaking to members of the **Middle Georgia Chapter**, he described how various products are manufactured, the plant facilities, layout, and organizational structure. Mr. Power discussed the incentive program and methods used to determine standards.

Editors offer guide to prospective authors

Robert Rice, Editor of *Industri* *Engineering* magazine, and Abl Cohen, Assistant Editor, were ,, ic speakers at a recent meeting of t **Philadelphia Chapter.** Mr. Ri presented a comprehensive gui to authors for *Industrial Engine* *ing* and listed the advantages publication. Mrs. Cohen spo about the basic rules of news repo ing, the kind of chapter news that desirable for the magazine, and t importance of using correct gra mar.

IE's suggest improvements for training center

Volunteers of the **Metropolita New York Chapter** have submitt recommendations for layout a methods improvements in t Training Center and Workshop f the Association for the Help of R tarded Children. The proposa were submitted by David Einbin er, Director of Community Servic in conjunction with the chapte community service project.

Physician talks on industrial medicine

The area of industrial medicine gaining in importance as a result the Occupational Health and Saf ty Act. To learn more about the i pact for industrial engineers, th **Canaveral Chapter** invited Dr. F. G. Pierce, Deputy Clinic Director of Industrial Medicine for Pan Am to speak at a recent chapter meeting. Dr. Pierce related the goals of industrial medicine to the engineering profession.

time this issue went to press:

Mid-Hudson Chapter
John Kristakis, senior member
Jack F. Jericho, fellow
Jim F. Wolbrink, senior member
John Weber, senior member
Robert S. Rice, senior member.

OPINION

What will the next two decades show ?

This issue of *Industrial Engineering* includes an index listing articles and papers published from January 1968 through December 1971 in *The Journal of Industrial Engineering*, *Industrial Engineering*, and AIIE *Annual Conference Proceedings*. Together with the Index published in 1968 we now have a complete and up-to-date compilation of literature published by the Institute since its founding. (The December 1971 issue of *AIIE Transactions* will include an update of its index.) As acknowledged in the introduction to our Index, we are grateful to William E. Lewis, H. H. Young, and their colleagues of Arizona State University's Industrial Engineering Department for this unique contribution to the members of AIIE and, indeed, to the industrial engineering profession.

Perusing the indices, one notes the development of IE technology over the relatively short span of twenty-two years — from innovations in work measurement techniques through applications of systems engineering to complex real-life problems. We note the unfolding of improvements in the methods of analyzing and solving the variety of problems with which IE's are traditionally associated. Too, the indices trace the expansion of IE concern and influence into enlarged areas of activity — into functions such as marketing, into service enterprises such as hospitals, for example. In short, the literature reflects rapid, substantial growth in IE technology.

The growth in stature of the industrial engineering profession parallels the maturation of the literature. Jim Wolbrink described and documented the new heights of recognition of IE in his OPINION in the November 1971 issue of *Industrial Engineering*.

Obviously, the rewards of recognition and assignments to larger responsibilities haven't been given just for perseverance. The reason has got to be that you IE's have been making contributions to more effective management of commerce, industry, and services that are earning these rewards. Now, what are these outstanding accomplishments that, in the aggregate, are carrying IE to new heights?

Even some current literature, and much of the unpublished literature to which we are privy reveals two disturbing facts: some IE's appear to be discovering techniques that have long been known to their mentors; others give evidence that they are spending too much work time on trivia, long hours devoted to developing elusive optimum solutions to minutia. Let us, instead, fill the literature with documentation of the accomplishments that are important enough to earn plaudits. Let the *Industrial Engineering* literature of the future reflect an ever-accelerating growth in IE technology. Tell us, you makers of progress, what you're doing — so that we can tell other IE's.

Robert S. Rice, *Senior Member AIIE*
Editor, Industrial Engineering

MEMBERS IN THE NEWS

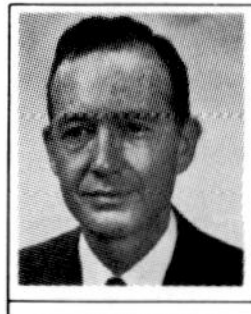

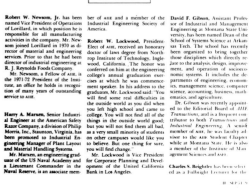

Robert W. Newsom, Jr.

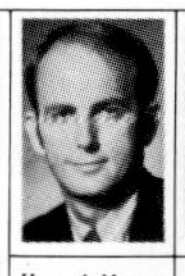

Harry A. Marxen

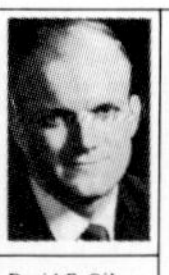

David F. Gibson

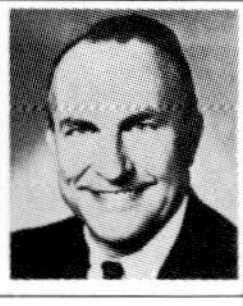

Robert W. Lockwood

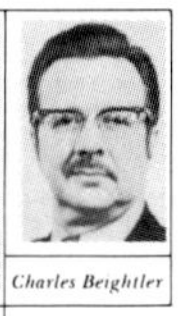

Charles Beightler

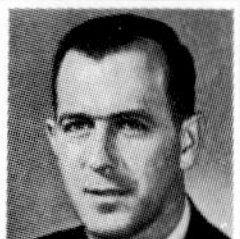

Thomas E. Peatross

Robert W. Newsom, Jr. has been named Vice President of Operations of Lorillard, in which position he is responsible for all manufacturing activities in the company. Mr. Newsom joined Lorillard in 1970 as director of material and engineering services. Prior to that he had been director of industrial engineering at R. J. Reynolds Foods Company.

Mr. Newsom, a Fellow of AIIE, is the 1971-72 President of the Institute, an office he holds in recognition of many years of outstanding service to AIIE.

Harry A. Marxen, Senior Industrial Engineer at the American Safety Razor Company, a division of Philip Morris, Inc., Staunton, Virginia, has been promoted to Industrial Engineering Manager of Plant Layout and Material Handling Systems.

Mr. Marxen, an engineering graduate of the US Naval Academy and a Lieutenant Commander in the Naval Reserve, is an associate member of AIIE and a member of the Industrial Engineering Society of America.

Robert W. Lockwood, President-Elect of AIIE, received an honorary doctor of laws degree from Northrop Institute of Technology, Inglewood, California. The honor was conferred on him at the engineering college's annual graduation exercises at which he was commencement speaker. In his address to the graduates, Mr. Lockwood said: "You will find some real difficulties in the outside world as you did when you left high school and came to college. You will not find all of the things in the outside world good; but you will not find them all bad, as a very small minority of students on other campuses would like you to believe. But one thing for sure, you will find change."

Mr. Lockwood is Vice President for Corporate Planning and Development of the United California Bank in Los Angeles.

David F. Gibson, Assistant Professor of Industrial and Management Engineering at Montana State University, has been named Dean of the School of Systems Science at Arkansas Tech. The school has recently been organized to bring together those disciplines which directly relate to the analysis, design, improvement, and operation of socioeconomic systems. It includes the departments of engineering, economics, management science, computer science, accounting, business, mathematics, and agriculture.

Dr. Gibson was recently appointed to the Editorial Board of *AIIE Transactions*, and is a frequent contributor to both *Transactions* and *Industrial Engineering*. A senior member of AIIE, he was faculty advisor to the AIIE Student Chapter while at Montana State. He is also a member of the Institute of Management Sciences and ASEE.

Charles S. Beightler has been selected as a Fulbright Lecturer for the

Columns by outside writers require special handling

The two examples shown here are typical: the headline must be highly visible; the portrait of the writer is essential, as is the byline and affiliation; the name of the column, if it is a repetitive one, must be clearly visible; the character of the page must be distinctive yet must retain its identity as one of a series of department pages.

The simplest, most effective solution to this perplexing set of requirements, is to invent a format which will become standardized, varying only in headline and copy.

The example from *Nation's Schools*, right, has a rigidly pre-scribed logo area (into which other writers' names and mugshots can be slotted, as required); it also has a standard number of lines to fill. The *House & Home* example, opposite, is equally rigid in its box but allows a random column length, letting the text vary considerably in length (making life easier!).

Obviously there is an infinite number of arrangements possible with these elements. But, unfortunately, there are not that many formats which will allow the necessary flexibility within the context of the column page. To strike a proper balance between individuality and systematic anonymity is not easy. But, as in all the department pages, it is necessary; who says that it must be *easy*?

Dotted lines are more interesting than plain rules, even if they may look like coupons to cut out!

LOOKING FORWARD / Arthur H. Rice

Revolution, not evolution will change American schools

The question is: Will readers of this column permit me to write about the revolution in education? It's not my idea, but the prophecy of a greatly respected and honored educator who, I believe, has a message for all of us.

Okay, you say, who is he and what is this "revolution"?

The author of the prophecy is Stuart A. Courtis, 93 years old, former professor of education at the University of Michigan and Wayne University, who is now retired and living in Cupertino, Calif. Dr. Courtis is probably best known nationally for his pioneering in arithmetic tests and the measurement of child growth.

How the revolt will start

Dr. Courtis anticipates a revolution in educational philosophy and practice. He is not content to take the easy road and say that eventually, by the process of *evolution*, we will arrive at the goals that he envisions. He asks: "How long will it be before the energy of parent dissatisfactions, teacher strikes, sporadic attempts to improve both curricula and practices will flare into violent, unplanned revolution?"

Dr. Courtis believes that much of what we call "teaching" is shal-

Dr. Rice, editorial adviser to NATION'S SCHOOLS *and professor of education at Indiana University, Bloomington, is coordinator, Instructional Systems in Teacher Eduaction, Indiana University.*

low or worthless verbalization. Learning, he says, is primarily "becoming." The function of teaching, he maintains, is to serve. He writes: ". . . my slant is that education is most helpfully defined as 'becoming,' the natural process of evolution by which every individual, without exception, as a result of the experience of living and as long as he lives, is continually becoming something different from what he was just before."

In seeking support for education, how often have we used the phrase "knowledge is power!" But Dr. Courtis reminds us that "while it is knowledge that gives power, the ends to which that power is directed are determined by the 'values' held by the persons who control the use of power. Down through the ages, tyrants like Stalin, Hitler and others have given many demonstrations of how men may use power for their own selfish ends. Democratic governments escape partially from such disturbances and try, ignorantly, to give equal opportunity for growth and development to all. But to this day, and in every kind of government we know of, individual men and women seek to manipulate constitutions and laws to their own benefit. Democracy, as we know it, is not the answer."

May I suggest that you read this again. I have done so a dozen times, and each time it takes on more meaning for me. It says to

me: How then have we failed in the education we give our children, and what we can do to bring about a better society?

How children will learn

Now let's read Dr. Courtis' answer to this question, even if we think that it is impractical or impossible.

"Try to imagine a Service Station in which children grew up in an environment *free* from the imposed control of parents, teachers, politicians and so forth, and were given opportunities to develop in terms of their own inner natures. . . . I believe that if children grew up always solving cooperatively the problems that arise, always learning from experiences, books or persons, given only when they are faced with a problem on which they asked and received the help they desired, evolutionary values would grow spontaneously. Then, when as adults, they gradually begin to face present world conditions, with conflicting interpretations from statesmen, artists and scientists, capitalists, labor unions, and so forth, and when they discover for themselves the misery, sickness, discontent and frustrations now existing, I believe they would aggressively set themselves to solving such problems cooperatively."

We may not accept Dr. Courtis' plan for the kind of education that would lead us to a better society,
Continued on page 16

*Mugshots should look into the page —
or forward, fullface, at the reader*

THE ZONING SCENE

"Regional planning sounds like a cure-all, but it could hurt more than it helps"

There's a new magic potion going around planning circles, and it's called "regionalization." Start with a housing shortage, add a stiff dose of developers' frustrations, a dash of zoning litigation, and season with professional planning principles. Stir well, using rules of thumb, and bring to a full boil.

The new brew has a bewitching flavor, but it may sit poorly in the stomachs of developers and citizens alike.

It is supposed to neutralize an overdose of local home-rule. Everybody wants to solve the housing shortage but no one wants it done in his neighborhood, and in the frontier townships, developers have faced increasing frustrations in seeking approval for new projects, particularly denser ones. Many developers believe that a higher-level planning authority would be more sympathetic to their views.

Professional planners rightly point to the need for a regional approach to such interlocking systems as sewer, water, and transportation. Many will argue for regionalization because it seems to offer a simpler way to save green belts, encourage logical land use patterns, and foster orderly cities.

But as planners ourselves, we're opposed to potions and panaceas. We think there's a better approach.

When local resistance is intense, zoning litigation is often the last resort of the developer. Frustrated by the delays and demands of local officials and the insistent queries of little old ladies at public meetings, developers have turned to the law office to take on townships that use large-lot zoning as a weapon.

But while courts usually rule against townships in such cases, the decisions have not provided real relief either for the developer or the consumer. Local authorities may pay nominal heed to the court by zoning impractical locations for high density development. In one case, for example, local officials responded by zoning an old quarry for apartments. And the local community has such other potential weapons like codes, and subdivisions ordinances, etc. Clearly, the practical solution to the problem lies outside the legal arena.

The positions of developers and local people are really not inherently irreconcilable. The developer can save up to $10,000 per acre by clustering, increasing densities, and reducing engineering costs, and he can still comply fully with health, safety, and welfare requirements. Through such techniques as PUD, he can offer the township considerable advantages in reduction of local service costs and preservation of the landscape. And the township stands to gain even more if the new project brings in considerably more tax revenue than it costs in schooling and municipal services—as a PUD usually does.

The process of negotiating plans for new development is, therefore, a grass roots affair. It's a process of equitably swapping until everyone is protected—developer, officials, and neighbors.

The people involved are neighbors, administrators, politicians, and developers. Neighbors will want a development that looks good and pays its own way. Professional administrators often feel obliged to protect their position by enforcing the highest standards. Politicians must hold down taxes in order to stay in office and are therefore anxious to minimize service costs. Developers, public or private, may need concessions in terms of higher densities in order to avoid onerous costs in construction.

All of these various interests can be accommodated much more directly by the local political process than by a regional bureaucratic labyrinth.

Frontier townships got into a bind because their rapid growth in the post-war period was spurred on, first by easy FHA financing, and then by interstate highways. This growth spread far in advance of services, without government support for sewage treatment systems, open-space purchase, maintenance and improvements on local roads, etc. The result has been disproportionately high taxes.

It follows that frontier township authorities are not optimistic about government promises of relief, particularly with the accompanying threat of government action to force acceptance of additional unprofitable housing. Understandably, the result of this outlook is restrictive zoning.

In the local political process, the developer has a chance to show how, on the basis of the services he provides—roads, utilities, community buildings, shopping areas, recreational facilities—his PUD will provide a large tax surplus. And he has the opportunity to develop local support.

If instead of this he finds himself dealing with a regional office, he may become enmeshed in additional layers of red tape, seeking relief from a bureaucrat who is much less responsive to the local problem, and probably even more unreasonable than the local administrator. Like the local bureaucrat, his position obliges him to enforce the least flexible standards, since that procedure tends to justify his staff and his budget. But while the local administrator works under the politician, who is very responsive to cost-saving proposals, the regional bureaucrat is guided by no locally responsible person.

A reasonable process of review serves the self-interest of good developers and good community government. Local communities are obliged to see to it that all new development has a positive impact on educational costs, open space reserves, and the whole spectrum of municipal services.

They have the police power to protect the health, safety, and welfare of their residents, which include establishing reasonable legal requirements for development and a process of township review. In the process of review, the developer must demonstrate that his project will benefit the community.

In the process of evaluation, developers meet with the local people face to face, swapping proposals and requirements until everyone is reasonably protected. Neighbors, administrators, politicians, and developers can accommodate each other, avoiding onerous costs in taxes and in impractical construction. If the developer and his planner have proper credentials they will get a fair hearing for most proposals. And if they produce a well-documented professional plan that shows a financial benefit to the community, chances are they will succeed. We're not convinced that this process can be replaced by the imposition of a once-removed authority on the regional level.

JOHN RAHENKAMP, PRESIDENT, RAHENKAMP SACHS WELLS AND ASSOC. INC., PHILADELPHIA, PA.

There is magic in numbers

In nearly every issue of *House & Home,* a feature story about a particular development is run, packaged as part of a continuing series. Since it is shown at considerable scale and uses at least six pages in full color, one would hesitate to label it a "department". Yet in the very fact of its continuity (and thus its familiarity), and in the repetition of the design of the opening spread, it fits the definition.

The design of each opening spread which helps to define it as a department-of-sorts consists of four simple elements: a very large, striking picture; a credit block citing facts and figures; an introductory text block describing the project in its context; a vertical black bar at left with label headline and number dropped out in white, or in color. The subsequent spreads vary in design, according to the requirements of the material, of course.

The key to the recognition-effect sought by the design is the numeral. The rest of the design may or may not appear familiar and reminiscent of a previously-seen story. But the number obviously implies that there have been umpteen such portfolios published before and others will most probably follow.

PROJECT
PORTFOLIO

16

PROJECT: Amherst Fields
LOCATION: Amherst, Mass.
DEVELOPER: Otto Paparazzo Associates Inc.
ARCHITECT: Callister, Payne, & Bischoff
INTERIOR DESIGNER: Anawalt & Myer
SITE AREA: 626 acres
NUMBER OF UNITS: 1,640 condominium townhouses,
   duplexes, fourplexes and detached units
   plus a 34-acre commercial center
PRICE RANGE: $23,500-$52,000

If the photo above gives you an impression of farmhouses set in an unmowed meadow,
the effect is not accidental. Developer Paparazzo and architect Callister, the men
most responsible for the landmark design of Heritage Village in Southbury, Conn.,
faced a problem here: how to maintain the site's strong rural quality at a
density of about three units an acre. Detached housing at that density would have
destroyed much of the natural landscaping—leaving, at best, tiny front lawns and
insignificant greenbelts. And clustered townhouses and apartments would have looked
suburban rather than rural. The solution: a combination of duplexes, triplexes and
fourplexes (plus an occasional detached unit)—all sited further apart than in
normal cluster practice and all in a contemporary version of New England design.

Four style changes in ESQUIRE

TRAVEL NOTES
RICHARD JOSEPH

"Forward!" is the word for this corner of Esquire's fortieth anniversary issue; you'll find no nostalgia here except as it proves useful in plotting the future—to find out where you're going it often helps to look back on where you've been. So what will travel be like forty years from now, in the year 2013, when Esquire will celebrate its eightieth anniversary, and the writer will have been its Travel Editor for sixty-seven years?

Chances are that you'll fly from coast to coast and across the oceans in transport rockets at speeds somewhere in the neighborhood of 17,000 miles an hour. That means New York to Paris in about thirteen minutes, New York to San Francisco in nine minutes, San Francisco to Tokyo in nineteen minutes, New York to Sydney in about an hour.

Sounds Buck Rogerish? Well, that's the speed of present-day rockets and satellites. And some time ago, on a radio show on which we were both appearing, rocket expert Werner Von Braun told me that rocket passenger transportation was well within the limits of technical feasibility; the main problem to be solved was deceleration.

The projected speed forty years hence is not at all out of line with the progress that has been made over the past two forty-year periods—and scientific and technical advances progress at an ever-increasing tempo. It represents a more than tenfold increase over the 1400-m.p.h. speed of the Anglo-French supersonic Concorde, now undergoing tests before entry into airline service in a year and a half. But the Concorde's speed is almost ten times that of the 160-m.p.h. DC-3 which was being tested forty years ago, before going into service for American Airlines—which became American Airlines—in 1936. Yet the DC-3 was less than three times faster than the fastest transportation—the railroad trains—forty years before that in 1893.

And if the whole concept of rocket travel still sounds outlandish to you, just back-project to 1933 to see the changes the past forty years have wrought. In the year that Esquire was born, college men, their hair parted in the middle, F. Scott Fitzgerald style, worked their way to Europe aboard cattle boats or sailed in class aboard the White Star liner Majestic, then the largest afloat, or the Ile de France, which carried Lorelei Lee, the blonde that gentlemen preferred, on her memorable voyage. But there was no North Atlantic air service (Charles Lindbergh had made his memorable solo flight only six years before).

The German dirigible Graf Zeppelin was flying the South Atlantic, though, carrying twenty-five passengers in ten staterooms on the three-day flight from Europe to Brazil. (Four years later, in 1937, the tragic crash of the Hindenburg just about finished lighter-than-air ships as passenger carriers.)

Transatlantic plane service didn't begin until 1939 when Pan American inaugurated its New York-Southampton service with Boeing 314 flying boats that carried twenty-four passengers across the Atlantic in twenty-seven hours, stopping at the Azores, Lisbon and Marseilles.

Domestic air travel was equally primitive. Forty years ago, TWA's

Ford trimotor planes flew from New York to Los Angeles in the same twenty-seven hours, stopping at Philadelphia, Harrisburg, Pittsburgh, Columbus, Indianapolis, St. Louis, Kansas City, Wichita, Amarillo, Albuquerque and Winslow. One-way fare was $160. Compare it with the present coach fare of $155.56, plus tax, and you'll see that air travel is no bargain that has survived recurrent waves of inflation. (In 1933 you could buy a Plymouth for $445, the latest model Chrysler sedan was $785, and New York's St. Regis Hotel charged $4 to $6 a day for a single room, $7 double, or $10 to $20 for a suite.)

In its 1933 timetables, American Airways was reassuring its pioneering passengers with notes to the effect that all its tickets were obtainable at offices of the Pennsylvania Railroad, Postal Telegraph, Western Union, Greyhound Bus Lines and from hotel porters.

But one item in the American Airways timetable is a reminder that passing years don't necessarily bring progress and improvement. Back in '33 it cost seventy-five cents and took forty-five minutes to ride the airport bus from Newark airport, then the main one serving the New York area, to midtown Manhattan. Now it costs two dollars and takes ten minutes longer, and the running time from JFK is an hour.

The timetable went on to explain that schedules had been arranged so that meals might be obtained at airports where adequate facilities were available. "American Airways," it said, "endeavors to see that these are palatable and that all costs are reasonable.

"Cabins of American Airways planes are comfortably heated and ventilated," it continued, so passengers were advised to "wear regular apparel regardless of season."

Nevertheless, travel agents still seemed unconvinced of the importance of air travel, and a Pan American official said they didn't appear to be interested in developing the air travel market. Which was understandable, replied A.S.T.A. (the American Society of Travel Agents Association), since such an airline as TWA (then called Transcontinental and Western Air) was advertising that its tickets were obtainable at offices of the Pennsylvania Railroad.

And Connecticut's Senator Lowell P. Weicker, who while not chivying Watergate malefactors serves on the Senate's Aeronautical and Space Sciences Committee and is a leading Congressional transportation buff and opponent of the highway lobby, points out that New York City traffic, which moved along behind horses at eleven and a half miles an hour in 1906, is creeping along today at an average speed approaching eight miles an hour "behind the highest performance engines Detroit can mass-produce."

We asked Senator Weicker what he thought travel would be like in the year 2013, and he told us, "The answer to what the transportation scene will be like in another forty years is very much merged with the question of what America will be like. To answer the question we can imagine a visitor from another world

22 ESQUIRE: OCTOBER

Esquire, Richard Weigand

1974

SPORTS   BY ROY BLOUNT JR.

Biorhythm and the Big Game
First count from your birth date, see . . . and you can prove anything

The first I ever heard of biorhythm as a sports factor was in 1973, the day after Steeler quarterback Terry Bradshaw came out of a big game with his collarbone broken. "Bradshaw was down," said Steeler patriarch Art Rooney. "Before the game he was telling me. There's a new study going on now. In your body, there are certain times you're at a low ebb. There are three waves in you. When these waves get below a certain level, you're in danger.' I was saying that's all the bunk. I hoped he didn't believe in that low wave. I said I'd been in that wave forty years. The minute I saw Bradshaw come off that field, I thought, There's no way to convince him those waves are the bunk now."

Since then, a considerable consulting touring industry has been founded upon the waves, THE FITH MAN IN HUDDLE: A BIORHYTHM EXPERT, read a recent headline in The New York Times. Many gamblers, some football coaches and even a few baseball managers and their doughtired owners, the Times reported, are consulting biorhythm charts to determine where to put their money, at whom to run their plays, how to rotate pitchers and when to race or breed horses.

The theory is that on the day you're born you embark upon three root-counting your phone bill) overlapping, recurrent cycles: a 23-day cycle of physical ups and downs; a 28-day cycle of emotional rhythms; and a 33-day cycle of intellectual fluctuations. (Incidentally, horsemen, no such figures have been postulated for beasts.) At high points of these cycles you have more potential for high performance, at low points you are more likely to be flat, and on those days cal" days when the curve recrosses the neutral or starting line between low and

high, you are shifting gears, so to speak, and are prey to rashness, instability and fumble-itis. When your three waves are all high, you should have a wonderful day—if there's no tornado—and when all three are critical, it's like being born again, which is to say awful.

To figure out anyone's biorhythms on a given day, add up the number of days from his or her date of birth. Then divide that number by 23, 28 and 33. Take the three remainders and plot them out on three simple graphs. It's fun—takes you back to the seventh grade. Tables, which are available in popular paperbacks, greatly expedite the process, and you can buy a pocket biorhythm calculator or retain a consulting firm, which makes it even easier, though more expensive.

My first reaction to all this was fine. I am inclined to believe in everything. T.M., Doan's Pills, Pat Boone, psychiatry, jogging, dream books, X rays, dynamic tension, a charm, a quark or any other conceivable subatomic particle, Sufism, Christian Science, medical checkups, Nietzsche, sprouts, solid geometry—everything but Republicanism and methadone maintenance. I don't practice any of these things, but as far as going along with them goes, I'm like the old boy who was asked whether he believed in infant baptism. "Believe in it?" he said. "I've seen it done!"

As soon as I heard the word "biorhythms," I did feel it should be replaced, in sports, by Art Rooney's term. "Waves" is better. Teams could "beat the waves" or "ride great waves into the crucial tilt," and players could say, "Hey, I don't make excuses, man. But I was playing on some waves you wouldn't believe. I'd try to cut back quick on that physical wave of mine and it was underflow.

The statistical opportunities struck me as tremendous. You could work out a scale of values to go with the waves and refigure everybody's stats from Francis

Ouimet on. Say a basketball player shot 41.3 percent from the floor while "playing critical." That might be as good as 68.7 achieved on a triple high. Pro-football scouts could plot out a prospect's waves for game Sundays over the next ten years and work that factor into his computer rating. Players could demand a sliding scale providing extra incentive pay for low days. That's the way my thoughts went surfing along until I looked further. Then the waves sank in my estimation.

For one thing, 23- and 28-day figures derive from Wilhelm Fliess's nineteenth-century research into fluctuations in the lining of the nose. One of Fliess's theories was that you could treat sexual dysfunction by applying cocaine to "genital cells" in your nose. Fliess operated on Freud's nose once, and Lord knows people would line up for his prescriptions today, but Einstein he wasn't. In her scholarly Biological Rhythms in Human & Animal Physiology, Gay Gaer Luce says, "Fliess's blatantly unsophisticated understanding of simple mathematics is evident in his formula, which is transparent junk. Yet, every year it is offered to the public in new books on biorhythms.

"Well, you still have people saying there's no value to vitamins," says Bernard Gittelson. "All I say is, if they help you, use them. Gittelson wrote two widely read books, Biorhythm—A Personal Science and Biorhythm Sports Forecasting. He is also president of Biorhythm Computers Inc., and he says he is under contract as a consultant to "a lot" of N.F.L. teams. I asked him about the formula. "There's no question there may be variations," he said. "You may find yourself on a twenty-four- or twenty-five-day cycle. But the rhythms for most people are standard, just as most women have a twenty-eight-day menstrual cycle."

Contributing editor Roy Blount Jr.'s biorhythms waves were all on an upward cycle when he wrote this column.

28 MARCH 14, 1978 ESQUIRE

Photograph by Ben Rose

Milton Glaser

1978

Politics   by Richard Reeves

The Iseman Cometh
Fred Iseman planned to take over N.Y.'s papers. So did Rupert Murdoch

Fred Iseman was very clever at Yale. He even put his philosophy into epigrams that his friends still repeat:

"You have to understand that half the world is asleep, and you won't disturb them if you step over the bodies."

"You're born with a full address book, and the purpose of life is to clean it up."

When he got out in 1975, he thought he should let the world in on the secrets—for a price. He decided to start a magazine called Moving UP! He put together a twenty-two-page prospectus, including a sample mailing to potential subscribers that began: "There's not enough room at the top for everyone. Join the Movers!"

Each month, the Movers would learn "How to acquire the hot new skills that mean big bucks in the near future." The prospectus promised articles with headlines like these: "How to Use a Connection." "How to Change Your Image Without Changing Yourself." "Phone Power—Winning Without Being There."

Another sample was "The Jock's Advantage," advising corporate climbers to find out their boss's favorite sports and then to learn golf or tennis or croquet.

Iseman was hustling around New York this year, trying to raise $2 million for Moving UP!, when he spotted some room at the top, the chance to make big bucks in his near future. On August 9, The New York Times, New York Daily News, and New York Post were shut down by striking pressmen. On August 21, a temporary newspaper called The New York Daily Metro hit the streets—500,000 copies at 25 cents apiece, and each named Frederick Iseman as president and publisher. The publisher was quoted extensively in the first issue—put out primarily by striking New York Timesmen being paid

$60 a day—and the quotes focused on rumors that Rupert Murdoch, publisher of the struck Post, was actually the power behind the Metro. Not so, the temporary paper reported:

"Mr. Iseman, normally an assistant editor of the op-ed page of The New York Times, said the bulk of profits from the publication would be contributed to charity. . . . Mr. Iseman said the New York Post had agreed to deliver 150,000 copies of the Metro each day through its home-delivery system. . . . [But] Mr. Iseman asserted that there would be 'no editorial or business control by Murdoch' in the daily operations of the paper. 'I can't say it more emphatically,' Mr. Iseman declared. 'This newspaper is mine. I am its sole stockholder.'

As we shall see, that statement was more emphatic than candid. Among other things, Iseman was expecting to make $100,000 a week with charity toward

none, and Rupert Murdoch could be making $1,000,000 a week while the Times and Daily News both would be subsidizing the establishment of a nonunion Murdoch morning paper to compete with them. But that is getting way ahead of the story, which should begin with the fact that what twenty-five-year-old Frederick Iseman really was on August 9 was a summer replacement at the Times who was scheduled to be let go on August 25 after just eight weeks on the Times's payroll.

Using his father, Joseph Iseman, a prominent lawyer, as his connection, young Iseman tried to organize a temporary newspaper with the cooperation or backing of Metropolitan News Company, one of the large New York newspaper distributors that desperately needed some kind of product to distribute. One of the difficulties with that arrangement was that it might create some antitrust problems because the distributor would be handling both a paper it owned and that paper's direct competitors, or, at least, there would be a sticky public relations situation. So Iseman consulted one of the city's best PR men, Howard Rubenstein.

"You're going to have to live a long time in this town," Rubenstein said. "You'll be asked about the Metropolitan News connection. The only way to handle it is candidly, honestly, openly. Okay, now present this is a press conference. I'm a television reporter: 'Mr. Iseman, what is the relationship between your newspaper and its distributor, Metropolitan News?' Now you answer and remember: candor, honesty, openness.'

Iseman hesitated for a second, then said: "No comment."

"No, no. You can't do that," Rubenstein said. Okay, Iseman said, he'd make something up. Rubenstein refused the account.

Anyway, the Metropolitan News deal

Illustration by David Levine

OCTOBER 10, 1978/ESQUIRE 11

April Silver

1978

TRAVEL
BY DAVID BUTWIN

THE PACIFIC/ORIENT CONNECTION
When to go, how to get there, where to stay, and what to buy

ONCE YOU'VE selected a beachhead in the South Pacific or Orient (see pages 64–71), it's time to plan the invasion. Here are the basic strategies.

HOW TO GET THERE: Choosing the best and cheapest routes west of Los Angeles has become as complex and challenging as the region itself. Whether you're going to the Pacific or to the Orient—and the two are separate spheres on airline schedules—the Advanced Purchase Excursion (APEX) is the best bet for the sporting, adventurous, independent traveler. Don't dismiss package tours out of hand, though. Tahiti, for example, can be a better deal if you book a tour that includes hotels and meals.

Although APEX fares may be more than 40 percent cheaper than normal economy fares to the South Pacific, you must buy tickets at least thirty days in advance. Moreover, you are usually limited to a single stopover en route and cannot switch airlines without paying a surcharge. An exception is the new APEX plan Pan American and Qantas have worked out. Using Qantas southbound from the West Coast, you may stop in Honolulu en route; going home on Pan Am, you may visit Auckland, New Zealand. Most airlines flying to the South Pacific (some others are UTA, Continental, and Air New Zealand) depart from Los Angeles.

APEX fares to the Orient generally require a stay of fourteen to sixty days and ticket purchase within twenty-one days of departure. San Francisco, Los Angeles, Seattle, and Anchorage are the main jumping-off spots to Tokyo, Taipei, and beyond. When bound for these regions, as for the South Pacific, it's important to inquire about other so-called promotional fares that may be better bargains than APEX. Northwest, for example, has a budget fare to Hong Kong that is lower than its APEX fare. And Philippine Airlines offers an

$852 round-trip budget fare from San Francisco ($1,048 from New York).

One way to travel without worrying about stopover restrictions is to buy a round-the-world ticket and stop pretty much where you please. At this writing, Pan Am's $1,719 ticket ($1,279 if you go standby) commits you to twenty-two to eighty days, with at least four stops of forty-eight hours or more. Flying from the West Coast, you could take in Honolulu, Tokyo, Hong Kong, Bangkok, Singapore, Delhi, and Bombay. Singapore Airlines and TWA have a joint pact that can get you around the world for $1,709 using Singapore's routes in Asia, TWA's in Europe and America. Northwest has a similar arrangement with Air India, Pakistan Airlines, and Cathay Pacific for $1,599 economy, $2,349 first class.

Japan Air Lines has a $1,300 APEX from New York to Tokyo, saving you $388 over the next-lowest economy fare, but no stopovers are permitted and reservations

must be made thirty days ahead. Japan Air Lines also runs flights from San Francisco and Los Angeles daily. In the cluttered, convoluted matter of booking a flight, at least you don't have to be concerned with seasonal fare changes. Whereas the fares to the South Pacific are figured according to high, low, and shoulder seasonal rates, they're the same year round to the Orient in economy class.

A final note: it's important to know that the inscrutability of the East still exists, and it can be found not only in back-street bazaars but at airport ticket counters.

WHEN TO GO: Down Under, summer is that balmy stretch from December to March when the air fares happen to be highest. From June to August is an economical time to visit Australia, but it can be a bit brisk for sailing in Sydney. The Whitsunday Passage, on the other hand, is probably best from May through August, when Qantas, for example, drops its APEX to $820 round trip. From Los Angeles or San Francisco, it may rain in New Zealand's Fiordland National Park in spring or the wet season of the year, but summer, particularly February, is the mildest (if not the cheapest) season. Tahiti is warm and dry, but also most expensive, in July and August. In September, as well as from April through June, Tahiti tends to be less crowded and less costly.

Except in Japan, which has distinct seasons (including steaming summers), count on a year-round hot time in the Orient. Manila's temperatures, however, are moderate from November to February, and Hong Kong is clearest and most comfortable (and most crowded) from October through December. Indonesia, Malaysia, and Singapore are close enough to the equator to be uniformly warm all year.

WHERE TO STAY: Some of the best and most colorful hotels are conveniently situ-

ESQUIRE: MARCH 1981

Robert Priest

1981

110

Four styling developments in SIGNATURE

Far Corners

The Road to Timbuktu

You take the first left...or is it a right?

by Carolyn Miller

The legendary city of Timbuktu, long a symbol of distant mystery and romance, well deserves its reputation as one of the world's most inaccessible places. I speak with some authority, having spent $1,500 and two weeks bouncing over desert roads in a Land Rover trying to get there and failing. The trip was not without its rewards, but, as it turned out, Timbuktu was not one of them.

I don't mean to imply the place can't be reached. If you want to cheat, Timbuktu has an airport that can handle anything up to a small jet. But that's hardly in keeping with the spirit that has made Timbuktu what it is today—hot, dusty and insect-ridden, according to what I've heard (remember, I didn't get there). Should you be wondering what I was doing in the Sahara courting failure in the first place, it is very simple. My life was in more than its usual state of disarray when I saw an advertisement for a tour going to Timbuktu overland, the hard way. The offbeat trip seemed like a natural method to put off a few hundred decisions, so I signed on.

Trips of this sort are touted in the travel industry as "adventure vacations." Usually these are off-the-trail jaunts utilizing something fundamental, like rafts, horses, camels, four-wheel-drive vehicles, or simply your own two feet. This particular trip, however, was more eccentric than most, a one-shot special put together by an English expedition company, Allen & Dunn (now Treasure Treks), to lure old Africa hands who have grown jaded by mere lions.

I was one of 16 would-be Stanleys from six different countries on the trek. Like most of the others, I had had previous adventures in Africa of a conventional nature. This time around I wanted something different. Well, a *little* different at least.

I paid $1,507 for all land costs and the round-trip airfare from London to Africa, and prepared to fly to Niamey, the capital of Niger, where the tour would assemble with our three-man crew and Land Rovers. From there we were to make a circle passing through Upper Volta and into Mali, reach Timbuktu, and then follow the River Niger back to Niamey. Much of the journey would either be through arid savannah or across the Sahel, the stark landscape that borders the Sahara Desert.

Today Mali is a land-locked, somewhat ignored West African republic, but from the 13th to the 17th centuries, Mali was a great empire and Timbuktu was an international city, exchanging ambassadors with important foreign courts. The city's location on the northern curve of the Niger River made it a natural for enormous traffic in trade. "Desert ships" made their way in caravans across the sands to the famous city. The overland route most often traveled to Timbuktu these days is from Gao in the east. We chose instead to enter from the west and travel up through the marshes formed by the Niger, crossing the river twice by ferry. Though the track was clearly marked on the Michelin map, not even our guide had been that way before.

The 19 of us on the tour (including leader, cook and mechanic) first came together late one night in the garden of a hotel in Niamey. Because (for reasons never discovered) there were no vacant rooms in the entire capital, we were to sleep by the swimming pool. In the meager illumination of our flashlights, everyone else looked impressively fit and ready for anything. I couldn't even find my mosquito repellent.

The next day we loaded our three Land Rovers and headed into the bush toward the Upper Volta frontier. At this point, primed by the tour's vivid itinerary and the local guidebook, I was eagerly anticipating a look at the "sacred crocodiles" so lavishly described. As part of an ancient rite (and current tourist draw) the local Mossi tribesmen sacrifice chickens to the crocodiles. As we pulled up to the edge of the water, we were greeted by a group of small boys carrying mangy pullets and noisily insisting on sacrificing one chicken for every two persons in our group. Nothing less would do. To everyone's relief, their idea of "sacrifice" turned out to be dangling a bird over a crocodile's head until the croc opened his jaws far enough for a good photo. The bedraggled chicken would then be swiftly jerked back, to be preserved for the next squadron of tourists. We moved on with no great reluctance.

A short time later, our leader, Roger Lloyd, pulled off the dirt track and stopped at a Hausa village of round straw huts. Roger, a tall, bearded Englishman, graciously greeted the shy women who came out to stare at us and gave candy to the children.

Soon, a crowd of giggling youngsters gathered around me, fascinated by my camera. When I finally detached myself to enter their village, I felt like a new friend, not a tourist. The walled compounds, the thatched roofs, the calabash vessels seemed totally untouched by Western influence. Everything looked exotic—the woman

32 Signature June 1978

Signature, Dave Stech

1978

TRAVEL WORLD

Detouring Through Austria

by Margaret Zellers

KUFSTEIN, AUSTRIA—An Austrian friend confidently told me that it's possible to drive from Innsbruck to Salzburg via Rosenheim, Germany, in about an hour and a half, and from Salzburg to Vienna in "three hours at high speed." But my advice is, don't do it. There are too many marvelous pausing places along that route—one of which is Kufstein. This Austrian border town lies between Innsbruck and Salzburg—about an hour's leisurely drive from each and on the main rail route.

Whether you drive through Austria or go by train (see below), there are many detours along the way that are well worth the time they take. Recent meanderings took me the better part of three weeks, and I would gladly have taken a lot more time.

Start at Innsbruck, where you can wander around the old town and enjoy the Goldener Adler Hotel (make a reservation for dinner and order cevapcici, spicy Hungarian-style meat, and palatschinken, paper thin crêpes with various fillings). Then head out in an arc that includes Igls, with its memorable Schlosshotel where the manager graciously spoils all her guests. The crossroads that is the village of Lans is a reasonable walk from Igls—or even from Innsbruck if you enjoy a couple of hours of country walking. Here, the Wilden Mann inn is the one to aim for. Hall, once a walled city, sits beside the Inn River, just outside Innsbruck. Its Ritter-Küchl (Salvatorgasse 6) serves an eight- or nine-course medieval banquet which includes suckling pig served with ceremony and singing. (Ask your hotel to book the reservation.)

From Innsbruck to Salzburg, the autobahn weaves up through Germany and then back into Austria. Kufstein sits right on the Austrian border, straddling the Inn River. It is a town of enchanting medieval inns on narrow lanes hidden amid modern buildings. Find the Auracher Lochl Hotel and walk up the stairs to its first-floor restaurant, which occupies a series of wood-walled rooms filled with benches and trestle tables. Sample the local cooking and—if you're here when the new rooms are finished in late 1980—stay a night or two.

Salzburg, known as a city of song (mostly Mozart's), surrounds the Salzach River. The left bank is the best part of town, in my opinion, with several imposing churches (the Cathedral, known as the Dom, St. Peterskirche and the Franziskanerkirche), as well as an assortment of intriguing restaurants that make up in atmosphere what they may lack in culinary proficiency.

The Peterskeller, with several cellar-style rooms and lots of *Gemütlichkeit*, serves meals, snacks and beverages well into the evening hours. For lingering and absorbing the local color, try the Cafe Tomaselli on the Alt Markt square, not far from the Dom, and the Podium, wedged into the walls near the Gstätten Tor, not far from the base station for the lift up to the Winkler café/restaurant/casino atop the Mönchsberg.

Take the three-minute ride up (10 Austrian schillings, up and back) and you'll see a lot more than the modern Winkler with its viewing platform and commercial pleasures. If you follow the path through the woods, it's an easy 10-minute walk to the humble café St. Hubertus. Chamoix horns punctuate the walls, and other woodsy décor sets the tone for your coffee or country food. Another 10-minute walk from here, in a triangle with the Winkler, is Schloss Mönchstein, an elegant castle hotel for about two dozen lucky guests.

Built in 1358 to be used as the guest castle for the archbishops of Salzburg, the Schloss still maintains the small chapel in an alcove off room 15. The tone, set by the late Baron von Mierke and maintained by the Baroness, is that of comfortable elegance. The main street hubbub of Salzburg is only a walk and an elevator ride away, but at

continued on page 22

20 Signature May 1980

Stanley M. Braverman

1980

The Selective Buyer

Glassy-Eyed on Fifth Avenue

Not long ago a package arrived in the mail bearing the famous Steuben snowflake logo. Inside was a carefully wrapped, engraved ashtray, first prize in a contest I'd entered. It was a massive, sloping bowl of clear, brilliant crystal, a work of art.

Curious to see more, I paid a visit to a nearby Steuben showroom. (Steuben glass is available in their showrooms in New York City, at the factory in Corning, N.Y., as well as in selected stores throughout the country.) The range of vases, bowls, presentation pieces and jewelry was dazzling. It was a magic show of light and shadow and confirmed the fact that there is indeed a distinctive "Steuben look."

The glass itself is as clear as a mountain spring with marvelous reflective qualities. Meticulous finishing lends a diamondlike quality, which may be one of the reasons why Steuben has recently introduced a selection of gemlike crystal jewelry—at gemlike prices. A heart pendant on an 18-karat-gold chain is priced at $2,600. Steuben's engraved pieces range in price from $2,200 to $75,000 and some are produced in limited editions, adding to the value for the serious collector.

For those in search of gifts in a more modest price range, there is a handsome crystal apple for under $200. New York's Mayor Ed Koch is fond of presenting these mementoes of The Big Apple to visiting dignitaries. In fact, Steuben glass has long been popular as an official state gift, and every President since Truman has presented heads of state with specially designed pieces. Recently, friends of Ronald Reagan ordered an engraved crystal plaque as a birthday gift for the newly elected President. It read: "The Buckeroo Stops Here."

Today, Steuben is the country's premier fine glass maker, a position it has not always enjoyed. In 1933 Corning Glass Works, the parent company since the end of World War I, considered shutting down the entire division. But Arthur H. Houghton, Jr., a member of Corning's board and a great-grandson of the founder, persuaded management to allow him to restructure the company. The original firm had been founded in 1903 by Frederick Carder, a respected glassmaker who produced quality colored glassware in the Art Nouveau style. Houghton believed that flawless *uncolored* lead crystal was the best medium for good design—and the best hope for Steuben. His strategy proved successful. Today the glass is made with sand from Africa, believed to be the purest in the world. All ingredients are carefully tested before mixing, then the glass is made in a melting furnace and stirred with corrosion-resistant platinum rods.

Quality control is important. Glass samples are routinely subjected to microscopic examination and sophisticated testing, even X-ray spectroscopy. Because the company sells no "seconds," each piece must be flawless—free of any color tint and such obvious flaws as scratches and imperfect engraving. There must be no air bubbles, specks of foreign matter or flow lines. Cleanliness is so vital to the manufacture of fine crystal that even the areas surrounding the factory are watered down to eliminate the airborne particles that are the natural enemy of the glassmaker.

It is efforts such as these—in production, design and workmanship—that have put Steuben in the forefront of American glassmakers, and convinced me that, if I ever win another Steuben ashtray, I'll be getting the best. —JOHN FOSTER

Steuben glass sculpture depicts silver Eskimo fishing in a crystal sea.

14 Signature May 1981

Stanley M. Braverman

1981

LETTERS OF A GLOBETROTTER

A Natchez Pilgrimage by Coskie Stinnett

The Edgewood estate in Natchez "speaks wistfully of the Old South."

If I had to select the one city of the old Confederacy which had been left behind to remind the world of the architectural and cultural glory that flourished in the antebellum South, it would be indisputably Natchez, Miss. This small Mississippi River town dominates nothing but the bluff upon which it stands; it was never, like Richmond or Montgomery, the capital of a vanished nation or even of a state, nor was it ever a significant center of river commerce, as were New Orleans, Memphis and St. Louis. Natchez is and always was an elegant little city—now an overgrown town of 21,732 people—that speaks wistfully of the beauty of the Old South, of the great families and the handsome homes they lived in, and, above all, it speaks of manners. This is not to say that Natchez was only a seat of grandeur presiding gloriously beside the river, because this is not entirely true. It felt the devastating whiplash of the Civil War, and even in peacetime it had the somewhat dubious distinction of being the western terminus of the famous Natchez Trace, the 450-mile trail extending from Natchez to Nashville. This was the chief overland trail for tradesmen, settlers, gamblers and ruffians who walked back to their homes after selling their goods or suffering reversals in New Orleans. They were a raffish and boisterous group, and while they didn't tarry long in Natchez, their visits were usually memorable.

Only 135 miles northwest of New Orleans, Natchez occupies pretty much the same latitude as San Diego, and although winter nights are likely to get uncomfortably cool, the days are usually mild. I went there recently in the autumn, which is probably as good a time as any, since spring—which is almost a floral explosion—brings great crowds of tourists eager to join the Natchez Pilgrimage of famous homes. Summer is hot, fiercely hot. But Natchez in the autumn is splendid: There is still a great deal of green showing, and the humid Mississippi River haze of summer has departed. Moreover, there is a languid feeling in the air, a pleasant sort of lassitude that seems to go hand in hand with the city's gentle manners, its grace and geniality, and its pride. I walked to the river at the foot of the bluff one day to watch the *Delta Queen*, the famous paddle-wheel river boat, tie up and unload, and before climbing back up the hill, I thought it appropriate to stop in a river tavern and have a beer. It's that sort of feeling one finds in Natchez in autumn.

There are the usual motor inns on the edge of the city, but I stayed at The Burn, one of the city's great antebellum mansions, and although I felt as if I were sleeping in a museum, it was an experience that I treasure. Built in 1832, this Greek Revival mansion was used as a hospital by federal troops during the Civil War, but in 1978 it was converted into an inn by Mr. and Mrs. Buzz Harper, an attractive young couple who had owned a large antiques store in Natchez and who furnished the house with pieces from their own collection. The Burn is located on North Union Street where the mansion is set off by three acres of terraced gardens. After I had been shown to my room, a quiet, elegantly appointed chamber whose only acknowledgment of the 20th century was a miniature television set on a night table beside the four-poster bed, I wandered through the downstairs rooms, half expecting to encounter a group of Confederate cavalrymen in one of the sitting rooms or the music room. There was an exquisite porcelain statue of Evangeline, Sèvres sconces on the walls, Sheffield silver wine

22 Signature January 1982

Stanley M. Braverman

1982

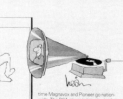

Change shows in a strip

Ovation, Ira Teichberg

Symbolic mezzotint photo

Keynote, Edward Spong

Personality quote

Capital, Helmut Schmidt-Rhen

Cartoon inside and outside box

Panorama, Norman S. Hotz

Fortune, Ronald N. Campbell

Two-line logos use stacked, butting type.

Audio, Frank Moore

Decorative outline typeface impaled on rule

Mechanix Illustrated, Andrew Steigmeier

Words, symbols, pictograms

Forest Industries, Peter A. Tucker

Shadow from title incorporates byline, mugshot, etc.

INDUSTRY NEWS

Development work progressing satisfactorily at Selby

UNITED KINGDOM

Sinking headframes and equipment at Nos. 1 and 2 shafts, Wistow mine site

AUSTRALIA
New Breeza coal discovery could rival Hunter Valley deposits

Large type dropped out of large, black field

World Coal, Neil R. Shakery

WORDVIEWS
Compulsive Browsing
FRANK GRAHAM JR.

Encyclopedist John K. Terres: a one-year project stretched to twenty.

Wording centered in narrow band, two rules

Audubon, Daniel J. McClain

InfoFile   A DIGEST OF STUDIES, SURVEYS AND STATISTICS

Economy

Energy

Review of the Energy Department

Foreign Policy

Public Policy

Urban Policy

Small black type over light gray screen

National Journal, Nancy M. Krueger

CHANNELS
O N   A I R

'I Heard the News Today...Oh Boy'

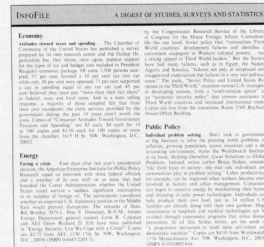

by Gloria Emerson

Bold type over pattern of horizontal rules

Channels, Dean Morris

DEPARTMENT HEADINGS IN UNUSUAL FORM

Geo, Susanne Walsh

Discover, Leonard Wolfe

Overlapping two words in two different faces

Logo and box placed at an angle

North Shore, Larry Sampson

Inquiry, Bruce McGillivray

Light outline logo; items in tinted boxes

Stylish graphic embellishment

WORKING

THE OFFICE AS FORTRESS

Something for the executive who lives dangerously: A New York-based company builds customized desks that function as security and surveillance command centers.

Ben Jamil, a spokesman for Communication Control Incorporated, says that the counterespionage desk console "was designed for the person who has everything and wants to keep it." Especially popular with foreign royalty and American oil magnates, the desk incorporates more than a dozen 007 features. A telephone scrambler and wiretap alert keep communications strictly confidential. A microwave video system can police locations up to 30 miles away. A voice stress analyzer and body response monitor are said to help assess the character of office callers. A bug alert foils electronic spying, and an infrared detection and alarm system warns of unwanted visitors.

If all this equipment fails to do the job, pushing a panic button will automatically dial a preset phone number and deliver a recorded message, or sound an all-out alert. Prices range from $3,000 for the basic console to a top-of-the-line $260,000.

EQUAL OPPORTUNITY FOR THE UNHEALTHY

The pre-employment physical may be on the way out.

The Federal Government recently ruled that its grantees and contractors could not use physical examinations to discriminate against people with health problems. That may signal the beginning of the end of a new form of discrimination: refusing to employ people on the basis of risk to their health. Physical exams may be conducted to identify such people in order to hire more of them, however.

"An employer can no longer deny someone a job solely on the basis of high blood pressure," says Larry Velez of the Department of Health and Human Services, "unless he can prove that high blood pressure renders that person unfit for that particular job—and the burden of proof falls on the employer."

WORK—DON'T RUN—THROUGH AIRPORTS

Executives may not have to sprint, hurdle or fly through airline terminals to get back to the office anymore. One car-rental company propaganda. The office—complete with secretarial help, telexes and word processors—is coming to meet them.

BRINGING WORKERS TO THEIR KNEES

Sitting down on the job may never be the same. Norwegian designers worked closely with physiotherapists

Balancing Act: Will these chairs shape office posture of the future?

to come up with a tonic for the deskbound backache: the Balans chair. Already in use in Europe, the chairs were introduced a few months ago in the United States.

Sitting in one is more akin to kneeling. Instead of back support, the chair has a seat that tilts forward, thrusting the weight of the body onto the knees, which are supported by a cushioned pad. The designers say that the chairs automatically make sitters balance their torsos by straightening their backs and causing them to open their diaphragms for easier, deeper breathing. A benefit not mentioned by the manufacturer: People seated in such chairs will undoubtedly spend less time lost in contemplation of the ceiling.

Electronic Moat: A desk console with everything but a trapdoor button.

92 NEXT MAY/JUNE 1981

Next, Lester Goodman

METHODS IN MANAGEMENT

By Bernard E. Pasierb

SAVING YOUR FIRM FROM A FLOOD OF PAPERWORK

Paperwork is like water building behind a dam. It rises so gradually at first that there's little cause for alarm. Then suddenly, as reports, memos, and forms begin to pile up, the dam breaks, swamping management and staff alike.

Soon, the paperwork that was supposed to keep operations running more smoothly does just the opposite. There isn't time to control the company. Too many people devote too much time to controlling paper. Costs escalate. According to recent surveys, the cost of processing a single page of typewritten information can now exceed $12.

Paperwork can be controlled. By recognizing the symptoms of an impending flood, managers can avert disaster. By attacking paperwork at each stage of the accumulation process—creation, capture, distribution, and storage—management can keep the levels safe. The results are a reduction of necessary paperwork, more relevant information available when needed, and better control of paperwork expenses.

The first step in controlling paperwork is to watch for 10 symptoms that signal a paper glut: (1) an expanding clerical work force, especially in relation to production levels, (2) consistently backlogged typing operations; (3) increasing use and cost of photocopying equipment and supplies, (4) numerous large reports, documents, or internal memoranda, (5) proliferation of "standard" forms; (6) growing requirements for file storage space and equipment; (7) "blanket" circulation of unimportant or irrelevant information; (8) extensive reporting requirements; (9) user dissatisfaction with existing paperwork; and (10) difficulty in retrieving needed information.

Do these sound familiar? If so, you may be inviting—or may already have—a paperwork problem. To begin solving it, identify the stage at which the problem exists.

Paperwork problems are often traceable to the first stage of the paperwork process—creation. A reduction in the amount of paper generated will automatically reduce the control problems that occur at later stages. Before any material is generated, the following questions should be answered:

☐ What is the purpose of this particular report, memo, letter, or other piece of paper?
☐ How is the information to be used, and who should receive it?
☐ Is the level of detail appropriate?
☐ Can similar information be found in other sources?
☐ Is this the right time to convey this information?
☐ Could this information be communicated without paper?
☐ If this information were suddenly not available or substantially reduced, what would happen?
☐ What should the recipient do with this paper after reading it?

Once these questions are answered, determine the best form for distributing the information. For example, could the information be transmitted by telephone? Would a one-page memo highlighting exceptional items be sufficient?

Assuming a written document is the best method of transmitting the information, the next stage in the paperwork process is capture. This stage includes writing, editing, and typing the message.

Provided that paperwork has been limited in the creation stage, controlling paperwork at the capture stage is primarily a matter of scheduling and processing. In this instance, automation, extra equipment, or improved work flows can keep paperwork under control. Measurable costs at this stage include manpower, filing systems, and supplies.

Distribution is the other stage. Managing paperwork at this point is more than a matter of how it's distributed—by hand, mail, or special courier, for example. Costs can be controlled by determining exactly who should receive the material. It may be possible to reduce the number of documents distributed.

The final stage is storage and retrieval. What information must be stored and for how long? Costs at this stage include manpower, filing systems, and storage space. Many companies put expiration dates on documents so that storage facilities don't become overloaded with obsolete information.

Controlling paperwork—and its costs—requires constant attention. But once that habit is developed, the control becomes second nature. The dam holds. ☐

The author is a consultant with Price Waterhouse & Co., New York.

THIRTEEN TIPS TO TRIM PAPER DISTRIBUTION COSTS

1. Eliminate superfluous parts of multipart forms.
2. Print on both sides of company forms.
3. Use one basic design for all company forms, with color changes to differentiate topics.
4. Periodically review the need for standard forms.
5. Put copying machines in more convenient locations to save personnel time.
6. Eliminate extra computer printout copies.
7. Make reports double as simple self-mailers for delivery to stockholders and customers.
8. Redeem "spoiled" meter mail: 90% of the face value of meter imprint errors can be recovered. Submit meter errors with claim form (POD Form 3533) to the post office servicing your meter.
9. Watch weight on large mailings. Check meter and weight of paper and tape used. Savings can run as much as $1 per mailing.
10. Discontinue all mailings to employee homes. Use interoffice mail instead.
11. Reuse interoffice envelopes. Eliminate stapling or taping them shut.
12. Eliminate use of expensive office envelopes for interoffice mail or informal communication with field staff.
13. Reward efforts to control paper costs.

INC./AUGUST 1979 83

Inc, Paul Schaffrath

Topic word anchored in clean space demarcated by rules.

Topic, head & byline float in space edged by text.

Una cápsula de bobina móvil (MC), vista por dentro.

Ajedrez

Entre el odio y el desprecio

Hi-fi

Bobina móvil

Fotografía

El centro de interés

Rostro y manos, centros de interés gracias a una iluminación selectiva, aumento del contraste y un fondo uniforme.

Video

Batalla de sistemas

El Diario, El País Semanal, David García

Unexpectedly deep head- and foot-margins define whole section.

CAREERS JOINING THE FOREIGN SERVICE

Diplomacy is the name of the game for Foreign Service officers. Women now are serving as ambassadors, political policymakers and key officers around the world—sometimes in trouble spots

BY NANCY J. WHITE

With flowered kimonos and made-up faces, the geisha girls bowed to the members of the US negotiating team. The dozen girls washed the Americans' hands, served them nine courses of Oriental specialties and sang lilting ballads long into the night. It was the traditional Japanese ritual, with one important difference. The guest of honor, the US Ambassador for Oceans and Fisheries, was a woman, Foreign Service officer Rozanne Ridgway. As if acknowledging a cross-cultural sisterhood, one geisha girl took Ridgway's hand and said: "Congratulations."

As the chief US delegate negotiating fisheries treaties, Ridgway had reached an unusually high position for a woman diplomat. But in the US Foreign Service these days, women are coming into their own. They are serving as ambassadors, political/military policymakers, and key officers in such global trouble spots as the Middle East. In 1971, only 5 percent of Foreign Service officers were women. Currently women make up 14.8 percent of all officers and about 30 percent of all new officers. The Foreign Service, the diplomatic arm of the State Department, has even set up a mid-level program to hire women and minorities with nine years of relevant experience—usually in international relations, administration or economic analysis.

Women have been a part of the Foreign Service since 1922, when the first woman officer, Lucile Atcherson, was appointed. Following the 1946 Foreign Service Act, which was designed to make the Foreign Service more representative of the American people, the first woman officer was appointed an ambassador in 1953 (Frances E. Willis, ambassador to Switzerland).

Dissatisfied with representation of women and minorities in the upper echelon of the Foreign Service, Congress mandated in the Foreign Service Act of 1980 that the State Department take affirmative action to increase opportunities for women and minorities.

Women have been part of the Foreign Service since 1922, when the first woman officer, but it has some definite drawbacks. An officer spends about 60 percent of her career overseas and moves every two to four years. A woman's movements may be somewhat restricted in posts where local women still are behind the veil, but terrorism abroad doesn't discriminate: Two women were among the hostages recently held in Iran. Back in Washington, the post isn't easy either. The old-boy network, some women say, still is an obstacle to good assignments and promotions.

The work itself is varied. An administrative officer supervises embassy personnel and plans embassy budgets; consular officers issue visas and help Americans abroad who run into difficulties; political officers analyze political events; economic officers report on business trends to aid American investors abroad. In addition, the US International Communication Agency (USICA), an independent agency, offers overseas jobs dealing with the press and cultural affairs.

CHANGING FOR THE BETTER

For many people, the Foreign Service offers a change from a sedentary career. Anne Holmberg, 30, was a commercial forecaster for the telephone company in Cheyenne, Wyoming. "After eight years with the phone company, I felt trapped," she says. "I wanted to travel and live overseas." She approached several corporations about assignments abroad, but most required that she speak a foreign language fluently and have an area of expertise. "The Foreign Service, on the other hand, taught me a language and used the skills I had," Holmberg says.

To qualify, Holmberg had to pass the Foreign Service written and oral examinations—considered to be among the toughest and most competitive in the federal government. From a list of 30 possible assignment locations, she selected six and was assigned to her first choice—Nicosia, Cyprus. After several years as administrative officer in charge of the embassy's operating budget, Holmberg transferred to the US International Communication Agency. Her next assignment will be working on cultural-exchange programs in Caracas, Venezuela.

Holmberg estimates that if she had stayed with the phone company her salary now would be about $34,000. Her Foreign Service salary is $24,500. "Occasionally I complain about the money," she says. "But the psychological renewal—the new ideas, faces and places—can't be measured in dollars." She receives housing and cost-of-living allowances and a differential for a hardship post, which Caracas is considered.

Ridgway's career choice, too, was a case of wanting to see new faces and places. She grew up in St. Paul, Minnesota, attended a grade school across the street from her home, a high school six blocks away and a university in the same neighborhood. "Everyone assumed that I would stay nearby and teach," says Ridgway, 45. A story in a Life magazine about a woman in the Foreign Service piqued her interest and she joined in 1957. She worked her way up through the ranks—issuing visas in Palermo, Italy, supervising personnel in Manila, Philippines, and touring various remote regions.

Ridgway's big career break came in 1970 when she was named desk officer for Ecuador at the State Department in Washington, DC. "That's when you're really in charge of something," she says. "A bank teller stint as desk officer that Ecuador, followed by other Latin American countries, seized several US tuna boats. Ridgway quickly became well acquainted with maritime law.

After Congress passed the 200-mile fishing limit in 1976 (the US has control over fisheries within this limit; foreign boats have to sign an agreement before they are allowed to fish—and then they are limited to catching only the surplus), Ridgway circled the globe, working up to 18 hours a day negotiating treaties with various countries. "We reorganized 25 years of ocean law and history in nine months," she says. In most of the talks, Ridgway was the only woman.

After the negotiations, Ridgway was appointed ambassador to Finland and then became the first woman counselor of the State Department, a senior advisory post. Ridgway currently is serving as a special assistant to Secretary of State Alexander Haig. She went to Canada with President Reagan in March and is working on unresolved World War II claims between the US and Czechoslovakia. After one more overseas tour, Ridgway, who earns the top salary of $52,750, plans to retire from the Foreign Service. She will be looking for a high-level corporate management slot with a six-figure income.

In her office in Washington, DC, overlooking the Lincoln, Jefferson and Washington monuments, Ridgway reflects on her career. "In moving around so much, I've said a lot of goodbyes—that's the trade-off. I don't know if I could have done this career if I had married."

FITTING IN A FAMILY

Teresita Schaffer has combined career, marriage and family successfully—something of a feat in the Foreign Service. Schaffer, who entered after graduating from Bryn Mawr Col-

Working Woman, Tony Iannotta, Petrella

Rule of same boldness as the topic word's type

The New Age Of Financial Services

Deregulation is changing your banking habits.

A young, enthusiastic reporter pounded out a sizzling story of a bank robbery on his old Remington Standard. He proudly dropped the pages into his editor's copy basket minutes before deadline and smugly waited for praise. Instead, the editor snarled, groaned and furiously blue-penciled the story.

"There was no 'bank robbery,'" growled the editor after shipping the story off to the composing room. "It was a savings and loan robbery."

The reporter was puzzled.

"A bank's where you deposit and withdraw money," said the reporter. "And the bank lends you money and pays you interest on your money. Right? This 'savings and loan' does all of that, so isn't it also a bank?"

The veteran, who had gone through the same scenario with dozens of reporters (and many other people who regularly confuse the two), explained the differences. For years afterward the reporter would remember: savings and loans make home mortgage loans; banks have credit cards, checking accounts and just about everything else.

A few years later, the reporter noticed that savings and loans were acting like banks, offering checking accounts and credit cards. And he already knew from personal experience that you could get a home mortgage loan from a "commercial bank."

The reporter also saw automatic, self-service bank teller machines in supermarkets and shopping malls. And then Merrill Lynch, the Wall Street brokerage firm, solicited him for a "Cash Management Account," which sounded an awful lot like banking.

Then what's the difference between a bank and a savings and loan and a brokerage firm?

Today, not much. The banking industry is in the midst of "deregulation." In effect, financial institutions are being allowed to sink or swim in the competitive marketplace. Deregulation means that financial institutions will eventually pay money-market interest rates to depositors. But it also means borrowers may pay more for loans. And everyone will have to pay for financial services such as checking accounts and credit cards.

Deregulation will also change our

> **Customers want convenience in the form of total financial services.**

banking habits. For one, many neighborhood branch banks will go the way of the mom-and-pop grocery store. They'll be replaced by teller machines—for such routine transactions as deposits and withdrawals. Some people may eventually bank at home by combining personal computer systems and cable television service. A bank in Knoxville, Tennessee, is already testing such a system.

"The branches that survive will be more like financial planning and service centers," says Biff Motley, a Chicago-based banking consultant. "Many banks are already training their personnel for that kind of life.

"Instead of offering a depositor a choice of six-month or four-year fixed-rate certificates of deposit," says Motley, deregulation would allow for a greater variety of options—such as money-market mutual funds, corporate bond funds, tax-exempt funds or even blue-chip equity funds.

"I don't expect banks to get into exotic investments for their customers, but they'll want to offer the kinds of investment vehicles their conservative clientele would like," Motley adds.

With the onset of deregulation, it would appear that brokerage firms are acting like banks.

Merrill Lynch's Cash Management Account (CMA), already used by some one hundred eighty thousand customers and available through about 70 percent of the firm's offices around the country, certainly skirts around the edge of banking. Using a complex computer program (the product of some one hundred man-years of talent), the Wall Street giant is blazing a new trail in one-stop financial management.

To join the CMA program, an investor needs a minimum of $20,000 in cash or securities or any combination of the two.

The program works like this: let's say you start with $10,000 in the CMA money-market mutual fund and $10,000 in marginable securities (just about all the securities listed on the New York Stock Exchange, most of those on the American Stock Exchange and many of the over-the-counter issues are marginable).

On the cash, you're earning the money-market rate. You can write a check against the funds, too, and continue to earn interest until the check clears. (Unlike most money-market funds with check-writing privileges, CMA has no minimum-amount rules.) Should you earn any dividends or receive proceeds from sales of securities, you can direct the

United Mainliner, Jerold Smokler

Thick-and-thin ("scotch") rules fit character of typeface

HEALTH AND RELIGION

Ministerial Burnout. This affliction of the "Bionic Minister" can be avoided by taking some common-sense precautions. Here's how.

by William Rabior

He was a colleague in the ministry whom everyone described as a human dynamo—certainly one of the hardest-working men we knew. He seemed to thrive on work, driving himself constantly toward new goals, new projects, new horizons. And then one day he simply found himself unable to function ministerially. It became necessary to seek medical attention. At the age of 42, he had burned himself out physically, emotionally, and spiritually.

Because we are ministers of the gospel, some of us get the idea that we are somehow invulnerable to the kind of breakdown my friend experienced. We are doing the Lord's work, we reason, and therefore are immune to the ills that affect ordinary mortals. Yet ministerial activity is often accompanied by a high degree of stress, which can prove overwhelming and take a terrible toll. Although called of God, we are, like other professionals, susceptible to what has been termed "burnout."

Boston University professor LeRoy Spaniol describes burnout as "a sense of dead-endedness, a feeling that you have nowhere to go, that nothing new is happening." Not infrequently it is accompanied by such psychosomatic complaints as insomnia, excessive fatigue, or severe headaches. In some cases it may actually take the form of some kind of emotional collapse. According to Professor Spaniol, burnout occurs in those people who ignore their own needs by trying to live a Spartan existence.

How can you avoid ministerial burnout? First, stop trying to be the "bionic minister." Remember that you are human and can accomplish only so much in the lifetime God has given you. Be realistic in setting goals and objectives for your ministry. Keep in mind that allowing them to build up inside. Pastors ministerto hundreds of people, but who ministers to the pastor? Who is the pastor's pastor? Many clergy are forming support groups that meet periodically not only for relaxation but to talk over problems, goals, attitudes, and personal feelings related to ministry. If the people in the group are willing to be honest and open with one another, they can provide excellent opportunities for emotional release and personal growth. The group to which I belong provides me a forum to let off steam, to share ideas, and to build friendships.

Finally, learn to relax and appreciate each day. The evidence from Scripture is that Christ Himself, despite His intensity of purpose, deeply enjoyed life. He appreciated a good meal, the beauty of nature, a quiet walk alone. He knew the importance of inner serenity and how to relax. This is one area of imitating the Master that we often forget or simply ignore, especially as the pace of our ministry accelerates and we strive harder to accomplish even more. We may actually become so busy doing God's work that He can't even get our attention!

We may be God's ambassadors, but we are also human beings with very real needs and limitations. Unless we pay some attention to those needs and take care of ourselves in some fashion, ministerial burnout is always a possibility. A sound mind in a sound body makes for a sound ministry, enabling us to serve God longer and more effectively.

Perhaps if my colleague, the human dynamo, had read this article a few years ago, he would still be pastoring today.

despite all indications to the contrary your church will go on after you are dead.

Second, make time for yourself. Even Jesus scheduled periods of time when He could be alone for prayer and undoubtedly just to relax. Each week try to build into your schedule one day with no professional duties. If that is impossible, try to find at least part of a day. Periodically break out of the grind.

Exercise is an excellent means of relieving tension and stress. More and more ministers are turning to jogging or some other form of active exercise as a means of combating the effects of work pressures. One colleague has been jogging for the past year and says that he feels ten years younger. I honestly have to admit that he looks it!

Try to find someone with whom you can share the frustrations that come with ministry. Ventilate your feelings by discussing them with that person instead

William Rabior is an associate pastor in the Roman Catholic Diocese of Gaylord, Michigan.

Ministry, Byron Steele

Decorative quality of triple rule adds graphic distinction

The National Interest/Michael Kramer

WANDERING IN THE DESERT

With open arms: *Reagan greeting Prince Fahd in Cancun last month*

Reagan's Mideast Mirage

"I have no hesitation in [branding the P.L.O. as a terrorist organization]. We live in a world in which any band of thugs clever enough to get the word 'liberation' into its name can thereupon murder schoolchildren and have its deeds considered glamorous and glorious ... If others wish to deal with them, establish diplomatic relations with them, let it be on their heads and let them be willing to pay the price of appeasement. The P.L.O. is said to represent the Palestinian refugees. It represents no one but the leaders who established it as a means of organized aggression against Israel."

THE MAN WHO SPOKE THOSE WORDS in September of 1980 was running for president of the United States. Now he has the job. But you'd never know it was the same Ronald Reagan—at least not from the president's recent statements. Reagan hasn't exactly done a 180-degree turn, but it is clear he now believes that the P.L.O. is the representative of the Palestinian people and must, sooner or later, be spoken to.

The president's secretary of state has gone farther. The P.L.O., said Alexander Haig recently, isn't a terrorist outfit after all. It's an "umbrella organization," said Haig, made up of both terrorists and non-terrorists. And this, said the secretary's aides, should be taken as a "signal" by the P.L.O.

The question is: a signal of what?

"Well, we don't know exactly," says a high government official. "But our policy is that the Soviets are the major threat in the region. Israel can't fend them off alone. The Arabs have to do it. And that means that we have to look at things through the Saudi prism, which means dealing in some way with the P.L.O."

In other words, says Senator Pat Moynihan, "we're back to a new version of the old Nixon doctrine. Nixon viewed Iran as our surrogate in the Middle East. The local nation on the scene that would do our fighting for us. When Iran fell, we placed most of our chips on Egypt, and now, after Sadat, we're turning to the Saudis. Sadat wanted to work through Camp David. The Saudis want nothing to do with Camp David; hence all this new talk about the P.L.O."

There are two problems with the notion that the Saudis can be a new American surrogate in the Middle East. The Saudis don't want the role, and their pitifully small army couldn't perform it if they did. Saudi Arabia, as the New York Times puts it, "has no friends, only business partners." They prefer neutrality and non-alignment. They want as little to do with the superpowers as possible. This doesn't mean they won't take America to the cleaners. They will and they are, beginning with awacs.

The Saudis want to be big shots in another way. Rather than be America's surrogate, the Saudis want to play middleman in the Middle East peace process. So Crown Prince Fahd, the king-dom's operating ruler, has come forward, again, with an eight-point plan, a proposal that would replace Camp David. The Europeans, who need Saudi oil, have fallen all over themselves in cheering Fahd's ideas while declaring that Camp David is just about "finished." And the United States, which rejected the Saudi proposal as nothing new, before Sadat's assassination, now professes to see "interesting" things in it. The Saudi plan, says President Reagan, is "a beginning point for negotiations."

Among the points in the Saudi proposal is one that calls for the creation of a P.L.O.-led Palestinian state on the West Bank, with its capital in East Jerusalem. This would require a pullback from "all" territory occupied by Israel following the 1967 war. "That's worse than what's called for in U.N. Resolution 242," says Senator Moynihan. "Two forty-two talks about a pullback from territory—not from 'all' territory."

Another point in the Saudi plan seems to imply that Israel will gain acceptance of its right to exist in exchange for agreeing to a P.L.O. state. The plan doesn't really say that, and there is a good deal of dispute as to whether the Saudis really intend recognition of Israel and what "recognition" would mean. In any event, even though the P.L.O.'s Yasir Arafat has welcomed the Saudi plan, it is hard to see how his group could recognize Israel. The P.L.O. has consistently reaffirmed its intention to "liquidate the Zionist entity, politically, economically, militarily, culturally, ideologically."

Now, it is possible that the P.L.O. might go along with a peace treaty with Israel (and there is even evidence that the P.L.O. actually drafted the Saudi plan), but what would happen then? Is it not possible that the P.L.O. would renege on its commitment? Of course. And even Ronald Reagan has acknowledged that "no country has ever observed the terms of a treaty if it suited its national purposes to break that treaty." Precisely, says Pat Moynihan. "If the P.L.O. got its state, I'd say there'd be war with Israel within two years' time. No question about it."

Israel, of course, agrees. Which is why Prime Minister Begin has rejected the Saudi plan (with the exception of a few minor points). "It's nothing but the old Arab formula for trying to liquidate Israel, albeit in stages," says Begin. Without Israel's interest—and Israel's lack of interest extends across the Israeli politi-

Photograph: UPI

New York, Roger Black

Rules of varied weights add color and organize space

prime time
finance

Life Insurance Options
If you're carrying more than you need, there are lots of alternatives to just paying more premiums.

REMEMBER THAT LIFE insurance policy you bought thirty years ago? You've faithfully paid the premiums ever since, but when was the last time you looked at the policy? It may or may not fit your current needs. It may or may not tie in with your other carefully made financial plans for your estate.

First look at the total picture. Individual life insurance is only one part of the support package. Your spouse may, depending on age, receive some tax-free Social Security benefits. He or she may be covered by a pension. And your group term life insurance may continue after you retire. This new "perk" typically provides continuing life insurance of one-quarter to one-half of the amount carried on your life before retirement. If your employer offers this benefit, it may make a big difference in the amount of individual life insurance you'll need.

After assessing your current needs, you may decide that you don't have enough life insurance. If so, you can buy more at just about any age, although you'll find it more expensive as you get older. If the need is for a limited purpose and time, such as being sure your survivors don't get stuck with a large business debt, you should consider term insurance. This form of insurance is "pure" insurance, without any cash surrender value; it can be written so that it is renewable, usually in five-year increments, until (for most companies) you reach the age of 70. It can also be written in a convertible form, so that it can be converted to a whole life policy. So if you want life-long insurance, to be sure that your survivors will have liquid assets whenever you die, whole life insurance will probably be your best choice.

If, after assessing your current needs, you decide that you don't need as much life insurance as you're now carrying, you have several options. You can simply cancel the policy, take the cash surrender value, and run. You could then invest the cash value (after any income tax that will be due if the cash value exceeds the premiums you've paid in over the years) in anything from the stock market to a trip around the world. But this choice, permanently foreclosing all other choices, might not be best.

You might, instead, borrow against the cash value, at a rate in most states of about 6 percent for such older policies, and invest the money elsewhere while keeping the policy in force. If you never repay the loan—and you don't have to—your beneficiary will receive the face amount of the policy minus the amount of the loan. If you have a participating or dividend-paying policy, you can protect its face value by electing "the fifth dividend option." You use your dividends to buy one-year renewable term insurance up to the amount of the cash value, while continuing to earn dividends and to accrue cash value.

You could also take the cash value but draw an annuity to assure steady post-retirement income. Or you can keep your life insurance in force, without any further cost to you, by converting it to paid-up whole life in a reduced amount. When you convert a policy to a reduced face amount, you keep the cash value intact. You can still borrow against that cash value or surrender the policy and claim the full cash surrender value.

Take the hypothetical case of George Smith. George is 50 years old and has a life expectancy of 25 more years. His wife, Lois, is 45 and can expect to live 35 more years. Their only child is 23 and self-supporting.

By Grace W. Weinstein

14   NOVEMBER 1980

Illustrations by Jim Harter

Prime Time, Judy Fendelman

Topic in light face, headline bold, deck italics.

Music/by Arthur Lubow

ENO, BEFORE AND AFTER ROXY

Brian Eno: Tackling writer's block by Oblique Strategies

When Brian Eno says he is unable to play any instrument well, he is celebrating the victory of mind over matter. Eno (an accidental anagram for "one brain") bears no obvious similarities to a rock & roll hero. Instead of arching his body lewdly above a shrieking guitar, he bends silently over a synthesizer keyboard or a computer terminal. He is the technician as rock star, composing mantras for the machine age. The instrument he finds most sympathetic is the tape recorder; he suggests that he owes much of his distinction as the critics' favorite synthesizer player to his lack of expertise.

"Rick Wakeman and Keith Emerson have a far more accomplished technique," he says cheerfully. "But with synthesizers, more than with other instruments, the thing is not to learn how to play, but what to play." In music, he says, one starts with no technique, "when everything is new and exciting," passes through a period "when things aren't interesting anymore," and finally arrives at a stage "in which the technique can be used, but it isn't a constraint." The temptation is to allow fluidity to gel, "to innovate a technique and then codify it, applying it to other situations even though it's only partially applicable." Eno's talent is a sci-fi version of swing or soul: he moves with the flow; he adapts to the environment. He doesn't gel.

It was intuition that led Eno, son of a Suffolk postman, to abandon a dubious career as an art student ("I could never finish a painting") and start experimenting with tape recorders. In early 1971 he was asked to join Roxy Music, a progressive yet unpretentious British band, to supervise electronic distortions and work with a synthesizer. Although band leader Bryan Ferry wrote and sang the songs, and guitarist Phil Manzanera was a far more accomplished musician, Eno rose quickly as the most notorious exponent of Roxy ultra-sophistication. He was charmingly quotable, delightfully avant-garde. And when it came to the band's sartorial ambitions, Eno was unequaled. Daubed with lipstick and mascara, sprouting peacock feathers over his leopard-skin shirts, he was uniquely photogenic.

The use of outrageous costumes, he now says, "was a deliberate decision by all of us to dress interestingly as well as to make arresting music." But it was more than a publicity pose. "I haven't ever done anything strictly to get attention," he insists. "That period is quite misty to me now. [These days, to enjoy the thrill of anonymity, the 29-

that word in a limited sense: deification of rational knowledge."

Eno regards rational knowledge with respect but suspicion. What interests Eno is flight and metamorphosis, motion and process. His great passion is cybernetics, the theory of information organization. "My interest is in attempting to describe musical and artistic evolutions," he says. "Cybernetics is the only science that deals with the evolution of systems as processes in time. It's a science that knows its answers are always inadequate, a science that deals with probabilities rather than certainties, a science that talks of a range of goals."

"I don't bother to question my intuition," he says, explaining his initial fascination with cybernetics. "If I feel like doing something, I do it, and figure that I'll understand it later. If I had questioned my intuition, I would probably be a bank clerk. In any person's life, the most important decisions are indefensible."

year-old Eno wears short hair, T-shirts and jeans.] But before I ever joined Roxy, I got interested in wearing various kinds of clothing that would have been considered effeminate. I didn't like masculine clothes. Masculinity is science. The Western version of masculinity opposes rational man against intuitive woman. The part of my being that interests me has always been my intuition."

After a couple of years and two albums, Eno left Roxy Music in the summer of 1973. From Eno's perspective, the group was the victim of commercial success. As sales and publicity multiplied, Ferry demanded that the band duplicate its formula. There was no room for another singer and writer with independent ideas.

Since leaving Roxy, Eno has written and performed four solo albums. He has played with tape recorders, synthesizers and treated guitars on two duet albums with Robert Fripp, guitarist of the defunct King Crimson. On his own label, Obscure, he has produced Discreet Music (which fades in and out of earshot "as part of the ambience of the environment") and the Portsmouth Sinfonia (an orchestra of untrained musicians playing classical favorites). Recently, he has collaborated with David Bowie on two albums, Low and Heroes; he is about to produce the second Talking Heads album. Because the sounds he produces are beautiful as well as interesting, Eno's cult is substantial—his first three song albums have each sold 50,000 copies.

Eno's songwriting technique might sound familiar to a medicine man. Af-

72   NEW TIMES 3/6/78

New Times, Kelley/Weigand

Topic and byline in light, headline in bold caps

UPDATE

Magazine Watch

New magazines

The Record
A monthly magazine covering rock music, *The Record* was launched in November 1981. Published by Straight Arrow Publications, Inc., the 8½-inch by 11½-inch tabloid will feature interviews, columns on records in progress, film and book reviews, as well as a centerspread pin-up. Circulation: 35,000 paid. Subscription price: $12. Cover price: $1. Ad rate: $880 for a junior page. Managing editor: David McGee. Address: 745 Fifth Ave., New York, N.Y. 10151.

Arts & Architecture
Arts & Architecture, a new version of the magazine that ceased publication in 1967, was launched in October. The quarterly, published by Arts & Architecture, Inc., features articles on fine arts, architecture and related subjects in the Western United States. Initial circulation: 4,000 paid and non-paid. Cover price: $6. Subscription price: $21. Ad rate: $850 for a black-and-white page. Editor: Barbara Goldstein. Address: 835 N. Kings Rd., Los Angeles, Calif. 90069.

Elan
The OAO Corporation introduced its new bimonthly, *Elan*, with a December-January issue. Geared to the affluent, college-educated black woman in the 25 to 54 age group, the magazine emphasizes career management, fashion and culture. Initial circulation: 150,000. Ad rate: $3,400 for a

black-and-white page. Publisher: Cecil Barker. Editor: Marie Dutton Brown. Address: 545 Fifth Ave., New York, N.Y. 10017.

Moviegoer
Moviegoer, a free, in-theater movie magazine published by 13-30 Corporation, was introduced in December. Distributed through 400 select theaters, the single-cancel-er monthly includes short items to be read in the theater as well as longer take-home features on film personalities and behind-the-scenes activities. Initial circulation: 1,000,000. Publisher: Chris Whittle. Editor: Frank Finn. Address: 505 Market St., Knoxville, Tenn. 37902.

Honky Tonk
A bimonthly devoted to country and western music, fashion, sports and food, *Honky Tonk* was introduced in October 1981. Geared to the 18- to 35-year-old market, the Honky Tonk Publication, Inc. magazine will feature interviews with noted country and western performers. Circulation: 150,000. Cover price: $1.95. Ad rate: $1,800 for a black-and-white page. Publisher: Dennis Gaskin. Editorial director: Shelley Levitt. Address: 75 Rockefeller Plaza, New York, N.Y. 10019.

Building Products Digest
The first issue of *Building Products Digest* will appear in March 1982. Aimed primarily at retail lumber and building materials dealers, home centers and mass merchandisers in the 13 Southern states, the monthly will feature in-depth studies of retail and wholesale operations as well as new-product news and editorial. Initial circulation: 10,000 non-paid. Ad rate: $750 for a black-and-white page. Publisher: David Cutler. Editor: Juanita Lovret. Address: 4500 Campus Dr.,

Suite 480, Newport Beach, Calif. 92660.

Windsurf
Formerly a newsletter, *Windsurf* becomes a bimonthly magazine this month. The Windsurfing International, Inc. publication covers all aspects of the rapidly growing board-sailing sport, featuring in-depth articles on, and interviews with, windsurfers from all parts of the world. Subscription price: $12. Cover price: $2.50. Ad rate: $1,550 for a black-and-white page. Publisher: Don Kremers. Editorial director: John Severson. Address: 561 Dana Point, Calif. 92629.

Appetizingly Yours
Billed as a magazine dedicated to Connecticut's better restaurants, *Appetizingly Yours* was launched in July 1981. The Horwitt Publishing quarterly serves as a forum in which executive chefs and owners can express themselves through anecdotes, as well as through their menus. Each issue will feature an area restaurant and include an interview with the owner and chef. Initial circulation: 25,000. Cover price: $2.75. Subscription price: $9.90. Advertising rate: $695 for a black-and-white page. Publisher: Jay L. Horwitt. Editor: Jocelyn Horwitt. Address: 58-60 Boston St., Guilford, Conn. 06437.

Complete Woman
Complete Woman was launched in August 1981 by Associated Publications, Inc. The bimonthly addresses itself to the changing role of today's

JANUARY 1982 39

Folio, Steve Phillips

Logo in tight, light face; topic in rich bold

PETER DOBEREINER
Tour stats uncover the secret of golf

Oh, very well then. You have been extremely patient. For something like 500 years you have been waiting to learn the secret of golf and finally I have decided to reveal it. As a matter of fact, it has been revealed it out. So did Bobby Jones. Ben Hogan realized it late in his career and told the world. Nobody listened because there was no way to prove that the secret worked.

Now that the U.S. tour is keeping full statistics, and people are paying attention to them, the secret of golf is uncovered for all to see. All you have to do is aim your drive down the left side of the fairway and *hit it with a high fade*.

Why, oh why, you ask, have I waited so long to divulge this information? Well, it all goes back to those far-off days when airplanes had propellers and a foolhardy U.S. Navy undertook to teach me to fly. Hatchet-faced instructors would assess the progress of us intrepid birdmen and grade us in terms of baseball statistics. Knowing nothing of baseball, and less of baseball statistics, I never knew how I was doing.

But anyway, we won the war and I emerged as a staunch disciple of Winston Churchill's dictum that "games are lies, damned lies and statistics." Particularly sports statistics.

This lifelong mistrust of sporting statistics drew me naturally to golf, a game blessedly free of decimal points and performance averages. Until last year. Then the U.S. tour started measuring and analyzing the game, and in the line of duty I have spent four months with a cold towel wrapped around my spinning head, trying to make sense out of the statistics.

The first thing to do is reject the obviously idiotic figures. The money list, for example, is meaningless since it makes no distinction between the golfer who played 40 tournaments and the player who teed it up only 12 times. Instead, we must look to the stroke averages for a measure of performance. Likewise, we can dismiss the tables for birdies and eagles, since these simply reflect a summary of golfing skills. And while we are

It was Arnold Palmer who remarked that all pros are fighting a hook.

at about it, we can toss those putting statistics into the trash basket because they are hopelessly biased in favor of the player who misses greens, chips up to the flag and holes out from 18 inches. They tell us nothing about putting skill as such.

The revealing tour statistics are those for driving distance, driving accuracy, hitting greens in regulation, sand saves and scoring averages. First, this exciting business of giving the ball a big bash off the tee. Driving distance is revealed as golf's major false god. Anyone who averages 260 yards off the tee must be rated a long hitter but those who strive for an extra 10 yards are simply slugging themselves into oblivion.

Driving accuracy (given a decent quantity of horsepower in the shot) is much, much more important than distance. Jack Nicklaus is the only player who drives the ball both long and straight and

his rank in accuracy off the tee (13th) is somewhat falsified by his tactics of occasionally deliberately firing his ball into light rough for position. It may sound trite, but the art of good golf as shown by the statistics is to put your shot into position from where you can hit the green in regulation figures.

That conclusion, which can now be backed by statistical proof, leads me to the all-important secret of golf. From personal observation I would say that nine pro golfers out of 10 draw their drives, as the result of an obsession for length. They start as kids, striving for every inch of length because of their simplistic reasoning that the shorter the second shot the lower the score. They won't be told. Explain that a faded drive down the left makes the fairway twice as wide and they reverse the argument, saying that a hooked drive down the right has the same effect. It doesn't. The high faded ball sits where it lands while the hooked ball pitches and runs—into trouble as likely as not. That is the real story of the tour statistics.

Are you still unconvinced? Then I invite you to run your eye down the scoring averages and, if you must, down the money list. In both cases the top-10 leaders of 1980 are players who fade the ball. The one incongruity is Andy Bean, whose natural shot is right to left. Three years ago I daresay that Bean would have been the leader in driving distance, for he used to give the ball an almighty smash and hook it back into the fairway. Today he is only just in the top 30 for distance off the tee for he has seen the light. He is a reformed hooker and that is vastly encouraging.

I believe it was Arnold Palmer who remarked that all pros are fighting a hook. In his case it was certainly true, but he never got the club into a position at the top to make a sweet pass at the ball and he had to turn himself inside out on the downswing to avoid a real snapper.

So there's the secret: fight that hook, and if the ball still goes left, then fight harder—until you have mastered that lovely, money-winning high fade. ■

14   APRIL 1981/GOLF DIGEST

Golf Digest, Pete Libby

Headline (small, light) overwhelmed by byline

Tennis, Michael Brent

Simply-handled typography of text inserted into full-color frame (repeated on several pages). Various colors, also overlaid on text itself. Pictures in color.

Travel & Leisure, Adrian Taylor

8-page form printed in red and black on distinctive, rough, tan stock is bound into the issue with four pages in front, four in back. Each half is handled differently: an attention-getting news format up front; an elegant, analytical presentation in back.

DEPARTMENT SECTIONS   FOUR-COLUMN MAKEUP

Attenzione, Paul Hardy

Lively composition of widely-varying story lengths, tiny-to-huge pictures, random patterned space allotment. Text set to conform to silhouetted picture shapes.

Technology Illustrated, Peter Hudson

Long stories provide sufficient text to establish simple, visible column pattern, so no rules are needed to hold it together. Space flows easily from column to column.

CONTINUUM

THE IMPORTANCE OF BEING TENTATIVE

Omni, Frank de Vino

Type in black over silver. Picture areas "knocked out" of silver background and photos run in duotones — two coordinated halftones on top of each other, rich black.

THIS MONTH

FEBRUARY 1980

White House Wants More Energy from Networks...Hollywood Comedy Goes Gay... How Loud Are Commercials?...Winston Churchill, Superstar...Talk to Your TV Set

Panorama, Norman S. Hotz

Embellishing rules and some panels dropped out from silver; others run in black on white or black on silver, creating rich diversity. Pictures run in horizontal line screen.

department

00

DEPARTMENT NAME

A long and useful headline goes in this space
BYLINE HERE

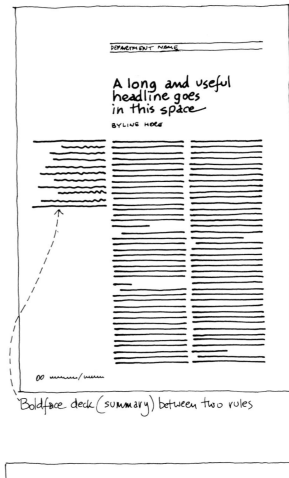

00 ~~~~/~~~

Boldface deck (summary) between two rules

NAME
OF
DEPARTMENT
The headline goes in this small space like this

Text could be broken up into short items...
but mugshot implies one-person's viewpoint about them

LOGO

PEOPLE

00

The lead story in wide-set, larger type

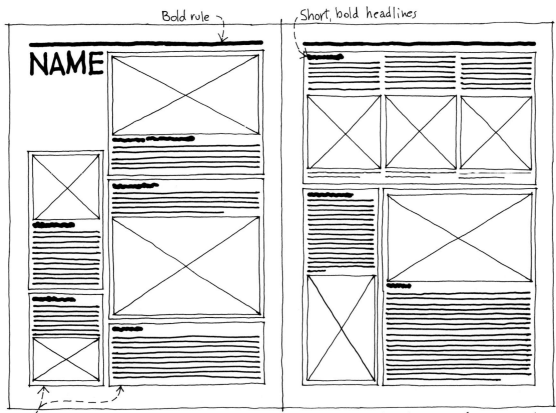

Bold rule

Short, bold headlines

NAME

Boxes (one per item) based on simple 3-column page makeup: stacked boxes to fill space available

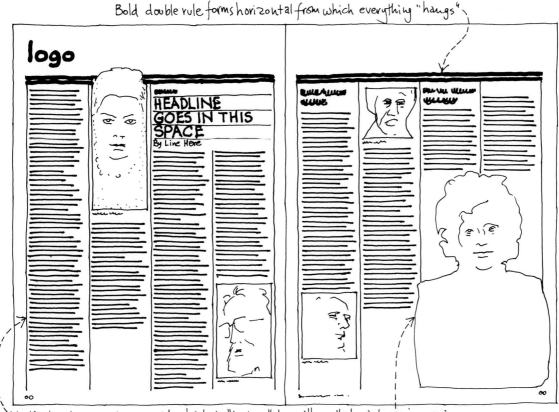

Bold double rule forms horizontal from which everything "hangs"

logo

HEADLINE GOES IN THIS SPACE
By Line Here

Vertical rules are strong grid which is "broken" by silhouetted pictures in various ways

EDITORIALS

It is quite normal to find a whole page of a publication's issue devoted to opinion, labeled "editorial" or some such title. Some devote more space, such as a spread or consecutive rights (especially if there are two or more editorial writers expressing their opinions); others squeeze in editorials on a vertical two-thirds of a page alongside the masthead, perhaps. But an editorial comment of some sort is usually there, somewhere.

This is a page that ought to look different since its content is different from the rest of the publication: the normal magazine pages show reports of outside goings-on. The editorial is an inward-looking page, giving the editor an opportunity to pontificate, see ←-- into the future, make pronouncements, warn of impending doom. It ought to look like what it is: serious of mien, weighty in tone, with large type, generous white space, wide columns.

The page consists of the following elements:

○ The text itself.

○ A headline. In informally written, chatty editorials that don't deal with earth-shaking events, the head is sometimes dropped, but there usually is a headline simply because the editors want to draw attention to their piece.

○ The "editorial" label (or its equivalent) somewhere on the page, usually at the top.

○ The writer's signature, either typeset or handwritten.

○ The editor's picture, sometimes: either because it helps to personalize the page, or because it is useful to the publication to show that its editor is the distinguished and well-known leader-of-the-industry Mr. So-and-so. It can also work the other way: Mr. So-and-so can become a spokesman for his readership because he becomes well known through his picture on the editorial page.

○ A cartoon; if the drawing is an illustration of the main direction of the argument stated in the words, then it is a cartoon-illustration; if, however, it is a separate, independent thought, then it becomes a true editorial cartoon and the cartoonist becomes a subsidiary editorial "writer." This hairsplitting of definitions is important because the placement of the cartoon on the page is affected by the kind of cartoon it is: if it is an illustration, it ought to be closely tied into the text or headline; if it is independent comment, it ought to be separated from the words as clearly as possible.

The placement of the editorial page within the issue varies from publication to publication, but it should *never* vary from issue to issue of the same publication. The reader should be able to find the editorial page immediately, whether the page is in the front of the book (right after the contents page, where it is most often found) or whether it is the first right-hand page of the feature section. It could well be the last page opposite the inside back cover — or anywhere else that makes some sense — as long as it is always to be found in the place the reader expects it.

Of greater importance than the page's position in the book, is the question of what goes on the page opposite. Since editorial pages are normally just a single page, and since they claim high readership because of their intrinsic interest, the opposite page is often sold to advertisers at a premium as a "preferred position." It follows, therefore, that the design of the editorial page must take this unpleasantness into consideration. Unpleasantness? Certainly, because the advertiser who invests extra money for the page is going to want to get maximum visibility for it and the ad will be as full of attention-grabbing graphics as the agency can devise (which tends to detract from the characteristics of quiet dignity and seriousness that the editorial page needs). The upshot is that we must be twice as careful in creating the proper climate for the editorial because of the competition for attention from the page opposite.

So, the desired characteristics are simplicity, larger-than-normal scale, smoothness, elegance. These are the design qualities we seek to create the maximum contrast betwen our important words and that distracting madness across the gutter. Perhaps the word *restraint* is the most accurate to describe the desired goal.

How do you achieve it? The examples that follow on the next

twelve pages will be analyzed with this specific characteristic in mind. They can be summarized as follows:

1. a wide moat of white space (or something acting as a "wall") to separate the two pages
2. type set larger, in longer lines than usual, but with ample extra space between the lines to make the words comfortable to read
3. no overcrowding: self-discipline and ruthless editing to prevent overfilling the page with words
4. setting the text ragged right, perhaps, to act as a contrast to the flush-right setting in the rest of the issue
5. standardized placement of signature cut, photo of personality, page slug, dateline, etc.

Now a word about this *standardization* problem. Most publications have worked out a format for this page and seldom vary from it. They know exactly how many words they need for the page, how long the heads can be, and so forth. Such standardization makes great sense both from the point of view of recognition value of the page, as well as in the workability of the page.

Yet straitjacket formats have an inherent danger too. They can rob the editors of incentive to do something larger or deeper or more revolutionary ("it won't fit anyway so why bother"). Further-more, sometimes the standard format is wrong for the material that is to be published; sometimes you need more space, or a different typographic handling, to do justice to the message. In such cases, let the page reflect those needs, whatever they may be, allowing flexibility where it is useful, and retaining rigidity where flexibility is unnecessary. So, if a single-pager suddenly has to expand to a spread, retain the slug in the top right-hand corner (if that's where it usually is), and let the signature cut be at bottom right (if that's where it usually goes), and set the headline in two lines at the far left (if that's how you normally handle it) — just expand the body space required to fit the copy. The elements placed in the standard positions will carry their own recognition value over into the unusual format and you can achieve the best of both worlds: an expressive, logical presentation which still signals "editorial page" at first glance.

Editorials: an aura of major pronouncement

Large type set ragged right is the major feature that attracts attention to this page from *Dental Economics*. The text is, in fact, quite short, but the type size masks that. The liberal use of white space also adds to the grandiose scale of the page (besides splitting it away from the ad across the gutter at left). The typeface of the body copy (Melior) is used in bold in the headline, and a similar, but more decorative face (Dominante) is used for the department heading. They work together to give the page its unified character.

Pale color tint

Editorial Comment

THE PUBLIC MUST REORDER ITS PRIORITIES

A news release from the November meeting of the American Medical Association was sharply critical of physicians who add a service charge to unpaid bills. Doctor Elmer G. Shelley, chairman of the AMA Judicial Council, stated that adoption of such collection methods "reflects adversely on the whole profession, especially on the countless doctors who extend credit willingly and even write off old accounts." He added that if a physician is not paid as promptly as are other creditors, "he should recall that he is a professional man, with all the perquisites that the term implies."

This seems to be the season to take pot shots at the professional man who is striving to improve his delivery of health services by upgrading his practice administration procedures. Hard on the heels of the AMA's attack comes a book reviling the dental profession for its alleged money-oriented motivation. The overtones are clear.

Our readers will recall that the September 1970 *Dental Economics* featured in-depth treatment of this timely subject. The authors were representative of four points of view—a dentist, a practice administration expert, a banker; and a dental tradesman. The dentist conceded that credit has become a national habit. The consultant objected that such a commercial practice is unprofessional.

The banker warned against entering the arenas of finance; and the dental tradesman defended the need for a service charge, because "business is business."

The individual practitioner should have the privilege of determining how to meet the problem of the unpaid bill. No one has the right to make this decision for him.

Further, it is our opinion that the public must reorder its priorities and stop hiding the doctor bill at the bottom of the pile month after month.

. . . or of cool, carefully argued opinion

This page is handled with the same graphic solutions as are the other departments of *Library Journal* (see page 84). But on this more dignified page, the text is set in two columns rather than the usual three. The lower rule of the logo is used as the top edge of the box that encloses the entire page. The amount of text can vary, within reason, to give the writer some leeway.

Ideally, a little more white space above the headline would have been preferable. As in the example opposite, there is a distinct relationship in character of the typography: the headline type (Stymie Extrabold Condensed) is very similar in structure and weight to the Egyptian Outline used for the specially-set department slugs. The "specially-set" describes the special artwork–handling the letters require in order to touch and overlap.

LJ:EDITORIAL

Fear of information

It is easy to understand, in these times of the ubiquitous tape recorder, how people in positions of authority could be increasingly afraid of the public disclosure of information, or the public statements of their subordinates. Anyone whose memory includes the last 25 years will remember that secrecy, surveillance, and closed meetings were the awful earmarks of those frightened fifties. There are depressing signs that this phenomenon is on the upsurge again, probably because of the current social and political climate. Very few public or private officials can utter anything without having to "eat" their words later because of public disclosure. (*LJ* has quite an appetite for its own.) The institutions of our nation, including the libraries, seem to be building a network of "secure" oval offices, and instead of announcing information to the publics they serve, they carefully leak it, piecemeal, to the press and others. One supposes that the spectacle of a U.S. President having to "eat his words" has scared every other public and private office holder. The result has been a growing threat to freedom of information, freedom of expression, and to the entire concept of an "open" society.

Librarians and libraries have a great deal at stake in times when the climate produces this kind of censorship through information "management." It threatens their access to all the traditional materials and information, but more important, it threatens those newborn programs that, in our view, may contain the seeds of the future public library. Community information programs depend for their viability upon the ability of the library to collect, organize, and make public not only the published and publicized information available, but also the unpublished and unpublicized data about community or neighborhood problems, life crises, and citizen's rights as they confront government, law, business, or employment.

On page 1650 of this issue we report the directive from the administration of the Cleveland Public Library warning the Cleveland staff to be "discreet when approached by representatives of the news media" and to refer to all requests for "nonpublic" information or "opinion" to their chief or face a reprimand and/or "disciplinary action." We don't mean to focus on Cleveland, which has other problems now, and the practice of muzzling the staff is common to nearly every major library, and it is virtually an untold story because of the muzzling. We've often tried to interview staff members from many libraries when there were problems, and in nearly every case their fear was sufficient to prevent them from any disclosure of information or opinion. For a journalist, even a library journalist, that kind of climate is the most dangerous because it usually means either one-sided reporting or that the story will remain a secret.

A few other examples will sharpen our point. Although it has been used to threaten a variety of activities and units of the American Library Association, there has still been no detailed disclosure of the complaint of the Internal Revenue Service against ALA, yet it is, in large part, our membership dues IRS wants to tax.

On the current ALA Conference Program, despite a 1971 policy specifically limiting closed meetings to discussions affecting "privacy of individuals or institutions," we note at least 25 groups that have scheduled nearly 60 time slots for closed meetings. Many of these are necessary, but what or whose privacy is threatened by the RTSD Organization Committee, the ACRL Academic Status Committee, the RTSD CCS Descriptive Cataloging Committee, the AALS Executive Board, the ERT Executive Board, COPES, the AASL Professional Relations Committee, or the host of others? One can't help suspect that here again is an example of committee members unwilling to say what they have to say on the record for their members. In this case, however, they are obviously in violation of Association policy, if not in legal terms, certainly in spirit. It is that difference between stated intentions and real intentions that raises serious questions.

The point of these few examples, and they are only examples, is that librarianship, like the society it serves, is quite willing to give lip service to the idea of freedom of information, but when that information or opinion is from "my library," "my staff," "my committee," or "my lips" then a different set of rules applies. This kind of intellectual schizophrenia can only damage our stand on freedom of information and make our formal pronunciamento mere mouthings. If we librarians, as the public's purveyors of information, are willing to accept, as we are asked to do, the idea that our first amendment rights are subject to administrative licensing, we really don't have those rights at all.

If we're willing, in the library, to disclose all the details of the workings of someone else's shop, how can we justify this secrecy about our own? *John Berry III*

Two-page editorial: major thought first, followed by afterthoughts on page two

The first page, shown at right, is a straightforward and not frightfully exciting graphic presentation. It could hardly be simpler. But it is effective for several reasons: first, its very simplicity makes it stand out; second, the huge white spaces are unexpected and surprising; third — something not discernible here but essential to understand — page seven of each issue is devoted to the editorial, come what may. The readers know where to find it (the page following the Contents) and they look for it.

The follow-up page, shown opposite, is looser and less formal. It carries its own title, yet it remains very much an editorial page since it is comprised of comments by the editor. The makeup varies according to the material, but the white band at top is standard, as is the three-column makeup.

What is significant about these two pages is the comparison between the two graphic images they convey. There is no question but that the real editorial page *looks* like one whereas the Perspectives page does *not*.

The difference lies in the detailing: the headline treatment — large and light versus small and black (which is much more ordinary); the amount of white space; the dignity of the page arrangement, tall and vertical versus squat and fully packed (which is more ordinary); and, of course, the atmosphere created by the words themselves — formal and serious versus informal and chatty.

Engineering for architecture: there's nothing to it but people

Said architect Lew Davis at our Round Table on energy conservation: "It's become so easy to be a good architect. All you need is good clients—and good consultants. We rely on our consulting engineers, and when new forms are required [as for energy conservation] we will rely on them to come with us and produce the new forms."

Well, Lew, who with his partners tackles some awfully tough jobs, does make it look easy—as many top-rank architects do. He also makes a point: The best architects know how to make the best use of their consultant engineers, and they know how to turn those engineers on so they do their very best work. I'd bet anything that on a Davis-Brody job the working arrangement is not between an architect and an engineer, but between Lew and Sam (Brody) and their friends/engineers Marvin (Mass), Jim (Leon), Bob (Rosenwasser), Dave (Geiger), and Art (Zigas).

Sure there's a contract—there's also a mutual commitment to give the client the best job that the architects and engineers working together know how to design.

Enthusiasm works! In his introduction to the article (page 100) on the work of KKBNA, engineers in Denver, senior editor Bob Fischer wrote: "In the course of reportorial conversations, the editors were struck by the energy and perceptiveness seemingly common to all members of the firm, and their unmistakable enthusiasm for their work. Our curiosity prompted us . . . to interview the firm's partners and associates, and some of their clients, to find out what accounts for the high quality of their work—and just why they have so much fun doing it." There's a chicken and an egg there!

In another introduction—to the case study section beginning on page 66—associate editor Grace Anderson wrote: "What becomes evident as one reviews the projects on the following pages is that there are a lot of people around with a sizable store of technical expertise—not only architects and engineers, but contractors and manufacturers as well. Talking with contributors to this section," Grace writes, "the editors also noticed the sheer enjoyment these experts take in tackling a knotty problem, whether it's big or little, and the great satisfaction they find in helping to make a building look more beautiful, or work more efficiently, or go together more simply, or cost less money."

I just finished reading—and making a few editor's hen-tracks on—the article on Frank Bridgers' work on solar energy. Having read more than my share of articles—in the popular and professional press alike—on the geewhizzeries of solar energy I approached my first reading of this article, even if Bob Fischer did write it, with a certain amount of . . . well, nervousness. Well, when I finished I had the feeling that I'd heard from an expert—that Frank Bridgers really *knows!*

Well, enough examples to make the point. As I wrote on this page for our first "Engineering for Architecture" issue just a year ago: "We wanted to do this issue because we think the place to search for solutions to our problems in this industry—problems like cost and energy conservation and new scale—is with people." This issue, like our first effort a year ago, demonstrates once again the enormous technical resources that we have available to solve whatever building or design problem comes up, and reinforces the unique relationships of architects to engineers that exists throughout the industry.

Finally, as it was last year, this issue is intended to honor the best work of the best engineers—to give recognition to engineers in building for their absolutely essential and all-too-often unrecognized inventiveness and resourcefulness in working with architects to achieve economical and rational and beautiful buildings.
—*Walter F. Wagner Jr.*

■ Some "essential and all-too-often unrecognized inventiveness" takes place in producing an issue like this, and—as I did last year—I'd like to give a little credit where credit is due. The editor-in-charge of this issue is Senior Editor Robert E. Fischer—the chief worrier, the chief gatherer of information, the chief writer on the issue, and (see photo credits everywhere) its chief photographer. Grace Anderson did such a fine job of assisting Bob last year that we managed to put her on the staff, so she is now Associate Editor Anderson and the assistant chief worrier, etc, etc.

One-time Associate Editor Peggy Gaskie (who moved to Denver just because she got married, for Pete's sake) wrote the KKBNA article for us with the style to which we were long accustomed. Production editor Annette Netburn managed to handle this issue with an extra arm she found somewhere, while her regular two arms produced the August and September issues. Muriel Cuttrell worked over and above on most of the handsome drawings in this issue. The issue was designed—I think with great style—by Jan White; and art production was handled by his Son the Design Student, Alex White.—*W. W.*

PERSPECTIVES

More great lines from the Round Table: an evocative potpourri

As you have probably seen already, beginning on page 92, is a report on RECORD's Round Table: Towards a Rational Policy on Energy Use in Building. One of an editor's frustrations in editing such an article is the enormous amount of thoughtful comment which gets edited. The transcript of the day-long meeting was 269 pages long, double-spaced; and clearly much worth hearing had to be left—as the film-makers say—on the cutting room floor. Herewith, with no attempt at organization, some of the most evocative comments:

. . . Paul Greiner of EEI on utility problems:
"The problems are serious. We are a highly capital intensive industry, and with the cost of money going up and the scarcity of capital increasing the problems get more and more serious. Add to that the evironmental constraints we have to deal with—the siting problems. And then there is the problem of shortages and choice of fuels.

"ASHRAE has now set up a source-evaluation committee—better known as 'the hole-in-the-ground committee'—to study the whole problem [of where the energy is to come from]. . . . We are studying the availability of fuels, the various environmental impacts, the economic impacts, the mix of various fuels at various times, and finally the mix of usage in buildings. . . .

"In the absence of a true national energy policy, we have an energy conflict and we are all seeing it."

And Mr. Greiner pointed out that different utilities have different problems: "You take the load profile on any particular utility company and it will be very different from another utility . . . Most of the major metropolitan utilities are summer-peaking—even in the northern climates. Some still have winter peaks. I will say that the industry is looking at peak-load pricing to try and level off those peaks and fill in the valleys. Inverse rates to penalize the heavy-user? Probably just for residences."

. . . Arthur Diemer of CC&F Property Management on developing a sense of urgency among users: "My problem as an owner-manager is to translate the urgency and seriousness of energy conservation to our tenants. At the peak of the energy crisis, practically everyone adhered faithfully to the 55-mph limit. But it took only four months before everyone started to change back to 65. . . . There was a noticeable reduction in energy consumption in buildings during the gasoline shortage, but our records for late last year and this year show consumption climbing again."

. . . Charles Ince of FEA on the need for public commitment and education: "Our concern is that the public really believe there is an energy crisis. In Washington, when the embargo was on, the growth rate was four per cent. It is already up to eight per cent again.

"I am not convinced that an energy-conserving system has to cost more. The technology exists. It is a matter of understanding that the technology must be used, of getting incentives or disincentives. . . . The Federal policy in the building field is absolute conservation. It is cutting back the consumption of energy used in the construction of buildings and in the operation of buildings. We have been looking and will continue to look at long-term programs that will have a significant impact. Here I am not talking about standards, but about an informational, educational program. And that is clearly needed because at your 1971 Round Table you were debating many of the same issues that we have today."

. . . Dr. Maxine Savitz of HUD on government and the private sector working together: "This era of more expensive energy and lower energy availability gives us an opportunity for new solutions to problems.

"The architect, the engineer, and the building owner will have to work together to develop the best design and best systems.

"It is an opportunity for government and the private sector to work together to make sure that whatever is developed is technically sound and reasonable to implement. . . . There is not going to be one solution to using energy more efficiently in buildings. There are new buildings and old buildings, and very different building types. These will have to be addressed separately, and by separate means. The government will offer some solutions. The private sector can do a lot on its own—not just with education, but with fee structures and ways of financing.

"There are lots of problems, but lots of opportunities that can be looked at from a positive point of view."

. . . Frank Coda of IES on a subject dear to the hearts of architects and engineers:
"The biggest problem for architects and engineers is that they don't get adequately paid for the kind of work involved in a really careful energy analysis. If we are going to have energy conservation, we are going to have to start treating professionals as professionals and pay them for the work that needs to be done."

A promotional-type word about RECORD's "Resources 76" seminar in October

In this issue with its special emphasis on engineering, permit me this special message to engineers on RESOURCES 76—the crash course on getting work in today's climate—which RECORD is holding Monday through Thursday, October 27th through 30th, at the Center for Continuing Education of the University of Chicago. As I said in an earlier editorial: "This is going to be a workshop—perhaps even a sweatshop. The program starts every morning at 8 o'clock and continues after dinner. We think this concentration of work is entirely appropriate. We're asking you to spend a fair amount of money and time—and no one has much spare money or time to spend these days." The tuition will be $400.

What do we offer worth $400? Please take the time to dig back into your July issue and look at the mammoth fold-out on page 65. It gives you in far more detail than I can here exactly what we think is worth your $400 and your time. Bill Marlin, ex-competitor and now compatriot who's done the organization for the conference, has assembled a truly extraordinary roster of speakers and panelists to tackle the subjects that are closest to the heart of the business problem of every engineer and architect—business outlook, legislation, cost control, office efficiency (for small and large firms alike), changing lender attitudes, new market opportunities, and on and on.

I hope you will, despite these troubled times, seriously consider attending. There's a coupon for registration in the July issue; and—since you're a reader—you should have gotten another promotion piece in the mail. If you can't find it, call me (at 212/997-4565) or Bill Marlin (at 212/997-4242).

—W.W.

Standard placement of editorial page: last-left

The example from *Engineering News-Record,* left, shows the simple handling of the editorial when placed opposite the inside back cover. This is an old, established position in the publication and all readers are familiar with it. The position itself can be relied upon to attract the attention it requires (especially since the opinions expressed in the editorials in this specialized newsweekly are of vital importance to the readership). This attraction is, in fact, so strong, that the page can be relied upon to pull the readers through the issue. And the makeup of the page need not be flamboyant for the same reason, so a straightforward two-column format using large type for easy legibility is satisfactory, especially since it allows full use of the available space.

ENR   EDITORIALS

Encourage energy development

The economic measures proposed last week by the President contain nothing to warrant dancing in the streets. But one can take heart at the move to at least try something different (p. 20).

How much of the present economic malaise arises from energy-related problems is an unanswered question. But certainly it is a substantial part. For that reason and others, there is cause for optimism at the President's recommendation that we unshackle and encourage those who would push development of additional energy in this country, not only new sources but coal-burning and nuclear powerplants as well.

Removal of unneeded obstructions to powerplant financing and construction could create new jobs and move the U.S. toward energy self-sufficiency.

Contrary to what some of the back-to-candlelight enthusiasts seem to think, we can't just quit building powerplants and make do with what we have. Energy conservation will be necessary just to stay solvent during the years immediately ahead while we gear up to exploit the resources available to us. And conservation is likely to become a normal part of our life style in the future. But it won't stretch today's energy enough to take care of 50 million more persons.

That is the approximate increase to be expected in U. S. population in the next 40 years as a result of the growth momentum left over from past baby booms. That estimate presupposes that the country will sustain a low fertility rate from now on.

Food, clothing, shelter and other necessaries of modern life for those extra people will take lots of power. There is no way for a society with the numbers and concentration we have today (both intensifying every year) to provide for itself except through the energy-hungry industrial system that has been evolving in the western world for the past 200 to 300 years.

The President seems to understand that. Congress and the public should understand it too and insist on liberation of our own energy resources from unrealistic restraints.

Encourage energy conservation

President Ford's proposed standards for housing and buildings come on the heels of some state and local actions already in legislatures or passed to conserve energy (p. 21). But if this country is serious about conserving energy and becoming independent of foreign suppliers, national standards adopted and enforced through the states is one way of doing it.

The standards for one and two-family housing will probably come from existing standards used by the Department of Housing and Urban Development.

The standards for apartment, office and industrial buildings are yet to be written, but one guideline mentioned is the standard the American Society of Heating, Refrigeration and Air-Conditioning Engineers (ASHRAE) is working on. This standard in its initial draft was given to ASHRAE by the National Bureau of Standards for review and further input. While both the General Services Administration and the Federal Energy Administration have already issued their own guidelines to conserve energy in government buildings, the ASHRAE standard has been researched to a much greater extent and has had input from thousands of industry sources. It is the only comprehensive energy design standard in existence and should be used as the basis for national standards.

Speeding deepwater oil ports

Two weeks ago a shipyard near Baltimore launched the 1,100-ft-long oil supertanker *Massachusetts,* the largest commercial ship ever built in the U.S. But the ship can't put into any U.S. port because they are all too shallow.

Dredging existing ports to an adequate depth would be, in most instances, economically unrealistic and environmentally disastrous. If the U.S. is to benefit from giant crude carriers like this one, the only way is port facilities standing offshore in deep water.

Backers of at least three deepwater port proposals are ready to request permission from the federal government to build them (ENR 1/16 p. 8). If everything goes as planned, they will be able to file their applications by May 1. Ideally, the federal Transportation Department, Environmental Protection Agency and other federal offices involved in the reviewing process will make every effort to expedite the applications. Should the applications bog down in red tape, construction could be delayed for at least another year.

All the environmental and economic arguments for and against deepwater ports have had ample time to be aired during the more than two years that two of these proposals have been in the wind. The argument that properly constructed and operated supertankers are safer environmentally than smaller ones makes sense. Fewer tankers crossing oceans lower the odds that collisions and spills will occur. Offshore docking of large ships eliminates the risks of spills during lightering, in which deep-draft tankers, while still at sea, pump their petroleum into smaller tankers that can enter inshore ports. Larger-capacity tankers also offer economies of scale in transportation costs.

There's no excuse for unreasonable, additional delays to occur once applications are received. If the government hasn't kept score in evaluating the arguments over the past few years, it should have. If it has kept score, debate on the proposals will be well-documented and concise and the decisions made will be the correct ones.

... or on page following the Contents

The placement on page 5 of this Letter from the Publisher (a slight variant of the normal Editorial and, in this publication, supplanting it every so often) shows how a smaller-scale editorial statement can be tied to the staff listing and thus use less space without losing any of its apparent significance.

The masthead, beneath its tinted color block acts as a wall separating the ad on the opposite page from the important text on this page (in the same way that white space does in the example on page 128). Furthermore, the contrast between the small type of the masthead and the larger text type of the editorial makes the large type appear even bigger than it in fact is. The ragged-right setting and spacing between paragraphs gives the typography a different texture and feel from any other page in the publication though the typeface is the same. The signature cut is a slightly more personalized way of presenting the byline than setting it in type, and it is a bit more graphically interesting and decorative.

Color

CHEMICAL ENGINEERING

EDITOR-IN-CHIEF
Calvin S. Cronan (212-997-2464)

EXECUTIVE EDITOR
Robert B. Norden (997-3077)

MANAGING EDITORS
NEWS: Nicholas P. Chopey (997-2197)
ENGINEERING: Frederick C. Price (997-2358)
PRESENTATION & SPECIAL PROJECTS
Joan M. Nilsen (997-2678)

NEWS EDITORS
SENIOR ASSOCIATE EDITOR: Mark D. Rosenzweig
ASSOCIATE EDITORS: John C. Davis
Raúl Remirez,
Nicholas R. Iammartino
ASSISTANT EDITOR: Larry J. Ricci

ENGINEERING EDITORS
SENIOR ASSOCIATE EDITOR: Edward H. Steymann
ASSOCIATE EDITORS: Steven Danatos,
Roy V. Hughson, Jay Matley, Ryle Miller, Jr.

PRESENTATION EDITORS
ART DIRECTOR: Noah Bee
ASSOCIATE ART DIRECTOR: Edward W. Libby
PRODUCTION ASSISTANT: Kathleen V. Nallen
CHIEF COPY EDITOR: Henry S. Gordon
ASSISTANT COPY EDITOR: George Ellis

REGIONAL EDITORS & BUREAUS
HOUSTON: James H. Prescott, Wilma Pryblek
LOS ANGELES: Guy E. Weismantel
DOMESTIC NEWS BUREAUS: Atlanta, Chicago,
Cleveland, Detroit, Houston/Dallas, Los Angeles,
San Francisco, Seattle, Washington
WORLD NEWS BUREAUS: Bonn, Brussels, London,
Milan, Moscow, Paris, Tokyo, Toronto.
Correspondents in 133 cities in 61 countries.

CIRCULATION
MANAGER: Paul W. Erb

EQUIPMENT BUYERS' GUIDE
MANAGER: Joseph A. Callahan

ADVERTISING & BUSINESS
ADVERTISING SALES MANAGER:
Thomas H. King (997-6547)
MARKETING SERVICES MANAGER:
Laurence J. White (997-3206)
MARKETING RESEARCH MANAGER:
Bertha Chase (997-6368)
SALES SERVICES MANAGER:
Joan Silinsh (997-2315)
DIRECTOR OF PRODUCTION:
Philip J. Hoelz (997-2312)
ADVERTISING MAKEUP:
William Graham (997-3696)
REPRINTS: Jacquelyn Ford (997-3068)

PUBLISHER
Alfred S. Reed

PUBLISHER'S PAGE

The Process of Change

The technology of printing and publishing, just like the technology of chemical engineering, is constantly changing. With this issue, almost a quarter of a million CHEMICAL ENGINEERING readers will be treated to a new graphic design aimed at faster, easier reading.
Since its origin in 1902, CHEMICAL ENGINEERING has undergone many changes to give readers the most advanced publishing techniques, such as computerized photo composition, web offset printing, and lighter but improved paper stock.

Still, CE's approach is not revolutionary. The editorial product, from Chementator to Plant Notebook, remains exactly the same. What we have substantially altered are the visual techniques that help you get the most out of CHEMICAL ENGINEERING. Indeed, you may not even notice some of these changes because they are working best when they are not obvious.

For those interested in technical details, our new typeface is Baskerville, which replaces Times Roman. Baskerville is an "open" face that is noted for its legibility. It results in slightly fewer characters per line, and to make up for the difference we have widened each page and added one line. The result: faster reading, with no sacrifice in number of words per page.

You will find a new logotype on the cover, more emphatic headings for departments, and an improved format for tables and figures. Our design consultant calls it a "coherent graphic image." Actually, we are even more interested in a coherent presentation of news and practical chemical-engineering technology for you, a technical-decision maker in the chemical process industries.

CHEMICAL ENGINEERING's new look is the result of almost a year of study and analysis, not unlike developing a new process system. We started with a conceptual design, evaluated the feasibility of alternate routes, selected the optimum approach, produced a prototype model for debugging, and finally brought the new system onstream.

We hope you'll find CHEMICAL ENGINEERING's new graphic presentation attractive, and even more informative and useful than before. Please give us your opinions, whether good or bad, since it's you, the reader, whose opinions we value the most.

Alfred S. Reed

5
CHEMICAL ENGINEERING AUGUST 4, 1975

Two Letters from the Publisher: a vertical-half

Split-page makeup, such as in *Midwest Purchasing,* right, is hard to handle, since the competition for attention from the ads on both sides is fierce. But if the typography is clean and neat and a bit "different" (as it is here) and if there is a modicum of personalization by means of a picture and a signature cut, then the material receives the visibility it needs. The headline here should have been a size larger and set in italics to tie it into the text more distinctly.

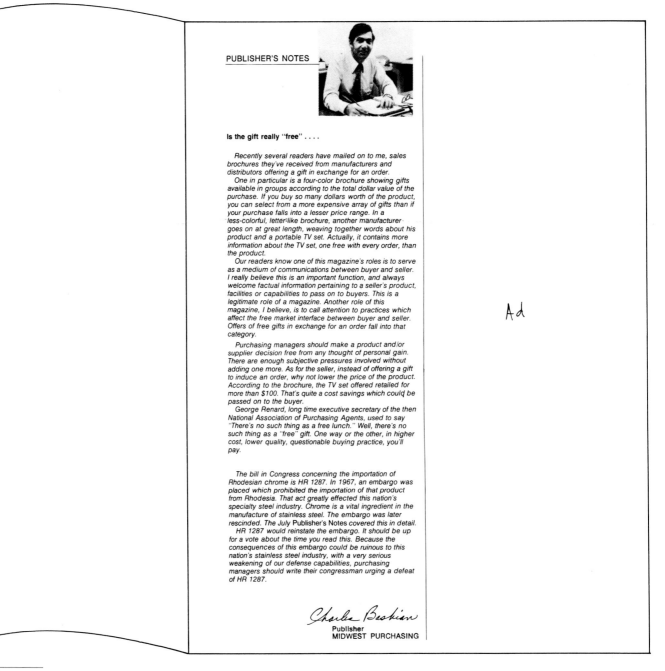

PUBLISHER'S NOTES

Is the gift really "free" . . . .

Recently several readers have mailed on to me, sales brochures they've received from manufacturers and distributors offering a gift in exchange for an order.

One in particular is a four-color brochure showing gifts available in groups according to the total dollar value of the purchase. If you buy so many dollars worth of the product, you can select from a more expensive array of gifts than if your purchase falls into a lesser price range. In a less-colorful, letter-like brochure, another manufacturer goes on at great length, weaving together words about his product and a portable TV set. Actually, it contains more information about the TV set, one free with every order, than the product.

Our readers know one of this magazine's roles is to serve as a medium of communications between buyer and seller. I really believe this is an important function, and always welcome factual information pertaining to a seller's product, facilities or capabilities to pass on to buyers. This is a legitimate role of a magazine. Another role of this magazine, I believe, is to call attention to practices which affect the free market interface between buyer and seller. Offers of free gifts in exchange for an order fall into that category.

Purchasing managers should make a product and/or supplier decision free from any thought of personal gain. There are enough subjective pressures involved without adding one more. As for the seller, instead of offering a gift to induce an order, why not lower the price of the product. According to the brochure, the TV set offered retailed for more than $100. That's quite a cost savings which could be passed on to the buyer.

George Renard, long time executive secretary of the then National Association of Purchasing Agents, used to say "There's no such thing as a free lunch." Well, there's no such thing as a "free" gift. One way or the other, in higher cost, lower quality, questionable buying practice, you'll pay.

The bill in Congress concerning the importation of Rhodesian chrome is HR 1287. In 1967, an embargo was placed which prohibited the importation of that product from Rhodesia. That act greatly effected this nation's specialty steel industry. Chrome is a vital ingredient in the manufacture of stainless steel. The embargo was later rescinded. The July Publisher's Notes covered this in detail.

HR 1287 would reinstate the embargo. It should be up for a vote about the time you read this. Because the consequences of this embargo could be ruinous to this nation's stainless steel industry, with a very serious weakening of our defense capabilities, purchasing managers should write their congressman urging a defeat of HR 1287.

Charles Beskian

Publisher
MIDWEST PURCHASING

Ad

... and a horizontal-third

The small space remaining on the page after the staff listings and masthead are placed, is used for a short note from the Publisher when it is not being used for Letters. The plain type shows off well against the typographic complexities beneath. The picture always refers to the subject of the note. The reason for using the top of the page is that the top of the page is the most visible and the more important material ought to go there. Thus the masthead was squashed down to the lower area, ensuring that the material on the upper portion of the page gets at least *some* readership. Compare the informality of this page with the formal Editorial page from the same magazine on page 132.

ENR

TO FILL YOU IN

James Stanford Fisher, McGraw-Hill World News Atlanta bureau chief, earned his journalism degree at the University of North Carolina-Chapel Hill and later a master's in East Asian history from Georgia State.

With that kind of education, he probably never expected to end up knee-deep in the mud of heavy construction sites for ENR. But 35-year-old Fisher this week has his second cover on ENR in less than three months.

In addition to this week's feature on the Tennessee-Tombigbee Waterway (p. 16), he reported the cover article on William Sangster, newly elected presi-

Stan Fisher

dent of the American Society of Civil Engineers.

He has been almost preoccupied with construction in recent months. He covered the heavy construction portion—both editorially and photographically—

of the Administration minisummit on housing and construction that was held in Atlanta in September.

Fisher also reported on the projects being undertaken by International City Corp., Atlanta; a three-pager on Atlanta that was actually four stories, an overview plus sidebar stories on architect John Portman's hotel, the Hilton hotel, and Omni International.

Earlier, Fisher was writing about the first use of the reinforced earth system in the U.S. in a marine environment, and he'll have two stories in the Tools of Construction issue (ENR 2/6).

EUGENE E. WEYENETH, *Publisher*

ENGINEERING NEWS-RECORD McGRAW-HILL'S CONSTRUCTION WEEKLY—101st YEAR OF PUBLICATION

Editor, Arthur J. Fox, Jr.

Managing Editor, Joseph F. Wilkinson

Executive Editor, James B. Sullivan

Manager, Business Data Department, Robert H. Dodds

Senior Editors, Charles J. Harding, William W. Jacobus, Jr., E. Allen Soast, Robert J. Stinson, Edward M. Young

Assistant Managing Editor, Howard B. Stussman

Departments:

Transportation: E. Allen Soast, Geraldine Galli Loose, James W. Fullilove

Buildings: Robert J. Stinson, Richard M. Kielar, David R. Breul

Water: William W. Jacobus, Jr., Rolf A. Fuessler

Management & Labor: Charles J. Harding, Roger Hannan, William F. Campbell

Business Data-Costs, Prices, Markets: Robert H. Dodds

Construction Reports, Pulse: Ursula Blakemore, Jonathan Tilden, Judy Stahl, Pearl Herndon, Marie Moravsik, Anna Mary Chan, Christine Galgano, Diane Terrana, Ann Shapero, Barbara Jackson

Economics, Statistics: Linda Marcotte, Sally Miller, Lorraine Taylor

Cost Trends, Prices, Wages, Indexes: Edward A. Downe, Etta Maye, Dianne Miller

Unit Prices: William G. Reinhardt

Copy & Production: Howard B. Stussman, W. Thomas Erskine, Dolores Ferreiros

Presentation: Harry W. Jensen, Rita Potocny Krider

Regional Editors, San Francisco: David G. Ellingson, Judith H. Dobrzynski; *Chicago:* Edward M. Young

Correspondents, Bureaus: Joan Spano

Editorial Research & Indexing: Gabriella L. Turnay

Assistant to the Editor: Beth Anderson

Planning & Development: James H. Webber

Consulting Editors: Waldo G. Bowman, Nathan A. Bowers

Advertising Sales Manager, James L. Rice

Circulation Manager, Edward F. Bressler

Controller/Business Manager, Hugh J. Carlson

Publisher, Eugene E. Weyeneth

McGraw-Hill World News:

Ralph R. Schulz, Director; Albert Wall, Editor

Domestic News Bureaus: Atlanta—Stan Fisher; *Chicago*—Mike Kolbenschlag, Daniel C. Brown, Dennis Chase, Marcia Opp, Jane Shaw; *Detroit*—William Hampton, Roger Guiles; *Houston/Dallas*—Robert E. Lee, Lorraine Smith, Nick Hunter, Helen Crawford; *Los Angeles*—Michael Murphy, Barbara Lamb, Darrell Maddox, Gerald Parkinson; *San Francisco*—Margaret Ralston Drossel, Jenness Keene, Robert Yeager, Alan Kennedy; *Seattle*—Ray Bloomberg; *Washington*—Robert Farrell, Bruce Agnew, Muriel Allen, James Canan, Herbert Cheshire, Jerry Edgerton, Boyd France, Charles Gall, William Hickman, John Higgins, Dexter Hutchins, Norman Jonas, Wilbert Lepkowski, Donald Loomis, Susan A. Meyer, Daniel Moskowitz, Seth Payne, Peter Philipps, Caroline Robertson, David Secrest, Roger Smith, Lee Walczak, James Wargo, Steve Wildstrom, Stanley Wilson.

Foreign News Bureaus: Bonn—Robert Ingersoll, Jon Fedler, Ty Marshall; Silke McQueen; *Brussels*—James Smith; *Buenos Aires*—Ernest McCrary; *London*—James Trotter, Dorsey Woodson, Roy Eales, Donald Ediger; *Milan*—Peter Hoffmann, Andrew Heath; *Moscow*—Peter Gall; *Paris*—Michael Johnson, William Kosman, Richard Shepherd, Michael Sullivan; *Singapore*—Colin Gibson; *Tokyo*—Michael Mealey, Peter Rutledge, Jiro Wakabayashi, Shota Ushio. Marvin Petal, European Manager. Axel Krause, Economic Correspondent.

Chief Correspondents: Madrid—Dominic Curcio; *Stockholm*—Robert Skole; *Zurich*—Laura Pilarski.

Correspondents in 90 principal U.S. cities and 70 foreign cities.

Published weekly, with an additional issue the last week of April, by McGraw-Hill, Inc. Founder: James H. McGraw (1860-1948). **Subscriptions:** Available only by paid subscription. The publisher reserves the right to accept or reject any subscription. Subscriptions to ENGINEERING NEWS-RECORD, solicited only from persons with identifiable commercial or professional interests in construction and building. Position and company connection must be indicated on subscription orders forwarded to address shown below. Subscription rates for individuals in the field of the publication: U.S. and possessions. $14.00 per year (single copies, $1.00 in U.S.—except the February 6, 1975, issue which is $3.00). Canada, $18.00 per year; other countries, $30.00 per year.

Executive, Editorial, Circulation and Advertising Offices: McGraw-Hill Building, 1221 Avenue of the Americas, New York, N.Y. 10020. Telephone 997-1221. Publication office: 99 N. Broadway, Albany, N.Y. 12204. Second class postage paid at Albany, N.Y. Title reg. (R) in U.S. Patent Office. Copyright (C) 1975 by McGraw-Hill, Inc. All rights reserved.

Officers of the McGraw-Hill Publications Company: John R. Emery, President; J. Elton Tuohig, Executive Vice President—Administration; David J. McGrath, Group Publisher—Vice President; Senior Vice Presidents: Ralph Blackburn, Circulation; Walter Stanbury, Editorial; John B. Hoglund, Controller; David G. Jensen, Manufacturing; Gordon L. Jones, Marketing; Jerome D. Luntz, Planning & Development.

Officers of the Corporation: Shelton Fisher, Chairman of the Board and Chief Executive Officer; Harold W. McGraw, Jr., President and Chief Operating Officer; Wallace F. Traendly, Group President, McGraw-Hill Publications Co. and McGraw-Hill Information Systems Co.; Robert N. Landes, Senior Vice President and Secretary; Ralph J. Webb, Treasurer.

Unconditional Guarantee: The publisher, upon written request, agrees to refund the part of the subscription price applying to the remaining unfilled portion of the service if service is unsatisfactory.

SUBSCRIBERS: Send all correspondence, change of address notices, and subscription orders to Fulfillment Manager, ENGINEERING NEWS-RECORD, P.O. Box 430, Hightstown, N.J. 08520. If possible, attach address label from a recent issue. Please allow one month for change of address to become effective.

Postmaster: Please send Form 3579 to Fulfillment Manager, ENGINEERING NEWS-RECORD, P.O. Box 430, Hightstown, N.J. 08520.

January 2, 1975 ENR **5**

Which is better: careful balance or apparently random arrangement?

Two approaches to the same problem: how to handle an editorial placed on the first-right page of the feature section (see the next chapter for more on this). Which is better?

House & Home's solution, right, with its small logo and dateline signaling the start of the feature section as well as dignifying the editorial page itself, and with a box around the entire space, reflects the logic and design-conscious makeup of the entire publication. There is no element out of place, nothing that has not been deliberately placed just so. Is it exciting? By itself, perhaps not. But in its context, it most certainly succeeds in drawing attention to itself, and, having done so, it succeeds equally well in imparting its own aura of seriousness and dignity to the overall editorial product.

Scientific Research's solution is just as successful in attracting attention to itself, because of both its informality of arrangement and the cartoon, of course. But the context in which the page appears is totally different from that of *House & Home*. Here is a biweekly newsmagazine using standard three-column makeup throughout, quite rigid and neatly organized, but obviously not nearly as design-conscious as *House & Home*, which is essentially a picture magazine. So for *Scientific Research* the contrast between the random-height columns (which are slightly wider than the normal ones) and the usual full-height ones elsewhere is striking.

House & Home/September 1975

Editorial

It's a freewheeling business you're in, but . . .

One of the things that makes real estate a vital, dynamic field is the opportunity it offers to the entrepreneur. An individual with an idea, some flair, enough drive and a little luck can create a big, successful enterprise out of almost nothing.

But there are other—and less desirable—possibilities.

Success may breed in the entrepreneur a blind belief that the intuitive, seat-of-the-pants way of operating that shot him to the top is the only way to go. So when the need arises for a systematic approach to some phase of his operation, he rejects it out of hand.

Or, success may convince him that he has found the one and only path. So he locks himself into that way of thinking or operating and refuses to budge.

The result is that while real estate—and especially the housing portion of the field—is the freest, swingingest industry of any, it is at the same time the blindest, most hidebound and slowest to grasp new concepts.

The entrepreneurial dichotomy is highlighted by the first two articles in this issue of House & Home, both of them dealing with the rental market. For example:

It is generally accepted that the current ratio of interest rates to obtainable rents makes it unfeasible to build rental housing. But a number of apartment developers have discovered that if you stop thinking of renters as second-class inhabitants of minimum cubicles and start thinking of them as people who, while they may prefer renting to owning, nevertheless want much of the same lifestyle as owners, you can open up a very feasible market. Or . . .

When the apartment-construction market was strong and maintenance costs were low enough not to cut deeply into profitability, most apartments were managed on a sloppy, it-doesn't-matter-too-much-basis. But now that maintenance costs—especially for utilities—have gone through the roof, that sloppiness has become ruinous. It can be eliminated only if apartment management is turned into a systematized operation that keeps track of every nickel spent.

None of the foregoing should be construed as an argument for crowding out the entrepreneur—or for turning firms into facsimiles of large, over-organized and inflexible corporations. The record of such corporations in the housing field is conclusive proof of where *that* approach leads.

What we are suggesting is that the successful entrepreneurial approach must also be a flexible approach. Some areas of the builder's operation should be run on a freewheeling basis—in particular, finding new markets and new ways to serve old markets. Others must be tightly, even rigidly, organized. And all areas are subject to change.

—Maxwell C. Huntoon Jr.

So, *House & Home*'s editorial is a formalized page in informal surroundings and *Scientific Research*'s editorial is an informal page in formalized surroundings. Neither of them is "better" than the other, because they both do their job well. But if they were exchanged, neither would any longer do its job as well. Here is an example of the necessity to see the publication as a product — with a total character — and use the graphic means that will reinforce that character and make use of its potential to the fullest extent possible.

EDITORIAL

To avoid 1984

The average person feels disturbed and suspicious about the growing encroachment of the digital computer on his daily life —and with good reason. In our report on computers in research in this issue, Bell Labs' George Hamming warns (see page 54) that the nightmare image of the computer as an omnipotent monster forcing a totalitarian society on us could well become a reality by the end of the century.

Of course, as Hamming points out, the digital computer—like nuclear fission—is inherently neither good nor evil. Obviously it is how mankind chooses to use computers that will determine their effect on society. For computer systems that interact with human beings, the key question will be whether the system will in each instance be designed to make things easier for the computer—or for the humans.

If computer programmers and their bosses can be persuaded consistently to refuse to sacrifice human freedom of choice and human convenience for the sake of machine efficiency, then, Hamming argues, the computerized society will be considerably more like a utopia than a nightmare.

A happy example in the scientific community of Hamming's advice is the Dartmouth Time-Sharing System (see page 27). This system, designed with the convenience of the inexperienced researcher or student uppermost in mind, marks the advent of practical time-sharing for the mass of scientists. The astounding commercial success of an earlier version of the system encourages us to hope that in free competition people-oriented computer systems will win out.

Unfortunately, a more ominous threat can be expected from those quarters in which competition does not exist—government and quasi-government agencies. If no one has yet succeeded in persuading government or corporate bureaucracies to consider individual freedom and convenience in designing such simple things as application forms, how, then, can we hope to preserve our personal freedom in the age of computerization?

For scientists, the struggle with government agencies over the use of the computer is already in full swing. On page 36 we report how the government is dragging its heels in changing the procedures used in charging computer time to research grants. Now geared to machine-oriented batch operation, the accounting system must be changed to accommodate user-oriented time-sharing and multi-programming operation.

If ever an ombudsman was needed to safeguard individuals against the abuses of the civil servant, it is in this new area of the computer programmer. We suggest that the Nixon Administration think seriously of creating a new office to carry out this ombudsman function. We also suggest that the office be heavily staffed with scientists (including social scientists)—for scientists invented and developed the computer and are in the best position to give advice on what it is able to do.

Kioyaki Komoda

Two examples of prepared formats into which the editorials can be dropped

The two examples are from Brazilian magazines and both include the masthead, etc. The one at right places it in the gutter, tying it to the rest of the page by complex boxing/shadowing rules (which are a natural graphic outgrowth of the logo lettering — a typeface called Pioneer). The one opposite places the masthead at the foot of the page, like a footnote, and devotes the top part of the page to the editorial statement.

The advantage of such strong shapes is twofold. First, the recognition value is immediate since the reader becomes familiarized with them quickly. Second, it becomes a simple process to write the editorial and drop it into its space without having to worry too much whether the page is "designed" correctly; it removes the necessity of redesigning the page every issue. Obviously it is hoped that the format does not become a straitjacket and that the number of words allowed (given the common sense amount of leeway) works out about right every time.

EDITORIAL

ENGENHEIROMODERNO INDÚSTRIA

VOL. IX — ABRIL, 1973 — N.º 7
Diretor do Conselho Diretivo
Robert T. Lund
Diretor de Redação
Alípio do Amaral Ferreira
Coordenador Geral
Sérgio Carrera
Redatores-chefes
Isabel Kumpera EM/Construção
Alfredo Leite EM/Indústria
Pesquisa Editorial
Célia de Leão Bensadon
Assistente Técnico
A. C. Amorim
Correspondente no México
Hugo A. Brown
Secretária
Maria Dulce de Oliveira
Fotografia
Windsor Borges e José Prezado de Jesus
Diagramação
Marco A. Tretel Reis e
Marcos M. Martins
Produção
Antônio Carlos F. dos Santos
Revisão
Natalino D'Olivo
Dept.º Comercial: Osvaldo K. Nakamura, Gerente de Desenvolvimento; Francisco A. Dolce, Gerente Administrativo; Hélio C. Faccin, Gerente de Projetos Especiais; Maria José Campagnoli, Assistente — **Publicidade no Rio de Janeiro:** Cláudio Rozenbaum, Gerente; Hilda Rodrigues, assistente.
ENGENHEIRO MODERNO EDITADA POR T/L Publicações Industriais Ltda.
Diretor Presidente: Robert T. Lund
Diretor Gerente: R. Christopher Lund
Rua Brigadeiro Tobias, 356, 4.º andar, Tels.: 227-2417, 227-3658, 227-5971, São Paulo, SP — Caixa Postal 30493, São Paulo, SP — Filial no Rio de Janeiro: Rua Santa Luzia, 776, Cj. 401 — Tel. 222-8462, Rio de Janeiro, GB.
Administração: Ademar A. Vitoriano, **Assistente da Gerência Geral:** Delcy G. Penteado, **Representante no Rio Grande do Sul** — Impar Representações Ltda. — Rua Vigário José Inácio, 547, 13.º, Cj. 1309; Tel.: 24-6011 — Porto Alegre — RS. **Representante no Paraná e Santa Catarina:** Roberto Peixoto de Souza — Representação Veículos de Publicidade — Pça. Zacarias, 46 — 25.º — Tel. 22-3273, Curitiba — PR.
Representante no Exterior: World Marketing Services, Inc., Larchmont New York — **Diretor para a Europa:** Tomasz Zamoyski — 28 Great Queen Street, London WC2B 5BB Tel.: 01-242 6346 Cables: Moderno London WC2. **Circulação:** M.Q. — Mercados Qualificados Ltda. Toda correspondência referente a pedidos de assinatura e mudança de endereço deve ser dirigida a Engenheiro Moderno, Depto de Circulação — Caixa Postal 30493, São Paulo, SP.
Engenheiro Moderno Editada e distribuída por T/L — Publicações Industriais Ltda. — Rua Brigadeiro Tobias, 356, 4.º andar S. Paulo, SP. Número avulso — Cr$ 6,00. Número atrasado — Cr$ 7,00. Assinatura anual — Cr$ 60,00. Assinatura para o Exterior: via marítima — US$ 40,00. Via aérea — US$ 50,00.

Membro do IVC

Composta e impressa na Cia. Litographica Ypiranga, Rua Dr. Alfredo de Castro s/n, São Paulo

■ Recentes pesquisas desenvolvidas nos EUA, no campo da comunicação, revelaram que a maioria das citações em textos técnicos e científicos recentes referiam-se a trabalhos de especialistas divulgados nos cinco anos imediatamente precedentes. A caducidade precoce de um grande volume de informações com mais de cinco anos de publicação, atesta a velocidade de "substituição" de conhecimentos, o ritmo da inovação tecnológica e a necessidade de intensificar o esforço de atualização profissional.

A partir destes fatos, a pesquisa mostra que a evolução tecnológica é diretamente proporcional à velocidade da difusão do conhecimento científico.

À vista destes dados ninguém mais pode estranhar a multiplicação e expansão das revistas especializadas, cujo sucesso, naquele país, como de resto em todo o mundo, contrasta com as dificuldades crescentes que enfrentam os veículos que pretendem "contar-tudo-para-todos".

Sensível às necessidades dos leitores, Engenheiro Moderno tem procurado cumprir missão do jornalismo especializado, consciente de que, dentro do processo de modernização tecnológica pelo qual passa o País, o tempo se torna cada vez mais importante e a oportunidade da informação cada vez mais crítica. O mais recente exemplo desta obediência às necessidades de seus leitores e do País está na seção PM — Produtos Modernos. Este mês, com quatro páginas, que serão oito na próxima edição, atestando a receptividade de uma iniciativa perfeitamente enquadrada nas tendências atuais, pois possibilita contato direto entre os que produzem equipamentos e aqueles que vão utilizá-los e difusão ampla e imediata das inovações, tão logo surjam no mercado.

Dinheiro, e mais dinheiro

Há momentos em que um *chairman* precisa sair do pedestal e resolver os problemas do cotidiano. E os momentos de recessão nos negócios estão seguramente nessa condição.

Contudo, o difícil é identificar esses momentos; é algo constrangedor — e freqüentemente dramático — intervir numa rotina que por anos a fio vai dando resultados para, mediante cirurgias aqui, transfusões ali, oxigênio acolá, deixar as organizações novamente em dia e com boa saúde.

Se Rodolfo Marco Bonfiglioli, nosso entrevistado para o *Artigo de Capa* desta edição (*Os novos poderes de um homem só*, na página 17), tem um mérito na história recente das duas maiores empresas que dirige (a Cica e o Banco Auxiliar), é esse: o de ter sabido enfeixar os controles operacionais do dia-a-dia antes que os problemas começassem a se manifestar.

Essa postura empresarial se dirige para uma controlada limitação do poder dos executivos, no âmbito de cada uma das empresas. Isso pode ser bom num momento em que os problemas parecem exigir respostas mais do conjunto do grupo e menos das partes isoladas que o compõem.

De fato, é muito fácil notar, nesse grupo, uma estrita preocupação com a integração entre a fábrica de conservas alimentícias (que já é, por sua vez, uma operação agro-industrial) e o banco comercial, como uma forma de não desperdiçar munição —

segundo se assinala na matéria, reportada e redatada por Jorge Wahl.

O que não quer dizer que os arsenais desse grupo estejam por baixo. Bem ao contrário, Bonfiglioli cunha uma expressão definitiva, pelo bom senso e picardia, quando se refere à crise de crédito — e que vale, de resto, para a recessão mais ampla de negócios. Ele diz: — O problema atual não é a falta de dinheiro e sim de mais dinheiro.

Os homens que decidem no Grupo Gerdau, outra das empresas enfocadas nesta edição (*Gerdau: a duplicação em 4 anos*, na página 28), às voltas com o onipresente problema da expansão nas indústrias siderúrgicas, talvez concordem com Bonfiglioli.

Quem se dispõe a investir num panorama de um certo desalento geral em relação ao futuro certamente tem de responder, antes, às perguntas cruciais: É hora de crescer? Como projetar o crescimento se os custos se inflacionam rapidamente? — e, mais especificamente: Como pensar em investimentos se o dinheiro é um produto a cada dia mais caro e, portanto, mais raro?

Entretanto, aparentemente a direção da Gerdau sabe que os períodos de crise não são senão períodos de desafio se se acredita no sistema e na sua capacidade de sobrevivência sem rupturas estruturais. E que a crise, para as empresas que contam, as que vão sobreviver, é apenas um pedaço na história das organizações.

Editor e Diretor-Responsável
Francisco V. Crestana
Diretor de Redação
Sidnei Basile
Secretário de Redação
Francisco da Costa Pinto
Redação: Fernando Guimarães, Jorge R. Wahl, Roberto Benevides, Regina Pimenta de Castro, Paulo Ludmer, Ana Maria Baccaro e P. R. Barbosa.
Pesquisa econômica: Antonio M. Furtado e Maria Elisa Carvalho Bartholo.
Produção: Edison Ribeiro, gerente; L. Fernando dos Santos.
Revisão: Alfredo Iamauti, chefe; Gabriel Arcanjo Nogueira.
Fotografia: Bob Schalkwijk, Michel Zabé e Ulrich Svitek.
Correspondentes: Roberto Salinas (México) e Alberto Safrán (Argentina).

Publicidade: Sergio B. Rosa, gerente comercial; Klibson José de R. Silva, gerente-Rio; Efraim C. Kapulski e Alexandre L. Pinto Neto, representantes-SP; Celso Murce, representante-Rio.

Sucursais e/ou representantes:
Belo Horizonte: Programar Publicidade Ltda., Avenida Afonso Pena 748, sala 802, fones 22-9552 e 22-3440.
Curitiba: Roberto Peixoto de Souza, Pça. Zacarias 46, 25.º andar, fone 24-3273.
Porto Alegre: Ricardo Corrêa Otero, Rua Gonçalo de Carvalho 22/24, Tel. 25-3178 e 25-0367. **Recife:** Sitral — Serviço de Imprensa, Televisão e Rádio Nordeste Ltda.-Rua Marquês do Recife, 119, cjs. 308/309, fones 24-4554 e 24-1698. **Salvador:** Sitral — Serviço de Imprensa, Televisão e Rádio Nordeste Ltda., Rua Conselheiro Dantas 8, sala 610, fone 2-1003.

Circulação: Rosa Maria Augusto.
Distribuição
Datec — Distrib. Mala Direta e Gráfica Ltda.
Impressão
COLIBRI — Comercial Litográfica Brasileira de Impressão Ltda. Clímaco Barbosa 659, São Paulo, SP.

EXPANSÃO — A Revista Brasileira de Negócios — é uma revista técnica de gestão de empresas, dirigida exclusivamente à alta direção, que se envia cada duas semanas a 15 mil executivos em todo o território nacional. Números avulsos a Cr$ 10,00, assinatura anual (Brasil) a Cr$ 200,00 e (Exterior) a US$ 80,00 (via aérea). Registrada na D.C.D.P. do Departamento de Polícia Federal sob o n.º 087 - P. 209/73.

EXPANSÃO — A Revista Brasileira de Negócios é membro do Instituto Verificador de Circulação.

Publicada por
Publicações Executivas Brasileiras Ltda., Rua dos Ingleses 150, Caixa Postal 30837, fones 287-7100, 287-7400 e 287-7433, CEP 01329, São Paulo, SP. Avenida Alm. Barroso 63, gr. 2502, fone 222-6748, 20000 Rio de Janeiro, GB.

Diretor-Superintendente
Francisco V. Crestana
Diretor Administrativo
F. Harvey Popell
Diretor Comercial
Persio Brait Pisani
Gerente Financeiro
Roberto Valdrez
Assistente da Diretoria
Rubens Brazil Folino

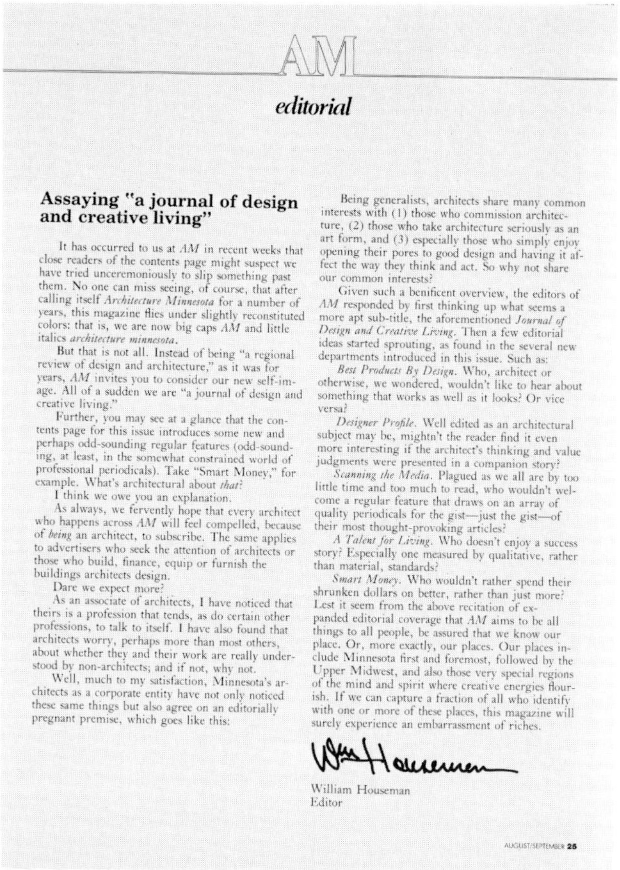

AM

editorial

Assaying "a journal of design and creative living"

It has occurred to us at *AM* in recent weeks that close readers of the contents page might suspect we have tried unceremoniously to slip something past them. No one can miss seeing, of course, that after calling itself *Architecture Minnesota* for a number of years, this magazine flies under slightly reconstituted colors: that is, we are now big caps *AM* and little italics *architecture minnesota*.

But that is not all. Instead of being "a regional review of design and architecture," as it was for years, *AM* invites you to consider our new self-image. All of a sudden we are "a journal of design and creative living."

Further, you may see at a glance that the contents page for this issue introduces some new and perhaps odd-sounding regular features (odd-sounding, at least, in the somewhat constrained world of professional periodicals). Take "Smart Money," for example. What's architectural about *that*?

I think we owe you an explanation.

As always, we fervently hope that every architect who happens across *AM* will feel compelled, because of *being* an architect, to subscribe. The same applies to advertisers who seek the attention of architects or those who build, finance, equip or furnish the buildings architects design.

Dare we expect more?

As an associate of architects, I have noticed that theirs is a profession that tends, as do certain other professions, to talk to itself. I have also found that architects worry, perhaps more than most others, about whether they and their work are really understood by non-architects; and if not, why not.

Well, much to my satisfaction, Minnesota's architects as a corporate entity have not only noticed these same things but also agree on an editorially pregnant premise, which goes like this:

Being generalists, architects share many common interests with (1) those who commission architecture, (2) those who take architecture seriously as an art form, and (3) especially those who simply enjoy opening their pores to good design and having it affect the way they think and act. So why not share our common interests?

Given such a benificent overview, the editors of *AM* responded by first thinking up what seems a more apt sub-title, the aforementioned *Journal of Design and Creative Living*. Then a few editorial ideas started sprouting, as found in the several new departments introduced in this issue. Such as:

Best Products By Design. Who, architect or otherwise, we wondered, wouldn't like to hear about something that works as well as it looks? Or vice versa?

Designer Profile. Well edited as an architectural subject may be, mightn't the reader find it even more interesting if the architect's thinking and value judgments were presented in a companion story?

Scanning the Media. Plagued as we all are by too little time and too much to read, who wouldn't welcome a regular feature that draws on an array of quality periodicals for the gist—just the gist—of their most thought-provoking articles?

A Talent for Living. Who doesn't enjoy a success story? Especially one measured by qualitative, rather than material, standards?

Smart Money. Who wouldn't rather spend their shrunken dollars on better, rather than just more? Lest it seem from the above recitation of expanded editorial coverage that *AM* aims to be all things to all people, be assured that we know our place. Or, more exactly, our places. Our places include Minnesota first and foremost, followed by the Upper Midwest, and also those very special regions of the mind and spirit where creative energies flourish. If we can capture a fraction of all who identify with one or more of these places, this magazine will surely experience an embarrassment of riches.

William Houseman
Editor

AUGUST/SEPTEMBER 25

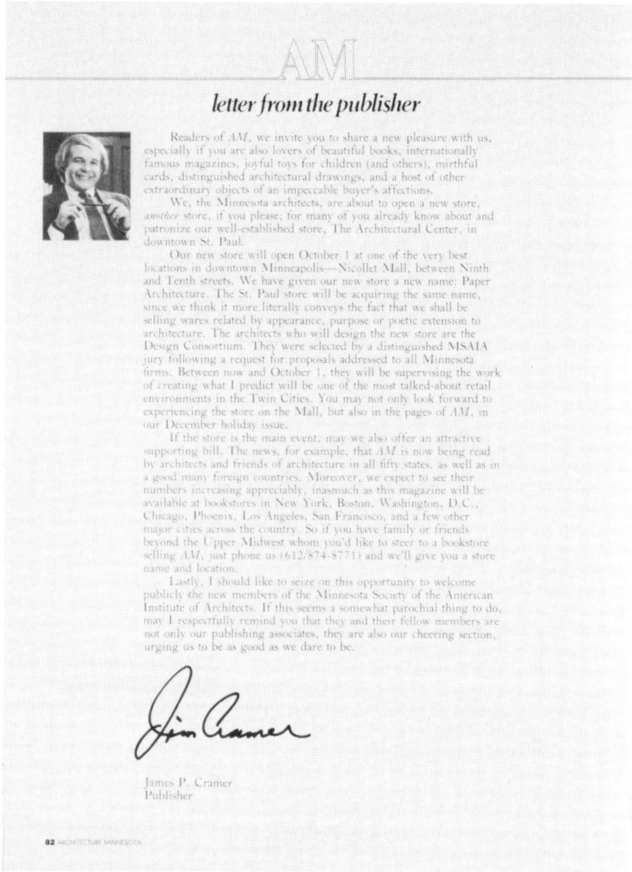

AM

letter from the publisher

Readers of *AM*, we invite you to share a new pleasure with us, especially if you are also lovers of beautiful books, internationally famous magazines, joyful toys for children (and others), mirthful cards, distinguished architectural drawings, and a host of other extraordinary objects of an impeccable buyer's affections.

We, the Minnesota architects, are about to open a new store, *another* store, if you please; for many of you already know about and patronize our well-established store, The Architectural Center, in downtown St. Paul.

Our new store will open October 1 at one of the very best locations in downtown Minneapolis—Nicollet Mall, between Ninth and Tenth streets. We have given our new store a new name: Paper Architecture. The St. Paul store will be acquiring the same name, since we think it more literally conveys the fact that we shall be selling wares related by appearance, purpose or poetic extension to architecture. The architects who will design the new store are the Design Consortium. They were selected by a distinguished MSAIA jury following a request for proposals addressed to all Minnesota firms. Between now and October 1, they will be supervising the work of creating what I predict will be one of the most talked-about retail environments in the Twin Cities. You may not only look forward to experiencing the store on the Mall, but also in the pages of *AM*, in our December holiday issue.

If the store is the main event, may we also offer an attractive supporting bill. The news, for example, that *AM* is now being read by architects and friends of architecture in all fifty states, as well as in a good many foreign countries. Moreover, we expect to see their numbers increasing appreciably, inasmuch as this magazine will be available at bookstores in New York, Boston, Washington, D.C., Chicago, Phoenix, Los Angeles, San Francisco, and a few other major cities across the country. So if you have family or friends beyond the Upper Midwest whom you'd like to steer to a bookstore selling *AM*, just phone us (612/874-8771) and we'll give you a store name and location.

Lastly, I should like to seize on this opportunity to welcome publicly the new members of the Minnesota Society of the American Institute of Architects. If this seems a somewhat parochial thing to do, may I respectfully remind you that they and their fellow members are not only our publishing associates, they are also our cheering section, urging us to be as good as we dare to be.

James P. Cramer
Publisher

82 ARCHITECTURE MINNESOTA

Architecture Minnesota, Bruce Rubin

Two editorials in the same issue: similar in style, identical in graphic raw materials, yet how different in effect and tone of voice!

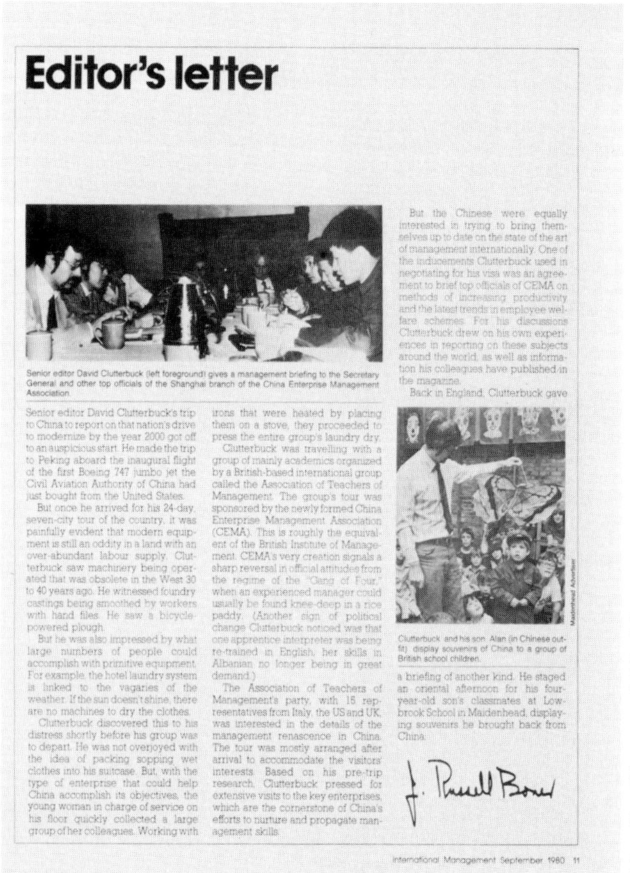

Editor's letter

Senior editor David Clutterbuck (left foreground) gives a management briefing to the Secretary General and other top officials of the Shanghai branch of the China Enterprise Management Association.

Senior editor David Clutterbuck's trip to China to report on that nation's drive to modernize by the year 2000 got off to an auspicious start. He made the trip to Peking aboard the inaugural flight of the first Boeing 747 jumbo jet the Civil Aviation Authority of China had just bought from the United States.

But once he arrived for his 24-day, seven-city tour of the country, it was painfully evident that modern equipment is still an oddity in a land with an over-abundant labour supply. Clutterbuck saw machinery being operated that was obsolete in the West 30 to 40 years ago. He witnessed foundry castings being smoothed by workers with hand files. He saw a bicycle-powered plough.

But he was also impressed by what large numbers of people could accomplish with primitive equipment. For example, the hotel laundry system is linked to the vagaries of the weather. If the sun doesn't shine, there are no machines to dry the clothes.

Clutterbuck discovered this to his distress shortly before his group was to depart. He was not overjoyed with the idea of packing sopping wet clothes into his suitcase. But, with the type of enterprise that could help China accomplish its objectives, the young woman in charge of service on his floor quickly collected a large group of her colleagues. Working with irons that were heated by placing them on a stove, they proceeded to press the entire group's laundry dry.

Clutterbuck was travelling with a group of mainly academics organized by a British-based international group called the Association of Teachers of Management. The group's tour was sponsored by the newly formed China Enterprise Management Association (CEMA). This is roughly the equivalent of the British Insitute of Management. CEMA's very creation signals a sharp reversal in official attitudes from the regime of the "Gang of Four," when an experienced manager could usually be found knee-deep in a rice paddy. (Another sign of political change Clutterbuck noticed was that one apprentice interpreter was being re-trained in English, her skills in Albanian no longer being in great demand.)

The Association of Teachers of Management's party, with 15 representatives from Italy, the US and UK, was interested in the details of the management renascence in China. The tour was mostly arranged after arrival to accommodate the visitors' interests. Based on his pre-trip research, Clutterbuck pressed for extensive visits to the key enterprises, which are the cornerstone of China's efforts to nurture and propagate management skills.

But the Chinese were equally interested in trying to bring themselves up to date on the state of the art of management internationally. One of the inducements Clutterbuck used in negotiating for his visa was an agreement to brief top officials of CEMA on methods of increasing productivity and the latest trends in employee welfare schemes. For his discussions Clutterbuck drew on his own experiences in reporting on these subjects around the world, as well as information his colleagues have published in the magazine.

Back in England, Clutterbuck gave

Maidenhead Advertiser

Clutterbuck and his son Alan (in Chinese outfit) display souvenirs of China to a group of British school children.

a briefing of another kind. He staged an oriental afternoon for his four-year-old son's classmates at Lowbrook School in Maidenhead, displaying souvenirs he brought back from China.

International Management September 1980 11

International Management, Peter Tait

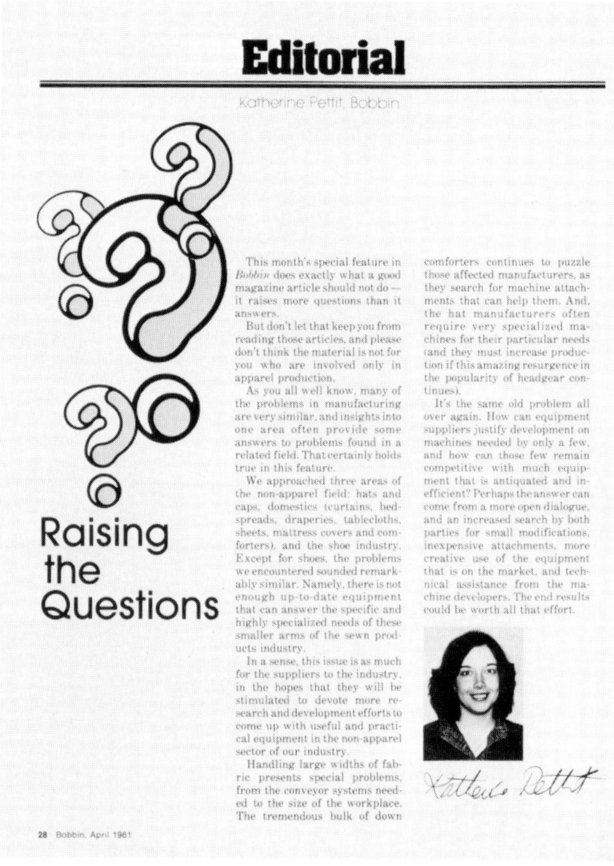

Editorial

Katherine Pettit, Bobbin

Raising the Questions

This month's special feature in *Bobbin* does exactly what a good magazine article should not do — it raises more questions than it answers.

But don't let that keep you from reading those articles, and please don't think the material is not for you who are involved only in apparel production.

As you all well know, many of the problems in manufacturing are very similar, and insights into one area often provide some answers to problems found in a related field. That certainly holds true in this feature.

We approached three areas of the non-apparel field: hats and caps, domestics (curtains, bedspreads, draperies, tablecloths, sheets, mattress covers and comforters), and the shoe industry. Except for shoes, the problems we encountered sounded remarkably similar. Namely, there is not enough up-to-date equipment that can answer the specific and highly specialized needs of these smaller arms of the sewn products industry.

In a sense, this issue is as much for the suppliers to the industry, in the hopes that they will be stimulated to devote more research and development efforts to come up with useful and practical equipment in the non-apparel sector of our industry.

Handling large widths of fabric presents special problems, from the conveyor systems needed to the size of the workplace. The tremendous bulk of down comforters continues to puzzle those affected manufacturers, as they search for machine attachments that can help them. And, the hat manufacturers often require very specialized machines for their particular needs (and they must increase production if this amazing resurgence in the popularity of headgear continues).

It's the same old problem all over again. How can equipment suppliers justify development on machines needed by only a few, and how can those few remain competitive with much equipment that is antiquated and inefficient? Perhaps the answer can come from a more open dialogue, and an increased search by both parties for small modifications, inexpensive attachments, more creative use of the equipment that is on the market, and technical assistance from the machine developers. The end results could be worth all that effort.

28 Bobbin, April 1981

Bobbin, Sisi Sims

Photos illustrating background of major story ... typographic symbols illustrating headline

"With all thy getting get understanding"

Fact and Comment
By Malcolm S. Forbes, Editor-in-Chief

WHERE'S THE ECONOMY GOING TO BE AT THIS NEW YEAR'S END?

MORE OF THOSE COMPANIES WITH CASH IN THE HAND

PAYING A DIVIDEND WHEN YOU'RE STRUGGLING

IT'S NO LONGER SHOOT-OUT TIME EVERY NOON

PRESCIENT STOCK PREDICTOR TISCH SEES A SIGN

THE ONLY THING WRONG WITH THE VIDEO GAME CRAZE

THIS REALLY *IS* AN OPTIMIST

THE MEMORY OF HAPPY MOMENTS
is often even happier.

ACT OF FAITH
To view the end as a beginning.

REAGAN'S YEAR OF TESTING
By M.S. Forbes Jr.

Forbes, Everett Halvorsen

Two successive right-hand pages of commentaries; generously leaded type, centered on the pages makes this mini-section appear different from the rest of the issue.

Preface

Philip Sheehan
Philip Brown Sheehan
Editor, The McGraw-Hill HomeBook

The McGraw-Hill HomeBook **11**

McGraw-Hill Homebook

Dignified, mood-setting editorial message treated as formal frontispiece/preface.

141

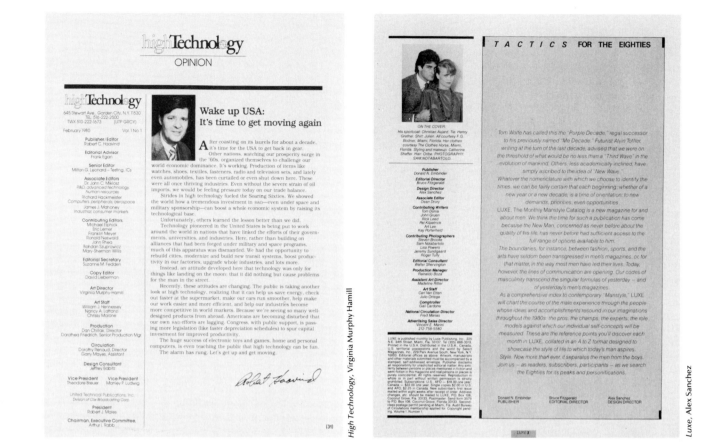

High Technology, Virginia Murphy Hamill

Luxe, Alex Sanchez

Three right-hand ↑ and three left-handy pages: mastheads usually close to gutter; note variety of material accommodated

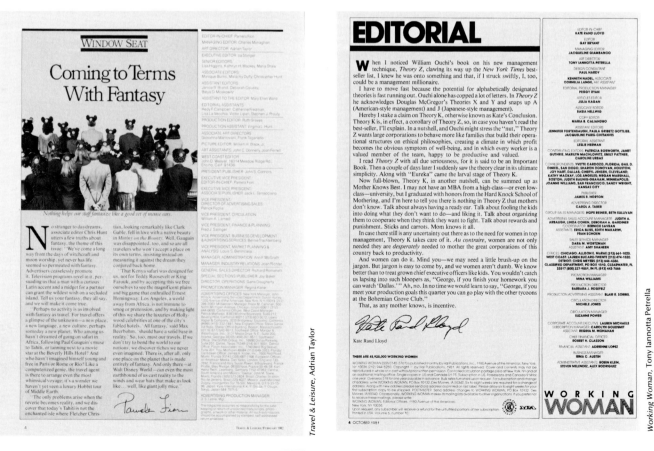

Travel & Leisure, Adrian Taylor

Working Woman, Tony Iannotta Petrella

LAST-LEFT IN BOOK

EDITOR: Paul J. Taylor
MANAGING EDITOR: Kelly A. Anthony
ADVERTISING/BUSINESS MANAGER: Janet Cestaro Mahoney
ART DIRECTOR: Richard A. Craig
ASSOCIATE EDITOR: Barbara Alice MacRobie
PHOTOGRAPHY DIRECTOR: Ovidio Gallo
CONTRIBUTORS TO THIS ISSUE: Mary Bishop, Dr. Rene G. DeSaulniers, Hilda Fried, Dr. Jeffrey Gold, Dr. Douglas W. MacRae, Dr. William H. Pehl, Rene R. Rivard and Elise Vider
CONTRIBUTING PHOTOGRAPHER: Doris Barclay

St. Raphael's **Better Health** magazine is published bimonthly by the Hospital of St. Raphael, 1450 Chapel Street, New Haven, CT 06511. Telephone (203) 789-3912 for advertising and business offices, and (203) 789-3507 for editorial offices.

Views expressed are those of the authors and do not necessarily reflect the opinions of the Hospital Board of Trustees or administration.

Better Health is designed to promote your understanding of how to maintain good health. It is not intended to help diagnose illness or to replace professional medical advice. Your family doctor should be consulted about health problems.

Circulation policy: More than 100,000 copies circulated free of charge six times a year to Hospital friends and other interested readers living in the Greater New Haven area. All others, $6 year subscription.

St. Raphael's

Better Health

November/December 1981

To our readers

Something different. **Better Health** usually focuses on the personal side of health care, featuring facts to help you stay healthy. An article in this issue jumps to the other end of the medical spectrum by looking at one of medicine's biggest advances in technology.

We call it "CAT." Its real name is "Computerized Axial Tomography" scanning but, by whatever name, this sophisticated form of radiology looks and sounds like a creation straight from "Flash Gordon" or "Star Wars." But science fiction it is not. I recommend investing a few moments to learn about this amazing diagnostic tool.

For years after CAT scanning first came on the scene more than a decade ago, it was not looked upon as the marvel it is today. Critics said it was just a "new toy" for doctors; another "expensive gadget" for hospitals to compete for; more "unnecessary" tests for patients to pay for. They were wrong, as you will read in the article by Mary Bishop.

The first patient was scanned on St. Raphael's CAT in September, after nearly 10 years trying to obtain regulatory agency approval to get a scanner. An end-all? Hardly.

Even more advanced technology is already available, in use elsewhere and being looked at by our physicians. For the present, CAT scanning is now readily available in Greater New Haven. Let's hope you never need it, but knowing about it in advance is a good idea.

• This issue marks the second anniversary of **Better Health.** Many of you have told us you enjoy our magazine. Please continue to let us know your opinions.

• It's early, but this will be my last chance to wish most of you a prayerful Thanksgiving and a joyous Christmastide. Enjoy your holidays to the fullest!

Sister Anne Virginie
President

Contents

Features		Departments	
2	Miracles of CAT Scanning	14	Caring
6	Coping With Ol' Man Winter	10	Forum Roundtable
19	How To Put The Economic Recovery Act To Work For You	32	Capsules
23	Are You An Alcoholic?		
26	Dealing With The Angry Child		

On the cover: The thrills, spills and ills of winter skiing in New England are dramatically captured in this photograph courtesy of Olin Corporation, Middletown, Connecticut.

Better Health, Richard A. Craig

Editorials

A big year for savers

The first year of the Reagan Administration has brought revolutionary changes in the ground rules of personal finance, as well as in the balance between investment and consumption in the U. S. economy. Tax reform has replaced the old penalties on saving with substantial incentives. BUSINESS WEEK's annual review of the investment outlook, which begins on page 75, shows that cautious savers, ambitious investors, and adventuresome speculators will all find that the new laws open major opportunities to them.

The liberalized Individual Retirement Accounts alone offer such generous tax shelters that they should prove a major source of new capital for the expansion and modernization of U. S. industry. And the across-the-board reductions of personal income tax rates scheduled for 1982 and 1983 will increase the net return on investments generally. Beyond that, for everything from rehabilitating old dwellings to speculating in financial futures, there are specific, if sometimes little-known, provisions that will make all sorts of deals more appealing on an after-tax basis.

Most investors, however, will have to count on collecting their rewards at some time in the future, not tomorrow morning. The U. S. is going into 1982 gripped by a painful recession and faced with the prospect of no real gain in the economy for at least some months. The determined effort of the Federal Reserve to bring the growth of the money supply under strict control is no less painful because it is long overdue. And in spite of the rising rolls of unemployed and the virtual collapse of such key industries as autos and housing, the Fed cannot yet loosen the monetary reins. It must convince consumers and investors alike that inflation is winding down. Otherwise, all the efforts of the Reagan Administration to promote capital formation will be washed out in a rush to get out of the dollar and into goods.

Times such as these are hard on investors' nerves, but the opportunities are there nevertheless. The revolution has truly been launched. The rewards the economy offers to investors with foresight and a modicum of courage are greater than at any time in the postwar era.

A tough test of policy

The coming year—the second year in the White House for Ronald Reagan—will be a crucial test of his economic theories and the policies they have produced. Most of the essential pieces prescribed by supply-side economics are now in place. Substantial tax reform for corporations has already been enacted, and massive tax cuts for individuals are scheduled for the next two years. The role of government in the U. S. economy has been reduced, and federal spending has been scaled down, except for military programs. If the private sector now responds with a vigorous expansion, financed by the new funds the tax cuts make available for investment, then the President and his advisers will get the strong second-quarter recovery they are predicting. If, instead, consumers mistrust the dollar and rush to put their money into goods, inflation will pick up speed, interest rates will set new records, and the economy will be threatened with a prolonged depression.

Paradoxically, the response of the private sector will be determined in large measure by the credibility of the President's promise to bring inflation under control, and at the same time, the ability of the Administration to check inflation will depend on the economy's response to its policies. The circularity—or feedback relationship—inherent in this situation leaves the President no choice. He must scale down the enormous deficits now projected for the federal budget in the years ahead. If he does not, he will be in danger of touching off a new round of inflation that could wreck the economy, discredit his economic policies, and demolish the Republican Party.

To assuage the psychological fears about these deficits by consumers and business people, the single most effective action President Reagan could take would be to accelerate the decontrol of natural gas prices and impose a windfall profits tax on old gas. The resulting revenue would go a long way to reduce the size of the deficits, and the increased exploration would be a stimulus for the economy. At the same time, the U. S. would take one more step toward solving its long-term energy problems.

Realism at the UAW

The executive board of the United Auto Workers showed a good deal of common sense, as well as a willingness to face reality, when it voted to allow union representatives to reopen agreements with General Motors Corp. and Ford Motor Co. before the expiration of the current contracts next September. The UAW leadership must now follow up by persuading the locals at GM and Ford that they will lose far more than they will gain by waiting to the last minute to negotiate changes that will help the U. S. producers meet the competition of imports.

The union has already made significant concessions to Chrysler Corp., which was threatened with collapse. But GM and Ford cannot hold their place in the market when Japanese carmakers have an advantage over them of roughly $8 an hour in labor costs. A gap of that size cannot be eliminated in a single move. But long-term contracts with a temporary wage freeze, limited future wage increases, severely restricted cost-of-living adjustments, and reductions in paid time off and health-benefit costs could narrow the gap significantly. In return, GM and Ford should offer some kind of job security tied to company performance, perhaps through profit-sharing.

The UAW says that, because of the Christmas holidays, the earliest it could convene the GM and Ford councils to make final decisions on reopening would be after Jan. 1. This should give the leadership time to sound out rank-and-file attitudes and point out the facts to local leaders. It should make the most of the opportunity. U. S. labor can no longer afford to take the attitude that negotiating for the survival of a company would jeopardize a union's position as an adversary institution.

Business Week, John R. Vogler

Editorial opinion page usually covers several subjects

EDITOR-IN-CHIEF Henry Anatole Grunwald
PRESIDENT J. Richard Munro
CHAIRMAN OF THE BOARD Ralph P. Davidson
EXECUTIVE VICE PRESIDENT Clifford J. Grum
CHAIRMAN, EXECUTIVE COMMITTEE James R. Shepley
EDITORIAL DIRECTOR Ralph Graves
GROUP VICE PRESIDENT, MAGAZINES Kelso F. Sutton
VICE CHAIRMAN Arthur Temple

FORTUNE

Founder Henry R. Luce, 1898-1967

MANAGING EDITOR William S. Rukeyser
ASSOCIATE MANAGING EDITOR Daniel Seligman
EXECUTIVE EDITOR Richard Armstrong
ASSISTANT MANAGING EDITORS William Bowen, Allan T. Demaree, Paul H. Weaver
ART DIRECTOR Ronald N. Campbell
BOARD OF EDITORS [illegible]
ASSOCIATE EDITORS [illegible]
REPORTERS [illegible]
CORRESPONDENTS [illegible]
ART STAFF [illegible]
COPY DESK [illegible]
COPY PROCESSING Joseph L. Mazella (manager)
PRODUCTION STAFF Sidney Skar (manager), Maureen Mallon Cluen (assistant manager)
EDITORIAL SERVICES Christiana Walford (director)

PUBLISHER Edward Patrick Lenahan
ADVERTISING DIRECTOR James B. Hoeter
BUSINESS MANAGER Marie Chenchetti
PROMOTION DIRECTOR Howard Kaplan
CIRCULATION DIRECTOR Lucy Pulien Wenner

The Editor's Desk

Campbell and Fasciano

It seems that no matter where art director Ronald Campbell goes, no matter what time of year, editors, designers, artists, photographers, and sundry laymen all want to know how he's planning to illustrate the next FORTUNE 500 cover. The 500 numerals, after all, have been rendered in compacted garbage, neon lights, molten bronze, and in the lit windows of the Time & Life Building on a dark and rainy night. "After so many years, it's getting increasingly difficult to come up with a new idea," says Campbell, who has been in charge for the past eight.

This year's new idea, to represent the industries in which most FORTUNE 500 corporations are classified, seemed simple enough. Originally the plan was to put models of easily identified products of these industries into a construction of the number 500. But early on Campbell decided to use real, full-scale objects, and he insisted that each of them be made by a FORTUNE 500 company. "Doing it with real things seemed much more rewarding than doing it in miniature or in painting," he says.

First, Campbell and free-lance artist Nicholas Fasciano, who has worked on three other 500 covers, selected items that would be easy to manage. For example, they chose a Black & Decker chain saw to represent the industrial- and farm-equipment industry instead of a tractor. Then, art researcher Leslie Yoo invited several companies, like IBM, GE, and Bausch & Lomb, to lend their products to the effort. Only with the objects in hand could Fasciano determine the size of the construction—the Formica-coated plywood structures stand four feet tall—and get to work building it.

Campbell's bias toward reality ended when it came to selecting the background. He chose a 10-by-20-foot canvas of painted sky done by former set designer Sarah Oliphant. "Now that we've found a sky, we might try skywriting," says Campbell, who figures it's never too early to start planning the next FORTUNE 500 cover.

Richard Armstrong
Executive Editor

Fortune, Ronald N. Campbell

THE LAST WORD
by Dick Lehnert

Feeding the hungry world: Some thoughts on food exports

Americans take pride in their high standards of morality.

We drove from office a President whose standards fell short. In many other countries he'd have held office for life — and made his children heirs to the position.

At the next opportunity, we elected a born-again Christian just to make sure of his morals. Religion has never been a guarantee of high morals, but Americans tend to associate the two. After all, America is the most church-going and the most God-fearing nation in the world, and that's the truth.

Combine our religiosity with our work ethic, and it makes a fearsome combination. We know what's right, we work like crazy and if those who don't would just move aside, everything would be right in the world.

Perhaps, then, that article by Ron Ferrell on page 12 of this issue seems an unkind cut. He says that American agriculture's overproduction is immoral because, in a thoughtless way, heedless of our children's needs, agriculture takes valuable, non-renewable resources and squanders them to produce commodities people aren't willing to pay the production price to get.

The export market

That thesis not only provides food for thought, it can be vastly extended into an even more intriguing area — that of food exports.

It has always baffled Americans that people like the Russians could have the gall to call us imperialistic aggressors when we invade virtually nobody.

But the point could be made that, as economic aggressors, especially in agriculture, American food has been an instrument of economic disruption in countries not sophisticated enough to handle it.

And on that front, the more moral we try to be, the less moral we seem to become.

Put yourselves for a minute into the shoes of an Indian farmer. Your crops have been poor and, just like an American farmer, you expect a higher price for what you have produced. But your price doesn't go up significantly, because the Americans are there, hovering over your market, ready for "moral reasons" to inundate your market with food not only cheaper than you can produce it — but cheaper than the Americans themselves can produce it.

You're trying to run a business, but your acreage is small, your varieties poor and your fertilizer costs are high because you have to compete with the Americans to buy it.

Then in comes American food at discount prices. Pretty soon you have to act like an American. Either you must buy out your neighbor and make your farm bigger, borrow money to buy fertilizer and better varieties, or move to Calcutta with the other 15 million already there to wait for the food ships to come in.

The American way

It is in this economic way that we are imperialists, for we cause people the world over to disrupt their traditional agricultural systems and join the American way.

And we insist that that's right, not just for India but for all countries.

Many other countries don't agree, and they make us angry.

American dairymen, for example, are convinced they could drive cows off the European continent if they were just allowed to compete freely. Instead, we find some of our own dairymen pushed out of business by skillful European traders who insist not only that we don't try to take their markets — but we open ours instead.

A bunch of dumpers, we complain. But actually both Europeans and Americans are dumpers of food produced at less than the cost of production onto the world market. The one difference is, European farmers are subsidized so they don't take it on the chin and our farmers are not.

A "free market," then, appears to be one in which farmers lose money and a "subsidized market" is one in which the subsidizing country loses the money.

The planned economies of the Communist world also don't play fairly, for, like the Europeans, they consider national goals. They buy or sell food based upon some game plan American farmers are seldom privy to.

The case of Japan

The problem American farmers have is a "mental set" problem of trying to see almost all countries as being like Japan. Japan falls far short of feeding itself, so it becomes a large market for food.

In this context, it is easier to understand the fierce competitiveness of the American Soybean Association, which resists American government loan guarantees and support prices on soybeans. Japan is open territory and the competition is with Brazil as to which country will get the market.

But few countries are like Japan. American farmers have been misled into thinking they can have a dramatic impact on feeding the world. In fact, we provide food for about 350 million people, a little less than 10% of the world's population.

But Americans are convinced of the morality of it all. We look at the low yields and inefficient methods of the Third World farmers and say, "If they all hung up their scythes, who'd miss 'em."

One must not allow oneself to be carried away by American agricultural capacity merely because we have few people to feed relative to our productive resources. But that does not mean we can drive the Indian farmers out of business and handily feed India.

In recent years, more people have come to see that. One is John Hannah. When he was president of Michigan State University, he hewed to the line that American farmers should be cut loose to attack the world food problem. Now, he says, Americans must be more careful not to disrupt the traditional agricultural systems of other countries — for the primary feeding base of any country must remain its own farmers.

Sometimes it's hard to see that one could be more moral by raising the price of what he sells than by lowering it.

"Food for Peace" can be "Food for Revolution."

What to do?

So what is the solution? Partly it's a matter of defining the problem, which is twofold:

First, American farmers tend to have trouble seeing the hungry world out there with all the food here. There is a natural tendency to discount that which is surplus.

Second, our own citizens see no reason why they should pay more for food than foreigners do, so they want the discount price for their own.

Top thinkers at USDA are considering the problem and you may see a proposal this year for a "two-price" policy: pricing exports higher, combined with government control over food exports.

This poses some real dangers for farmers and, thus, brings us back to why we aired Ron Ferrell's views in the first place. If such a mechanism is set up — and it should be — farmers should have control of it. ■

Michigan Farmer, Raymond L. Gibson

Personal editorial opinion page in tabloid-size publication

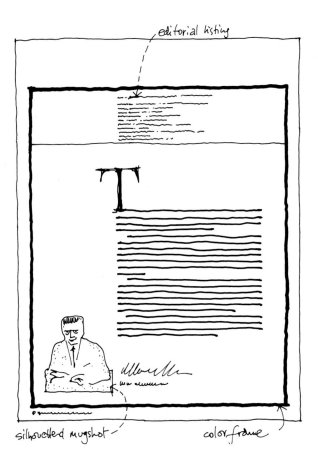

editorial listing

silhouetted mugshot

color frame

unexpeded color "shadows"

MEMO

LOGO

EDITORIAL / DATE

Short headline

LOGOTYPE

The headline of this piece

EDITORIAL

editorial

The headline hides here

Headline goes here

THE VIEW FROM HERE

p

thelast word

editorial

145

OPENERS

This is a tricky page to handle, but it needs handling well. It announces the start of the feature section — the main and most valuable part of the product. Here is where the editors put their maximum effort and where their work ought to receive greatest visibility and most memorable presentation. So it ought to be started off with a **bang** instead of with a *whimper.*

But the trouble is that the single-page, right-hand opener is small. Constricted. Vertical. And it appears opposite an ad, which requires that the gutter space that separates the two pages be widened. Thus this essential visual buffer encroaches upon the page further, leaving just a narrow vertical sliver within which to display the wares. That is why the page is tricky to handle.

Another consideration to bear in mind: since this is a page that recurs in every issue, there may be good reason to work out some format pattern that can be repeated from issue to issue, creating recognition value that will attract attention, and thus help overcome some of the limitations imposed by the constricted space available. The disadvantage of such a pattern, of course, is that the pattern itself can become a straitjacket, preventing the editors from moving in the way the subject and material demand. The format must therefore be flexible enough to allow maneuvering within a clearly articulated framework of recognition-symbols. (See page 162).

Some publications solve the problem by using the first-right as an editorial page (see p.136). Strictly from the point of view of effectiveness of presentation, this tends to work well. The page can be designed to be a definite break from the ad opposite; it can have a clearly recognizable standard format; it can function nicely as a starting signal. But an editorial page tends to be a weak introduction to a hard-hitting feature section unless the subject of the editorial happens to deal with the same material as the subsequent feature stories. How often does that happen, though? Normally an editorial deals with a subject other than those covered in the feature stories. So you can say that, although an editorial placed on the first-right works well graphically, journalistically it is unlikely to do so, except on rare occasions.

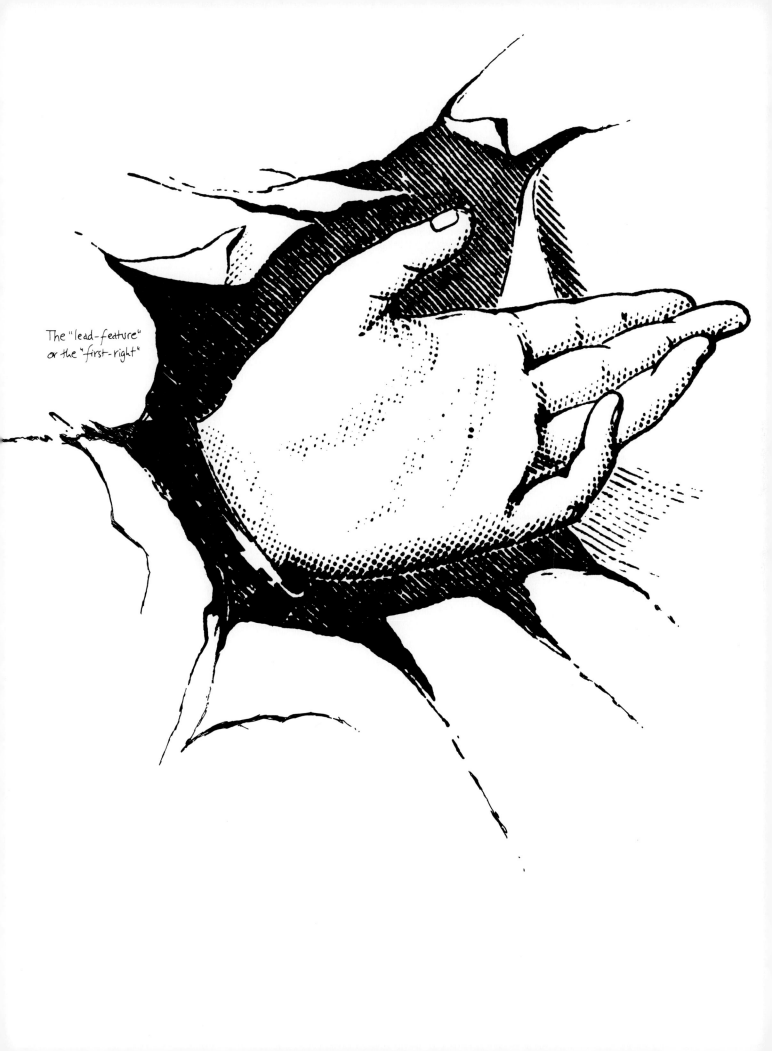

The "lead-feature" or the "first-right"

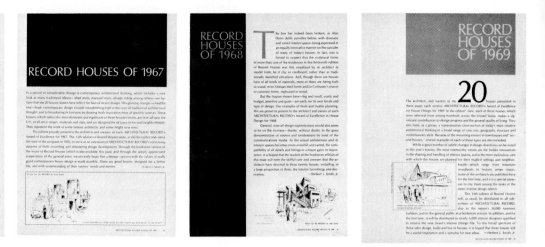

Sixteen solutions to an annual problem: how to make the first-right opener of this special annual issue different from last year's, yet show the identical material in just about the same way, in the same proportions every time. (Also in the same typeface, except in one aberrant case in 1972). The purpose of showing these is to prove that ingenuity can be used to useful effect in seemingly hopeless situations.

Perhaps editorials are red herrings placed in the path of clear thought. Perhaps they belong elsewhere. The final decision is dependent on the publication's character, and so it becomes a strategic decision made by the editor in light of clear analysis of the material, market, and goals.

To give the page its required poster value (startling visibility) and tie it in with the feature section for which it is the starter, it should be designed to be as simple and UNbusy as possible. Not only does this mean that the design must be "edited down" to *appear* simple, but also that the elements to be accommodated on the page must be equally edited down to their irreducible minimum. It is perfectly true that *less is more*. The less there is on the page, the greater the likelihood of that which is there being noticed. Extraneous elements obfuscate that one major eye-catching and brain-appealing element that really matters to the story. The result is lack of attention, low impact, failure to grasp an opportunity — and a nasty aftertaste of messiness.

When the material has been edited down to that minimum, the residue must be thought through further in terms that will define the hierarchy of importances: the most important element will probably be the headline (ideally nice and terse, so that it can be set in strong type). The secondary element will be — what: the deck? the byline of the distinguished author? the picture of the author? the illustration? The tertiary element: the text? It all depends. There is no one hierarchy better than another. What matters very much, though, is to articulate clearly what the hierarchy is in each specific instance, so that the designer can express it and pass it on to the reader in easily understandable form. The reader should get an orderly sequence of thoughts instead of an undigested jumble. The very orderliness helps to get the idea across quickly and effortlessly, and it increases the likelihood that the editors will evoke the reader response they want. If the page is a jumble, then the poor reader will have to work his way through it (assuming he'll bother to begin it), and that involves time, effort, and risk. After all, the reader can easily come to a conclusion different from the one the editors had in mind for him — or he can flip the page.

Many publications run a miniature logo, some accompanied with issue date, somewhere at the top of the page. This is helpful in reassuring the reader that this page is, indeed, editorial matter rather than an ad (should such reassurance be needed, although one hopes not). But the second logo has a more important, subliminal function: it helps to define this opener as a sort of secondary front cover, signaling the beginning of something. But there must be enough material following this page to make such a subcover worthy of its name. Twelve pages is the minimum; anything less looks foolish.

The typography of the page ought to be consistent with the pages that follow. It is better to design the page using the graphic materials (type, etc.) used throughout the publication than it is to change them in order to make the page more "visible." Certainly the body type-face and headline typography should be the same, forming a visual bridge between the opener and the pages that follow. The only difference should be a slightly more flamboyant design for the opener. The body copy could, perhaps, be double width (two columns, leaving the gutter column open as a moat separating the matter on this page from the ad opposite). And the copy could, perhaps, start with an interesting initial, or tiny postage stamp-size picture, as a focal point.

Illustrations are, like everything else on the first-right, hard to handle. The opener, by virtue of being an opener and therefore somewhat different from the normal page, is in a position where unusual or atypical illustrations might make good sense: mood shots or background-to-the-story pictures. The trouble is that the more atypical the pictures are, the more difficult it becomes to recognize them as "editorial" matter and the easier it becomes to mistake them for ads. Obviously that sort of confusion ought to be avoided. Such unusual pictures ought, perhaps, to be reserved for use on spread-openers where there is more space available and only editorial matter to rival. On the limited space of a first-right, the precious and unusual picture is likely to be squeezed into insignificance — and thus wasted. Perhaps the ideal place for such a picture is at the very end, as a tailpiece, big and worthily displayed. Besides,

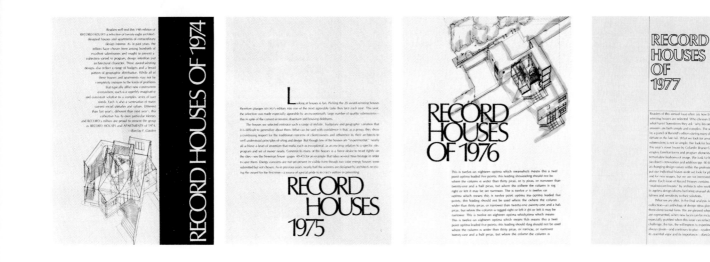

such a tailpiece can also act as an opener to all the many ornery
readers who insist on reading magazines back-to-front!

The best illustration to use on the first-right is one that echoes
the front cover — perhaps even reproducing the cover in miniature.
(Assuming, that is, that the cover and the first story have some
relationship to each other.) The reason is, simply, that the front
cover image is already established in the mind of the reader as
important simply by virtue of being on the cover . . . and therefore
it is likely to have quick recognition/remembrance value that is
useful in attracting the reader's attention to the page.

But, given the dictates of the small space available, experience
shows it is wiser to depend on words rather than images to catch
the reader's attention, except in very special situations. On the pages
that follow, there are a number of examples of opening page
treatments, both with and without pictures, that might be useful as
comparisons and idea-starters. Page arrangements should always be
secondary, however; the material itself must come first. If the first-
right is well edited, well organized, well articulated in its hierarchy
of importances, then a logical, expressive, and effective page
arrangement will grow out of these qualities naturally.

What about spread-openers? Many publications do not have first-
right positions at all, preferring to open the feature section on a
spread. The magazines lose the "preferred positions" that sell at
premium cost to advertisers this way, but they gain the capability to
create greater editorial impact. The scale of the full spread is far
larger than twice-a-single-page. This is not just because that
necessary river of (wasted) white space in the gutter is now at the
disposal of the designer; nor simply because there is no ad across the
gutter to fight against — though this is certainly a distinct advantage;
but, more importantly, because the shape of the space is horizontal
instead of vertical, that is, broad, instead of tall. And a wide space,
such as two contiguous pages, is capable of far greater design impact
than a narrow, single page. This design capacity is covered in detail
in Chapter 2 of *Editing by Design* and need not be discussed here.
However, one point is well worth making with respect to the
opening of a feature section on a spread: the illustration can have

tremendous impact (by virtue of giant sizing). As a result, such spread-openers can, indeed, be infinitely more effective than first-rights. BUT there has to be a picture worthy of such play every time. This is, alas, not always the case, except in publications whose stock in trade happens to be highly pictorial (such as architectural magazines, for instance). Unless a supply of blockbusters is assured, it is perhaps the better part of wisdom to avoid committing the publication to an opening of this kind as standard operating procedure.

A number of publications have predicated their story openers — including the first, i.e., feature-section opener — on a repetitive series of standardized arrangements, where the left-hand page has a full-bleed illustration acting as frontispiece, and the right-hand page carries the headline and text. This system can work well and is easier to produce simply because the graphic image is smaller. That illustration must be reliably exciting every single time, however. This is the same as saying that the publication must have lots of money available to spend on frontispiece illustrations — and talent and imagination to create them. If these requirements are problematic (and they are for most publications), then this ideal solution tends to be a trifle less than ideal.

If stories must open on left-hand pages, however, there are two possible variations for openers, depending on whether the stories are interrelated as part of a package or whether they are unrelated ones.

If they are related, then everything possible to make that interrelationship evident ought to be done on every opener. The first opener must be designed as a pattern setter, and the subsequent openers must become repetitions of the form at smaller scale, or variations of it, clearly recognizable but differing in detail. An example of both the repetitive and the theme-and-variation technique are shown on pages **168** and **172**. Both are nonpictorial, though both are distinctly visual, using graphic symbols and type to create recognizable character.

If the stories are unrelated, then the first opener ought NOT to be a pattern-setter. It is better to vary the openers as much as possible in format, so that the reader perceives story "starts" as clearly as possible.

Big pictures as openers: vertical barrier

The large vertical picture is an excellent barrier between the ad opposite and the start of the feature section if two conditions exist: (1) the ad must be in color and the picture in black-and-white ✳ so that there is an immediate difference between the two images that splits them from each other, and (2) the direction of the image in the picture itself must force the viewer's eye to the right, drawing it towards the head and text. If the picture in this example were flopped left to right, it would pull the reader's attention towards the ad opposite — distinctly not the purpose of the exercise.

The headline typography also should be quite large, to act as backup attention-getter if the vertical picture in the gutter is missed by the reader who merely flips the pages while holding the magazine by the spine with the other hand, and missing the picture altogether.

THE NEW BOSTON CITY HALL

Now complete except for the square, Boston's great new landmark, begun during the administration of Mayor John F. Collins, will be dedicated this month. A triumph for Gerhard M. Kallmann, Noel M. McKinnell and Edward F. Knowles—three comparatively young and, except for Kallmann, unknown architects who, in 1962, won the chance to build it in a national competition—the Boston City Hall will increasingly become the focus of wide-spread interest and will be evaluated from many points of view.

Those who may be perplexed by the building can be grateful to Kallmann, the eldest member of the team. Some years ago he produced a number of speeches and manifestos, establishing the philosophical, ethical and stylistic criteria by which his work, when he would eventually get some, could be interpreted, understood and judged. The writing of manifestos, as everyone knows, had been almost a daily activity for the founders of the modern movement —masters whom the most gifted young architects quite naturally hope to supplant— but for Kallmann's generation it was a lost art. His was almost a solitary voice because he was among the first with something new to say. Born in Germany in 1915, and like the English-born McKinnell, British-trained, he was known to the British and American architectural avant-garde as a brilliant spokes-

✳ or vice versa!

152

... or horizontal magnet for the eye?

A large picture used as an enticement for the eye and attention of the reader, must have intrinsic interest as well as size. Just making any old picture big cannot be expected to do the requisite job: the picture must also be journalistically meaningful. If it manages to fill the bill well enough, then the typography beneath it can be quite small, since the picture itself can be depended on to yield the poster effect. The numeral one, here in bright red, is also a subsidiary aid in signaling the start of something (obviously some sort of series). Incidentally, the numbering trick is used so often that it can become a bit of a bore, yet I have never succeeded in persuading editors to substitute A, B, C for the ever-present 1, 2, 3. They maintain that alphabetizing is too obscure a system. One wonders why?

Align *Align*

Two elegant new buildings by Skidmore, Owings & Merrill's Chicago office, with Myron Goldsmith partner-in-charge of design, use carefully detailed steel to reflect an existing college campus, and to demonstrate a steel company's products.

1 A NEW MULTI-USE GYMNASIUM FOR I.I.T.

This shimmery, glass-skinned sports facility remarkably maintains its own individuality, yet wholeheartedly echoes the spirit of the well known steel and glass architecture which already exists on the Illinois Institute of Technology campus. A very small site posed some severe space problems to incorporate all the large recreation areas needed. This was solved by building up to three levels below grade: the lower levels contain all locker areas, swimming pool, handball courts and mechanical rooms; the upper level provides for many spectator sports and for convocations.

ARTHUR KEATING HALL, Illinois Institute of Technology, Chicago. Architects-engineers: *Skidmore, Owings & Merrill (Chicago)—Myron Goldsmith, partner-in-charge of design; Kenneth Mullin, project manager, Michael Pado, project designer; Paul Marxen, job captain; contractor: A. J. Maggio Co.*

Most effective starting signal: a different stock

There is no question that a colored stock or textured stock insert makes the start of a new section quite obvious. This holds true for feature sections as it does for "flash forms" (see page 82). The book often breaks at this point, and combined with a different stock suggestive of a different product, these characteristics scream for attention. If, then, the material that is displayed on the paper is in fact a little more special than average (such as this, which is an opener to an eight-page album presentation of beautiful drawings) the impact is undeniable.

ARCHITECTURAL RECORD
APRIL 1967

Paul Rudolph's design for Stafford Harbor, Virginia, a new town that will be located on the Potomac about 38 miles south of Washington, D.C., reinforces the natural topography by placing the major groups of buildings along the ridges and harbor, leaving the intervening valleys free.

A new town that conserves the landscape

... or, as a substitute, a background color

If a different stock cannot be used because of cost, time, binding, or any other technical or practical reason, then a good substitute can be "homemade" different stock: the regular paper tinted with colored ink, used solid or in tints, or even plain old black, used solid or in tints of gray. The purpose is to create an illusion of differentness, using whatever means may be available. One step higher in sophistication is the use of some sort of pattern as background. (See *Editing by Design*, page 206). To retain the full illusion of separateness, however, it is essential — if obvious — that consistent stock treatment throughout the entire presentation must be retained. You cannot persuade the reader that your pages are of-a-piece if the ink that is supposed to tie them together is pink on one page and purple on another. And, again, as in the example opposite, the graphic techniques applied to the pages must be appropriate to the material disposed thereon. Here, for instance, the pictures are in color against a solid black background — and this is the first of twelve pages so treated. Black background is ideal for showing off color pictures, since it makes the colors appear rich and jewel-like.

What makes people like places? David Kenneth Specter, now a practicing architect in New York, used an Arnold W. Brunner Scholarship of the Architectural League of New York to look for design guidelines in some of Europe's great places, and took hundreds of photographs to show how people react to them. His photographs and commentary in this presentation suggest

SOME ESSENTIALS OF SUCCESSFUL URBAN SPACE

BARE, BARREN, UNCROSSABLE, MERELY EXISTING AS THE "SPACE BETWEEN" . . .

BECOMES SOMEHOW HUMAN, APPROACHABLE, LIVE, URBAN . . .

AND MAY EVEN ACHIEVE A SENSE OF PLACE.

The art of making this happen requires manipulation of both intangible and tangible elements of the urban environment. These elements—though often occurring accidentally—function in predictable and positive ways, and are a legitimate concern of the designer.

ARCHITECTURAL RECORD *January 1969* 131

Boxing the elements: separately

Any sort of pattern that is clearly discernible can be used to make the opener different, and thus, more noticeable. Whatever pattern is established on the opening page, however, must carry over onto the succeeding pages. For the story opener is never seen as an isolated, static unit but as a unit within a fairly fast flow of units (the speed depending on how interested the reader is in the material); thus the opener's individual impact must be reinforced by whatever follows it. Besides, if that opener is designed to be exciting, and the excitement is allowed to evaporate on the succeeding pages, each of those succeeding pages will be thought of as yet another opener; the main opener then becomes isolated and begins to "look like an ad" — and the article's impact is concentrated on one page and turns dull elsewhere.

The boxing in the example at right is "internal"; each element is surrounded with its own box — each box, in turn, becomes part of a bigger box arrangement. The net thus created holds the disparate elements together neatly, unifying them into a coherent image. Shown here is the first of a sixteen-page story in which all elements are encased in hairline boxes similar to the ones here.

Headline in orange/red

6 INTERIORS

Not too many years ago, the phrase "architectural interiors" could mean little else than four Barcelona chairs and a glass-topped coffee table set precisely into a pristine room. The six projects which follow indicate that such is not true today. The focus, for instance, on architectural matters at the recent NEOCON meeting in Chicago (see page 38 for a report), is an index of the growing interrelationship of interior design and architecture. Furthermore, many offices are now deeply involved in renovation with its heavy emphasis on interior architecture. The question becomes not who is doing what but how well it is being done. Not every person capable of producing such work is an architect, of course, but the standards are high. One such is sculptress Aleksandra Kasuba, whose New York City apartment, (right), not only presents new and dynamic concepts of interior space, but is realized with extraordinary attention to detail. As the next two pages make clear, it is certainly "interior architecture."

...or within a whole page

Given peculiar material of ragged outline, a simple geometric box enclosing the entire page can be used as an excellent foil. Not only is the raggedness-versus-precision an interesting graphic contrast, but also enclosing generous white spaces is an unexpected technique. The boxing formalizes the design, articulating each element, giving each an edge and demarcation line. What could easily appear as a thrown-together group of pages, is pulled together in a formal fashion. This is the first of eight pages enclosed in a neat, unpretentious box like the one shown here.

Pictures in black and brown duotone

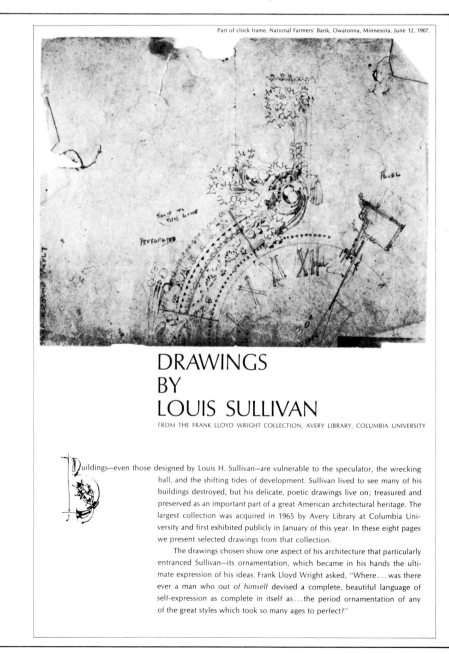

Part of clock frame, National Farmers' Bank, Owatonna, Minnesota, June 12, 1907.

DRAWINGS BY LOUIS SULLIVAN

FROM THE FRANK LLOYD WRIGHT COLLECTION, AVERY LIBRARY, COLUMBIA UNIVERSITY

Buildings—even those designed by Louis H. Sullivan—are vulnerable to the speculator, the wrecking ball, and the shifting tides of development. Sullivan lived to see many of his buildings destroyed, but his delicate, poetic drawings live on; treasured and preserved as an important part of a great American architectural heritage. The largest collection was acquired in 1965 by Avery Library at Columbia University and first exhibited publicly in January of this year. In these eight pages we present selected drawings from that collection.

The drawings chosen show one aspect of his architecture that particularly entranced Sullivan—its ornamentation, which became in his hands the ultimate expression of his ideas. Frank Lloyd Wright asked, "Where...was there ever a man who *out of himself* devised a complete, beautiful language of self-expression as complete in itself as...the period ornamentation of any of the great styles which took so many ages to perfect?"

Full-bleed pictures used as a background for type

Spectacular pictures can be as startling (and thus as useful for openers) as white space or huge type set sideways. If they happen to be color, so much the better. But a good black-and-white can do the job as well. One proviso: if the editors find themselves lucky enough to have such a spectacular picture, they must restrain themselves from spoiling it. They must allow it to speak for itself, merely laying claim to its being "editorial" by adding an inescapable minimum of words. In the example on this page, the only additional material is the headline; the way in which it is handled allows the picture to dictate the style and placement of the words. The strong direction within the picture calls for reinforcement by the use of italics (similar in slant) and their angular positioning (parallel to the direction of the sulky's travel). The type *improves* the picture by underlining the photograph's inherent dramatic qualities.

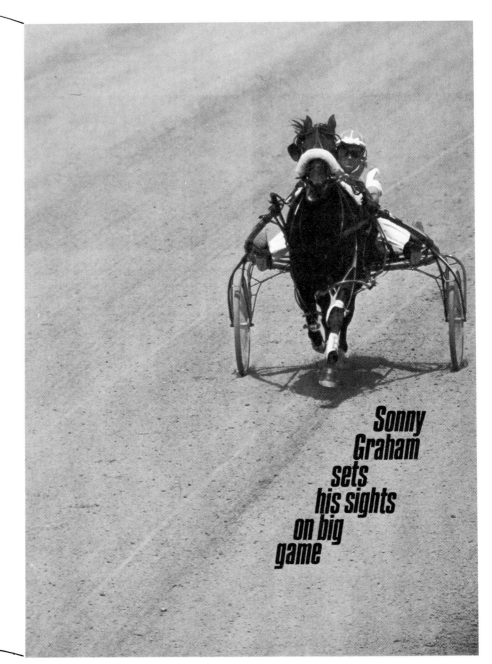

Sonny Graham sets his sights on big game

...and as basis of montage design

Using a good picture as a background to create a desired atmosphere, and superimposing upon it additional images as well as the specifics of headlines and blurbs, is another way in which photographs can be exploited. The example shown opposite is, in effect, a montage of five different elements, yet the simple arrangement into which they have been manipulated pulls them together logically so that the page synergistically "says" more than the sum of its individual parts, which is precisely the quality that makes it a good opener.

Both of these examples as well as the next two→ are in full color.

HOOF BEATS

SPRING

We are now in the season of life, and all living things know it. The new foal nursing at its mother's side, and the wildly free young colts wheeling at play on a warm and lazy April day, feel the pulsing beat of springtime. It is a time of genesis. Now is born the future king, and on some green plot a new champion walks today. Who knows his name? Better that we don't, for lacking that certain knowledge you and I can lie back, look at the blue sky, and know full well the champion is ours. It's spring! and in this field at least, if nowhere else, all is serene and well with the world.

Two more big-picture/peculiar-headline combinations

An attractive picture of a well-known personality catches the eye, and curiosity makes one turn the page sideways to read the headline. The name is well known to be an attention-getter on its own accord, but the way in which the deck is written describes the man's character and pinpoints what one suspects about him just by looking at the picture. It uses splendid word/picture relationship; the verbal/graphic liveliness makes it an effective opener.

Clint Hodgins

Harness racing's bluff, gruff curmudgeon of the sulky enters the sport's Hall of Fame

If one picture is good, are two better? Only if they can be combined into a startling unit. The **montage on page 159 does this** by superimposition. The example shown here gains attention by gluing together the elements with strong visual adhesive: the black band between and alongside the photos. The peculiar typography is the extra touch needed to establish the priority in which the reader will examine the several elements. By being peculiar, both in face and arrangement on the page, and by being good and large, the type will draw the reader's attention first. This is desirable, since it is the words that give the clue to the combination of the pictorial images surrounding them. So this one-two, words-then-picture sequence communicates logically, making a very complex page an effective opener.

Kentucky honors its no.1 product — The horse

Standardized recognition flag incorporated within a flexible format

The wide variety of material that must be placed on the first-rights of *Industrial World* demands a loose format with minimum restrictions. The necessity for flexibility is increased by the publication of each issue in English as well as Spanish, so that enough leeway must be allowed in the design to accommodate variations in headline and text lengths.

The varied editorial material makes it necessary to introduce some highly visible and characteristic graphic element to signal the start of the feature section and — more importantly — to do so in a consistent and familiar way in issue after issue.

Hence the introduction of the heavy vertical rule with the logo attached. It is positioned well into the page, alongside the gutter, and is sufficiently strong to allow the balance of the page to be handled in whatever manner the material demands. Five examples chosen at random from the twenty-five so far published using this pattern prove the efficacy of the system.

INDUSTRIAL WORLD

APRIL 1975

Are you ready for the new breed of robots?

Programmable industrial robots like the Unimate model above have many new skills

Industrial robots are staying on the job. Even as layoffs of workers are going on in many industries worldwide, the robots are joining the work force in more numbers than before.

In 1970 there were only about 200 robots at work in the U.S. and about 50 in Japan. Three years later, the worldwide robot population was estimated at 2600. Last year, the number jumped to 3500—1500 in Japan, 1200 in the U.S. and 800 in Europe.

At the 4th International Symposium on International Robots held last November in Tokyo, 300 experts from 18 countries attended. Forty-five robot makers exhibited their models. As host of the show, Japan is demonstrating that it is spearheading the newest developments in robot technology.

"Labor shortages and spiraling wages are among the factors that catapulted Japan to the forefront of this industry," reports Fred Saito, *Industrial World's* contributing editor from Tokyo. "Unlike West Germany, Japan has not been able to import foreign labor. Hence robots filled the labor shortage."

Over 75 Japanese companies are now in the robot business, most of them entering it within the last five years. In the U.S., two companies—Unimation Inc. and the Versatran Div. of AMF—dominate. More than 440 of their robots have been installed in Europe and in Japan. Other major U.S. firms are listed in the accompanying table.

Europe's robotmakers The more notable ones are: Swiss Assembly Products, Hawker-Siddeley Vaughn Associates—all of the U.K.; in Germany, there are Rheinische Nadelfabriken, VFW-Fokker GmbH, Robert Bosch GmbH; in Sweden, Ekstroms Industri AB, R. Kauueldt AB, Electrolux AS; in Norway, Trallfa-Nils Underhaug, and Tesa.

Robot experts say that 1975 is the year that will see the entry of a new type or generation of robot—the sensory-controlled machine. In contrast to the standard, widely used "pick-and-place" robots of the first generation, the newer versions will have a wide variety of sensors to recognize and manipulate work-pieces, parts and tools. The sensors may include pressure, torque, electro-optics, vision, force-sensitive touch, or proximity sensors.

Their memory-controlled program movements can be interrupted by closed-looped minicomputers. And their programmed control can be overridden by signals from sensor inputs. Robots of this type cross a new threshold: the ability to manufacture and test products.

15
INDUSTRIAL WORLD APRIL 1975

Leu Keller

¿Son vuestros métodos excesivamente complicados?

La simplicidad suele producir buenos resultados

Por LEE GROSSMAN*

Todos convenimos en la conveniencia de llevar las cosas con la mayor simplicidad posible, probablemente como reacción a la tendencia actual de la vida a complicarse. Sin embargo, no siempre conocemos de cierto la razón específica

*El Sr. Grossman es frecuente colaborador de INDUSTRIAL WORLD sobre temas de interés gerencial, y presidente de Lee Grossman Associates, 240 Sunset Drive, Wilmette, Ill. USA 60091

para simplificar, y no podemos probar que la simplicidad siempre produce buenos resultados. Pero, por otra parte, muchas veces tampoco podemos probar que no los da. Podemos no obstante aprender algo de ejemplos reales de lo que ocurre cuando las cosas se complican de propósito.

En su libro, *The Practice of Management* (el desempeño de funciones gerenciales o administrativas), Peter F. Drucker informa sobre un caso ejemplar, concerniente al presidente de una compañía que adquirió un pequeño establecimiento industrial de Los Angeles.

Harry Stavrakas

THE BEST IN PLANT MODERNIZATION

The 10 plants from 10 different countries described in the following pages are outstanding examples of innovative management. Each one includes ideas that may be adaptable to your operation

---

NEW WAYS TO TEST ROOFS FOR LEAKS

Repair work on your plant roof can be costly. Nondestructive techniques such as a radioisotopic meter (above) that reveals trapped water can cut maintenance costs

BY J R NORMAND CASAUBON

In these days of shrinking budgets and increasing responsibilities the plant engineer must take a hard look at all his expenses. He must be sure that money spent on roof maintenance is not wasted

Built-up roofing is particularly vulnerable to high maintenance costs. The fifth wall, the roof, is the hardest working wall of a structure. It is subjected to the brunt of all the elements and will perform its function only if it is properly main-

Mr Normand Casaubon is assistant engineering manager for the American Telephone & Telegraph Co of 195 Broadway, New York, N.Y., USA 10007. This article is extracted from a paper presented in Chicago, Ill. at the 1975 Plant Engineering & Maintenance Conference.

tained using reliable methods.

The cost of maintaining a flat or low-pitched roof varies greatly. Even a token periodic maintenance program can be costly. But ignoring a roof will sooner or later result in roof failure. It seems counter-productive to wait for a failure since the cost for repair can be large and will far exceed the expense of periodic maintenance.

With few exceptions materials used on conventional plant roofs are organic. The bitumens and impregnated felts deteriorate when exposed to sunlight. The oils and plasticizers evaporate from the bitumens leaving a brittle film which cracks with expansion and contraction of the membrane. Bitumens flow down from blisters leaving the dried felts which can absorb water and produce more blisters and even splits in the membrane.

Fiberboard insulations are also partly

Security steps to protect your plant against rising crime

BY ROBERT SHLASKO

The biggest cause of theft? A leading consultant says it's simply—opportunity.

That, in one word, is the good news and the bad news about crime. Bad news because it means there are people both inside and outside your plant who are ready to steal given the chance. Good news because it means you can cut theft by following some basic security guidelines.

Sadly, crime in this troubled world is on the increase. In the U.S. rising shoplifting has forced many retailers out of business, while in manufacturing, theft is estimated to cause annual losses of $1,800 million. The U.S. is not alone. In France, the rate of theft has risen 30% in the last two years.

Looking at the French crime rate, one observer saw conditions common to many lands: "New life styles have de-

Entrance door will not open unless valid identity card is inserted into card reader. Up to 64 readers can be controlled by an IBM System/7 computer located 1½ miles away

Echoing the cover gives ultimate recognition value to the opener

If a strong and memorable image is established on the front cover, its repetition will surely arouse the reader's interest when he comes across it again. This simple principle is applied to *Hoofbeats'* presentation of its annual profiles of the year's winning horses. The graphic handling is, of course, based on the "impossible figure" frames that appear logically three-dimensional until they are examined more closely and their subtlety becomes apparent. Each frame contains a color portrait of the subject, with subframes for the names and the biographies. The headline typography is equally elusive, since one cannot determine whether one is looking down or up at the lettering. Shown here are the cover, the first-right, and a spread from the story.

JANUARY 1975

HOOF BEATS

HORSE OF THE YEAR — DELMONICA HANOVER

THE CLASS OF '74

THE CLASS OF '74

Here is the class of 1974 as selected by the U.S. Trotting Association's coast-to-coast poll of more than 400 harness writers in the United States and Canada and by the racing secretaries of the 50 members of Harness Tracks of America. Class is that quality that sets leaders apart from those who follow. In horses it can be the tangible factors of speed, earnings and the ability to win the "big ones." There are good years and just average years. The year 1974 was a vintage year.

Horse of the Year, Aged Trotting Mare: Delmonica Hanover

Harness racing had a Queen in 1974 as *DELMONICA HANOVER* was voted best by North America's harness writers. The 5-year-old *SPEEDY COUNT-DELICIOUS* mare becomes the fifth mare ever to be so honored and the second developed by Delvin Miller. Miller trained 1954 winner *STENOGRAPHER*. Delmonica earned $252,165 in 1974 and raised her lifetime total to $709,799. She won both the Prix d'Amerique in France and the Roosevelt International. Miller, co-owner with *Arnold Hanger*, bought Delmonica for $5,000 as a Hanover yearling and sold her in November for a record $300,000 at Tattersalls. She will defend her Prix d'Amerique title in January.

All full-color illustrations. Type and frames in black

Four-Year-Old Trotting Mare: Colonial Charm

COLONIAL CHARM, now the fastest trotting mare in harness racing history, was judged the top 4-year-old trotter of 1974 by North America's writers. In 1972 she won the "2-Year-Old" award and in 1973 Castleton Farm's homebred daughter of **SPEEDSTER-DARN YANKEE** was chosen the "3-Year-Old Filly" queen. The **Glen Garnsey**-trained mare topped the 36-year-old world mark of the immortal **ROSALIND** (a 1:56¾ time trial) with her 1:56.1 victory over **DREAM OF GLORY** in Lexington's historic Transylvania Trot. This clocking also shattered **FRESH YANKEE'S** 1:57.3 all-age mare standard and bettered **SPEEDY SCOT'S** 1:56.4 Red Mile mark. For the year, Colonial Charm won nine times, including the Reynolds, Volo Van and Maple Leaf Stakes, and earned $106,440.

Aged Trotting Horse: Savoir

SAVOIR, shown with his veteran trainer **Jimmy Arthur**, didn't win very often this past season, but when he did, the 6-year-old gelding did so with a flair. The Allwood Stable's son of **STAR'S PRIDE-SPICY SONG** captured the $30,000 Goldsmith Maid on June 8 at Roosevelt, beating **AIKEN** and **COLONIAL CHARM**. Four months later he downed "Horse of the Year" **DELMONICA HANOVER** at Hollywood in 1:59.3, with **Jim Dennis** aboard. Savoir then climaxed a topsy-turvy year with a near-world record triumph in the $108,000 American Trotting Classic at Hollywood Park. He won this 1⅛ miles test in 2:13.3 (one-fifth off the world mark). He had $145,700 in '74 earnings, $693,806 overall.

165

These examples were picked pretty much at random, and reflect the current widespread practice in the use of boxes, borders, rules, and typographic embellishment of all sorts.

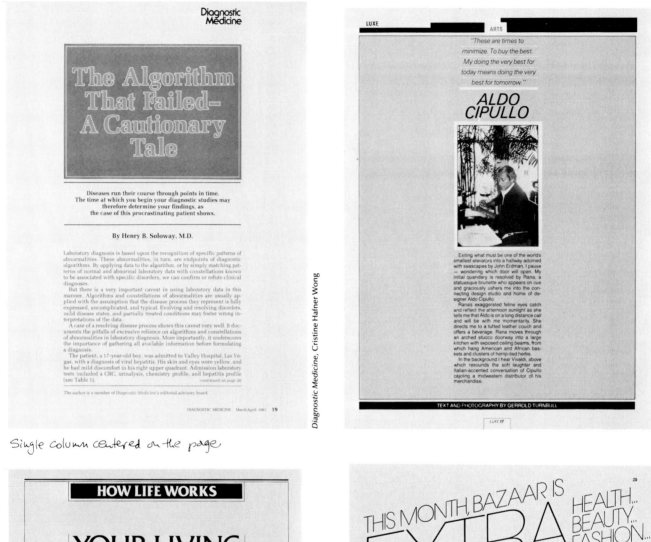

Diagnostic Medicine, Cristine Hafner Wong

Luxe, Alex Sanchez

Single column centered on the page

Science Digest, Frank Rothmann

Harper's Bazaar, Jerold Smokler

Two narrow columns centered on the page

Two narrow columns placed to the right of the page

Two wide columns across the page

Three normal columns with daring and conservative display above.

TWA Ambassador, Alfred Zelcer

Atlantic Monthly, Judy Garlan

Esquire, April Silver

Town & Country, Melissa Tardiff

Spread-openers for interrelated series: the theme-with-variations technique

In a special issue of *Architectural Record* on the relationship of engineering to architecture, each story deals with a particular aspect of the subject. Thus, to tie together the issue, each opener had to be designed within a recognizable format — similar, yet flexible enough to allow each story to be designed in the way the material naturally suggests.

The basic graphic element, the tall box on the left-hand page, is in color or various tints of gray. The text blocks vary in length as required, but are all placed in similar positions on the page for the sake of rhythm. The headlines are all handled differently: some dropped out in white from the dark gray background; others surprinted in black over light gray; the Lighting one is both dropped out and surprinted since the medium gray allows both techniques to be used while retaining legibility. The heads are set in whatever type size seemed right, but all in Optima all caps.

The simplicity and rigidity of the overall shapes is enough to make them stand out distinctly in contrast to the various pages opposite; these latter give some slight indication of the different page treatments applied within the stories themselves, though, alas, the most visually interesting treatments do not show on the openers.

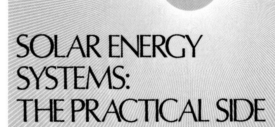

SOLAR ENERGY SYSTEMS: THE PRACTICAL SIDE

In the 1974 engineering issue, we showed how engineer Frank Bridgers has been putting solar energy to good use in buildings for 20 years. His latest endeavor is the preparation of a design procedure for solar-assisted heat pump systems for the National Science Foundation and ERDA. To validate the procedure the solar system in the Bridgers and Paxton office building (across page) has been revamped and highly instrumented to get the kinds of data needed. The information is sent over leased wires to Penn State, where Professor Stanley Gilman is analyzing and plugging it into a computer model that he programmed of the Bridgers and Paxton system. This article reviews some of the current attitudes about solar systems, some of the developments on the solar front, and then describes what Bridgers and Gilman are doing.

Black type over yellow background

**Data is being taken
on this solar building
to validate a
design procedure
for solar systems**

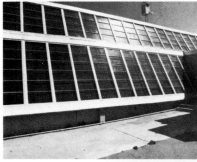

Frank Bridgers' comment that he has had more inquiries about solar heating in the last year than in the previous 15 is hardly surprising. What is different about now and 20 years ago, when Bridgers and Paxton built their own solar building, is the escalated cost of energy, for one thing, and the considerable dollar backing for solar-energy research by the Federal government, for another. Of the 138 solar-heated buildings reported by William A. Shurcliff in his May 1975 survey,* nearly 100 of them were initiated after 1970. As might be expected, most of the buildings are houses, though several schools and office buildings are listed (including a pilot project for a 10-story office building).

Solar-heated buildings that work well have been and are being constructed. Technology is not the basic question. The question, really, is how do the economics work out? Solar-heated buildings are capital-intensive because solar radiation is "low-level" energy. Large areas of collectors have to be provided to collect it, and some means has to be provided to store it to make up for nights and cold, cloudy daytime weather. Even so, solar-heated buildings are competitive now with conventionally heated ones at present energy costs when there is low-interest financing, as with

*Solar Heated Buildings, A Brief Survey, ninth edition, W. A. Shurcliff, Cambridge, Massachusetts.

Data from a weather station and from instrumented equipment in the Bridgers and Paxton building is acquired by computer and sent to Penn State for analysis.

public buildings. The really tough question is what is going to happen to the cost of electricity, gas and oil in the next 10 years. In 1973, engineer Bridgers estimated a 300 per cent increase in the cost of natural gas by 1990, and a 125 per cent increase in the cost of electricity. Now, he views these figures as very conservative.

Though the completeness and accuracy of weather data (solar and temperature) leaves a lot to be desired; though there is no commonly accepted design procedure (right now) for solar-heated buildings; and though, strictly speaking, the economics are far from simple, still a pretty good evaluation can be made of owning costs for solar-energy sys-

tems right now. The costs of owning a solar heating system include the amortization of the collector, the storage unit, the pumps and piping (or fans and ducting), and the cost of associated controls. Frank Bridgers reports that the increase in construction cost for buildings with solar-assisted heat pumps in the Mountain States is about 10 per cent for large commercial buildings, and about 20 per cent for small commercial buildings and for houses. A $60,-000 house, then, would cost $72,-000 with solar heating. Operating costs include the power for pumping fluid or moving air in the system, and maintenance of the system including any repairs to the collectors.

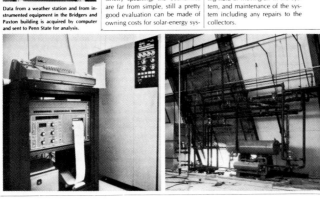

IDEAS
INGENIOUS, BOLD, PLAYFUL

The ten projects shown on these pages, the kind of stories journalists call "short takes," are all buildings that the editors couldn't stand *not* to publish, even though space was limited. Some impressed us with their inventiveness—an unexpected application of a common material, say, or unusually adroit integration of structure and services. Others we found downright amazing—see the incredible unfolding apartment house on page 124. In any case, the collection demonstrates, if further evidence was needed, the remarkable range of designers' ingenuity.

 **1** The graceful concrete picnic shelters at Denver's Cherry Creek Reservoir were cast in a singular forming system of fanned timbers. Architect Cabell Childress, inspired by Robert Behrens's sculptures and assisted by structural engineers KKBNA, devised a reusable form composed of stacked 3-by-6 timbers, threaded near the base on a pipe. The upper edges were then splayed like a Japanese fan. Rainwater drains through outsize scupper on the fan's spine. Because the recreation area is subject to floods during the spring run-off, picnic shelters and other structures in the park are submergible, needing only hosing and painting to ready them for visitors.

Robert E. Fischer photos

2 The facilities of a boilermaker's plant were employed to shape the ¼-in. weathering steel plates above park shelters at Yonkers, New York. The prefabricated hexagonal "flowers," designed by architect Joseph Roth and structural engineer Robert Silman, rest on flared hexagonal "stems." Each flower has six identical segments joined by continuous welds. Welding rods were also weathering steel, rendering seams virtually undetectable when ground smooth. Inverted flowers become fireplaces, stems become chimneys. Fabricators were United Iron Inc.

QUALITY LIGHTING WITH FEWER WATTS

Electric energy consumed by all forms of lighting is substantial—as much as 20 per cent of the total usage. So it is no wonder that government, owners and architects, and engineers are scrutinizing lighting design for energy savings, even in the absence of a coherent Federal energy policy. It is also no secret that significant savings are achievable. Logically, no single approach has been seen as an answer to all clients' needs. Fortunately, too, the simplistic advocacy of markedly lower footcandle levels has not taken hold. In seeking rational approaches, architects and lighting designers are giving a lot more attention to the different requirements of different spaces, to obtaining a greater appreciation of what quality means in the range of tasks to be lighted, and to whether the objective is "light to see" or "light to see by," or both.

This article is devoted to the main approaches that have developed to obtain quality lighting with fewer watts: 1) less reflected glare from tasks achieved by (a) location of luminaires geometrically with respect to tasks, and/or (b) control of light distribution of luminaires themselves; 2) use of luminaires with high efficiencies and improved light distributions; 3) electrical power distribution arranged to permit flexible lighting arrangements; 4) switching to turn lights off when not needed, and diminished lighting for janitorial services; and 5) use of lamps with higher efficiencies.

• Many ways for designers of lighting systems to cope with the need to use energy prudently are suggested by the lighting studies and case histories discussed here and on the following eight pages. One trend readily apparent is design for the discrete lighting of tasks: putting the right light in the right place.

If task locations can be predetermined, and will remain fixed, ceiling luminaires can be arranged to put more light on the task than on the surrounding areas; furthermore, the luminaires can be located to minimize reflected glare on the task. Or, conversely, the tasks can be located in areas with least reflected glare, hence, better vision. These principles are illustrated on the following two pages in the article by Louis Bello of Syska & Hennessy.

With task-oriented lighting, if desk locations will change frequently, then the luminaires will need to move with the locations. This can be accomplished in two ways. First, the luminaires may be relocated in the ceiling. Second, the luminaires can be incorporated in office furniture and the lighting moved with the furniture. (See record, March 1973 and mid-August 1974.)

Several methods are possible for relocating ceiling luminaires. To a limited extent this is possible with the 6-ft length of flexible metal conduit allowed by the National Electrical Code for making a connection between rigid conduit and luminaires in accessible air-handling plenums. Flexibility is greatly enhanced, though distribution costs may be increased, by providing means for plugging in luminaires on a modular basis. Two Toronto buildings (pages 118-120) will take this approach. In the first case a checkerboard grid of electrical raceways has plug-in capability, and also supports luminaires and acoustical panels. Furthermore, the grid conceals sprinkler piping and has openings for air outlets.

In the second example, outlet boxes are provided in the bottoms of concrete floor slabs that allow luminaires in the ceiling below to be plugged in on a modular basis. Luminaires are supported by acoustical louvers that also shield the fluorescent lamps.

If the lighting needs to be fixed in the ceiling, and task locations will change, then the only solution is to provide uniform illumination in spaces where the tasks occur—though circulation, storage, and other ancillary spaces can have reduced lighting levels.

Even at that, very good general lighting can be obtained for slightly less than 2 watts per sq ft to 2½ watts per sq ft, as is demonstrated in the examples on page 116. In both examples, the luminaires are louvered, parabolic-reflector, twin-beam types. These luminaires have high visual comfort values, and they are designed to reduce reflected glare, the preferred viewing direction being parallel to the length of the luminaires.

There has been a lot of flak about the Illuminating Engineering Society's recommended footcandle levels. While the presumed rigidity, and also the magnitude, of these levels have been questioned by a lot of people, in many cases their alternative proposals have had questionable or limited technical support. The trouble is that scientists in the field have not

integrated all the psychological and physiological factors that affect human performance and well-being to arrive at numbers that are valid in every respect. Obviously this is a gargantuan task that seemingly has no end, though some researchers, such as architect John Flynn, professor at The Pennsylvania State University, are trying to whittle it down. Flynn, for example, has used people as test subjects to rate lighted room appearances according to their preferences (when quantity and patterns of light are varied) for certain types of space usages. Dr. H. Richard Blackwell has proposed adjustments to illumination levels to account for eye adaptation factors, and his wife has done research on the effect of aging on visual acuity.

In response to its critics, the IES emphasizes that their recommended levels always did apply to task illumination. That they were many times applied indiscriminately across the board, can be attributed, among other things, to: 1) the public's lack of concern in the past about energy; 2) the requirement for space-use flexibility, real or imagined (or perhaps the owner will not commit himself); and 3) the greater amounts of thought, time and skill required to design task lighting properly. Not to be ignored is the fact that *more* came to be equated with *better*, even though sometimes it could be worse. Owners in competitive rental situations usually met their competition's footcandles, and more often than not in more.

From an energy-usage standpoint, the IES recommendations, properly interpreted by the lighting designer, with cooperation by the owner, need not result, at all, in high energy consumption, even though these recommendations undoubtedly were originally derived from some judgmental decisions, including economic acceptance by owners, along with Blackwell's and other research.

With offices, for example, recommended levels are 30, 70, 100, or 150 footcandles, for a range of tasks from easy to difficult (but not most difficult). At roughly 25-35 footcandles per watt from general lighting systems, this could mean about 1 to 5 watts per sq ft for the areas involved. One example in this article shows that 65 footcandles of general illumination can be achieved with 1.8 watts/sq ft.

One factor affecting design is that people have to some extent become accustomed to the bright-appearing levels in office buildings and schools. (But would people prefer desk lamps, or the equivalent, if they could have them?) Though space brightness is not necessarily related to footcandles of general illumination, it takes more thought, skill and experience to dispose illumination in the most advantageous ways for desired room brightness and task illumination.

In achieving owner and occupant satisfaction with room and luminaire appearance—i.e., the light one sees, which, more often than not is the basis upon which people appraise lighting—there is no substitute for experience in regard to what footcandle levels will be satisfactory. In a room with dark finishes, lit from ceiling luminaires, 80 footcandles of illumination may result in a room that seems dingy. In a room with nearly white fin-

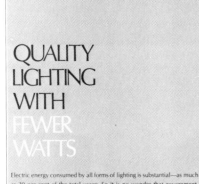

A. Improved visibility of reading tasks through optimum location of luminaires leads to less energy use (pages 114 and 115). B. Visibility can be enhanced through use of twin-beam-type luminaires. One lamp of this two-lamp unit can be switched off for energy savings (page 116). C. Task-oriented illumination, which allows more efficient utilization of luminaires, is possible with plug-in distribution systems (pages 117-120). D. Higher efficiency lamps mean more light for fewer watts (page 121).

White headline, black text on 50% screen of black

12 EXAMPLES

OF EFFECTIVE ARCHITECT-ENGINEER COLLABORATION

What becomes evident as one reviews the projects on the following pages is that there are a lot of people around with a sizable store of technical expertise—not only architects and engineers, but contractors and manufacturers as well. Talking with contributors to this section, the editors also noticed with interest the sheer enjoyment these experts take in attacking a knotty problem, whether it's big or little, and the great satisfaction they find in helping to make a building look more beautiful, or work more efficiently, or go together more simply, or cost less money. These examples range from a potential landmark—a one-of-a-kind commission with one-of-a-kind technical problems—to more common problems uncommonly well solved, such as two thoughtfully detailed curtain walls and a tightly reasoned mechanical system for a Colorado high school with a serious fuel shortage.

LANDMARK IN THE MAKING: "PEOPLE WORK HARD TO MAKE THINGS LOOK SIMPLE"

Superb execution is as important to a finished work of art as inspired design, a principle that is always reflected in the work emanating from the office of I.M. Pei & Partners. This principle is stretched very nearly to its limits at the National Gallery of Art, where extensive additions are presently under construction. The building contains more than a few technical tours de force, among them a space frame measuring 150 by 225 ft with supporting members weighing as much as 5 tons, a 135-ft concrete girder only 4 ft deep, and cast-in-place concrete of extraordinary beauty.

The new building's triangular plan derives from its trapezoidal site at the intersection of Pennsylvania Avenue and the Mall. The main elements in the plan include a large office-library wing, three "pods" for exhibitions, and a central court, roofed by a skylighted space frame, for circulation and sculpture display.

The dimensions and angles of the plan's adjacent and overlapping isosceles triangles cannot, of course, deviate, and the fixed geometry made the integration—an architectural given—of appearance, structure and services a rigorous exercise, requiring constant cross-conferences between architects, structural engineers, mechanical engineers, contractors and suppliers.

Another factor, although it is not evident in either materials or craftsmanship, was budget. The $75 million in donated funds from Paul Mellon (this is a private gift to the nation) carried no carte blanche for the designers, and expenditures, which must cover extensive underground facilities as well as the marble building, are carefully monitored for value.

NATIONAL GALLERY OF ART, Washington, D.C. Architects: *I.M. Pei & Partners—I.M. Pei; Leonard Jacobson, project architect.* Engineers: *Weiskopf & Pickworth* (structural); *Syska & Hennessy* (mechanical/electrical); *Mueser, Rutledge, Wentworth & Johnson* (foundation). General contractor: *Chas. H. Tompkins Co.* Construction consultant: *Carl A. Morse, Inc.* Space frame fabrication: *Chicago Heights Steel.*

KKBNA: ENGINEERING PRACTICED WITH ZEST

For last year's engineering issue, three impressive and diverse buildings were submitted by KKBNA, a Denver firm of structural engineers, or by their architect-clients. (We published all three.) This year, we got three more—again impressive, again diverse. In the course of reportorial conversations, the editors were also struck by the energy and perceptiveness seemingly common to all members of the firm, and by their unmistakable enthusiasm for their work. Our curiosity prompted us to ask Margaret Gaskie, an engineer by training and a former RECORD editor now working in Denver, to interview the firm's partners and associates, and some of their clients, to find out what accounts for the high quality of their work—and just why they have so much fun doing it.

The Denver-based consulting engineering firm of Ketchum Konkel Barrett Nickel Austin, with its New York affiliate Ketchum Barrett Nickel Austin/Besier, enjoys a widening reputation for sound, innovative solutions to tough structural problems.

That the reputation is earned is evident in the sampling of recent projects shown in these pages. That it is relished is evident in the partners' shoptalk, which is laced with terms like "challenging," "exciting," and, pervasively, "fun."

That it is no accident is also evident. KKBNA's fruitful collaborations with architects spring first and last from a reservoir of exceptional engineering talent. But they flow too from organizational policies and patterns well calculated to nurture that talent.

These, say its beneficiaries, are a legacy of the firm's founder, Milo S. Ketchum, who now teaches at the University of Connecticut but who continues to serve the firm as consultant, and his long-time partner, the late E. Vernon Konkel.

Michael H. Barrett, KKBNA's president, speaks of Ketchum as a teacher at heart, who saw the "practice" as just that: an ongoing effort to learn and hone skills. Believing that little learning derives from rote solutions to routine problems, Ketchum steered the firm instead toward the pioneering work in new methods, systems and products that is its stock in trade today.

Barrett is quick to point out that, for every structural tour de force, the firm engineers a dozen relatively unexceptional, and unsung, projects, adding that the firm's reputation for tackling the difficult and unusual can be a mixed blessing.

"It's discouraging," he says ruefully, "when a potential client hands a nice straightforward high-rise to another firm and tells us, 'There's nothing special about it. When I want a 500-foot free-form clear span, I'll come to you.'

"Sure we like the hard jobs, but even on ordinary jobs we have fun coming up with imaginative ways to save money, or speed construction, or do better justice to the architect's design."

Underlying KKBNA's openness to new concepts is a genuine empathy with the firm's architect-clients. The partners take pride in a cultivated ability to attune themselves to the architect's thinking and problems. And while convinced of the propriety of the architect's role as head of the design team, they do not see the role of the structural engineer as thereby reduced to "just a matter of designing connections and telling the client why he can't do what he wants to do."

Barrett likens the relationship between structure and architecture to a marriage, observing that while such elements as mechanical and electrical services can to an extent be divorced from—or appended to—the total design concept, structure and architecture are indissolubly wed.

. . . it is in the conceptual stages that the partners' time and talent yield the client the best value for cost. "A few clients have learned to get the most out of us, bringing us in early to explore all the possibilities, so the structure can really become a determinant part of the design. This, we love."

A similar analogy is drawn by long-standing KKBNA client William Muchow of Muchow Associates. "I use them for all my projects, right down to a creak in my living room floor," he says. "We work as if we were one office. . . My architecture is as much their structure as it is anything I put into it."

Such happy marriages don't just happen, however. Muchow emphasizes the value of continuity in his collaboration with KKBNA, believing that both parties gain by familiarity with the other's thought processes.

G. Cabell Childress, another self-described "old shoe" client, concurs, but inserts a practical note. At least in its work with frequent clients, he says, KKBNA encourages loose arrangements under which the firm undertakes the structural design on all of a given architect's project—large or small, simple or complex—for the same fee. "That way, if the architect really wants to go way out, KKBNA can afford to fly right along with him, and hope to make up any extra costs on future jobs."

Childress, himself not averse to the odd creative flight, likes to bring in KKBNA "as soon as I've determined 'what wants to happen' in the building, so we can work together to make sure what happens is contained in the simplest, most direct, most economical way."

Muchow agrees: "The best architecture comes from a team relationship where we stimulate each other to think creatively about basic objectives," but emphasizes that this is a process best begun in the beginning, before key design concepts are frozen.

To which KKBNA would add a hearty amen, pointing out that it is in the conceptual stages that the partners' time and talent yield the client the best value for cost.

"A few clients," Barrett says, "have learned to get the most out of us, bringing us in early to explore all the possibilities, so the structure can really become a determinant part of the design. This, we love."

Even so, KKBNA gets its fair share of problems posed in the mode of "the span is 327 feet and it has to be flat," as well as frequent commissions specifying structural forms—notably thin shells and space frames—that the firm has successfully executed in the past.

The partners accept the constraints of working within such pre-established design concepts philosophically. "Depending on how good the architect is—and a lot of them have a real feel for structure—things can often be done as well as if we'd been included at the beginning. An architect like Jim Ream, who has that innate sense and collaborates to the *n*th degree, winds up designing more of the structure than we do," Barrett says. "Our job isn't to originate design, but to refine the architect's concept and make it work."

At the same time, the partners are persuaded that too rigid parameters set too soon often add needlessly to the costs of a project. "We can figure out how to do almost anything if there's enough money," Barrett comments. "But we'd rather figure out how to do something better for less."

Fee schedules being what they are, KKBNA's appetite for adventure is not without impact on the firm's own finances. Barrett tells with a certain perverse pride of a recent "challenging" project entailing three stories and thirty-nine different floor levels. "On that one, our costs were two and a half times the fee," he relates, "plus twenty years of my life." But he adds, "If our main motive were to make money, we'd none of us be engineers to start with. There are all kinds of compensations."

The firm's official posture toward the profit motive is considerably less cavalier. While insisting on the superior satisfactions of creative work, KKBNA is also at considerable pains to maintain the efficient, productive—and profitable—organization needed to produce it.

Though formally a corporation, KKBNA operates as a partnership—and sometimes, says Barrett, "more like a commune." Of a staff of sixty, eleven are partners, who share equally in decision-making, and nine more are associates or project engineers, who also have a voice in the firm's management.

The resulting ratio of one chief for every two Indians, the principals admit, is sometimes unwieldy. But it reflects their conviction that clients hire people rather than firms, and that the firm should therefore afford the people within it the fullest possible scope for action and initiative. KKBNA believes its relatively large number of relatively independent principals enables it to offer clients the best of two worlds: the personalized attention of a one-man shop, backed by the combined experience and resources of the firm as a whole.

Accordingly, every project is overseen by a principal from start to finish. On comparatively small jobs, the partner-in-charge may also act as project manager—and often project engineer and chief draftsman as well. More usually, though, the task of project manager is delegated to an associate or project engineer, with the remainder of the project team drawn as needed from a pool of engineers, junior engineers and draftsmen. In either case, the partner in charge retains full responsibility for over-all management.

Given the autonomy KKBNA partners enjoy, there is little rigid specialization within the firm. In principle, a deliberate effort is made to distribute work so that all firm members have opportunity to gain experience on a variety of project types. In practice, though, since jobs coming in do not always oblige by lending themselves to a random match with the people available to work on them, some of the firm's engineers have acquired more experience with certain types of structures than have others. And since some also have more interest in particular structures than do others, a certain amount of concentration has evolved among them.

Except in the case of the civil engineering department, however—which now accounts for some 35 to 40 per cent of the firm's business—such specialization can be attributed more to happenstance than to planning.

The flexibility KKBNA espouses in its professional functions extends also to the management of the firm, which boasts no "business" partner as such. Rather, each principal is first a practicing engineer, and secondly a proprietor with administrative responsibility for certain aspects of the firm's operations.

President Michael Barrett, for example, also has major responsibility for long-range planning and business development. Donavon Nickel, trained in business administration as well as engineering, manages personnel and finances, while David Austin handles general operations. And so through the roster of partners.

Since divisions of labor are based less on organizational logic than on the propensities and proficiencies of the several partners, KKBNA's smooth functioning is perhaps in some degree serendipitous. But it can also be credited to a shared philosophy that overrides the principals' individual differences in approach and emphasis. "We've all grown up together in the firm" Barrett explains. "We've learned to do things pretty much the same way, and we see things pretty much the same way."

Not surprisingly, in light of the import the principals place on

"When you get down to it, the only way to get business is to do a superlative job. We all seem to grow by taking on challenges. . . . We like to think we add to the profession by doing it—and we have our share of fun."

their common heritage, KKBNA's policies toward its younger members are geared to produce similar opportunities for fruitful apprenticeship and ongoing association.

"Ketchum," Barrett says, "looked at the shop almost as a prep school. He'd bring guys in fresh out of school, train them in the real world for a couple of years, and then suggest they go on for more experience. Well, we feel for people to operate at maximum efficiency for the firm, they almost have to grow up with us, so

Black type on 30% screen of black

Spread-openers for interrelated series: the repetitive technique

This special issue of *House & Home* dealt with various aspects of the crisis in homebuilding (labeled "Homebuilding at the Crossroads" and hence the yellow and black traffic symbol used on the cover and in miniature on all openers).

Since the stories were made up of a great variety of material ranging from plain text to photo essays, the openers needed to be particularly strong in graphic character to ensure recognition as features in the confusing context in which they would be seen. To make matters more difficult, shortage of space required that no more than half a page be devoted to each opener.

Maximum use was made of just four raw materials: a solid black, full-bleed area (strong enough just on its own as a signal); the miniature symbol from the cover; angled headlines; and introductory text blocks which anchor the headlines to the bottom of the panel. There is no question about where stories begin or that they belong to a package.

Making private rehab pay

Every town has its share of rundown buildings in areas that are ideal for multifamily housing. Here is how one such building was rehabbed to produce a gross return of more than 20% on the original investment.

This private rehab job—a warehouse turned into apartments—generates a $20,400 rent roll on a total investment of only $95,000.

The investment by James R. Mowry, who is both owner and architect, was low for two reasons. First of all, the former warehouse *(shown below)* was reasonably priced because it's in a relatively dormant section of Binghampton, N.Y. Nevertheless, the location has attracted tenants because it's near public transportation and within walking distance of downtown theaters, the library, restaurants and offices.

Secondly, Mowry did surprisingly little remodeling. Instead, he capitalized on the structural soundness of the building, retaining—and exposing—the solid brick walls, the rough-sawn wood beams and the stone foundation.

In fact, except for steam-cleaning the brick and painting window frames, the only exterior work was at the entrance level. New arched doors were framed by brick reclaimed from the building's old meat smoking kilns.

To dress up the front a curved lattice overhang was installed above the recessed entry, and a wrought iron railing was set around a new light-well that brings daylight to the lower level of the front duplex *(plan overleaf)*.

Inside work consisted of the installation of new electrical, plumbing and heating systems and partitioning to set up the apartments.

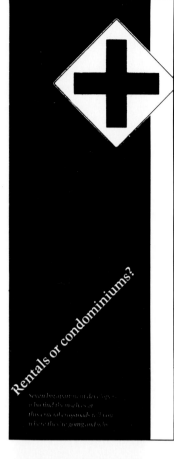

Rentals or condominiums?

Seven big apartment developers who find themselves at this crucial crossroads tell you where they're going and why.

"We're staking our company on the proposition that condominiums will go over big."

So says John W. Kessler, president of Multicon Communities, a subsidiary of Multicon Construction Corp., Columbus, Ohio.

Kessler is the only one of the several builders interviewed by HOUSE & HOME who was willing to state flatly that condominiums will represent his major marketing effort for both the immediate and long-range future.

Of some 2,000 total units Multicon now plans to build in several markets throughout the East, Midwest and South in 1972, all but four will be for sale as condominiums (most of them condominium townhouses). **The big market, Kessler says, will be in the $20,000 range.**

Pride of ownership, along with tax benefits, is still a major motivating force in the shelter market, Kessler believes. And the condominium concept retains these advantages at considerable cost savings compared with single-family houses, a factor which he feels will make condominium owners out of many home-owners as well as current renters.

Builders, faced with maintenance and management costs that will probably continue to outpace rental income rises, should find in condominiums a much brighter investment picture, Kessler says, especially since the net return can be booked soon after the project is completed. And this argument goes double in the case of an earnings-hungry public corporation (Multicon's parent company is Bethlehem Steel Corp.).

What are the key points to consider in condominium building? Kessler sees two: location and company organization.

The best site, in Kessler's experience, is a predominantly single-family neighborhood with nearby multifamily housing. Specifically, "A nice residential area where single-family homes are 10% more expensive than what we can offer."

The rule is: "A good condominium location is a good rental area, but a good rental area is not *necessarily* a good condominium area," Kessler says. Environmental factors are the reason for this. Rental tenants are primarily attracted by a site's conveniences—access to freeways, shopping centers, etc. But they are relatively much freer to move out if, say, the levels of noise and dirt are too high, than are condominium owners. Therefore a potential condominium owner will check out possible negative factors

John W. Kessler is president of Multicon Communities, a division of Multicon Properties Inc., located in Columbus, Ohio. Founded in 1962, with Kessler as a general partner, Multicon specialized in the joint venturing of rental projects. The company incorporated in 1969 and became part of Bethlehem Steel Co. in 1971. This year's Multicon starts are expected to be in the 1,800-2,000 range.

per square foot for new construction of condos and single-family houses in your area, plus the rentals per square foot for similar rental apartments.

Those figures will show you with precision your competitor's strength, says Lyons. Surely, you won't succeed in selling two-bedroom condos at $21,500 when around the corner from your building some other builder is offering two-bedroom single-family houses for $19,990.

Once you know what your competitors are charging, you'll need to determine the most you can spend on exterior improvements to make your building competitive with new construction in the area.

You can usually forget about the cost of interior repairs because 1) you'll strive to sell your units as is and 2) you'll simply charge more for a unit you've modernized.

Next, put a selling price on each unit. Here's a rough rule of thumb Lyons offers to help you arrive at the price: An apartment in a converted condo ought to sell at 100 to 120 times that apartment's monthly rental. And an apartment house in a desirable location—near a park, transportation or shopping—can command as much as 130 times monthly rentals.

There's one caveat: Your sales price should be 20% to 30% lower than new for-sale construction—condos or single-family houses—in the area.

Finally, determine how much each unit's owner will have to spend each month to live in his condo home. That's critical because today's prospective buyers consider monthly payout ahead of everything else.

The list should include, in addition to mortgage payments, taxes and insurance, all maintenance charges for the upkeep of the condominiums. And of course you should point out in that breakdown those items—taxes and mortgage interest—which are tax deductible.

Your monthly total should either be the same or lower than rentals for comparable apartments in your community.

Financing: Conversions need a new technique

Ask the bank that holds your present permanent mortgage to agree to give you—when you ask for it—a bridge mortgage equal to the amount outstanding on your old mortgage. The bridge mortgage, a newcomer to the financial community, was invented to solve the conversion problem. It does two things: It gives you the money to pay off the old mortgage. And it allows the release of the lien on each unit as the unit is sold—something the permanent mortgage would not do. Typically, you'll pay a slightly higher interest rate for this short-term money than for conventional mortgage funds.

At the same time get the bank to agree to provide the mortgages on the condominium units as you sell them.

If you need money to dress up your apartment's exterior, tack on those costs to the bridge's total, and then get an advance on those extra dollars. You'll run no real risk. For if you don't convert, you probably can refinance the original mortgage to repay the bridge advance. And the spruce-up job on the building may allow you to raise the rents.

Once you declare that your building is a condominium—a right only you can exercise—you accept the bridge mortgage, pay off the existing mortgage and then repay the bridge as you close on each condo unit.

On the other hand if you decide not to convert, you run no financial risk because the bank will not charge you for a bridge mortgage you never used.

Outside New York State, your banker will require that at least half of the apartments be sold *before* he'll grant the bridge mortgage, thereby allowing you to declare the building a condominium. But, Lyons says, you may set the percentage of sales still higher, if you choose. By law 35% of the existing tenants *in residence* in a New York apartment house must buy a unit before conversion can take effect.

Marketing: Present tenants are the first target

They have proven over the years to be an apartment owner's best condominium customer. So concentrate on selling them first, Lyons says. You can expect about 40% of them to buy. Typically, they'll buy their own apartment—as is—within the first 30 days.

"When the tenants don't buy within the first month," says Lyons, "we know we have a bomb on our hands."

It's critical, Lyons says, that no tenant learn about the impending conversion until the owner is ready to announce it. A leak will stampede tenants into somebody else's apartment house.

When you're ready, mail a letter to all tenants explaining your intention to convert. Include in that mailing magazine articles and newspaper clippings that explain positively the benefits of condominium ownership. "One item we included," Lyons says, in speaking of the conversion of Bedford Towers in Stamford, "was an article called 'To Rent or To Buy' by syndicated columnist Sylvia Porter. She's well known and highly regarded by the public."

Once the letter has been sent, you'll need to set up an office in a vacant apartment where the tenants can get their questions answered. And staffing that office must be a new breed of salesman—one knowledgeable in the economics and tax implications of condominium ownership.

Tenant sales will move swiftly—provided management has been good over the years, Lyons says. But if tenant resentment exists, your salesmen will have to overcome that ill feeling.

The best way to win over an irate tenant, Lyons says, is to explain that once the building has become a condominium, the villain landlord will be gone. From that time on the tenants-turned-owners will run the building—through their condominium association.

TO NEXT PAGE

Converting to condominium

More and more apartment owners, caught in the squeeze, are deciding they'd rather switch than fight. Two companies tell how to do it as painlessly—and profitably—as possible.

Conversion specialists

A new kind of company spawned by the rental squeeze

It was an unexpected request that got Largo Properties, a Connecticut builder-developer since 1969, into the condominium conversion business.

Late in 1970 the owners of a 144-unit rental apartment house in Stamford tried to unload their building on another investor. When there were no takers, the owners decided to try the conversion route. They hired Largo to handle the switch.

Largo in turn set up Largo Condominium Co., a wholly-owned subsidiary, and hired Robert Lyons, a former director of marketing and sales for U.S. Steel's Realty Development Div., as its director of marketing and sales. Now, with its initial conversion successfully completed, the new company is moving into others.

The first step: an in-depth market study

You need to determine whether or not the apartments you want to sell are the apartments the public wants to buy, says Lyons. For example will they be attractive to confirmed city dwellers—that 36-to-65-year-old group that wants homes without the suburban drawbacks? Will they perhaps attract empty-nesters whose present houses are too large and too much bother to maintain? Or are they suited to the 65-and-over retirement or senior-citizen market?

It's quite possible that your apartment has everything wrong with it—maybe 3- and 4-bedrooms in an urban community where young singles willing to buy their units want studios and one-bedroom facilities.

Lyons says it's all too easy for an owner to view his apartment house through the well-known—and deceptive—rose-colored glasses. And that's all the more reason for a third-party market study. That way you'll get a professional, objective evaluation.

With the market study you'll also have to compute the price

much more carefully before putting his mortgage on the line.

The local rep. This ties in closely with what Kessler believes is the next most important point in developing the condominium market: finding (and keeping) a man or company to represent Multicon in a local market area. Since this local representative will be responsible for finding and buying land, overseeing development and marketing the finished project, he is obviously a vital cog in Multicon's machine.

So after Kessler decides to go into a certain area, the first thing he does is look for a local entrepreneur who knows both the industry and the area. Sometimes this even means buying out a local homebuilder, then offering enough pay, incentives and responsibility to make him want to stay with Multicon.

When he finds his man, Kessler brings him to his Columbus, Ohio headquarters for several months. This gives both the man and the company ample time to know each other, and the local rep time to receive training in Multicon's business and construction methods.

These methods include a fine balance between centralized operation for coordinated planning and maximum purchasing clout and local management to get the best use out of the land and the most effective marketing and merchandising.

"My local representative is a vitally important member of the company and the key man when it comes to selling our condominium units," Kessler says. "If he's really good, he's hard to get and hard to keep. We require an entrepreneur. But a good entrepreneur, by definition, wants to work for no one but himself.

"That's why we give him almost complete responsibility for developing the area, subject to the barest minimum of authority from headquarters. And we do take away the risk factor for him."

What kind of condominium? Except for a few high-rises for retirees in Florida, all Multicon's sale units are townhouses. They are more similar to conventional houses than are apartments, and they don't require the common areas—corridors, large entry areas, etc.—that garden apartments do.

Moreover, the townhouse form of construction should eventually be a natural for modular housing, an idea whose time "just has to come," Kessler believes.

"With their potential advantages in high volume and production control, modulars should eventually provide better value, even though not all of them do at the present," he says.

"Today, they cost more to finance, and transportation is another big problem. But I'm sure there will be much more modular in the future."

Converting rentals. Kessler is even studying the feasibility of converting part of a Chicago project into condominiums. If the prospects look favorable, he will probably offer the apartments in one of the buildings for sale to its present tenants. Those tenants who don't want to buy will have the opportunity to move to a similar rental unit in another building in the project, with Multicon paying the mover's tab.

The vacated units would then be offered as is at a discount instead of being renovated.

Possible dangers. What factors in the future could change the outlook for condominiums? One is the tax shelter problem. If condominium building takes off the way Kessler thinks it could, rental owners whose vacancies went way up could pull their rents way down and operate more for tax shelter than for current income. This could pose competitive difficulties for the condominium builder, Kessler acknowledges.

Another fly in the ointment might be the growing demand for second homes. Since these are in most cases purchased rather than rented, a boom in the vacation home market could eat up the capital which would have gone into the down payment for the primary home. And Kessler sees the possible advent of the four-day week as giving a big boost to both the travel industry and the second-home market, again at the expense of the condominium builder.

But Kessler doesn't see these as major problems. He sums up his case like this:

"The public wants condominiums for ownership and tax write-off reasons.

"The builder should see in them the chance to take his earnings and look for new projects."

"The rental market is just now coming of age, and we're going to stay with it."

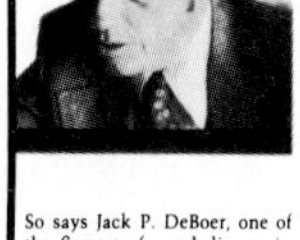

So says Jack P. DeBoer, one of the firmest of non-believers in condominium housing. He has no intention of leaving the rental market in which he has grown to one of the country's largest building firms.

DeBoer sees the best way of staying healthy in the squeezed rental market as increased efficiency—in his words, "taking the slop out of rental costs."

DeBoer thinks that until now, rental builders have been able to show black ink without being too careful about building and maintenance costs. That situation does not exist any more, and builders who want to stay in business will have to clamp down hard on excess costs.

DeBoer's own experience has been that there are costs to be cut and quality to be improved in virtually every area, from basic construction materials to carpets and light bulbs.

Looking ahead. A major reason for DeBoer's optimism towards the rental market is his conviction that condominiums will soon begin to price themselves out of the market.

"I believe we're going to see in condominium building exactly what has happened to the single-family market over the last twenty years," he says. "What happened there was a case of too good a selling job by the industry.

"The period from 1946 to 1956 saw an interesting evolution. First you had a two-bedroom house on a slab, then three bedrooms, then three with basement and so on up the line. Now people can't afford single-family houses any more, even though today you can still build a two-bedroom on a slab at nearly the same relative cost as you could in 1946.

"The industry sold itself out of the market in single-families, and it's going to do the same thing with condominiums.

"On the other hand our multifamily building quality is 200% better than it was three years ago, because we've learned that we can't afford to make mistakes any longer."

The better quality, DeBoer says, means that maintenance costs have been substantially reduced.

"And we keep the lid on even tighter by stringent and regular inspections of all our projects. This is the responsibility not only of the local management but of what we call our Environmental Department, which is based here in Wichita but is within two and a half flying hours of all our developments."

DeBoer's attack on high costs is two-pronged: full-time schools for managers and maintenance men, and a department whose job is to keep a log on the performance of maintenance hardware—a sort of Consumers Union in miniature.

This can make a big differ-

TO NEXT PAGE

Founded in 1965, Jack P. DeBoer Associates of Wichita, Kans., is presently doing an annual volume of close to $100 million in rental apartments. Geographically, DeBoer's projects extend from Las Vegas to Raleigh, N.C., and Lansing, Mich., to Houston.

Making the small site pay

Every town has its share
of small land parcels,
usually in prime locations where
multifamily zoning is possible,
if not actually in force.
Here you see how two such parcels
—each about half an acre—
were put to optimum use.

PHOTO: GERALD RATTO

Below-grade parking saves space on a small site in San Anselmo, Calif. For a closer look at the project, turn the page.

4/color

Making the problem site pay

A lot of potential apartment sites
get bypassed because of some
serious problem of land or location.
Here are three examples of
how such problems were solved—and
even turned into assets.

PHOTOS: E.R. GRENSTED

ONE BEDROOM UNIT

TWO BEDROOM UNITS

Building plans include storage
rooms (triangular sections) and
ground-level walkways (shaded
sections) over which six studio
units were built.

1

On this five-acre site in Monterey, Calif., a construction problem—how to work around big trees on irregular terrain—was turned into a design and marketing asset. Result: The 141-unit project has been fully rented since five weeks after its opening in April 1970. Rents, slightly higher than those of competing apartments, range from $200 to $250 for one- and two-bedroom units.

Saving the old oaks and Monterey pines called for more than the usual open space. So three-story buildings were necessary to reach the desired density of 28 units an acre. Aside from the trees, the project's most distinctive feature is a large plaza on the site's highest land. Buildings enclose the plaza and step down the hillsides.

The project, built by Tom Trollope, was designed by Barrie H. Groen & Associates, whose solution of a very different site problem is shown on overleaf.

Central plaza, shown above from the project's main entrance and at right from the north end of the recreation building, was planned around old trees. One-story recreation building has a rear entrance, shown below, and includes pool tables, saunas, a bar and a large room used by tenants for parties and meetings.

175

PRODUCTS

This seems to be the least glamorous part of a publication. The manufacturer-supplied picture (normally of doubtful quality) and press release copy (normally of prejudiced content) seem far away from journalism. So they are. And usually the chore of assembling the items for inclusion in the publication is delegated to the junior members of the staff: the assistant editor and the assistant art director (who just got their names on the masthead so can't in conscience object!). But, let's face it, rewriting press releases and scaling product pictures is no great fun.

So why have new products reports at all? Simply because the vast majority of specialized publication readers are vitally interested in them; readership surveys invariably show the product pages near the top of the "interested-in" and "did-something-about" listings.

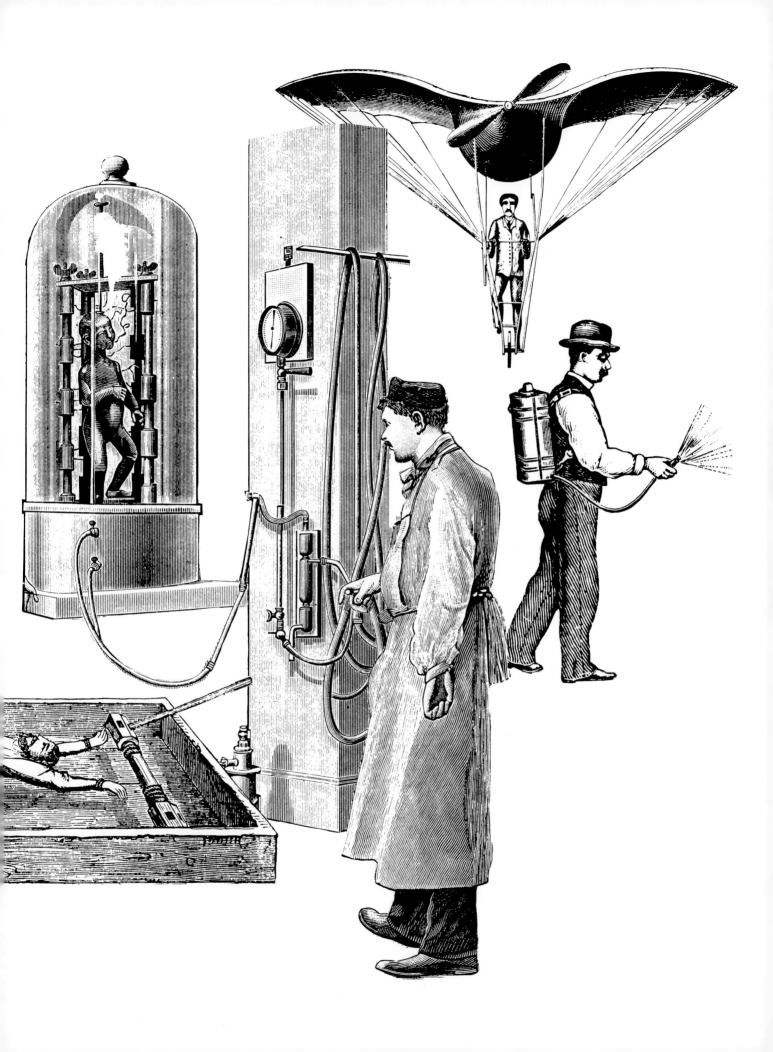

The widespread use of "bingo cards" (Reader Service cards on which the reader circles the number of the item he is interested in and mails back for more information) bound into the magazines also proves the drawing power of new product information.

The usual image that comes to mind when thinking of "new products" in a typical magazine is column after column of filler material separated by small space ads in the back of the book. This is, of course, a justified image, however sad and unimaginative the treatment may be. But this mechanical, regurgitated presentation is by no means the only — or the best — way of showcasing new products. It seems to be the easiest, simplest, most efficient way to kill several birds with one stone: to fill up those spaces, to give the ads editorial support, to keep the junior staffers busy, to publish useful information, and to keep advertisers happy (though perish the thought that editorial integrity and space be affected by anything so crass as plugging materials under commercial influence!).

The usual three-to-a-page presentation, with picture and small headline for each, plus those usually-too-black lines that say something like "for further information check No. 000 on Reader Service Card" needs no illustration.

Of greater interest, however, are some of the other presentation patterns illustrated on the pages that follow. Naturally, as in everything editorial, the choice of technique depends on the editorial and publishing goals. If the new products reports are just fillers, then a throw-away technique is adequate. But if higher ranking is desired, then varying degrees of importance can be given to the reports, as tactically appropriate.

New products as "story"

This is usually a technologically interesting item, and by delving into the item's background, purpose, ability to improve current techniques or practices, the editors can bring out its significance more fully than in a simple product description. Naturally, such a story-in-depth requires more space, more text, more pictures, and larger headline treatment. Also its interest value can be counted upon to attract the reader's attention. This is a very useful stratagem with which to begin a news section; not only is interest generated, but the seriousness of the report lends stature to the rest of the product reports and makes it clear that they are more than mere press release rewrites. An example is found on page 186 on which *House & Home* combines the major article with an index of products to be found on other pages (one of which is also shown).

New products as "news"

A slightly different angle from the product-as-a-story is used here, resulting in a slightly different presentation; the product-as-story can (and should) be laid out as a regular feature. (The *House & Home* example is, perhaps, too restrained in format to be an ideal example of this.) The product-as-news is laid out according to the news section format, so that it appears as a normal news story that happens to be about a manufactured product rather than about a political action, let's say, or somebody getting an award. As such, the piece has a headline which describes the news significance of the item, and the picture will probably not be a picture of the product itself but of the people who made it or something else that illustrates its *news* worthiness.

The example from *Chemical Engineering* shown on page 188 describes a process rather than a manufactured product, but products can be handled the same way. Page 189 illustrates a typical page which might follow such an opener on which two degrees of importance are shown: short product reports, illustrated and unillustrated, as well as a "boxed item" which signals the product's attention-worthy importance. All the layout formats, however, are exactly the same as those used for nonproduct "news."

New products as "show windows"

This is a group of related items presented as a major report — the emphasis is on the *group* rather than on any individual item. Thus the umbrella headline (normally a simple label is most effective) is the focal point of the presentation, and the design problem is tying together the disparate elements into arrangements that make sense graphically. Such design chores can become quite arduous and ultimately thankless, since the result will probably not be terribly exciting, no matter how much effort and talent are brought to bear. Usually there is just too much material to shoehorn in and everything is just too small to be graphically stimulating. A camouflaging format, therefore, is needed to provide spaces into which the items can be dropped, yet which will become — in itself — the apparent "design" of the page. An example from *Industrial World* is shown on pages 190 through 193. The ruled-box "net" gives the pages unity; and since there are a number of pre-drawn interchangeable nets available, the page makeup, issue to issue, becomes child's play. (Compare this to the Contents Page example, on pages 52 and 53 for treatment based on the same principle.)

What makes the *Industrial World* example significant in the context of this analysis, though, is that a normal, ordinary, mixed-bag new products section is also run in the same issue every month. Comparing the two makes the point about editorial purpose quite clear. (See page 193).

New products as "catalog"

Some publications devote major space to new products in every issue. Others do so only on occasion (such as once a year in a special issue). But whatever the frequency, certain catalog techniques are followed which should be pointed out. First of all, however, it is necessary to mention that the catalog business is burgeoning. Selling by mail from illustrated catalogs fills a proud and glorious page in this country's social history, though the graphic design of catalogs has only recently received the attention it deserves. An art it certainly is. Glamorous-looking, fashionable catalogs from expensive department stores receive tremendous design attention, and the illustrations are made by highly trained specialists. The investment involved is met in part by fees charged to the manufacturers of the various products shown in the catalog, though the catalog is made to *appear* to represent a single client, i.e., the department store. What holds these catalogs together and gives them their unity as a visual entity (in spite of the hundreds of individual items shown) is that they are a mosaic assembled according to an overall design plan. This plan may be based on a co-ordinated color scheme, or on groupings of pictures, or on groupings of items within larger pictures, or on overlappings, or on framings or on silhouettings, or on any number of other graphic gimmicks that will make an attractive package from the mass of unrelated items. The attractiveness makes the recipient react positively to it. It is meant to cajole him into liking it, spending time studying it, making it easy for him to absorb it, and persuading him to use it.

Alas, new product departments in magazines — however much they may wish to emulate these catalogs — cannot achieve such selling glamour; except in a few very special circumstances, they have neither the requisite funds, materials, nor time to produce such a package. They must get whatever glamour is possible within the practical restrictions in which they work, and make up for their more modest format by other means: primarily, service to the reader, by which they achieve the same goal as the glossy-format catalogs by persuading him to use the new products page(s).

Once the job of attraction has been accomplished the goal is to require of the reader minimum effort at maximum speed. Efficiency and ease of legibility are the touchstones. Items should be grouped logically in whatever groupings make most sense; the descriptions must, obviously, carry the requisite information; but — the most important criterion of all — the relationship between picture and description must be immediately apparent. Having to hunt around the page for the caption that fits the picture is time-consuming, irritating, and, as such, counter-productive.

Some sort of numerical labeling has been found to be the simplest, so long as the numbers can be found. On pages 194-197 are examples from *House & Home* and *Architectural Record*. The first one shows grouped pictures with large numbers dropped out of them referring to the descriptions at the foot of the page. The second is similar except that the text runs vertically and the numerals are in the interstices between the pictures. The *Architectural Record* presentation shows a typical page from a special issue in which a simple-to-apply system was invented to fit the picture requirements as well as give some flexibility in the length of descriptions. The spaces for pictures are standardized but the pictures that go in them are variable (as long as they are in a lower-left corner in each). The spaces for text are standardized also, but the text lengths are variable (as long as they are flush left and the first line in each column starts at the same position on the page). The dummy sheet indicates the system clearly. Without a system such as this, it would be likely that 768 separate items (each with its picture, number and blurb) on 67 pages could be a direct road to insanity for all.

Another possible catalog treatment is shown in the example on pages 198 and 199, typical of pages in the Book Review section of *Library Journal*. As far as graphics is concerned, this is simply a variation on the catalog theme; each of the many items consists of a group of predetermined elements, varying in length but of a predictable sort; all the items are grouped by subject, and they flow on page after page after page (which is yet another characteristic of catalogs).

Given the varying degrees of emphasis and their concomitant techniques of presentation, it is possible for a publication to generate great interest in its new products reports; there is no reason why all of these techniques could not be used on occasion, or why any one technique must be the standard one for a given publication forever. It is not the products that are dull; it is usually the unimaginative presentation that is the bore.

Plain new products columns dressed up

A perfectly standard presentation technique of headline, picture, text, address, and "circle" line had to be improved, in order to give the material greater visibility, the pages more oomph, the section coherence (especially since very

WHAT'S NEW

IN PRODUCT DESIGN-FUNCTION-ASSORTMENT

The purpose of this department is to provide convenient, up-to-date new product information. It is compiled from manufacturers' information. Listing does not imply Dental Economics endorsement. For additional information write to the manufacturer or return the Convenient Card, Page 16. Any quoted prices are subject to change without notice.

...SS HEAT GUNS—
...dental laboratory pro-
...Clean, flameless heat
...to 1000° F. is deliver-
...ly from a safe, con-
...jet that allows den-
...ed up setting time of
...acrylic plastic resins,
...drying of x-ray films
...res and decreases the
...kes to soften thermo-
...The newly developed
...hment fits entire line
...s and can be attached
...fferent positions. The
...irectional air diffuser

also pre-heats the gosport tube which provides concentration of high temperatures on a specific small area. *Master Appliance Corp., 1745 Flett Ave., Racine, WI 53403*
For information circle 126 on postcard.

VERSADENT—A new fully-portable dental unit with basic concept eliminating frills and cabinetry construction. Designed for sit-down, two or four-handed dentistry, left or right-handed operation. Working mechanism employs standard industrial components so that replacement parts may readily be obtained. Unit lends itself especially to

use in satellite offices, hospitals, nursing homes, dental schools, etc. Comprehensive general practice, orthodontic, dental hygiene, and assistant units are offered, each with several options. *Versadent, P. O. Box 4225, Davenport, IA*
For information circle 129 on postcard.

UNI-CHAIR—A new series of chair-mounted tables and instrumentation providing total convenience for either two-

handed or four-handed dentistry. Designed for dentist and assistant to provide fast, efficient, trouble-free dentistry in the smallest of operatories. The "His" model is ideal for dentist who already has existing suction equipment and who wants to convert to over-the-lap instrumentation. The Hygienist model provides all equipment needed for hygiene dentistry, with added benefit of compact design and ease of installation. The Uni-Chair "Hers" conveniently provides the assistant with all the tools she needs to help dentist work faster and easier. *Den-Tal-Ez/A-Dec., 1201 S. E. Diehl Ave., Des Moines, IA 50315*
For information circle 130 on postcard.

TMJ RECORDING ASSEMBLY—Is for accurate centric bites and split cast checking. Consists of Upper and Lower Slotted Plates, adjustable 120° Center Bearing Screw, Spacer Paralleling Ring and 6 Plastic Cones for injecting stone. The Slots function as split case mounting in checking accuracy of stone cen-

(Continued on page 53)

DENTAL ECONOMICS

What's New

DISCLOSING TABLETS IN BULK

Preventodontic Disclosing tablets are now available 1000 tablets in a single package. The tablets are individually sealed in cellophane sheets. Each sheet,

which contains ten tablets, can be easily dispensed to patients. *Mynol, Inc.*
For information circle 124 on postcard

ELECTRIC EYE SINK

The Aquatron electric eye sink affords sanitary working conditions with complete efficiency and safety. Water flows automatically when hands interrupt the self-contained electric eye

The purpose of this department is to provide convenient, up-to-date new product information. It is compiled from manufacturers information. Listing does not imply Dental Economics endorsement. For additional information write to the manufacturer. For additional information circle the appropriate number on the convenient Reader Service Card. Any quoted prices are subject to change without notice.

beam. stops when hands are pulled from the flow. The sink features preset water temperature, adjustable pressure regulation, absence of exposed knobs to contaminate hands and an easy-to-install design. Basins are available in vitreous china. porcelainized cast iron or stainless steel in a variety of standard or oval configurations. Price. $189.00 *Qualco.*
For information circle 125 on postcard

IMPRESSION COMPOUND

Cardex-Super impression compound is a silicone-rubber base material developed to take impressions of inlay cavities — crowns and stumps to be fitted with dowels. It is used in connection with the copper ring method. The compound consistency is similar to that of thermoplastic impression compounds so that the operator can continue his accustomed work method with copper rings. Cold curing (five minutes) is said to be its major advantage. *Peerless Dental Corp.*
For information circle 126 on postcard

DRYING AGENT

Prep-Dry is a liquid that when dabbed on enamel or dentin, completely removes oily surface film and moisture, thus improving the performance of adhesives requiring a dry field. It is nonirritating to soft tissue and is available in

a kit containing two 4-ounce bottles. *Lee Pharmaceuticals.*
For information circle 127 on postcard

CUSTOMIZED DENTAL KITS

A single dental health kit cannot meet the needs of everyone. Dentists can now customize dental health control kits for their patients' home use. Included in the kit is — a toothbrush. avail-

able in a variety of shapes and styles, a mouth mirror. unwaxed dental floss. disclosing tablets and a brochure. *John O. Butler. Co.*
For information circle 128 on postcard

MOULD GUIDE

A mould guide for Myerson's Porcelain Special Anterior teeth is now available. The leatherette mould guide includes samples of each mould with dimensional data, articulations and other necessary information. *Myerson Tooth Corp.*
For information circle 129 on postcard

DISPOSABLE CARTRIDGE

The new ball-bearing air turbine cartridge used in the Whispering Tornado now only requires oiling once a week. This new type disposable cartridge will operate for two hundred hours or 70,000 cutting operations at 200 grams pressure. Price. cartridge alone, $36.00. *Lincoln Dental Supply, Co.*
For information circle 130 on postcard

CHEEK RETRACTOR

Made of non-conductive plastic. Ora-Shields slip around the corner of the mouth to retract and protect the cheek. For greater retraction. a rubber band can be attached to the catch and looped over the ear. Ora-Shields are disposable, light in weight, and remain in place without being held by the patient or assistant. They also protect the lips.
Continued

peculiar spaces among the small ads had to be filled). Problem: no changes allowed in the material itself.

The solution: to enclose each column in vertical rules with wide spaces between them, so that each column becomes a freestanding vertical unit and to separate the headline from the text and overscore it with a heavy rule, underscore it with a light rule and thus give it "color." The spacing was, of course, coordinated with the line-by-line typesetting system so that makeup would be simple. The resulting pattern of dark and light strokes became the "design" of the pages, highly visible and individual.

Here is a much simpler technique than the one from *Dental Economics,* opposite. Again we have a three-column makeup (shown here is the opener of the section which devotes the outside column to a vertically run logo); the individual text pieces are somewhat longer than is usual, so that there are fewer elements that can be "dressed up" per page. The headlines are enclosed between two rules in the same way as *Dental Economics,* opposite, but here the lower line becomes the top line of a standardized box into which the illustrations are dropped. Because the great majority of the illustrations are pictures of medicines (i.e., boxes or bottles of some sort) it makes sense to decree that all illustrations be silhouetted, since it is easy to silhouette simple shapes such as boxes or bottles. So in this solution, the handling of the illustrations becomes the visual signal characteristic of the section.

novos produtos

NICOTILÉSS Pastilhas

Indicações — Medicação auxiliar na erradicação do tabagismo.

Fórmula — Em cada pastilha: sulfato de lobelina, 0,5 mg.

Modo de usar — Deixar dissolver uma pastilha na boca, todas as vezes que sentir necessidade imperiosa de fumar, até o máximo de 10 pastilhas por dia.

Apresentação — Caixa com 20 pastilhas.

Produzido por Boehringer do Brasil S.A., Av. Brasil, 5843, Rio de Janeiro, RJ.

BIPENCIL

Indicações — Infecções determinadas por germens sensíveis à ampicilina.

Fórmula — Em cada frasco-ampola: ampicilina benzatina, 250 e 500 mg; ampicilina sódica, 50 e 100 mg; citrato de sódio, 10 e 10 mg; carboximetilcelulose sódica, 40 mg; polivinilpirrolidon (PVP), 20 mg; lidocaína, 20 mg.

Modo de usar — Via parenteral: um frasco de 12 em 12 horas ou de 24 em 24 horas.

Contra-indicações — Sensibilida-

de à penicilina; infecções por estafilococos penicilino-resistentes; primeiro trimestre da gravidez.

Precauções — Podem ser verificadas superinfecções por germens resistentes ao antibiótico, quando o produto for usado por longo tempo.

Apresentação — Embalagem com 1 frasco-ampola e 1 ampola diluente.

Produzido por Colúmbia do Brasil S.A., Indústria Farmacêutica, Rua Magalhães Castro, 170, Rio de Janeiro, RJ.

AMOXIL Cápsulas e Xarope

Indicações — Infecções das vias aéreas superiores e inferiores, infecções urinárias e entero-infecções, inclusive febre tifóide.

Fórmula — Em cada cápsula e em cada 5 cm³ de xarope: alfa-amino-p-hidroxibenzilpenicilina, 250, 500, 125 e 250 mg.

Modo de usar — Via oral: 250 a 500 mg, de 8 em 8 horas, para adultos e 125 e 250 mg, 3 vezes ao dia, para crianças.

Precauções — Suspender a medicação na eventualidade de reações alérgicas, principalmente em pacientes com antecedentes de asma, urticária etc.

Contra-indicação — Pacientes hipersensíveis à penicilina.

Apresentação — Caixas com 9 cápsulas de 250 mg e com 6 cápsulas de 500 mg. Frascos com pó para preparar 45 cm³ de xarope.

Produzido por Laboratórios Beecham Ltda., Divisão Villela, Rua das Oficinas, 188, Rio de Janeiro, RJ.

Plain columns manipulated in space

The example on this page is based on a very simple trick: using a four-column width in a three-column space. The text is set to fit in narrow, four-columns-to-the-page measure, but put in vertical one-thirds or two-thirds spaces. The white area thus left over appears "wasted." But perhaps one ought to consider the attention-getting value of such "wasted" space: it may be a good investment, especially when there are many such mixed pages that have

4-column makeup ("A") used in 3-column space ("B")

to be filled and ought to be made recognizable. The upper example shows a vertical-third space, with the pictures sized to the full one-third width; the lower one shows the effect of keeping the pictures within the confines of the narrow one-fourth column; perhaps having the pictures poke out into the white space would have been more interesting. But that wedge of clean, white space certainly splits the editorial matter from the ad!

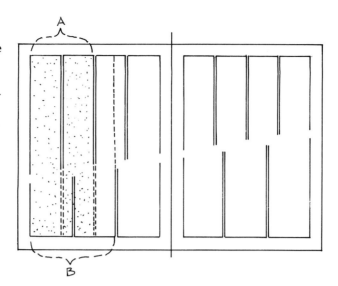

Here the space is arranged differently: the emphasis is on the horizontal flow from page to page (see page 96 for the context from which this page is taken). The columns' verticality has to be chopped down. By pulling the pictures away from the text and suspending them as random-size units from the logo, the space for the text becomes a square. This square is emphasized by the tight way in which the type is placed in it. To add literary interest — and to tease the reader a little — the picture captions are worded differently from the way in which the headlines are written.

LJ BUYERS' GUIDE

Every effort is made to evaluate carefully the products listed. However, mention here is not an endorsement. Prices are subject to change, and may vary in different geographical areas.

PERIODICAL HOLDERS

SECRET SURVEYOR

BLADE REFINER

CHANGE BAGGER

Magazine binders

A new type of publication binder from the Highsmith Co. is a reasonable cost solution to the problem of avoiding loss of valuable magazines while keeping them available for frequent use. These multi-copy binders feature blade-lock security for each periodical, assuring that the magazines remain in their original sequence; 13 steel strap-rods are inserted through the center of the magazines and locked into place with a key.

Blade-Lock binders come in 16-gauge textured vinyl buckram, covering extra-heavy binder's board. They are available in eight sizes, ranging from 8" to 16" in height with a 3" capacity, and in four colors—orange, blue, green, and charcoal—with color corresponding to size.

For more information write to the Highsmith Co., P. O. Box 25, Fort Atkinson, Wis. 53538. (414) 563-6356.

Personal security device

Library staff working in security hazardous areas might welcome the "U"Gard, a thumbsize personal security device that can be worn or hidden in clothing or pocket. The device is a miniature battery-operated electronic generator that emits a constant ultrasonic signal which continues for over one hour when triggered and is picked up by receivers hidden in a room. These receivers can be specially wired or utilize existing wiring in the building to bring the signal back to a control panel in a security office.

Every room can be provided with a receiver which picks up signals as the person wearing the transmitter moves from room to room. Thus a path is indicated on the control panel for rescue at the point of emergency. Since the ultrasonic beam will not go through room walls, the location of the emergency can be pinpointed to a specific room or rooms.

Once turned on, the "U"Gard cannot be turned off. It will resist crushing, cutting, and similar attack. An exclusive signal turner prevents the device from being falsely triggered by keys, TV controls, dog whistles, etc.

The cost of "U"Gard equipment is approximately $100 per room depending on the wiring required. Transmitters are available in various designs—ladies pendant, pens, belt clip-on, etc. For further information contact Bergen Laboratories, Inc., 60 Spruce St., Patterson, N.J. 07501. (201) 278-3020.

Knife sharpener

Applicable to all paper cutters from 18" up, the new Michael Electric Knife Sharpener makes it possible to keep the knife sharp without removing it from the paper cutter. Differing from previous sharpeners, it has a one arm grinding wheel swing to meet all knife levels down to the cutting stick. The bevel angle setting is never altered from the initial setting, giving a constant bevel to any level of the knife. Another important feature is an adjustable metal stop-pin which eliminates burrs and double grinding in spots.

Available from Michael Business Machines Corp., 145 West 45th St., New York, N.Y. 10036. (212) 582-2900.

Label protectors

A new adhesive, transparent label protector of tough plastic is now available to keep book labels or direct lettered call numbers permanently in place. Highsmith See-Thru Label Protectors will adhere to textured material such as book cloth, leather, and vellum, as well as film cans, reel boxes, record labels, and book jackets.

Protectors come in two sizes: 1½" x 3¼" and 2" x 5". A plastic box contains 200 labels. For free samples and information write: The Highsmith Company, Inc., P.O. Box 25, Fort Atkinson, Wisc. 53538. (414) 563-6356.

Coin-wrapping machine

This compact, lightweight coin-wrapping machine counts and packages a roll of coins in 40 seconds. Designed to package quarters, the unit also has tube and tray attachments for pennies, nickles, and dimes. Price is $14.95 from T.Y.U. Enterprises, P.O. Box 59, Harbor City, Calif. 90710.

Rotary files

A new line of rotary index files from Bostitch will be useful for maintaining easily changed listings, e. g. periodical files. Molded of G. E. Lexan and Cycolac plastic—the same high impact materials used in space and football helmets, these files will stand up to heavy abuse and will not crack, dent, chip, or peel. The files also feature a no-slip clutch which makes the job of turning the cards easier.

The four models of the Bluemark line come with cards and alphabetical guides included, in grey or biege with (or without) a bronze color cover, at these suggested prices: RF 245, 500 cards 2¼" x 4", no cover, $11.95; RFC 245, 500 cards 2¼" x 4", $16.95; RFC 245 Twin 1000 cards 2¼" x 4", $27.95; RFC 355, 500 cards 3" x 5", $22.95. Available in office supply, department stores, etc. From Bostitch Div. of Extron, Inc., Briggs Dr., E. Greenwich, R. I. 02818. (401) 884-2500.

Section opener features a product as a "story"

The opener is signaled not just by the large logo with its bold vertical rule, but also by the index beneath it. The index may or may not be used as such by the reader, but it is extremely useful as an indicator of the *beginning* of something as well as a suggestion of the *amount* of that something.

The product report on the opener is oriented less to the product as a product than it is to the effect that the product might have on the industry as a whole — which, of course, affects more readers than just those who happen to be in the market for the specific item. To open a products section with such a wide-ranging report adds stature and seriousness to the entire section.

The subsequent pages, each organized about a subject, are carefully assembled to give them an information-packed (i.e., full-of-value) look and to glean the greatest possible variety of arrangements from the four-column format. The page arrangements are anything but random, taking into account, as they do, the scale of the material shown in the pictures, the balance of the page as a whole, the necessity to square off elements against each other as well as to tell the stories clearly.

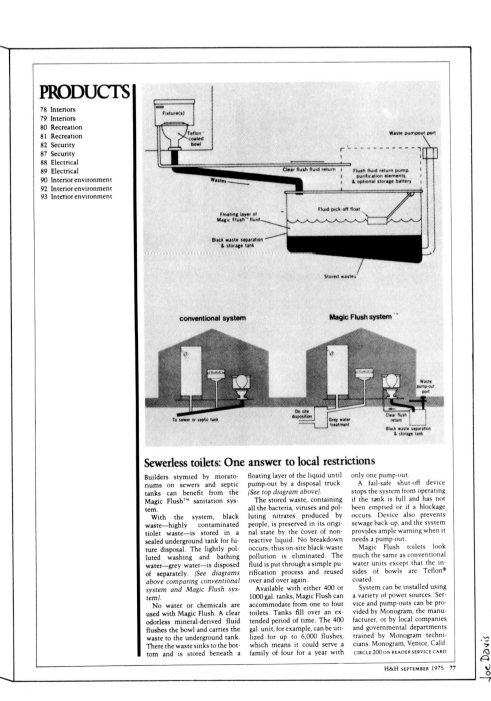

PRODUCTS

Sewerless toilets: One answer to local restrictions

Builders stymied by moratoriums on sewers and septic tanks can benefit from the Magic Flush™ sanitation system.

With the system, black waste—highly contaminated toilet waste—is stored in a sealed underground tank for future disposal. The lightly polluted washing and bathing water—grey water—is disposed of separately. (See diagrams above comparing conventional system and Magic Flush system).

No water or chemicals are used with Magic Flush. A clear odorless mineral-derived fluid flushes the bowl and carries the waste to the underground tank. There the waste sinks to the bottom and is stored beneath a floating layer of the liquid until pump-out by a disposal truck. (See top diagram above).

The stored waste, containing all the bacteria, viruses and polluting nitrates produced by people, is preserved in its original state by the cover of non-reactive liquid. No breakdown occurs; thus on-site black-waste pollution is eliminated. The fluid is put through a simple purification process and reused over and over again.

Available with either 400 or 1000 gal. tanks, Magic Flush can accommodate from one to four toilets. Tanks fill over an extended period of time. The 400 gal. unit, for example, can be utilized for up to 6,000 flushes, which means it could serve a family of four for a year with only one pump-out.

A fail-safe shut-off device stops the system from operating if the tank is full and has not been emptied or if a blockage occurs. Device also prevents sewage back-up, and the system provides ample warning when it needs a pump-out.

Magic Flush toilets look much the same as conventional water units except that the insides of bowls are Teflon® coated.

System can be installed using a variety of power sources. Service and pump-outs can be provided by Monogram, the manufacturer, or by local companies and governmental departments trained by Monogram technicians. Monogram, Venice, Calif. CIRCLE 200 ON READER SERVICE CARD

... followed by carefully patterned pages

Natural stone surfacing material, ASTRO-STONE®, *(above)* is composed of epoxy-coated aggregate or marble chips. Surface is slip-proof, resistant to temperature extremes and needs little maintenance. Astro-Stone, Lake Success, N.Y.
CIRCLE 225 ON READER SERVICE CARD

Billiards table with solid slate bed, "Spirit of '76," features a bicentennial look. Cloth and vinyl aprons are red; legs and rails are black. Table with ball return is 4'x8'. Ebonite, Miami Lakes, Fla.
CIRCLE 222 ON READER SERVICE CARD

Mechanical ice hockey table, "Power Line Play," *(below)* is for institutional use. Game has unbreakable men and rigid aluminum control rods. North American Recreation, Bridgeport, Conn.
CIRCLE 223 ON READER SERVICE CARD

"Whirlwind" slide *(left)* offers safety and maintenance-saving features. Top platform is enclosed, ladder has safety treads and stainless steel slide bed is rust-free. Miracle Recreation, Grinnell, Iowa.
CIRCLE 226 ON READER SERVICE CARD

Portable basketball backstop *(right)* can be moved by tipping it backward onto two rubber-tire wheels. The 370-lb backstop is stable when in position and its base is equipped with non-marring floor protectors. Sportsplay, St. Louis.
CIRCLE 227 ON READER SERVICE CARD

Canopy table *(below)* is constructed of 2"-thick redwood. Large enough to seat 12 people, table is smoothly sanded and treated with preservatives. Vinyl-coated canvas canopy is offered in ten colors. Omar Products, Lake Zurich, Ill.
CIRCLE 228 ON READER SERVICE CARD

Versatile playground unit, "Playtank," includes slides, fireman's pole and ladder ring. Translucent fiber glass components make inside activities visible from the outside. Fire-retardant resins are used throughout the equipment. Kilgore Corp., Reedsville, Pa. CIRCLE 224 ON READER SERVICE CARD

more products on page 82

New products reports handled as "news"

The first three or four product reports that open the section in *Chemical Engineering* are approximately three pages long and are handled in precisely the same way as straight news stories are: the typographic treatment (as well as the phrasing) of the heads is identical, as are the decks, opening paragraphs, etc. In fact, the best way to find out whether the item is a product report is to check the end of the story, to see whether it has a "circle" number for the Reader Service Card. The logo at the top of the page is a clue, too.

The subsequent pages of short reports are straightforward three-column makeup pages, with overscores on the headlines except where pictures are shown.

One additional element is shown on the page opposite: the boxed item. This handling is reserved for items deemed to be of special interest to the readership as a whole and thus deserving of a degree of emphasis greater than the regular, short report. Graphically it is handled the same way as boxed items in the news section.

Products-as-News page
↓
and
News-as-News page —↗

NEW PRODUCTS & SERVICES

Treatment trio tames organics, kills bacteria

Gamma rays, ozone, and activated carbon join forces to decimate even the hardiest viruses and bacteria in wastewater—and slash COD as well.

☐ Here's a pilot-plant-proven wastewater treatment process that eliminates chlorine disinfection and its related woes (see p. 49 for other chlorination alternatives).

Basically, the system consists of two pieces of hardware—an oxidation chamber and an irradiator/activated-carbon hybrid. The irradiator disinfects the stream and enhances oxidation of organics captured on the carbon surfaces. As an added plus, the gamma rays continuously regenerate the activated carbon, overcoming a major shortcoming of conventional activated-carbon columns—the need to be shut down and reactivated when the adsorbent becomes saturated.

And, because the brunt of the radiation dose is concentrated just on the organics—rather than on the entire wastewater stream—the system's operating efficiency reportedly is substantially higher than competitive radiation schemes, while costs are lower. For example, total costs for a 500,000-gal/d facility (with an organics loading of 250 mg/l) amortized over 20 yr are 28¢/1,000 gal.

HOW IT WORKS—Compressed air agitates the wastewater in an oxygenation chamber. The air bubbles through the wastewater, pressurizing the chamber to 32-35 psi, and ensuring that the optimum amount of oxygen dissolves in the water. From the bottom of the chamber, ozone is injected into the wastewater.

The ozone removes some color and kills some viruses in the chamber, but the primary purpose of both ozone injection and oxygen absorption is to raise the dissolved oxygen level to about 25 mg/l, which is necessary to oxidize the organics completely to carbon dioxide and water. The wastewater is then pumped from the oxygenation tank to the irradiator—a concrete vessel lined with 304 stainless steel and filled with activated carbon. In the center of the column are cobalt-60 rods. The organics attach to the column and are irradiated by the rods, dropping the dissolved oxygen content to 2-3 mg/l and reducing color by 90-99%.

Then, ozone is injected into the discharge line to boost the dissolved oxygen level to about 14 mg/l.

The combination of radiation and ozonation produces synergistic effects, the firm claims: studies show that, alone, ozone kills just 95-96% of viruses and bacteria, and gamma rays kill only 99%. Together the kill is virtually 100%.

PILOT SUCCESSES—In pilot testing at Marietta, Ga., a 5,000-gal/d system has routinely processed poultry-plant wastes. The process consistently pares organics by 95%, the company says, even with influents that contain up to 1,150 mg/l.

The unit houses four cobalt-60 rods in a 2-ft-dia., 8-ft-high column that holds 600 lb of carbon. Wastewater is screened to remove solids, is then held in a 15,000-gal tank, and finally flows by gravity to an 8-ft³ oxidation chamber. Baffles split the chamber into five equal compartments, and air lines supply 35-40 ft³/h of air into each section. Wastewater residence time is 16 min in the oxidation chamber, and 30 min in the 110-gal irradiator. The organics, which are irradiated with 100,000 rads/h, have a 10-h residence time in the carbon column.—*International Purification Systems, Inc., Atlanta, Ga.*

351

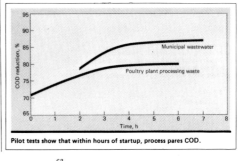

Pilot tests show that within hours of startup, process pares COD.

Noah Bee

Plastics fair dazzles, but exhibitors complain

With current demand and prices at rock-bottom level, European producers have to look hard for a silver lining. Most of them are trying to raise prices back to old levels in the hope of boosting profits.

☐ There were ups and downs at the world's biggest plastics fair (K '75), which ran for one week (Oct. 7-14) in Düsseldorf, West Germany. Compared with the previous exhibition, held in 1971, this quadrennial event glittered with expensive-looking booths and boasted both a higher number of exhibitors (1,200) and stronger foreign participation (over 40% of the total). But attendance dropped 13%, to 153,000 visitors, participation by U.S. firms declined,

and some major European exhibitors interviewed during the show were concerned over the poor current performance of Western Europe's plastics industry.

Even though most producers expressed optimism for the future—albeit modestly—they seemed to concur that the present situation is downright grim. Western Europe continues to be plagued by overcapacity in plastics. At K '75, exhibitors complained that cutthroat com-

petition had forced down prices of Western European bulk plastics by about 35% this year. Meanwhile, raw materials prices have risen—e.g., by 15-20% in the case of naphtha. Benzene prices, after weakening in early 1975, have gone up too, due to increasing demand in the U.S.

Plant-capacity utilization is down to 50-60%. And expansion plans for plastics throughout Western Europe have been stalled by anticipation of an average annual growth in output of only 6-8% and a severe profit squeeze.

THE GERMAN CASE—In many ways, Germany's plastics industry is a microcosm of Western Europe's. Its output, after dropping 3% last year to 6.27 million metric tons, slumped by 24% in the first nine months of 1975, thereby falling to the 1972 production level.

Capacity utilization now stands at 50-60%, and a marked improvement is not in sight as long as exports, which account for as much as 45% of total production, remain sluggish. German companies pin some hopes on the U.S. economic recovery, but the U.S. market absorbs only 7% of German plastics exports, compared to 45% of the still-ailing EEC market. "For the next few months we do not expect a substantial improvement," says Günther Metz, deputy head of Hoechst's plastics and wax department.

The domestic [...] in Germany doe[...] trend. Still, prod[...] whether the Ger[...] bear the 10-15%[...] plastics introduce[...] pliers in the secon[...] ber. "This merely[...] to the February/[...] phasizes Gernot[...] BASF's polystyr[...] "but without reac[...] erage."

All German firm[...]

Modern structure at Düsseldorf housed exhibits from 30 countries

motor styles and capacities, normally in the 2-hp range, are optional. Headed for tough industrial applications, such as pumping hot titanium dioxide slurries, hot concentrated sulfuric acid, and Freon/nitric-acid mixtures, the unit features a Teflon/Buna-N double mechanical seal.—*R. S. Corcoran Co., New Lenox, Ill.* 360

Portable monitor

A portable opacity measurement system, the RM41P, can be used for accurate visible emission measurements, or for precise adjustments, fault isolation, and performance testing of electrostatic precipitators, baghouses, and other emission-control equipment. An optical transmissometer measures light transmittance through an optical medium such as smoke or dust. A 5-ft probe that fits into the stack

houses the instrument's retroreflector. A portable control unit indicates optical density and opacity corrected to stack exit-conditions.—*Lear Siegler, Inc., Englewood, Colo.* 362

Alloy

This iron-base alloy provides corrosion resistance midway between that of austenitic stainless steels and nickel-, chromium-, iron-, and molybdenum-copper alloys. In the solution heat-treated state, the Haynes alloy No. 20 Mod has a room-temperature tensile strength of 84,500-94,900 psi. In the as-welded condition, a 3⁄8-in.-thick plate has a room-temperature tensile strength of 95,100 psi; a 0.166-in sheet, 77,900 psi.

The alloy has proven itself in corrosion tests, the developer claims: no crevice corrosion or pitting occurred after immersion in boiling sea water

for 432 h, or testing in a 2% sodium chloride plus 2% potassium permanganate solution for 120 hr at 90°C. In stress-corrosion cracking tests in a 42% magnesium chloride solution, specimens lasted 10 times longer than Type 316 stainless steel. Alloy No. 20 Mod is available in sheet, strip, plate, wire, pipe, tubing and forging stock.—*Stellite Div., Cabot Corp., Kokomo, Ind.* 361

Valves

This family of high-quality, low-cost industrial valves encompasses 253 sizes in 32 configurations, including iron-body gate, globe and check valves from 2-12 in, bronze-body gate, globe and check valves from 1⁄4-4 in., and bronze ball-valves from 3⁄8-3 in. All the valves are available from the company's 15 regional warehouses, providing 24-h delivery to customers within 300 mi of these key cities.

The iron gate valves feature a fully guided solid wedge disk, deep stuffing box, ductile iron handwheel, and flanged ends. They are available with rising or nonrising stems, and bronze or iron trim. For corrosive applications, a special nickel-iron bodied, stainless steel trimmed, gate valve is also offered. The bronze valves are all shell-molded for porosity-free casting, and the four different ball valves boast 15% glass-filled Teflon seats.—*Red-White Valve Corp., Carson, Calif.* 357

Protective coating

Fibre/Glaze CR, a chemical-resistant, fiberglass-reinforced protective coating, is said to be ideal for use on structural steel, piping, overhead railings, walls, floors, ceilings and tanks. Designed to withstand chemical fumes, abrasion and repeated

Boom contains oil spills in fast-flowing water

The first oil-spill-cleanup boom demonstrated to be effective in flowing water with medium and fast currents (up to 2.8 mi/h) resembles two parallel strings of sausages floating on water. Each "sausage" is, in fact, a 50-ft-long flotation device that is coupled to the section next to it. The boom, which weighs only 2 lb/ft, can be shortened and lengthened as desired, by adding or removing sections. Netting, fastened to a nonwoven material, runs the full length of the boom and links the parallel floats beneath the surface of the water. In operation, the boom is placed across the current flow at an angle. The oil and water flow under the leading float and through the netting. The water passes through the fabric while the oil comes to the surface between the two floats. A tangential current produced between the two floats carries the oil to the downstream end of the boom, where it is collected and recovered.
Steltner Development and Mfg. Co., Ltd., St. Catharines, Ontario, Canada. 353

Normal products page

New products handled as featured groups by subject

The emphasis here is on the group rather than the individual item; the clue to the grouping is, of course, the label headline. In the examples shown here from *Industrial World,* the "before" and "after" show the same approach to the same problem, but the "after" is considerably easier to assemble and it is, perhaps, a little more formalized and stylish. It is certainly more recognizable as a featured element in the magazine, issue by issue. On the following page is an example of the same technique used on a full spread. The first change is to split the recurring title of the department (Product Update) from the heading describing the specific subject in this issue (Air Compressors). This was done to allow the pages to become a part of a continuum of department pages, instead of being in a no-man's-land between department and feature. The second change is to establish design patterns that would simplify the process of page assembly without giving up the random, light-hearted quality of the pages to which the readers had become accustomed. A number of grids was prepared, allowing a variety of shapes as well as a different number of items to be accommodated per page. The items can be dropped into these spaces easily, thus avoiding the necessity to "design" each page separately every issue. A spin-off advantage: the modular grids which incorporate the department heading are the recognition symbol of the section.

On page 193 is a normal new products page from this same publication. It is handled as a normal three-column products page which usually has an item of double-column width to start off the section. Comparing the two sorts of product pages makes it quite clear how important it is to define the editorial and publishing purpose before graphic solutions that make expressive sense are attempted.

Product Update: FOOD PROCESSING

For skinning beef at a fast rate (up to 60 heads an hour) with less waste and only one operator, a Hide-Down Puller pulls up instead of down. The hydraulically powered rotating drum is raised and lowered by a telescoping piston. Hide rolls onto a drum when pulling and reverses to release hide. Write Anderson IBEC, 19699 Progress Drive, Strongsville, Ohio, USA 44136 or circle No. 451 on inquiry card

An automatic unit that separates bone from meat contains less parts than former models, resulting in simple operation and maintenance. Only two major components move. The mechanical deboner is made from stainless steel. For more information, write Stephen Paoli Int'l. Corp., 2531 Eleventh St., Rockford, Ill., USA 61108 or circle No. 452 on Reader Service inquiry card

The Hydrolock (left) is for the high speed sterilization of food product containers, up to 1,000 per minute. It is suitable for glass jars, rigid formed metal or plastic packages, for multiple-sized cans or multiple grades of products. Write Rexham Corp., 1665 Elmwood Road, Rockford, Ill., USA 61101 or circle No. 453

An X-ray imaging system in the Borden Model 1000 scanner detects foreign material in glass containers at speeds up to 300 containers per minute. Rejects are automatically sorted out. Write Borden Int'l, 711 3rd Ave., New York, N.Y., USA 10017 or circle No. 454

PRODUCT UPDATE

A line of packaged, stationary screw compressors consists of 50 models, from 50 to 500 hp. Three of these Pac-Air models are shown, from left, the 50-60 hp unit, the 75-125 hp, and the 150-300 hp. Units are either air or water-cooled, operate at 85 dBA. Write Ingersoll-Rand Co., 200 Chestnut Ridge, Woodcliff Lake, N.J., USA 07675 or circle 456

AIR COMPRESSORS

The portable 185 cft Model Singl/Screw compressor offers balanced compression to reduce axial and radial forces that cause wear and friction. It operates at 30°F lower than twin screw types of similar capacity and discharges air at about 70°F over ambient. Write Chicago Pneumatic, 608 Country Club Dr., Bensenville, Ill., USA 60106 or circle 457

A BT compressor can be set on any flat firm floor without need for bolting. The air-cooled line comes in single unit packages ranging from 100 cfm to 250 cfm, and operates at below 80 dBA. Write Atlas Copco, Boomse Steenweg 957, Antwerp, Belgium or circle 458

The Electra-Screw is a 30 hp oil-flooded, screw compressor available on a tank and base mount. Capacity is up to 132 cfm and maximum pressure of 175 psig. For more details, write Gardner-Denver Co., 1860 Gardner Expressway, Quincy, Ill, USA 62301 or circle No. 459

Designed for large volume air users, the Series 32 screw type unit is available from 200 to 350 hp. It is directly driven without gears by a 1770 rpm motor. The compressed air generator features two 13 in. diameter steel screws which eliminate wear. No foundation is required. An oil separating system is standard. For more details, write Sullair Corp., 3700 E. Michigan Blvd., Michigan City, Ind., USA 46360 or circle No. 460

191

PRODUCT UPDATE

Model 6654 gas-flow analog computer is designed to meet the needs of the natural gas industry. It's computational accuracy is ±0.1% full scale. A single run metering station is used to compute flow rate and total flow. Write Leeds & Northrup Co., North Wales, Pa., USA 19454 or circle No. 456

Fluids ranging in temperature from −45° to 310°C can be measured with the Brooks-Oval Flowmeter equipped with the model 4020 differential inductance converter. The oval rotors are the only moving parts in the metering system. It handles viscosities of less than one centipoise to in excess of 500,000 centipoise. Output is an electronic signal which is computer compatible. Write Brooks Instrument Div., Emerson Electric Co., Statesboro, Ga., USA 30458 or circle No. 457

This no-moving-parts, vortex shedding flowmeter is suitable for use in pipelines six through 48 in. in diameter. The model 2510 provides a pulse-type output. It uses flush-mounted thermal sensors that enable slurries and dirty fluids to be measured. Write Eastech Inc., 2381 S. Clinton Ave., South Plainfield, N.J., USA 07080 or circle No. 458

Leak testing and pneumatic testing is made easier with the DFF series Hastings fast response flowmeter. It has a dual relay control to operate an alarm or rejection device if the product being tested does not conform to specifications. Response time is one second for both flow rate indicator and limit relays. Write Teledyne Hastings-Raydist, Hampton, Va., USA 23661 or circle 461.

Model 400 is a light industrial gas meter with a maximum flow rate of 400 cfh. Maximum working pressure can be 10, 25 or 50 psi. Unit features weight saving aluminum alloy case with iron tops on aluminum center and covers. It has lubrication free internal components and bearings. Write Sprague Meter Co., 35 South Ave., Bridgeport, Conn., USA 06601 or circle No. 463

FLOWMETERS

An ultrasonic electrode cleaning system is available with 50 mm to 900 mm 2800 Series Magnetic Flowtubes. This prevents fouling from coating buildup on the electrode. The Series 2800 flowmeters can be used with any conductive fluid and are unaffected by temperature, viscosity or pressure. Write Foxboro Co., Foxboro, Mass., USA 02035 or circle No. 459

Designed for pollution control systems, this American Gas Sampling Meter accurately measures the volume of gas passing through a sampling train. The meter is usually placed between a gas analyzer and vacuum pump. It has a capacity of 140 cu ft per hour at ½ in. water column pressure across the meter. A front-mounted index with a large dial and a four digit readout displays meter reading. For details, contact American Meter Div., Singer Company, 13500 Philmont Ave., Philadelphia, Pa., USA 19116 or circle No. 460

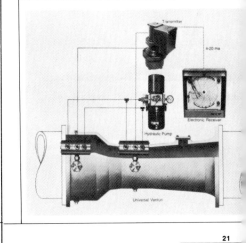

These spherical case meters are designed for reliable liquid metering in the range of 5 to 350 gpm. They have high strength and pressure resistance. Write Liquid Controls Corp., P.O. Box 101, North Chicago, Ill., USA 60054 *or circle No. 462*

Reduced power consumption and precise factory established zero stability are features of the new Mag-X magnetic flowmeter. Measurement signal is continuously sampled and stray signals are subtracted from it. The unit is available for 6 to 96 in. ID pipe. Installation costs are low since only one conduit is required between flowmeter and receiver. Write Fisher & Porter Co., 556 Jacksonville Rd., Warminster, Pa., USA 18974 *or circle No. 464*

...es and sewage, the SBF (Solids Bearing ...wmetering system eliminates problems of ...fouled pressure lines and gas entrapment. It ...sensitive detection of flow signals produced ...uri tube. Readings can be verified with a ...anometer. Write BIF, a unit of General Signal, ...sion Rd., Warwick, R.I., USA 02893 ...No. 465.

Harry Stavrakas

NEW PRODUCT REVIEW

Fork Lift Truck
The 6,000 lb capacity Model 1 MA-60H fork lift has a six-cylinder, 72 hp gasoline engine. Gradeability with rated load at 1 mph is 29.3%. Forward and reverse travel speed is 11 mph in high range, 6.75 mph in low range. Unit has full forward-reverse power shifting in low and high range.—White Materials Handling Co., White Motor Corp., 130 Ninth Ave., South, Hopkins, Minn., USA 55343 *or circle No. 395*

Process Pump
The Model 5A-VBD sanitary process pump has a built-in gear reducer for use where low material flow is desired. Supplied with an 1800 rpm motor, pump speed is reduced through belts and a built-in 3 to 1 gear reducer to about 350 rpm. Pump capacity: .8 gal per 100 revolutions. Ports are 1 in. x 1 in. Can be used with temperatures to 525°F, pressures to 450 psi.—Tuthill Pump Co., 12500 S. Crawford Ave., Chicago, Ill., USA 60658 *or circle No. 411*

Oil Burner
The HP series Iron Fireman oil burner is a compact forced draft pressure atomizing burner. It includes a burner, forced draft blower and a totally enclosed electrical control panel. Packaged unit is wired, piped, tested and ready for installation. It can be used in high or low pressure boilers. Available in 8 models from 7½ to 30 gph.—Dunham-Bush, Inc., 175 South St., West Hartford, Conn., USA 06110 *or circle No. 385*

Can Tester
Automatic testing wheel with 40 stations tests cans for tightness and rejects those with leaks. Cans enter revolving testing wheel individually where open end is clamped against a rubber seal and covered with a bell filled with compressed air. Pressure in testing bell is measured with sensors, calibrated in mm water gage. Faulty cans are automatically ejected.—Capacity: 400 cans per min.—Fried. Krupp GmbH, Altendorfer Strasse 100, 43 Essen, W. Germany *or circle 420*

Coil Stacker
Automatic coil stacker stacks coils on pallets positioned on a turntable after larger coils have been slit to size and banded. Palletized coils are removed from turntable by a discharge conveyor for weighing and processed for shipment. Unit which is equipped with ID and OD gripping mechanism handles coil up to 10,000 lb, OD to 72 in., height to 16 in.—Braner Engineering, Inc., 9355 W. Byron St., Schiller Park, Ill., USA 60176 *or circle No. 400*

Dust Collector
The Compact cell filter uses a non-woven filter cloth with a surface weight of over 0.1 lb per sq ft. Filter material is arranged in 40 kg cells constructed in modules of 3 or 4 units. By using cells, instead of bags, space occupied is $^1/_7$ of conventional bag filters. Filter is cleaned by short blasts of compressed air. Inspection and maintenance is done from the outside. Cells can be replaced in 3 min; cleaning interval: 2, 4 or 8 min.—AB Bahco Ventilation, S 19901 Enköping, Sweden *or circle No. 389*

Anchoring System
A polymer anchor in the form of a glass capsule contains a synthetic resin glue with stronger adhesion than conventional anchoring systems. After hole is drilled in concrete or other material the capsule is inserted and anchor rod is rotated into the capsule, crushing it and causing complete mixing of resin. After curing, the synthetic resin glue binds the anchor rod to the building material providing a powerful, stress-free support in the entire hole with no lateral mechanical pressure on the building material.—Bolidt Elementenbouw B.V., Edisonweg 14, Alblasserdam, Netherlands *or circle No. 419*

New products turned into glamorous catalogs

Here and on the next spread are examples of typical catalog organization for large numbers of product items. The essence of the arrangement is to assemble the pictures into handsome groupings, keying each item to its descriptive text run elsewhere on the page. The problem, of course, is to devise a system so strong that the very variety of elements that must be accommodated serves as a visual advantage, rather than disintegrating into a disorganized grab bag of odds and ends.

One fact must be faced — the pictures are handouts (99 percent of the time), and there is neither

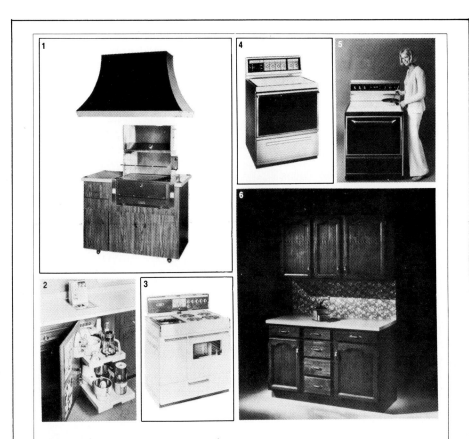

← This page shows product items in black-and-white. Some are plain halftones, others silhouettes within an area articulated by ruled outlines. Reference figures are surprinted or dropped out from the pictures themselves, and the space between is white, to add lightness to the page.

The spread opposite → is a montage of pictures all in full color. The frame in which they are encased is solid black, which yields good, decorative contrast. It is also a good (and cheaper) background for all the reference numbers.

PRODUCTS: KITCHENS

1. Gas-fired built-in barbecue unit, "Hacienda Star," has gas burners, fire pan, ceramic briquettes, stainless steel smoke-flavor compartment and rotisserie. Heat is adjusted by raising and lowering fire pan or by gas-flame control. When unit is not in use, positive shut-off is provided. Easy-to-clean, grills fit in the dishwasher and slide-out drawer collects debris. A selection of venting systems is available. Goodwin, Berkeley, Calif. *Circle 351 on reader service card*

2. Built-in all-purpose appliance, "Foodmatic," includes a blender, juicer, knife or scissors sharpener and mixing bowls and beaters. Unit, which can be installed in any cabinet of adequate size, closes flush with countertop when not in use.

Latches hold each attachment firmly. Solid state control offers an infinite choice of speeds. Unit can be set for manual or automatic use. Optional attachments include a meat grinder. Ronson, Ronson, N.J. *Circle 352 on reader service card*

3. Dual-fuel electric range is ideal for vacation home use. Unit includes "stand-by" coal/wood or oil kitchen heater with two-burner cooking surface. Protection for woodwork and circulation of heat are provided by steel shield behind back flue. Continuous cleaning oven stays spatterfree at regular roasting temperatures. Combination heating range is also available in gas and "Duo-Oven" models. Monarch, Beaver Dam, Wis. *Circle 353 on reader service card*

4. "Smooth-top" electric range features easy-to-clean cooking surface of ceramic glass. Continuous cleaning oven is fully automatic. Fast preheat and adjustable broiling are provided. Surface units have infinite heat controls. Range has elegant black-glass oven door with stainless steel trim. Classic White, Antique Copper, Avocado Green and Harvest Yellow are available colors. Optional rotisserie kit is offered. Kelvinator, Grand Rapids, Mich. *Circle 354 on reader service card*

5. Top-of-the-line electric range has self-cleaning oven and one-piece smooth top. Special "Autolatch" control eliminates need for manual locking of oven door before self-cleaning process. Each cooking area is clearly marked on smooth top.

Unit also includes control console with easy-to-read digital clock for automatic timing, infinite heat control, and black finish on oven door. Line also features models with continuous cleaning ovens. **Tappan,** Mansfield, Ohio. *Circle 355 on reader service card*

6. Traditional cabinetry, "Patrician Pecan," complements almost any decor. Doors feature pecan-veneer panels within solid frames. Panels are removable and a choice of decorator inserts can be used. Line has self-closing hinges and adjustable shelves in single-door wall cabinets. Base cabinets are 24" deep, 34½" high. Wall cabinets are 12" deep. Optional antique finished hardware is offered. Home-Crest, Goshen Ind. *Circle 356 on reader service card*

Joe Davis

time nor money to get alternates. If the basic pattern into which the various elements are slotted is strong, chances are that the internecine warfare between the pictures can be diminished, even if it cannot be overcome entirely.

The most effective camouflaging ruse is to have a strong overall shape into which the pictures are dropped. This shape should be easily discerned — simple — and, as such, ought to be a geometric shape with clear outlines, as the examples shown here.

The next essential requirement is a highly visible and easily followed cross-referencing system between picture and accompanying text. Opposite, the numbers are superimposed on the pictures; below, they are dropped out of the grid between them; in both cases the numbers are large enough to be read easily.

The last essential requirement is flexibility of picture and text handling — for the editors' sanity if nothing else. The example from *Architectural Record*, on pages 196 and 197, reproduces the grid dummy and a typical page, to illustrate the ultimate in flexibility and efficiency: the pictures can be any shape and the text can be any length (within reason). Their placement, however, is rigidly controlled. Each picture must fit into the lower left-hand corner of the allotted individual space; the text columns must all start off at the same position on the page, though their length may be random. This rigid patterning is what holds the pages together and makes the entire sixty-seven-page issue (with 768 items) succeed as an organized catalog, easy to read and easy to tell edit pages from ads in spite of the fact that they both deal with essentially identical materials.

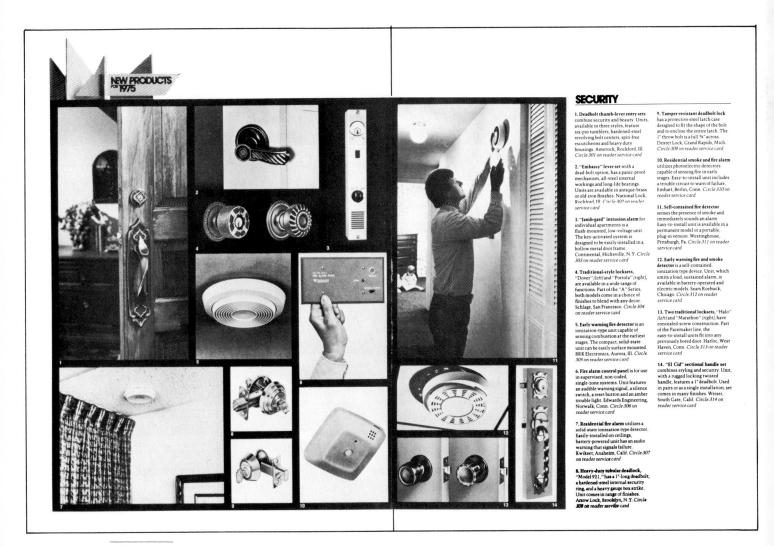

SECURITY

1. Deadbolt thumb-lever entry sets combine security and beauty. Units, available in three styles, feature six-pin tumblers, hardened-steel revolving bolt centers, spin-free escutcheons and heavy duty housings. Amerock, Rockford, Ill. *Circle 301 on reader service card*

2. "Embassy" lever set with a dead-bolt option, has a panic-proof mechanism, all-steel internal workings and long-life bearings. Units are available in antique-brass or old-iron finishes. National Lock, Rockford, Ill. *Circle 302 on reader service card*

3. "Jamb-gard" intrusion alarm for individual apartments is a flush-mounted, low-voltage unit. The key-activated system is designed to be easily installed in a hollow metal door frame. Continental, Hicksville, N.Y. *Circle 303 on reader service card*

4. Traditional-style locksets, "Dover" (*left*) and "Portola" (*right*), are available in a wide range of functions. Part of the "A" Series, both models come in a choice of finishes to blend with any decor. Schlage, San Francisco. *Circle 304 on reader service card*

5. Early warning fire detector is an ionization-type unit capable of sensing combustion at the earliest stages. The compact, solid-state unit can be easily surface mounted. BRK Electronics, Aurora, Ill. *Circle 305 on reader service card*

6. Fire alarm control panel is for use in supervised, non-coded, single-zone systems. Unit features an audible warning signal, a silence switch, a reset button and an amber trouble light. Edwards Engineering, Norwalk, Conn. *Circle 306 on reader service card*

7. Residential fire alarm utilizes a solid-state ionization type detector. Easily-installed on ceilings, battery-powered unit has an audio warning that signals failure. Kwikset, Anaheim, Calif. *Circle 307 on reader service card*

8. Heavy-duty tubular deadlock, "Model 921," has a 1"-long deadbolt, a hardened-steel internal security ring, and a heavy gauge box strike. Unit comes in range of finishes. Arrow Lock, Brooklyn, N.Y. *Circle 308 on reader service card*

9. Tamper-resistant deadbolt lock has a protective steel latch case designed to fit the shape of the bolt and to enclose the entire latch. The 1" throw bolt is a full ⅝" across. Dexter Lock, Grand Rapids, Mich. *Circle 309 on reader service card*

10. Residential smoke and fire alarm utilizes photoelectric detectors capable of sensing fire in early stages. Easy-to-install unit includes a trouble circuit to warn of failure. Emhart, Berlin, Conn. *Circle 310 on reader service card*

11. Self-contained fire detector senses the presence of smoke and immediately sounds an alarm. Easy-to-install unit is available in a permanent model or a portable, plug-in version. Westinghouse, Pittsburgh, Pa. *Circle 311 on reader service card*

12. Early warning fire and smoke detector is a self-contained, ionization type device. Unit, which emits a loud, sustained alarm, is available in battery-operated and electric models. Sears Roebuck, Chicago. *Circle 312 on reader service card*

13. Two traditional locksets, "Halo" (*left*) and "Marathon" (*right*), have concealed-screw construction. Part of the Pacemaker line, the easy-to-install units fit into any previously bored door. Harloc, West Haven, Conn. *Circle 313 on reader service card*

14. "El Cid" sectional handle set combines styling and security. Unit, with a rugged locking twisted handle, features a 1" deadbolt. Used in pairs or as a single installation, set comes in many finishes. Weiser, South Gate, Calif. *Circle 314 on reader service card*

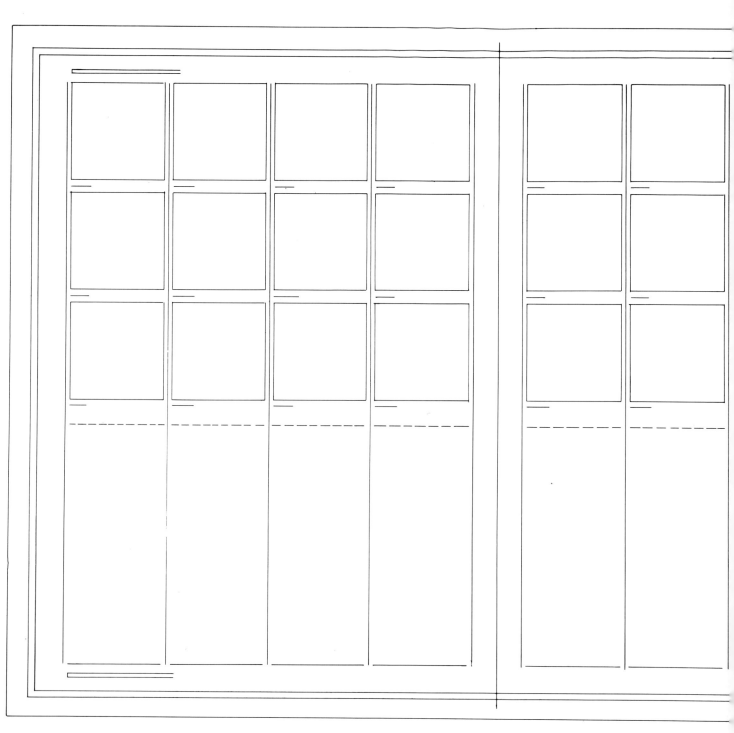

This grid is the basis for the layout of the entire issue...

... of which this is a typical page. Pictures are in both black-and-white and color. Where there is no section-opener headline as shown below, the fourth column would be used to accommodate three additional product reports.

Alex Sti Illano

uci 6

wood and plastics

ARCHITECTURAL WOODWORK
LAMINATED & PROCESSED SHEETS
LUMBER
PLASTIC FABRICATIONS
PLASTIC LAMINATES
PREFABRICATED STRUCTURAL WOOD

177

178

179

180

181

182

183

184

185

ARCHITECTURAL WOODWORK

177 ACRYLIC/WOOD / This is a prefinished product composed of natural hardwood impregnated throughout with acrylic plastic, subsequently hardened by irradiation. Oak, walnut, and ash moldings are available in four shapes. / Julius Blum & Co., Inc. A,I

178 CARVED WOOD / The company produces over 60 carved wood patterns that can be used for flexible wall set-ups, built-in furnishings, and room dividers. Systems include a choice of Walnut, Red Oak, Beechwood or select grades of White Pine with other woods available on special orders. / Stanwood Corp.

179 STRIP PANELS / Constructed of ¾-in.-wide strips of tempered hardboard with genuine teak, walnut or other hardwood veneers, or primed for painting, strips are mounted on a flexible fabric backing. Standard panels are 24 in. wide and 96 or 120 in. long. / Forms & Surfaces.

180 WOOD AND MIRROR / *Sculpturewood* wall panels are available with *Plexiglas* mirror in ¾-in. wide strips, set in grooves cut into modular panels of Redwood, hardwoods and in woods with durable color finishes. Panels are 11 in. wide and 96 in. long. / Forms & Surfaces.

LAMINATED/PROCESSED SHEETS

181 METALLIC LAMINATES / Suitable for fixtures and accent walls in banks, airports, hotels, retail firms, and theaters, *Metallic Laminates* are genuine aluminum and copper foils in a high pressure laminated sheet. The 12 patterns are embossed and antiqued. / Wilson Art Co.

182 PLANK FILM / ''Random Plank,'' a pattern in woodgrain vinyl film, is laminated to board and used in consumer and institutional furniture, kitchen cabinets and bathroom vanities. It is available from stock, or it can be custom printed in the colors of choice. / Phillips Films Co., Inc.

183 PRELAMINATED PANEL / The panel, with a polyester surface thermoset to particleboard, comes in several woodgrains and solid colors and patterns, including ''Butcher Block'' as shown. Panel thicknesses range from ¼ to ¾ in. in nominal 4- and 5-ft widths by 8- and 10- ft lengths. / Ralph Wilson Plastics Co.

184 SHEATHING / A fire-resistant structural sheathing can be used under most exterior finishes. It is clad in water-repellent paper, and attached with nails on staples. / United States Gypsum Co. A,L

185 STRUCTURAL FOAMS / The material is reported to have higher impact resistance and increased thermal stability over other thermoset foams. Materials are composites composed of integral skin foams with reinforcing filaments, in sizes up to 10 ft wide by 45 ft long. / Xentex Co., Div. of Exxon Enterprises, Inc.

Literature reports and book reviews: a variant of new product presentation

Unillustrated text items of varying lengths but following some basic pattern are, in essence, another form of catalog presentation. The usual column width is based on three-columns per page, simply because this is the sort of material that is ideally suited to placement in the interstices between small space ads in split makeup pages.

Shown here are two pages from a highly specialized area of *Library Journal,* the Book Review section, which devotes some twenty to thirty pages per issue to this material. To add a modicum of variety to such extremely important but, alas, visually colorless material, several *ars gratia artis* elements were introduced:

1. To lend variety and texture to the type itself, the titles are set in boldface, and the ancillary bibliographic information is set in smaller, indented type. Thus the start of each item is clearly signaled by a different color and texture. Note that this is helped along considerably by setting the last few lines of the preceding item, carrying the reviewer's name and affiliation, in italics.

2. All department headings are set in a different, decorative typeface for visual variety: they are the raisins in the oatmeal. A choice of faces that express the meaning of each title by visual punning and

LIT

obedience," and *A Week* have been misunderstood and misused. By seeing Thoreau whole instead of in fragments, Wolf clearly demonstrates that Thoreau is "one of the great American mystics and creative religious thinkers . . ., theologian of creation, apostle of wilderness, and prophet of social action," in addition to being a skilled literary craftsman. His ideas on religion, state, ecology, and nature are as relevant today as they were in 1862. A necessary book for libraries big and small, school, church, and city. *William White, Journalism Program, Oakland Univ., Rochester, Mich.*

Yunck, John A., tr., intro. & notes. **Eneas: a twelfth-century romance.**
Columbia Univ. Pr. (Records of Civilization). Sept. 1974. 272p. bibliog. LC 74-8543. $10.   LIT
This book represents an outstanding and vital contribution for students of medieval narrative. The introduction sketches succinctly the major issues: manuscript tradition, sources and influences (good discussion of Veldeke), the main omissions from and additions to the *Aeneid,* the poem's structure, the medieval translator's humor, his didactic concerns and attitudes towards antiquity. The adaptation, composed for an audience delighted by "narratives of the establishment and growth of civilization in Western Europe," offers a chivalric theme—a secular pilgrimage. The poet, ostensibly aware of the inner man in the long amplification on Lavine, presents also "a landmark in the history of erotic narrative." Yunck has provided a superbly written and mostly smooth translation. The five-page critical bibliography is quite thorough. Available now for the first time in English, the work is indispensable to anyone interested in the birth of romance. *Raymond J. Cormier, Dept. of French & Italian, Temple Univ., Philadelphia*

MUSIC

Faurot, Albert. **Concert Piano Repertoire: a manual of solo literature for artists and performers.**
Scarecrow. 1974. 338p. bibliog. LC 73-15567. $10.   REF/MUSIC
This handbook provides a survey of piano recital literature, with thumbnail biographical sketches of composers, short descriptions of individual works, and indications of the degree of difficulty. Unfortunately, although this volume is fairly comprehensive, it suffers from a number of failings. A major fault is the lack of uniform references to available published editions, particularly necessary for contemporary scores which are often published by small, relatively unknown companies. The author's highly prejudiced, subjective, and even offensive opinions about composers, compositions, and performers only serve to discourage inexperienced pianists from investigating the literature on their own. The artist or performer will be much better served by Maurice Hinson's thorough and scholarly *Guide to the Pianist's Repertoire* (*LJ* 7/73). *Susan Kagan, Dept. of Music, Bronx Community Coll., CUNY*

MUSIC

Rabson, Carolyn. **Songbook of the American Revolution.**
NEO Pr., Box 32, Peaks Island, Me. 04108. Jul. 1974. 112p. illus. by Nancy Hansen. bibliog. index. LC 73-81353. $8; pap. $4.   MUSIC
A harbinger of the bicentennial, this thoroughly documented collection contains ballads, hymns, and national songs, presenting both the rebel and loyalist points of view. Most of the texts originally appeared in newspapers and broadsides with only the names of the tunes to which they were to be sung (it was then safe to assume that everybody knew them), so much sleuthing and fitting has been necessary. Most of these selections, except for the hymns and national songs originally published in score, are presented with only the melody line and guitar chords. Each song is headed with a historical note, and additional verses occupy the facing page. The illustrations "are mostly based upon details and border designs from colonial prints." Undoubtedly the book will meet a demand. *Philip L. Miller, formerly at N.Y.P.L.*

Shanet, Howard. **Philharmonic: a history of New York's orchestra.**
Doubleday. Jul. 1974. 792p. illus. bibliog. LC 72-96256. $20.   MUSIC
Shanet has delved into the early history of the orchestra, into correspondence, diaries, and contemporary accounts to give a thoroughly documented, scholarly history of the orchestra from its beginnings in 1842 until 1970. His account of cultural life in New York during the 1840's, with its rich literary, theatrical, and musical activity, is particularly interesting. The reports of the Mahler and Toscanini years are especially valuable and the records of the orchestra during two world wars and one civil war are of substantial interest as well. The appendixes include backnotes, copies of early criticism, and a full record of performances, 1942-1970. This excellent study is a valuable addition for American studies, New York history, and music collections. *William Shank, C.C.N.Y. Graduate Sch. Lib.*

Shestack, Melvin. **The Country Music Encyclopedia.**
Crowell. Sept. 1974. 400p. photogs. index. LC 74-9644. $13.95.   REF/MUSIC
Much of the appeal of country music lies in its directness and its reflection of the simple dramas of life. Shestack uses this straightforward unsophisticated approach in his intimate portraits of several hundred country music personalities—singers, songwriters, instrumentalists, and producers. The basic biographical facts and the most important songs of the musicians are worked into slick personalized critical essays which often quote their song lyrics and sayings. The book is apparently modeled after Stambler and Dandon's *Encyclopedia of Folk, Country and Western Music* (*LJ* 11/16/69) and as a reference tool is similarly helpful, although it is, of course, more up-to-date. Many musical terms are defined, sometimes with a country twist. Hundreds of photographs, a lengthy discography, a few well-chosen printed scores of country classic songs and a rather redundant index accompany the text. For country mu-

MUSIC

sic enthusiasts this book is a joy to browse through and a fascinating compendium of personal anecdotes. *Stephen M. Fry, Northwestern Univ. Lib., Evanston, Ill.*

Walton, Charles W. **Basic Forms in Music.**
Alfred Pub. Co. 1974. 218p. illus. index. LC 73-81046. $7.95.   MUSIC
Written by a widely respected theory teacher, this book provides a brief description and analysis of the various forms which have been used in music for centuries. The explanations are relatively simple and easy to follow. Analysis is aided by including the complete musical score when each form is presented for the first time. Although this book breaks no new ground, it is recommended for medium-sized and large libraries because of the clarity of the explanations, and its inclusion of many examples from 20th-Century music. *Hillel Ausubel, New Rochelle P.L., N.Y.*

Young, Percy M. **A Concise History of Music: from primitive times to the present.**
David White. Jul. 1974. 168p. illus. index. LC 72-83990. $8.95.   MUSIC
This brief, readable survey emphasizes "music as a collective art." Relatively little attention is paid to musical styles, individual musicians, or to the various periods of music. However, the relationship of music to religion, magic, nationalism, social institutions, technology, and to other arts is explored in depth. Recommended for YA and adult collections. *Hillel Ausubel, New Rochelle P.L., N.Y.*

Philosophy

Berry, Adrian. **The Next Ten Thousand Years: a vision of man's future in the universe.**
Saturday Review Pr.; Dutton. 1974. 256p. LC 73-16795. $9.95.   PHIL
This is no ordinary book on the future, too many of which are infected with a combination of myopia and social hypochondria. Berry's outlook is much broader and deeper than the views of such people as Ehrlich or the Club of Rome, whom he dismisses briefly. This is a broad treatment outlining in general terms what kinds of things we might expect in the future: the harnessing of greater amounts of power, the taming of the planets; and then beyond, to the stars, where our destiny must ultimately lie. Bacon, he claims, has set us on a course we cannot alter. This work is everything it promises to be: a vision, that all too rare thing, of what is forseeable in man's future. An essential purchase. *Robert Molyneux, Virginia Polytechnic Inst. & State Univ. Lib., Blacksburg*

Dufrenne, Mikel. **The Phenomenology of Aesthetic Experience.**
Northwestern Univ. Pr. (Studies in Phenomenology & Existential Philosophy). 1974. 578p. tr. by Edward S. Casey & others. bibliog. index. LC 73-76806. $17.50.   ART/PHIL
Dufrenne is a prominent French philosopher and one of the few French phenomenologists to explore aesthetic phenom-

humor was attempted, but there are many interpretations possible and what may be an innocuous tease to one is an offensive slur to another. So in the end the only one we all agreed on was MUSIC, for which the lettering is multi-lined and thus reminiscent of a music staff. Oh well . . .

3. Vertical hairlines are inserted between columns, since this is done elsewhere in the publication, used as a splendid light foil to whatever blackness may be around and hence an increase in "color-fulness" by contrast.

4. The hairlines are extended into the top margin where tiny flags are attached to them, each referring to the subject area of the column below in much the same way that the telephone directory runs alphabetical syllables in the top corners of each page to help easy reference — a highly utilitarian element which yields decorative and unique value in the bargain.

5. The few illustrations in the section are suspended in boxes attached to the vertical rules. Why? Well, when one has little to work with, it is essential to make the most of every opportunity to do something a bit different and original. An overall impression is actually built up of a large number of tiny details.

SCI

format book was designed by the Swedish publishing firm of Tre Tryckare. The text is relatively brief, but in conjunction with the substantial captions to the illustrations, manages clearly and effectively to trace the development of ships, trains, cars, and aircraft from their beginnings to the present. The real strength of the book, however, and the heart of the story, is visual. The hundreds of illustrations are almost all line drawings, many washed with color. The style is semi-diagrammatic and rich in detail. This is not the kind of book likely to be read from cover to cover, but it's a pleasure to browse through it.—*B.C. Hacker, Dept. of History, Iowa State Univ., Ames*

Social Science

Braroe, Niels Winther. **Indian and White: self-image and interaction in a Canadian plains community.**
Stanford Univ. Pr. 1975. 206p. photogs. index. LC 74-25927. $8.50.   ANTHROPOLOGY
Braroe's analysis of social interaction between a small group of Canadian Cree Indians and their white neighbors is an important contribution to societal studies. Especially significant is the persistence of ethnic identity which he finds. There is little evidence of "melting pot" activities between the Indians and the whites; in fact, relations between them appear to be deteriorating over time. Braroe concentrates on showing how the two groups respond in daily life to perceived "facts" of their social existence, with fulfilling roles for both groups consisting of both "substantive and symbolic transactions" between Indian and white. Braroe describes the historic development of the relationship between the two groups, as well as the current daily life of the groups. Well-written and of value to the general reader as well as the anthropologist.—*Ruth E. Olson, Nauset Regional H.S. Lib., North Eastham, Mass.*

SOC SCI

Campbell, Joseph. **The Mythic Image.**
Princeton Univ. Pr. (Bollingen). 1975. 552p. illus. index. LC 79-166363. $45; until May 31, 1975, $37.50.   MYTHOLOGY
Campbell lets "the spirit of the pictures rule," arranging his text "so that the reader might enter into its pages at any turn he liked." The result is a fascinating compendium of mythological stories which illuminate the book's more than 400 illustrations—and what illustrations! Drawn from nearly all parts of the world and all epochs, they luminously support Campbell's dual thesis that the ultimate source of myth is man's unconscious, and that many of the most prominent mythic motifs have diffused from a single center. These arguments are commonplaces, but they are seldom made with such concreteness and beauty. My only quarrel with Campbell is that he neglects Islam and devotes rather too much space to Buddhism, where many of the key terms have almost ceased to function symbolically. But this is my preference; in the structure of *Image* the attention paid to Buddhism is apposite and, for me, is in some measure redeemed by Campbell's unfailing lucidity and attention to details.—*John Agar, Dept. of English, Valdosta State Coll., Ga.*

Gottehrer, Barry. **The Mayor's Man.**
Doubleday. 1975. 326p. index. LC 73-10538. $8.95.   PER NAR/URBAN AFFAIRS
Gottehrer writes of the Lindsay years from the viewpoint of his own unique job: the quelling of violence. The task-force network of black community relationships and communications he patiently established to achieve this became a model for other cities. But the author also writes here with clear brilliant perception of white violence: e.g., the Columbia University riot, and Shanker school strikes. Gottehrer's book offers a solid, detailed, meticulously accurate history which nonetheless disappoints in one way. This reviewer worked in New York black communities at that time and witnessed firsthand the tremendous power of the mere name Gottehrer to prevent riot and reduce police brutality. He was never

SOC SCI

more than one telephone call away, and all factions knew that. So one would have liked to know: who was Gottehrer himself, and how did he inspire such trust and friendship in blacks? Because that was largely why New York did not burn. This he does not tell us, perhaps because he never knew himself. The book reveals him only as watching from the sidelines, considering all the facts, and doing what he could, which he didn't think was much.—*Elisabeth Hutchins, New York*

Kelly, M. Clark. **Hoboes.**
Drake. May 1975. 192p. illus. LC 74-22594. $12.95.   HIST/SOC SCI
Now, as in the past, Kelly tells us, hard times are compelling people to hit the road; and perhaps current wanderers will be interested in knowing something about the history of the hobo. His focus is on the early 20th Century, when the searching of the itinerant industrial workers reached a characteristic style: riding the rails, hanging out in hobo jungles, eating mulligan stew, etc. (I was interested to learn that there's a difference between hoboes, tramps, and bums—hoboes look for work.) Kelly describes the hobo's life style and the hard times, and talks about some famous ones, including Jeff Davis, "A No. 1," Jim Tully, and "Steamtrain" Maury Graham. Not a bad lot, as it turns out. It's hard to know what to make of the book itself. It's not very well written, but does have some charm nonetheless; and though it's by no means a major study, it does add to our knowledge of a little-known subject. Not essential, but recommended if you can afford it.—*Sheldon Kaye, Rochester P.L., N.Y.*

Mintz, Sidney W., ed. **Slavery, Colonialism, and Racism.**
Norton. 1975. 213p. index. $10.95.   HIST/SOC SCI
Each of the 11 essays in this broad-ranging and important collection surveys a major aspect of the black experience in Africa and the Americas. Historical perspectives are stressed, but attention is also given to literature, music, and education; the historical development of the literature of each of these subjects is emphasized throughout. Besides Mintz (an anthropologist who specializes in the Caribbean), well-known contributors include David Brion Davis (slavery), Philip Curtin and J. F. A. Ajayi (African history), and Benjamin Quarles (American history). Most of the contributions are sure to be regarded as seminal commentaries on their respective fields; and the book will be sought out by a variety of scholars, teachers, and students, especially as it comes during a major transitional phase in a field of enduring importance. Essential for academic libraries.—*R. Kent Rasmussen, Dept. of History, U.C.L.A.*

Perlman, Robert. **Consumers and Social Services.**
Wiley. 1975. 126p. index. LC 74-13540. $9.95; pap. $5.50.   CONSUMER AFFAIRS/SOC SCI
This book defines the recipient of social services as a consumer who seeks to acquire those services that will satisfy his needs. It examines in detail the interaction between consumer and supplier, with consideration of the types of con-

One of Kelly's "Hoboes"—part of the American Waste Land

Literature reports displayed in legible, modular pattern

Reducing the space allotted to each report from a sixth of a page to an eighth occasioned a re-examination of the entire graphic presentation technique leading to a complete overhaul of the typography, though the picture size was retained. The headlines were set in two bold, tight, stacked lines — and placed aligned across the page for speed of scanning, as a service to the reader. Descriptive text, set narrow and ragged right, can vary in length. The "for more information" line was reworded and the numeral strongly emphasized, as a service to the reader. (The success of this publication is measured by the number of items requested. After the new format was introduced, the requests were increased some 350%). As yet another service to the reader, checkboxes next to the headlines were incorporated into the vertical rules needed to separate the items. As in the case of *Industrial Equipment News,* a sister publication, see page 16, it was impor-

tant to devise a modular system for speed and simplicity of assembly: as a result, all the ruled lines and "for your copy" lines are standing art in film, and the headlines and body copy, as well as the pictures, can be stripped into indicated positions very easily.

☐ **Cold air gun**

Four-page idea brochure describes the Vortec 606 Cold Air Gun for production spot cooling, and comes with a handy machining feed and speed sliderule calculator. Clean, efficient cold air gun generates a steady stream of air at 10°F, without electricity or moving parts. It helps extend tool life and maintain production tolerances without oil residue or dangerous chemicals. Brochure shows typical applications for air guns, highlights advantages, and explains operating principle. **Vortec Corp,** 10125 Carver Rd, Cincinnati, OH 45242

For your copy circle ILR **103**

☐ **Reconstruction, renovation work**

Twelve-page brochure has case histories and before-and-after photos that dramatically illustrate Robertson building reconstruction and renovation services. Extensive retrofitting and remodelling capabilities make old structures attractive and energy efficient. Included are industrial, institutional, and residential projects, with specific energy savings. Brochure also details insulated roof and wall systems, outlines company's maintenance services, and discusses computer analysis capabilities. **H.H. Robertson Co,** 400 Holiday Dr, Pittsburgh, PA 15220

For your copy circle ILR **104**

☐ **Industrial intercoms**

New catalog shows intercoms designed to give efficient communication in areas where high ambient noise levels make conventional voice systems ineffective. Typical applications include stations adjacent to heavy production machinery, on loading docks, in steel mills, etc. Heavy-duty intercom housing is fully sealed against dust and dirt, corrosion-proof, weather-proof for use indoors or out. Simple installation requires plug-in power, ordinary 2-wire connection. **Atkinson Dynamics,** 14 Orange Ave, South San Francisco, CA 94080

For your copy circle ILR **105**

☐ **Power cylinders**

Pneumatic-hydraulic cylinders are just one of nine complete product sections featured in the Full Line Product Guide section of Schrader Bellows new Product Digest PD-3. All necessary technical specifications on the entire line of Schrader Bellows products are given in a special 20-page product section to make selection easier. Guide also has an 8-page, 4-color section on available services. **Schrader Bellows,** 200 W Exchange Street, Akron, OH 44309

For your copy circle ILR **106**

☐ **Energy saving exhaust damper**

Four-page brochure details the Protectaire energy saver and fire protection system for paint spray booths, welding enclosures, and other work areas served by exhaust fans. Motorized damper closes automatically when spraying is done, to keep heated or cooled air in. Temperature sensing switch also closes damper in case of fire to prevent flames from spreading to roof. Illustrated Bulletin PA 141 explains system operation, shows elements, and calculates specific cost savings for typical applications. **Protectaire Systems Co,** 1353 N McLean Blvd, Elgin, IL 60120

For your copy circle ILR **107**

☐ **Contract manufacturing**

Color-illustrated, four-page brochure explains how to meet special manufacturing or parts production needs with Gleason contract machining and assembly services. It highlights company's more than 115 years' experience in building machine tools. Shown are Gleason's complete machine shop with more than 900 machine tools, expert assembly facilities for complete machines or components, and large assembly areas. Bulletin also covers company's expert design assistance capabilities. **Gleason Machine Div,** 1000 University Ave, Rochester, NY 14692

For your copy circle ILR **108**

☐ **Electrical assembly**

Concise data sheet tells how Gleason contract assembly services meet almost any electrical standard, anywhere in the world, including JIC (USA), IEC (International), and VDE, VDI, or UVV (Germany). Assembly capabilities include relay control panels, pushbutton control stations, printed circuit boards, junction box and switch gear assemblies. Flyer outlines company's more than 115 years of electrical assembly experience. **Gleason Machine Division,** 1000 University Avenue, Rochester, NY 14692

For your copy circle ILR **109**

☐ **Precision spindles**

Four-page brochure details Gleason high precision spindles, delivered on time and designed to meet customer's needs for boring, drilling, and other machining operations. Design guide has dimensions of cartridge-type spindles with all bearings, block-types with ball bearings, and block-types with front taper roller bearings. Gleason has more than 115 years' experience building machine tools, and uses the latest equipment and computerized design and manufacturing facilities. **Gleason Machine Div,** 1000 University Ave, Rochester, NY 14692

For your copy circle ILR **110**

CENTRIFUGAL COMPRESSORS

Detailed eight-page brochure describes Paxton planetary drive compressors. Far smaller and lighter than conventional types, gearless compressors deliver oil-free air or gas quietly and without pulsation. Flow capacities are 50 to 1,000 cfm, pressures to 5 psig, and vacuums to 7.5 in. Hg. Compressors work with V-belt, electric motor, gasoline engine, or other drives. Bulletin compares planetary drive compressors with other types and has cutaway drawings that illustrate operation. It also lists applications, shows accessories, and includes performance charts and specifications. **Paxton Products Inc,** 929 Olympic Blvd, Santa Monica, CA 90404
For more information, circle ILR 133

SPRING ASSORTMENTS

Eight-page catalog shows time-saving Select-A-Spring assortments. Conveniently indexed cabinets help workers find springs when needed, eliminating delays and extra cost involved in hunting for parts. Each assortment has a display board with actual springs mounted and numbered. Specification sheet on the back makes reordering easy. Catalog describes assortments, gives prices, and lists ordering information for stock and custom springs. It also has decimal equivalent and wire gage tables and charts showing end styles of compression and extension springs. **Select-A-Spring Corp,** 39 Ave C, Bayonne, NJ 07002
For more information, circle ILR 134

INFRARED THERMOMETERS

Detailed Catalog MO 108 describes Modline non-contact temperature measurement and control systems. Color-illustrated, 16-page guide shows different modular elements combined to create custom control systems. Linked to a choice of remote sensing heads, any of sixty standard controls can be used to cover temperatures spanning 0 to 5000°F and 0 to 3,000°C. Systems can be outfitted with peak and valley pickers, BCD outputs, and other control and recording accessories. Catalog shows sensors and controls, describes functions, and charts performance for different applications. It also lists complete specifications. **Ircon,** 7555 North Linder Ave, Skokie, IL 60077
For more information, circle ILR 135

SPRAY NOZZLES 25

Spraco's new fully illustrated catalog 79 shows company's extensive line of spray nozzles. Sixty-eight pages have specifications, flow rates, flow patterns, and design details for a wide variety of fluid nozzles. Types include full and hollow cone styles in center jet, wall mounted, cluster, and pin jet configurations with assorted spray patterns. Flat fan nozzles come in wide angle, high pressure, and other styles. Included are pollution control nozzles, atomizing nozzles and guns, spray jets, humidifying equipment, and accessories. Brochure gives general engineering data to help customer determine his own nozzle requirements. Metric catalog also available. **Spray Engineering Co,** East Spit Brook Rd, Nashua, NH 03060
For more information, circle ILR 136

BEVEL GEAR MANUAL

Sixteen-page catalog and engineer's manual describes a full range of stock and standard-size spiral bevel gears. It has helpful information on the installation and use of spiral bevel gears. Illustrations and tables describe proper mountings, power and horsepower ratings, and explain backlash, deflection, and thrust factors. Specifications cover standard bevel gears in sizes up to 24 in. pitch diameter. Also included are stock bevel gears in ratios of 1:1, 2:1, 3:1, 3:2, and 4:3, in sizes from 1 to 14 in. pitch diameter. Teeth are case hardened and crown lapped, and sets are speed tested before shipment. **Arrow Gear Co,** 2301 Curtiss St, Downers Grove, IL 60415
For more information, circle ILR 137

INDUSTRIAL WOOD PRODUCTS

Full-color 1979 industrial wood products catalog gives specifications on products including plywood, particleboard, lumber, industrial panel, and hardboard. Information on sizes and specifications, applications, grades, species, code acceptability, and certification are included. G-P's expanded distribution and industrial capabilities provide nationwide service with reliable inventory and delivery of cost effective materials. Product packet includes the industrial wood products catalog and information on G-P cut-to-size capabilities. **Georgia-Pacific Corp,** 900 SW Fifth Avenue, Portland, OR 97204
For more information, circle ILR 138

A word or two about new product pictures

Most new product pictures are handout shots, literal, poorly composed, unimaginative, and atrociously printed in bulk . . . in sum, depressing and awful. Yet we are forced to run them since we have no alternative. We must not despair nor pretend that they are better than they are. It behooves us to make the best of a difficult job. One fundamental point to remember (whose result can be seen several times over in this montage) is to think of each such product shot as raw material ripe for manipulation, rather than as a final work of art. So, by all means blank out the background to leave an interesting silhouetted shape; or cut away just a part of the background so an element appears to poke out from the picture into the surrounding space in partial silhouette; or overlap one picture with another; or establish visual relationships of alignment from one to another and so on. The group shown here is, clearly, made of excellent originals in vibrant color. Even so, it would have been much less interesting, had they been displayed as little rectangles arranged in shooting-gallery fashion.

Housing, Joe Davis

NEW & NOTEWORTHY
By Mike Ballai

Pentax ME-F & SMC Pentax AF 35→70-mm f/2.8

The Pentax ME-F is the first camera to provide automatic focusing, or focus guidance, with a range of interchangeable lenses. Subject contrast is measured directly through any standard Pentax (or other brand) K-type bayonet-mount lens, using electronic circuitry originally "designed for video applications."

When used with conventional lenses, the ME-F's focus-guidance system simultaneously beeps and lights a light-emitting diode (LED) in the viewfinder when the point of proper focus has been set manually. Pentax AF (Auto Focus) lenses, of which the 35–70-mm f/2.8 is the first, use information that is provided by the same system to set the focus automatically.

The ME-F's autofocus system is said to be highly accurate at all distances, even with strongly patterned subjects or those located behind glass (conditions that tend to fool some autofocus systems).

In addition, "some moving subjects that even the eye cannot follow quickly" are claimed to be within the system's capabilities.

Pentax suggests that other "particularly effective" autofocus applications include close-up and macro photography, perspective correction with special "shift" lenses, and photomicrography. Manual focusing is possible with all lenses.

Aside from its focusing system, the ME-F is a conventional, aperture-priority automatic-exposure 35-mm SLR, similar to the Pentax ME Super. One novel feature of both cameras is a pair of push buttons that is used in place of the usual dial to set manual shutter speeds.

The Pentax ME-F and AF 35–70-mm lens will be available early in 1982, at a suggested retail price of about $1,000. Their U.S. distributor is Pentax Corp., 35 Inverness Drive East, Englewood, Colorado 80112.

Kodak Ektachrome 14 Paper

Ektachrome 14 is described by Kodak as an improved version of its current color-reversal (slide-to-print) paper. Changes are said to include improved (presumably lower) contrast, better highlight and shadow definition, cleaner whites, more realistic flesh and neutral tones, greater printing speed, and closer batch-to-batch emulsion uniformity.

The paper is also described as being more resistant to curling than previous types and less sensitive to variations in time or temperature during processing. Glossy (F) and semi-matte (N) paper surfaces are available, in a wide range of sheet and roll sizes.

Price and further details are available from the manufacturer, Eastman Kodak Company, 343 State Street, Rochester, New York 14650.

Canon Speedlite Models 577G & 533G

Two new handle-mount electronic-flash units from Canon—Speedlite models 577G and 533G—sport guide numbers (at ASA 25) of 78 and 59 respectively. That should satisfy the needs of most photographers. These energy-saving, multi-stop auto-exposure flash units provide dedicated operation with all Canon A-series cameras. In conjunction with the Canon A-1, AE-1, and AE-1 Program, dedicated functioning includes the setting of both shutter speed and f-stop; only the former is set with other Canon models.

Canon Speedlite 533G with A-1 camera.

These "potato-masher" flash units are versatile, and offer many similar features. One notable difference is that the 533G uses an internal power supply with the option of using an external battery pack, while the 577G is designed for use only with external battery packs. Each flash unit accepts alkaline or nickel-cadmium power sources.

Both models have five-position bounce heads that also rotate horizontally up to 120° in either direction. In addition, each uses a separate sensor that mounts on the camera's hot shoe. Both units cover the image area of a 35-mm wide-angle lens; adapters are available for use with 20-mm, 24-mm, and 100-mm lenses. For off-camera-flash applications, an accessory sensor, the 100G, has a 39-inch coil cord.

Since both of these units are energy-saving types, they have fast recycling times in automatic operation. However, only the 577G is agile enough to keep up with a motor-driven camera at five frames per second.

The 577G weighs just over 21 ounces, the 533G is slightly over 23 ounces—reasonable weights considering their output. The 577G sells for $340 including sensor, quick-release bracket, and 24-mm adapter; an alkaline battery pack is $105; nicad pack and charger, $220. The 533G with sensor, quick-release bracket, and 24-mm adapter is $280. They are distributed by Canon, U.S.A., Inc., One Canon Plaza, Lake Success, New York 11040.

98 Camera Arts

Camera Arts, Thomas Ridinger

Items handled like dignified news stories with elegant typography and subtle variation in weight of rules.

HARDWARE

OFF-LINE

```
New developments in magnetic
bubble memory research were
presented by AT&T and IBM
researchers at the International
Conference on Magnetic Bubbles
(sponsored by the Magnetics
Society of the IEEE).  Andrew
Bobeck, a Bell Labs pioneer in
the field, described a method
for eliminating the coil
windings used in existing
devices to rotate the magnetic
field that moves the bubbles
around their predetermined
paths.  Bobeck and his team cut
the size of their package by a
third by replacing coil windings
with one or more wafer-thin
conducting layers punctuated
with oval-shaped holes.  A
current applied to the
conducting layer causes the
bubbles to move -- at up to 10
times the previous speed.

IBM researchers reported on two
projects leading to denser
bubble memory chips.  One
project developed a working
test chip storing bubbles one
micrometer in diameter (2- or
3-micrometer diameters are
used conventionally).  The small
diameter is made possible by
using "contiguous disk" circuit
patterns to guide the bubbles;
the bubbles trace a path along
the outside edge of the guides,
instead of under the guide as
in conventional devices,
removing constraints placed on
bubble size by current
technology that limits bubble
size to the width of the
guide it passes under.

Another IBM research project
lead to a fourfold density
increase through the
two recognizably distinct
types of bubbles.  The group
built operational 15,000-bit
devices using chevron guides
half as tall and half as wide
as usual, resulting in a
density of 3.3-million bits
per square centimeter.
```

8-INCH RIGID DISK

Packaged in a unit said to by physically interchangeable with popular 8-inch floppy drives (down to the screw holes), this vendor's initial entry into the hard disk market comprises drives with 9MB, 27MB, and 45MB capacities. The oem drives are intended for use with small mainframes, minicomputers, and microcomputers. As many as three nonremovable platters are used in each drive; each recording surface has an unformatted capacity of 8.7MB. The drives use Winchester technology, with the disks, heads and positioner environmentally sealed in the lower half of the unit. The rigid disks have average access times of 45msec and rotational speeds of 3,600rpm. In 1,000-lot quantities, the 27MB drive sells for $1,350. An optional intelligent controller board goes for $500 in the same quantities. The controller is said to allow a choice of a number of hard-sector formats, and it can support up to four drives, direct or buffered data transfers, and error correction. Evaluation units are slated for availability next month, with production shipments expected by year's end. MICROPOLIS CORP., Canoga Park, Calif.

FOR DATA CIRCLE 351 ON READER CARD

MAINFRAMES

IBM's E-Series announcement may be a tough act to follow, but this PCM, playing by the established rules, has countered with three new machines offering more for less. The smallest of the new offerings, the M80/32, is said to provide three times the performance of the IBM 4331 at roughly two-and-a-half times the price. Next, there's the M80/42, priced $10,000 over an IBM 4341, and offering 10% more performance. At the top, there's the M80/43, with 30% more kick than a 4341, and a price tag $50,000 greater. All of the M80s run processors with 100nsec processors and use 600nsec memory. Memory prices for the new processors have been brought into line with the IBM-established standard of $15,000 per megabyte. The /32 can have from three to six channels, the /42 from three to 16, and the /43 from six to 16. The two larger machines have cache, 16KB for the /42 and 32KB for the /43. Maximum memory sizes are larger than IBM's offerings: 8MB for the /32, and 16MB for the /42 and /43. The vendor plans to lag IBM's initial shipment dates by three months to make sure its microcode is totally compatible with IBM's. Existing M/80s can be upgraded. The M80/32, with 1MB and three channels, sells for $185,000. The M80/42 goes for $275,000 with 2MB and three channels. A 2MB M80/43 with six channels sells for $315,000. Additional channels are priced at $5,300 each. Availability is slated for the second quarter of next year. MAGNUSON COMPUTER SYSTEMS, Santa Clara, Calif.

FOR DATA CIRCLE 352 ON READER CARD

TRANSACTION TERMINAL

The Computer Communications Group of TransCanada Telephone System has come up with a short inquiry/response transaction terminal with a target tariff rate of $29.50 per month. Known as Vutran, the terminal communicates in ASCII at 300bps via an internal originate only modem. The microprocessor-based terminal, not much larger than a telephone, has a 16-character LED display, 20-button keypad (10 numeric and 10 function keys), and a magnetic stripe reader (ABA Track II) for financial applications. An integral memory of 452 characters is partitioned into 254 characters of transaction data, 89 characters of protected data, and 109 characters for telephone numbers used by the modem's autodialer. Vutran can work on the Datapac packet switched network, the regular telephone switched network, and on two point private lines. Outside Canada, Vutran will be marketed by Northern Telecom Ltd. THE COMPUTER COMMUNICATIONS GROUP, TransCanada Telephone System, Ottawa, Ontario, Canada.

FOR DATA CIRCLE 353 ON READER CARD

262 DATAMATION

Datamation, Cleve Marie Bintell

At left, a news report on technological development is set off by typewriter type from the ordinary reviews at right.

NEW
THINGS

New Ideas for That New House

Function is both art and beauty in this wall mounted clock (right) from the Howard Miller Clock Co. of Zeeland, Mich. The "King William" grandfather clock (far right) from Ridgeway Inc. of Ridgeway, Va. stands more than seven feet in height. Available in a choice of finishes and chimes, this proud clock costs $4,000.

The "Regulator" clock has been a sturdy part of many American households for more than 100 years. And while this Regulator is a reproduction, it would be difficult to tell it from an original. From Ridgeway Inc. of Ridgeway, Va.

19

New Things

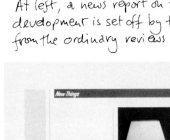

Every new house could use a gold brick. Especially one that with a flick of a switch becomes a 24 karat burst of light (far left). Actually the lamp from Deena Products Co. of High Point, N.C., is a gold finished ceramic. This proves that all that glitters is not gold. At left The Glendale Iron Works of Pacific Palisades, Calif., had wired these brightly painted pails.

So you love to cook. Here (right) are some lighting fixtures for the gourmet. From Artisan House Inc. of Los Angeles. The refrigerator no longer has exclusive rights over the electric light bulb anymore.

Designer Paul Evans has created a series of hand-painted tables for Selig Manufacturing Co. of Leominster, Maine. To protect the finish, the entire table is lacquered under plexiglas. This table is inspired by the work of Matisse.

22

Moving House & Home, Nancy Steiny

The generous white space is carefully articulated by hairline rules that establish the four-column-plus-wide-margin structure. Product pictures and descriptions are dropped in strategically, establishing a stylish look with the simplest of means.

CADEIRAS

Two radically different approaches from the same publication: Above, a regular catalog format with carefully controlled photos of similar objects against a neutral-color background. Below, a deliberately jumbled collection of odds-and-ends in lively notebook fashion.

Casa Claudia, Omar Grassetti

Tricks or treats that make scents for Halloween are candles and soaps from Carolina. Available in individual-selling units or as an assortment in a free, plastic counter display, these soaps and candles retail for the following suggested prices: 65 cents each for guest washballs; 75 cents each for pumpkin or witch guest soaps; $5 each for witch candles; and $6.50 each for pumpkin candles. Carolina Soap & Candle Makers Co., Oshkosh, WI 54903; (414)233-7700.
Circle Reader Service No. 115.

Combining the beauty of art glass with the utility of floral vases, ashtrays or paperweights, the Prismatic Collection of fine crystal represents singular works of art. Mouth-blown and hand-cut, each piece has diamond-like prisms which reflect light from every angle. Individual variations, which sometimes appear as small air bubbles or differences in thickness, height or width, distinguish this crystal from its machine-made counterparts. The vases range in height from 8 inches to 12 inches. Suggested retail prices range from $30 for the paperweight to $80 for the tallest vase. World of Porcelain & Glassware, Inc., 16926 S. Keegan, Unit B, Carson, CA 90746; (213)979-0404.
Circle Reader Service No. 136.

Fall is just around the corner, and these scarecrows are ready for any kind of autumn arrangement, from harvest designs to Halloween bouquets. Ranging in size from a 4-inch version on a pick to a 45-inch free-standing figure, these scarecrows all have a hand-crafted look. Modeled in raffia and rice straw, the scarecrows are all sold in assortments of dress. Suggested retail prices range from 99 cents for the picks to $30 for the 45-inch figures. Minimum orders are 144 for the picks; larger pieces can be purchased singly. A square basket display unit is available for the picks which displays 144 at a time. Caffco, P.O. Box 3508, Montgomery, AL 36109; toll free (800)633-5888.
Circle Reader Service No. 117.

Home entertaining can be both casual and elegant with these tabletop serving pieces. Handcrafted of wicker in delicate, airy designs, this Wicker Lace line includes ten pieces, finished in either white enamel or antique brown stain. Suggested retail prices range from $10 to $25. American Wicker, Inc., Rt. 3, Church Rd., Box 541-C, Boone, NC 28607; (704)963-4345.
Circle Reader Service No. 139.

Flowers &. Elaine Anderson, Dugald Stermer

One of several spreads in each issue devoting two-to-a-page space to significant product reviews. Precise alignment at the middle of the pages allows the pictures to be sized to any convenient height, and the text to be written to any length. Lack of headlines underscores soft-sell atmosphere.

NEW & INTERESTING

Pickup, Van & 4WD

Gray background within boxed area gives unified flavor to this fully-packed presentation. Rigid adherence to sizing all pictures to the full column width can, however, play havoc with the perceived scale of the objects to each other. (That spray can is somewhat large!)

204

Masterful handling of a variety of silhouetted pictures to achieve maximum graphic impact from the composition as a whole ... pictures superimposed onto an underlying five-column grid shown by vertical hairline rules and regular placement and width of text blocks.

Graphic organization of these catalog pages is achieved by means of light-ruled boxes that encase groups of items. The arrangement is enlivened by the fact that several pictures interrupt or overlap the boxes, thus creating a "trompe l'oeil" illusion of dimension.

205

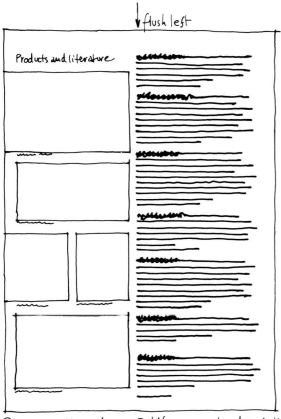

↓ flush left

Products and literature

Pictures neatly random   Boldface repeats description
beneath pictures

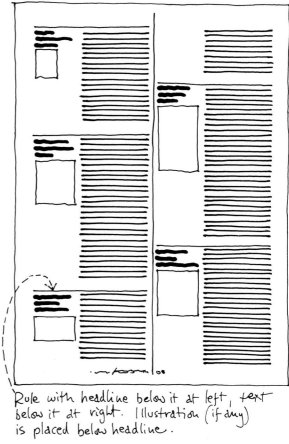

Rule with headline below it at left, text
below it at right. Illustration (if any)
is placed below headline.

Logo dropped out of color in white

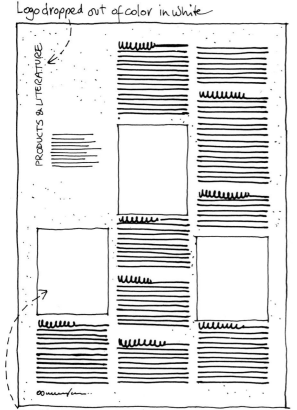

PRODUCTS & LITERATURE

Full-bleed color over whole page, except
the illustrations, which run in plain black ink

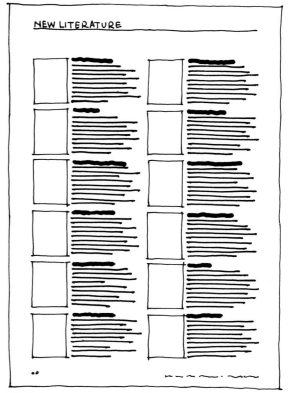

NEW LITERATURE

Modular arrangement of covers and
descriptions

Frame (in color or bold rule) encloses arrangement

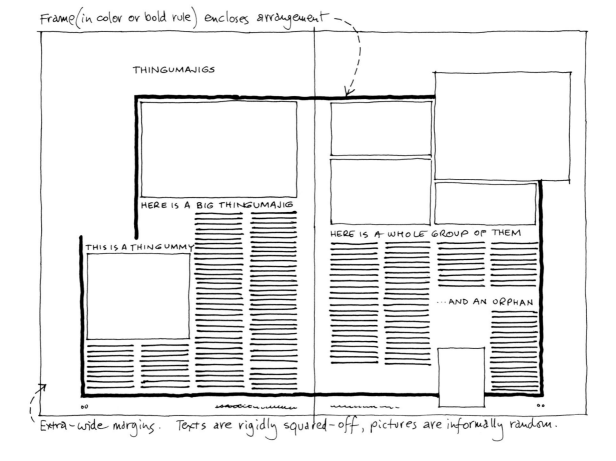

THINGUMAJIGS

HERE IS A BIG THINGUMAJIG

THIS IS A THINGUMMY

HERE IS A WHOLE GROUP OF THEM

...AND AN ORPHAN

Extra-wide margins. Texts are rigidly squared-off, pictures are informally random.

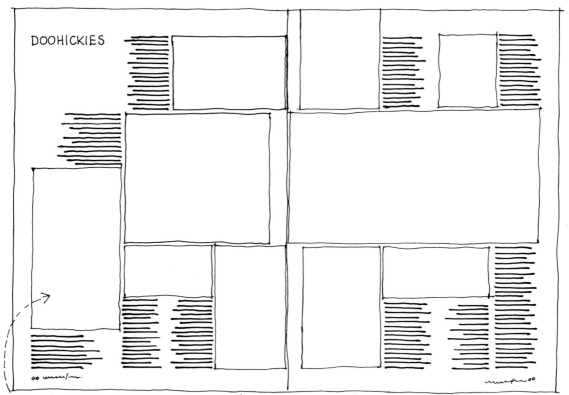

DOOHICKIES

Informal picture arrangement surrounded by individual product captions

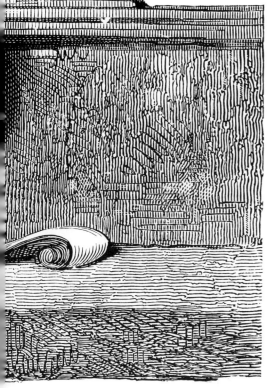

INDEX